INSIDE AutoCAD®

A Teaching Guide to the AutoCAD
Microcomputer Design and Drafting Program

Daniel Raker and Harbert Rice

 New Riders Publishing, Thousand Oaks, California

INSIDE AutoCAD®

A Teaching Guide to the AUTOCAD
Microcomputer Design and Drafting Program

By Daniel Raker and Harbert Rice

Published by:

New Riders Publishing
Post Office Box 4846
Thousand Oaks, CA 91360, U.S.A.

First Edition, 1985
Second Edition, 1986

Printed in the United States of America

Library of Congress Card Catalog Data

Raker, Daniel S. & Rice, Harbert V.

INSIDE AUTOCAD ®
A Teaching Guide to the AutoCAD
Microcomputer Design and Drafting Program

Library of Congress Card Catalog Number: **86-611228**
ISBN 0-934035-08-3 Softcover

Cover Shuttle Drawing Courtesy of Autodesk, Inc.
Cover 1903 Flyer Drawing Courtesy of Palisades Research Inc.

AutoCAD Screen Menu (Version 2.5) and AutoCAD Tablet Template (Version 2.5) Reprinted By Permission of Autodesk, Inc.

Printed by Day and Night Graphics, Santa Barbara, California

WARNING AND DISCLAIMER

This Book is designed to provide tutorial information about the AutoCAD microcomputer program. Every effort has been made to make this Book complete and as accurate as possible. But no warranty or fitness is implied.

The information is provided on an "as-is" basis. The authors and New Riders Publishing shall have neither liability nor responsibility to any person or entity with respect to any loss or damages in connection with or arising from the information contained in this Book.

If you do not agree to the above, you may return this Book for a full refund.

TRADEMARKS

AutoCAD ® is a registered trademark of Autodesk, Inc.

dBase II® and dBase III ® are registered trademarks of Ashton-Tate, Inc.

HICOMSCAN Tiger Digitizer Tablet ® is a registered trademark of Hitachi Seiko Ltd.

HIPAD Digitizer Tablet ® and HIPLOT DMP Plotter ® are registered trademarks of Houston Instrument, Inc.

IBM PC/XT/AT ® are registered trademarks of the International Business Machines Corporation.

Lotus 1-2-3 ® is a registered trademark of Lotus Corporation.

MS/DOS ™ is a trademark of Microsoft Corporation.

WORDSTAR ® is a registered trademark of MicroPro International Corporation

ABOUT THE AUTHORS

Daniel Raker

Daniel Raker is president of Design & Systems Research, Inc. a Cambridge, Massachusetts-based management consulting firm specializing in computer graphics applications and market research.

Mr. Raker is the editor of the A/E SYSTEMS REPORT, a leading monthly newsletter on automation in design professional organizations. In addition to the newsletter, Mr. Raker's column "CAD Angles" appears monthly in Plan and Print magazine.

Mr. Raker is an avid writer and educator in the field of computer graphics. Mr. Raker developed and taught the first full course on CAD at the Harvard Graduate School of Design. Recently, he has delivered dozens of presentations and authored articles under the auspices of the AIA, the National Design Engineering Conference, the National Computer Graphics Association, Computer Aided Engineering, and the International Reprographics Association.

Mr. Raker's experience in computer graphics comes from General Telephone and Electronics (GTE) Laboratories where he worked as an assistant research director, and from the Harvard University Laboratory for Computer Graphics where he held the position of Director of Services and was responsible for applications development, and graphics education and training. Mr. Raker earned his Bachelor of Arts degree from Harvard College.

Harbert Rice

Harbert Rice is the owner of New Riders Publishing in Thousand Oaks, CA. He divides his time between writing and publishing books on computer engineering software.

Mr. Rice writes about computer graphics software from practical interests in using microcomputers to publish technical books, and a long-standing interest in pattern recognition software.

Before moving to the west coast and forming New Riders, Mr. Rice was a Vice President of the Ziff-Davis Publishing Co. Based in Burlington, MA, he headed up a computer group providing engineering databases to utility companies. His publishing group distributed data electronically from central site minicomputers.

Originally trained as a plant biochemist, Mr. Rice earned his PhD from Harvard University. While at Harvard he became interested in using computers to model non-linear systems. Mr. Rice gained his computer software experience at ERT, an engineering consulting subsidiary of COM-SAT Corp., and the Raytheon Company in Burlington, MA. where he held research and development positions. He applied pattern recognition methods to large scale computer simulation problems, and co-developed a series of system identification programs called the Group Method of Data Handling program. This software is used on mainframe and minicomputers to extract non-linear engineering models from test and experimental data.

CONTENTS

Contents

Contents

CHAPTER 11

ATTRIBUTES AND DATA EXTRACTION
Assigning Information to Graphic Elements in Your Drawings (And Getting It Out Again)

CHAPTER 12

CUSTOMIZING
AutoCAD and Me

APPENDIX A

MS-DOS AND CONFIGURING AutoCAD

APPENDIX B

AutoCAD SCREEN MENU COMMAND STRUCTURE

ACKNOWLEDGEMENTS

The authors wish to thank John Walker of Autodesk for his continuing encouragement and support for this second edition of INSIDE AutoCAD. Our special thanks to Dan Drake and Duff Kurland of Autodesk for their reviews and comments. Thanks also to Fred Hoppersted, Eric Lyons, and Mauri Laitinen for helping with the review.

The authors wish to thank B. Rustin Gesner for his thorough and complete reviews of both text and tutorials, and for providing yet more helpful hints and useful tips to this edition.

Thanks to Carolyn Porter for again overseeing production, and to Todd Meisler for plotting and reproducing the drawings.

INSIDE AutoCAD was written and illustrated on an IBM PC/XT and an IBM AT. AutoCAD (Version 2.5) was supplied by Autodesk, Inc. for both machines. Houston Instrument supplied a HIPLOT DMP-52MP pen plotter and a HIPAD digitizer. Hitachi Seiko Ltd., provided a HICOMSCAN "Tiger" digitizer tablet.

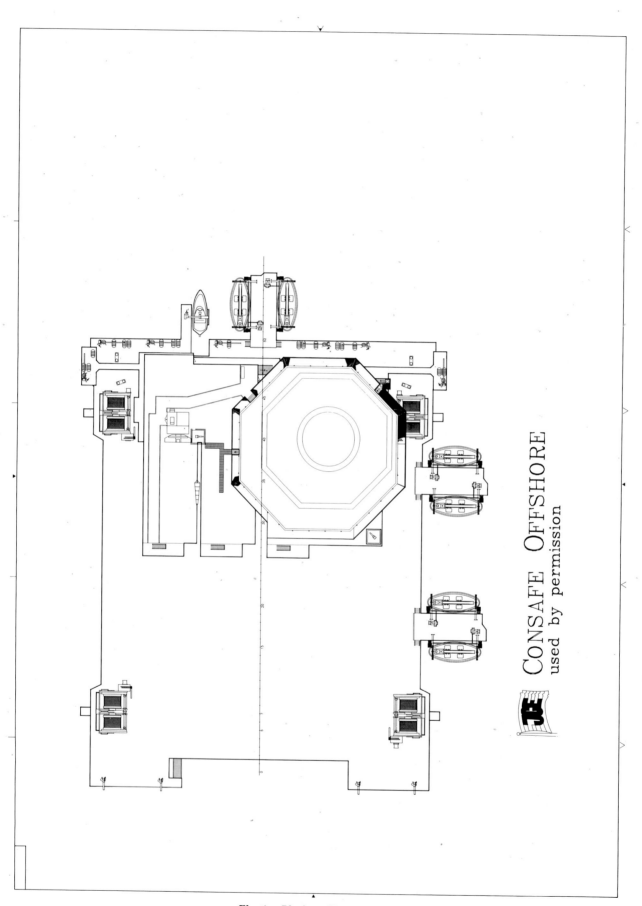

Floating Platform (Top View) Drawn with AutoCAD (Courtesy of Autodesk Inc.)

CONSAFE OFFSHORE
used by permission

INTRODUCTION

LAY OF THE LAND—WHAT WE WANT TO DO

Presenting INSIDE AutoCAD!!! A Complete Teaching Guide to the AutoCAD Computer Aided Drafting and Design program.

Our aim in this Guide is to introduce you to AutoCAD, the most popular CAD program. We want to help you learn how to use AutoCAD and to understand its drafting and design power. We want to help you unlock AutoCAD's power to get your design and drafting work done quickly and easily.

INSIDE AutoCAD is organized to show you how AutoCAD works and how you can benefit from working with AutoCAD.

The AutoCAD Program

You will find that the AutoCAD program is comprehensive. But the program is broken down and grouped into easily managed drawing operations. You can master each operational group in a few hours. At the same time you will find that AutoCAD's drawing capabilities are virtually limitless—bound only by your imagination and the skills that you develop using the program.

When you draw directly at your drafting table, your pencil and paper are all the tools you need. When you draft and design with AutoCAD, the program acts as an intermediary between your hand and the finished hard copy drawing. As an intermediary, AutoCAD will not slow you down. Quite the contrary—think of AutoCAD as a supercharger for your elbow.

The AutoCAD program knows a lot about drawing. It knows how to draw straight lines and right angles. It knows how to insert standard symbols for details that you want to use frequently. And it knows how to redraw entire drawings after you have made a simple correction.

Using INSIDE AutoCAD, you will learn how to operate the AutoCAD program. You will learn how to get AutoCAD to do work for you, and you will learn what you must do on your own to get your drawings done.

HOW INSIDE AutoCAD IS ORGANIZED

INSIDE AutoCAD is organized for the beginner as well as regular AutoCAD users. The Book does not contain any programming and it keeps microcomputer jargon to a minimum.

1

The Book is organized in Twelve Chapters. The Chapters take you sequentially through building drawings with the AutoCAD program, starting with **Setting Up**, and finishing with **Customizing AutoCAD** for your own use.

The First Chapter, **Setting Up**, teaches the basics about turning the AutoCAD program on and off, and storing your work. It teaches you how AutoCAD communicates with you. By the Chapter's end, you will be able to create an AutoCAD drawing file on disc, add lines to the drawing, display the drawing on the screen, and save the drawing for future use.

Chapter 2, **Getting Around**, explains AutoCAD's electronic tools for controlling where you are in your drawing file, and controlling what you display on the screen. By the Chapter's end, you will have a "map" for getting around your drawings with AutoCAD.

In Chapters 3, 4, 5, and 6 you will learn how to create drawings using simple electronic elements like lines, arcs, and text. You will learn to use AutoCAD's drawing aids like grids. Chapter 3 will teach you the **Drawing Basics** and you will start some actual drawings.

These drawings are continued in Chapters 4, 5 and 6. Chapters 4 and 5 will teach you how AutoCAD's drawing editor works. You will learn how to move and copy pieces of your drawing, and how to use CAD techniques like creating and tracing over construction lines. Chapter 6 will show you how to create and store permanent drawing **symbols**. We call this drawing process **"herding objects into symbols"**.

Chapters 7, 8, 9, and 10 will teach you how to save drawing time using AutoCAD's electronic bag of tricks. In Chapter 7 you will learn how to use AutoCAD's **drawing enhancement** tools. These are tools like automatic hatching to highlight drawings and special pattern libraries. Chapter 8 will teach you everything you need to know about plotting and getting good clear drawings onto **hard copy**.

In Chapter 9, you will explore AutoCAD's third dimension. AutoCAD has facilities for creating **isometric** and **3-D wireframe** drawings. You will learn how to create 3-D drawings and view these designs from any angle.

In Chapter 10, you will learn how to add **drawing intelligence** to your drawings by adding spatial dimensions and annotations.

The last two Chapters describe just how powerful AutoCAD can be in your hands. Chapter 11 will show you how to add non-graphic information to your drawing that you can later extract as Bill of Materials, specifications, schedules, or other data lists.

Chapter 12 will show you how to **Customize AutoCAD** using special AutoCAD tools and tricks to create your own drawing menus and automatic command sequences.

Appendices

INSIDE AutoCAD is a hands-on Tutorial. If you just read the text and look at the drawing examples, you will learn a great deal about AutoCAD. To solidify your working knowledge of AutoCAD, you need to sit down at an AutoCAD equipped microcomputer and work through the drawing sessions.

Appendix A gives the **Workstation Configuration** assumed for this Book. We assume you are using an MS-DOS "work-alike" microcomputer. The AutoCAD program has a **Configuration Utility** that allows you to configure your workstation hardware to run with the AutoCAD software. You have to configure your system before you can use AutoCAD's drawing editor.

In Appendix A, we run through the AutoCAD configuration for our "tutorial workstation configuration". If your setup differs from Appendix A, take the time to get familiar with the differences between your workstation setup and ours.

Appendix B gives a map to the **AutoCAD Screen Menus** which the Book covers in individual Chapters. This map is a guide to AutoCAD's screen menus and commands.

Appendix C gives a **Plotter Setup**. Plotters require some hardware setup and self-testing outside the AutoCAD program. Appendix C gives the Book's assumptions for plotter setup and self-testing.

Appendix D gives procedures for setting up AutoCAD's standard **Tablet Menu**. Appendix D gives the Book's assumptions for tablet menus.

HOW TO USE INSIDE AutoCAD

INSIDE AutoCAD is designed as a self-teaching Guide to the AutoCAD program. For your convenience, we separate working computer sessions and screen displays from text explanations. You can work through the teaching examples independently from the text.

Drawing Examples

Each Chapter has one or more tutorial drawing examples. Each example is separated from the Book's text. Screen display text is printed in computer-style type.

To help guide you through the tutorial exercises, each tutorial example has a target drawing. Example drawing screen displays are "illustrated" with drawings (made with AutoCAD!) to show the target drawing. Step-wise intermediate drawing displays, corresponding to the teaching steps used to create the target drawing, also are "illustrated". An intermediate drawing is shown in the SAMPLE DRAWING. This drawing shows how the Book represents an AutoCAD graphics screen display and the use of a pointing device.

A Sample Drawing. Graphics screen shows line being drawn. Pointer indicates drawing points.

The Book's Assumptions

The Book assumes that you can:

☐ Load your MS-DOS operating system from a system disc, or have loaded it onto your hard disc.

☐ Load the AutoCAD program, having configured it yourself or had it configured to work with your hardware.

☐ Select your responses to AutoCAD's prompts by typing from your microcomputer keyboard.

☐ Or select your responses from AutoCAD's screen menu or tablet menu by using a pointing device like a digitizer stylus, puck or a mouse.

If you are using your keyboard to enter responses to AutoCAD's prompts, you need to press **RETURN** (or **ENTER**), or the **SPACEBAR** after each typed response.

How Teaching Examples Look

If you turn your machine on, load the **MS-DOS** operating system, and load the AutoCAD program, you will see the following prompt sequence on your display screen:

```
C>
C> ACAD (RETURN)


(Note. This is the Book's format for describing AutoCAD
 program prompts and your responses.)
```

How "Illustrated " Example Displays Look

As soon as you type **ACAD (RETURN)**, AutoCAD will take over your micro-computer and display its MAIN MENU. The AutoCAD screen display is:

```
                    THE  MAIN  MENU


                    A U T O C A D
          Copyright (C) 1982, 83, 84, 85, 86 Autodesk, Inc.
          Version 2.5 (06/15/86) IBM PC
          Advanced Drafting Extensions 3
          Serial Number 12-3456789


          Main Menu

               0.  Exit AutoCAD
               1.  Begin a NEW Drawing
               2.  Edit an EXISTING Drawing
               3.  Plot a drawing
               4.  Printer plot a drawing

               5.  Configure AutoCAD
               6.  File Utilities
               7.  Compile shape/font description file
               8.  Convert old drawing file

          Enter selection:
```

```
Main Menu

0.  Exit AutoCAD
1.  Begin a NEW drawing
2.  Edit an EXISTING drawing
3.  Plot a drawing
4.  Printer plot a drawing

5.  Configure AutoCAD
6.  File Utilities
7.  Compile shape/font description file
8.  Convert old drawing file

Enter Selection ____
```

AutoCAD's MAIN MENU

The MAIN MENU illustration shows how the Book represents an AutoCAD text screen display.

Selection 5 is AutoCAD's Configuration Utility covered in Appendix A.

Selections 1, 2, 3, and 4 are where the drawing action is. This is where we will take up in Chapter 1.

Learning AutoCAD Menus and Commands

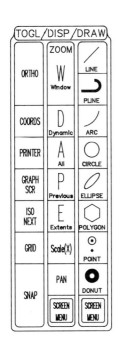

Sample Tablet Drawing Menu

Like any good microcomputer program AutoCAD uses menus and commands. You can get anywhere you want in the program by following the menus. Or you can execute individual drawing commands directly by using the keyboard or any input device without working through the screen menus. The SAMPLE TABLET DRAWING shows how the Book represents drawing commands on AutoCAD's standard tablet menu.

There are two basic tricks to learning AutoCAD. The first is to learn the AutoCAD menus and commands that you need for the drawings you want to produce. The second is to practice drawing by "playing around" with these AutoCAD commands.

We encourage you to play around with different commands. To help you learn the AutoCAD menus and commands, the first illustration in each Chapter contains a drawing of the AutoCAD tablet menu and the commands used in the tutorial exercises in that Chapter. To help you locate commands, portions of the screen menus also are repeated in the Chapters. Appendix B contains a complete screen menu map to AutoCAD commands.

AutoCAD Versions and INSIDE AutoCAD

This second edition of INSIDE AutoCAD is designed to be compatible with the AutoCAD release known as 2.5. In the Book we assume that you are working with AutoCAD 2.5 as well as the most up-to-date Advanced Drafting Extensions ADE-1 through ADE-3.

▶ Means New and Revised Material

To help you locate new material in this updated INSIDE AutoCAD, we have marked new and revised sections with a "triangle symbol" = ▶. You can find new material by looking for this "symbol" at the top of the page where the "running heads" are located, or in the INDEX.

If you have a different release of AutoCAD, don't be alarmed. INSIDE AutoCAD is perfectly useable with the earlier AutoCAD versions 2.0 and 2.1. If your AutoCAD version differs from the one assumed here in the Book, you will notice slight differences in screen displays, menus, and command prompting sequences. None of these differences will keep you from getting the full benefit of training and support that INSIDE AutoCAD provides.

If you are using an international release of AutoCAD, you will most certainly find minor differences among AutoCAD software versions, depending on the version number and the drafting extensions added.

In all cases, depending on your individual installation, you may find occasional differences in commands available (or absent) from screen menus. We assume that you are using AutoCAD fresh out of the box. AutoCAD is a highly adaptable and malleable program. If someone has installed AutoCAD on your system and altered its command or menu structure, your prompts, screen menus and tablet menu may be slightly different from those represented in the Book.

References, "Tips", and Occasional One-Liners

Besides working drawing sessions with AutoCAD, INSIDE AutoCAD also contains AutoCAD menu and command references, "tips" which we have collected from other AutoCAD users, and an occasional one-liner. The references are lists that explain AutoCAD's program assumptions or give settings for different drawing commands. These AutoCAD references along with users' drawing "tips" are set off as checklists for your convenience. Our one-liners also are set off as an occasional respite.

"It is time to bait, or cut fish".

—Fortune Cookie

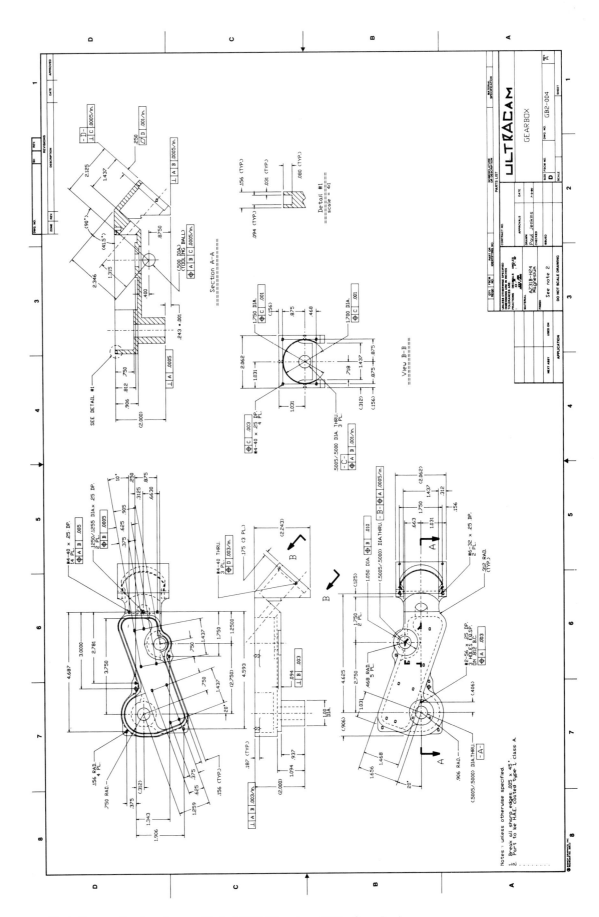

Movie Camera Gearbox drawn with AutoCAD (Courtesy of UltraCam, Inc.)

7

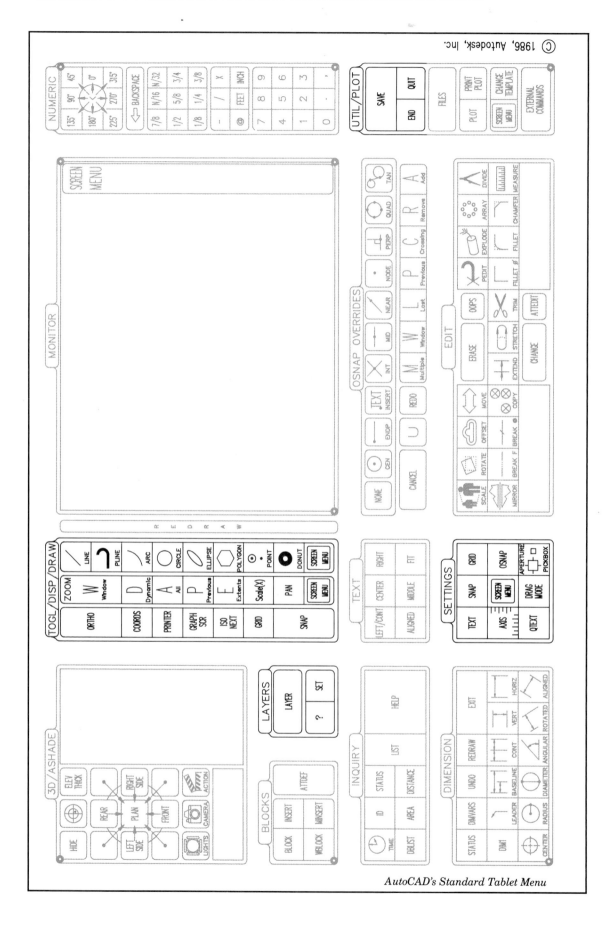

AutoCAD's Standard Tablet Menu

CHAPTER 1

SETTING UP AutoCAD

GETTING TO KNOW HOW THE PROGRAM WORKS

Lay of the Land—What We Want To Do. Let's Get Into the Drawing Editor and Play Around. The Main Menu. ▶ How the System Communicates With You (And Vice Versa). ▶ Keeping Track—Status and Prompt Lines. What To Do About Errors. How to Get Help! ▶ Setting Up and the AutoCAD Prototype Drawing. ▶ Scale, Units, and Limits. Layers, Colors, and Linetypes. One More Utility—Saving Your Work. Summing Up. Checklist for Setting Up. Here We Go.

LAY OF THE LAND—WHAT WE WANT TO DO

This is a tutorial about AutoCAD. In this Chapter we cover the basics on how to set up the program, how to turn it on, and how to draw. By the end of the Chapter you will have created an electronic CAD drawing file, selected a size and unit numbering system for your drawing, played around with a few lines, and saved the drawing.

The Benefits of Learning to Communicate with AutoCAD

The benefits of learning how to set up and store an electronic drawing file are obvious. Your real drawing benefits will come from learning about AutoCAD's command structure and how you and AutoCAD can interact to produce the drawings you want. Learning to communicate well with AutoCAD will unlock the CAD power and versatility inherent in the program for your own use.

A BRAZILIAN CABBIE IN NEW YORK

A few months ago we went uptown in Manhattan with a Brazilian cabbie who spoke no English when he came to the United States four years ago. In fluent English he told us how, in his first few months here, he would only take fares who knew where they wanted to go and were willing to direct him through any kind of communication—with English thrown in so he could learn the language. Now, he not only speaks the language fluently, knows the streets like the back of his hand, but he even helps people make up their minds about where they want to go.

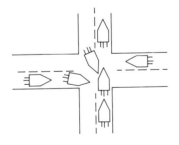

Manhattan Street Intersection

Your learning period with AutoCAD is going to be easier and much shorter than a Brazilian cabbie learning English AND Manhattan streets. But, like the cabbie, you will start with structured, simple tasks and graduate into more flexible and creative AutoCAD use.

So move into the front seat with AutoCAD!

LET'S GET INTO THE DRAWING EDITOR AND PLAY AROUND

Make a clean slate by venturing through door number **1. Begin a NEW drawing**. Call your drawing **CHAPTER1** and store it on disc drive **C:**. (If you do not have a hard disc and you are using floppies, you will want to call your working file B:CHAPTER1 to keep the example drawing file separate from the ACAD and operating system files.)

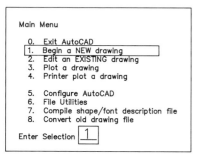

AutoCAD's Main Menu Showing Option 1 Selected

CHAPTER1 DRAWING

Enter selection: **1** (RETURN)

Enter NAME of drawing: **chapter1** (RETURN)

AutoCAD goes ahead and sets up a file on disc **C:** called CHAPTER1 and puts you into the drawing editor, clears the screen of text and sets you up for drawing.

The Command Communication Channel

If you are like most microcomputer enthusiasts you face the first screen with anticipation. "Can I get away with entering a few commands just to see what happens?" (I saw the guy at the store do it and the program didn't blow up.)

AutoCAD's first drawing screen displays a graphics drawing area and its ROOTMENU down the right hand side of the screen. If you look at the bottom of the AutoCAD screen, you'll see a **Command: prompt**. This is AutoCAD's communication channel.

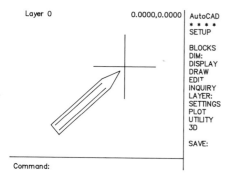

The First Drawing Screen Showing AutoCAD's ROOTMENU

Command:

This line is known as the **prompt line**, and we will learn to keep an eye on it to read messages from AutoCAD.

Make your pointer move the crosshair on the screen towards the commands listed in the ROOTMENU. When the crosshair passes into the menu area, a command lights up. Now move the pointer up and down to light up different commands.

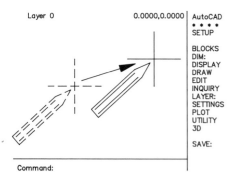

MOVE the pointer to get the crosshair to the Screen Menu

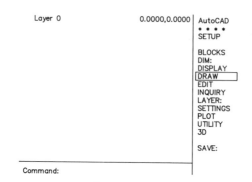

Getting to the DRAW Commands

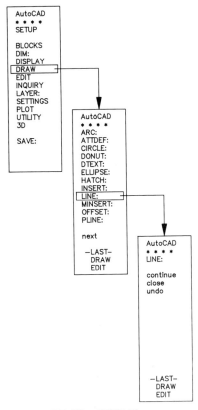

ROOT to DRAW to LINE Menu

The DRAW and LINE Menus

You can execute a command from the menu list by pressing the pointer button. Pick the **DRAW** command. As soon as you do, you get a new menu of commands.

Now move the crosshair to the **LINE** command and pick it. When you do this, both the screen menu and the prompt line change.

AutoCAD responds by saying (in so many words), "I understand what you want me to do . . . I will get ready to DRAW . . . a LINE . . . Please tell me where to start . . . Give me a—**From point:**"

Let's play around and draw a line.

Move the pointer to the center of the screen's drawing area, and pick a point. Good! You've locked in the **From point:** of your line. The prompt line changes:

```
Command: LINE From point:
To point:
```

As you move the pointer around the screen, you'll see the beginning of a line trailing behind the crosshair. Press the pointer again.

You did it! You have created, placed, and stored your first line inside AutoCAD!

AutoCAD assumes that you want to keep drawing lines so it again asks for a **To point:** on the prompt line. Create some more lines by picking a few more points.

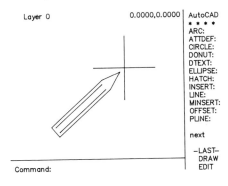

The DRAW Menu

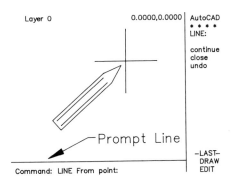

LINE Menu and the Prompt Line

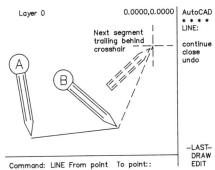

DRAWing a line

When you're done drawing connected lines, hit **RETURN**. You'll be free from the connected lines. You can draw a second set of connected lines. Hit RETURN again when you are done.

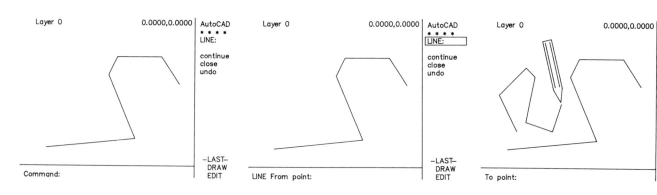

Getting out of DRAWing continuous lines with a (RETURN)

Restarting the LINE Command from the Screen Menu

Two sets of continuous lines

You've used the pointer, now try this with the keyboard:

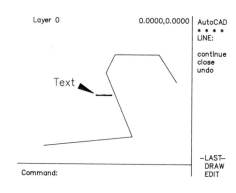

Welcome to INSIDE AutoCAD

Welcome to INSIDE AutoCAD (ZOOMed)

WELCOME TO INSIDE AutoCAD

Command: **TEXT (RETURN)**
Start point or Align/Center/Fit/Middle/Right/Style:
   6.5,4.5 (RETURN)
Height <0.20000>: **.05 (RETURN)**
Rotation angle <0>: **(RETURN)**
Text: **Welcome To INSIDE AutoCAD (RETURN)**   (Type the text.)
Command:

(So where is the welcome?)

Command: **ZOOM (RETURN)**
All/Center/Dynamic/Extents/Left/Previous/Window/<Scale(X)>:
   2 (RETURN)
Command: **ZOOM (RETURN)**
All/Center/Dynamic/Extents/Left/Previous/Window/<Scale(X)>:
   3 (RETURN)
Command: **ZOOM (RETURN)**
All/Center/Dynamic/Extents/Left/Previous/Window/<Scale(X)>:
   4 (RETURN)
Command: **ZOOM (RETURN)**
All/Center/Dynamic/Extents/Left/Previous/Window/<Scale(X)>:
   5 (RETURN)
Command: **ZOOM (RETURN)**
All/Center/Dynamic/Extents/Left/Previous/Window/<Scale(X)>:
   6 (RETURN)
Command: **ZOOM (RETURN)**
All/Center/Dynamic/Extents/Left/Previous/Window/<Scale(X)>:
   7 (RETURN)
Command:

(Now you see it . . . . .)

```
Command: ZOOM (RETURN)
All/Center/Dynamic/Extents/Left/Previous/Window/<Scale(X)>:
 1 (RETURN)
Command: ERASE (RETURN)
Select objects: L (RETURN)
1 found
Select objects: (RETURN)
Command:

(Now you don't!)
```

A Quick QUIT

Where are you? Where are you going?

Okay, you've played around and gotten that out of your system. How big were those lines you drew? You used the DRAW option on the ROOTMENU. What were all those other options? Take a closer look at the Main Menu.

Follow the prompts below to clear the screen and to get out of the drawing editor:

```
Command: QUIT (RETURN)
Really want to discard all changes to drawing? Y (RETURN)

(Main Menu appears)
```

THE MAIN MENU

```
Main Menu

0.  Exit AutoCAD
1.  Begin a NEW drawing
2.  Edit an EXISTING drawing
3.  Plot a drawing
4.  Printer plot a drawing

5.  Configure AutoCAD
6.  File Utilities
7.  Compile shape/font description file
8.  Convert old drawing file

Enter Selection ____
```

AutoCAD's Main Menu

As soon as you type **ACAD (RETURN)** from the MS-DOS operating system the AutoCAD program takes over control of your microcomputer and displays the Main Menu for you. The Main Menu gives you the choice of creating or editing drawings, plotting drawings, installing (configuring) AutoCAD, and a whole list of special utilities.

Here's a listing of what each Main Menu selection does:

Option **0** gets you back to the operating system. You will use this option every time you finish an AutoCAD session. If **ACAD (RETURN)** gets you in, option **0** gets you out. Selecting **0. Exit AutoCAD** from the Main Menu returns you to the MS-DOS operating system.

Options **1** and **2** are where you create, edit, and store your drawings inside AutoCAD. You will spend the majority of your AutoCAD hours inside the drawing editor. The drawing editor is the AutoCAD equivalent of your drafting board — the interactive part of the program that allows you to create and modify drawings.

There are two ways to get into the drawing editor. If you are starting a new drawing file, type a **1 (RETURN)** in response to the Main Menu selection prompt. AutoCAD will prompt you for the name of a NEW drawing file. If you want to edit a drawing that already exists, type **2 (RETURN)** and AutoCAD will prompt you for the name of the existing disc file you want to work with.

Options **3** and **4** are where you get drawings out to hardcopy.

Option **5. Configure AutoCAD** steps you through AutoCAD's interactive utility to let the **ACAD** program know what hardware you are using. Who ever set up AutoCAD for you used the configure routines to get AutoCAD to work on your hardware. More detail about this option can be found in Appendix A.

Option **6. File Utilities** allows you to perform disc file maintenance operations just as if you were using the MS-DOS operating system. You can use the AutoCAD File Utility to perform housekeeping chores on your files. If you feel more comfortable using the MS-DOS commands directly from the operating system prompt, there is no harm in doing so—they perform the same tasks:

AutoCAD File Utility Option	MS-DOS Equivalent
0. Exit File Utility	
1. List Drawing files	DIR.DWG
2. List user specified files	DIR Filename.ext
3. Delete files	DEL
4. Rename files	REN
5. Copy file	COPY

Options **7. Compile shape/font description file** and **8. Convert old drawing file** in the Main Menu are special situations and will not be covered in this Book. See the AutoCAD User Reference for details.

HOW THE SYSTEM COMMUNICATES WITH YOU (AND VICE VERSA)

If the drawing editor is where the action is, that's where you want to be. Let's go there again.

```
Main Menu

0.  Exit AutoCAD
1.  Begin a NEW drawing
2.  Edit an EXISTING drawing
3.  Plot a drawing
4.  Printer plot a drawing

5.  Configure AutoCAD
6.  File Utilities
7.  Compile shape/font description file
8.  Convert old drawing file

Enter Selection  1
```

AutoCAD's Main Menu Showing Option 1 Selected

```
Enter selection: 1  (RETURN)

Enter NAME of drawing (default chapter1):  (RETURN)
```

There are commands and then there are commands. AutoCAD has a flexible command structure that allows you to execute just about any command at any time. This means that you can execute a command from the keyboard by typing the name of the command and hitting (**RETURN**).

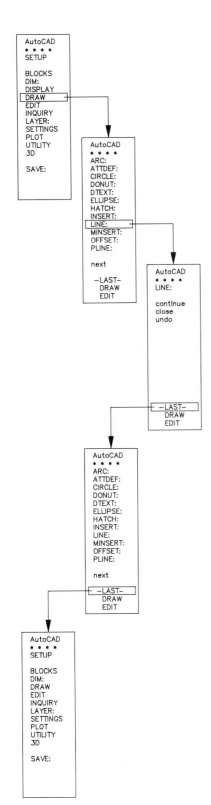

ROOT to DRAW to LINE. LAST-MENUs to DRAW to ROOTMENU

The Menu Option

But, because many of us are somewhat handicapped when it comes to typing, AutoCAD provides alternate ways to enter commands.

At the right hand side of the display screen, AutoCAD lists a set of key words that it thinks you might want to use to enter commands or get around in the program.

You've already seen that when you first turn on the drawing editor in AutoCAD, this group of options is known as the ROOTMENU. You know that options on the ROOTMENU lead to further menus, which in turn lead to more menus. Is there a pattern to this progression?

Menus, Keys and Commands

AutoCAD has more than 120 major commands and hundreds of subcommands. Because we often want to group commands together for convenience or simply to prompt us to use several commands together, AutoCAD provides the ability to create menus or groups of commands.

☐ A **MENU** is a listing of commands or keys. This list is for convenience only and has no effect on the AutoCAD command structure. A command can be executed any time you see a **Command:** prompt.

☐ A **KEY** is the name of an AutoCAD submenu. A key does not actually execute an AutoCAD command—it simply activates another menu page.

☐ A **COMMAND** is what makes AutoCAD go. A command actually performs an AutoCAD function. An executable command is shown in the menu with a colon, **:**, after it.

☐ Note, too, that **subcommands** exist on screen menus. These are shown in lower case letters. A subcommand can only be executed within a command.

AutoCAD Factory Settings

AutoCAD comes from the factory with a preset structure of **Screen Menus** and a preset **Tablet Menu**. These menus list keys or commands that you can use during an AutoCAD drawing session. The ROOTMENU that is showing on your screen now is an example of a screen menu. **AUTOCAD** is the key of the ROOTMENU. The menu list contains two commands (words followed by a colon—**DIM:** and **LAYER:**) and several keys (**BLOCKS, EDIT, DRAW,**) to get to other screen menus.

When you pick a command from the screen menu it will appear on the COMMAND: prompt line like this:

```
Command: LINE From point:
```

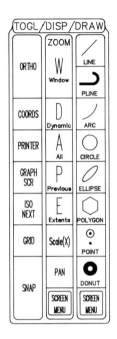

Tablet Menu with DRAW Commands

Tablet Menu

If you have installed AutoCAD's standard tablet menu, you also can pick the LINE command from the tablet with the same result. At the beginning of each Chapter in the Book is a map showing the tablet menu commands that will be used in the Chapter. You may want to mark the tablet menu map at the beginning of this and successive Chapters with a paper clip and keep it near your AutoCAD setup.

Screen and tablet menus aren't the only way to execute AutoCAD commands.

Typing the Command

The most direct way to issue an AutoCAD command is to type the command name at the keyboard. As you type, the letters appear following the Command: prompt, and the command will be highlighted on the screen menu if it is showing. Let's say we want to play around with the **LINE** command. Here's how you type a command: (If you make an error see WHAT TO DO ABOUT ERRORS. If you get completely lost see HELP!)

```
Command: LINE
```

You can also select a menu command from the keyboard. If the desired command is highlighted (even due to an abbreviation) you can select it from the menu by hitting the MENU CURSOR key (usually Ins).

In order to execute the LINE or any typed command, you must press the **(RETURN)** key on your keyboard to let AutoCAD know that you're finished typing. On some systems this is the **ENTER** key, on others it is a broken arrow (↵). If AutoCAD doesn't understand what you've typed after you press **(RETURN)** it will let you know:

```
Command: LI (RETURN)
Unknown command.  Type ? for list of commands.
Command:
    (This is AutoCAD saying "No hablo your lingo"  if you need
    more help type ?)

Command: LINE (RETURN)
From point:

(A note on notation. Authors' notes appear in parenthesis, ().
 RETURN = (RETURN) when it is pressed in response to a
 prompt. Responses to prompts also are bold typed.)
```

Coordinate Entry—Drawing a Square

Not only can you enter command names from the keyboard, you can also give AutoCAD locations by typing coordinates. While you are at the keyboard, let's pick up again with the **LINE** command. Type the LINE Command or pick it from the DRAW Menu:

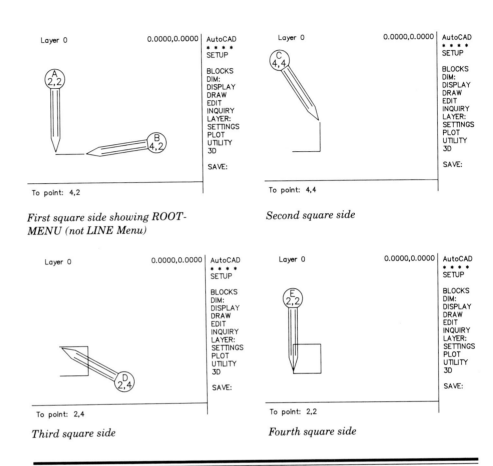

First square side showing ROOT-MENU (not LINE Menu)

Second square side

Third square side

Fourth square side

DRAWING A SQUARE

```
Command: LINE  (RETURN)
From point: 2,2  (RETURN)     (Type 2,2 followed by  (RETURN)
To point: 4,2  (RETURN)
To point: 4,4  (RETURN)
To point: 2,4  (RETURN)
To point: 2,2  (RETURN)
To point:  (RETURN)
Command:
```

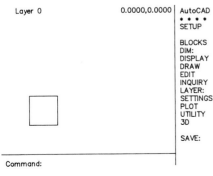

Finished square

AutoCAD uses a Cartesian coordinate (X,Y) system. The X-axis is left-right, and the Y-axis is up-down. Coordinates are entered X first, followed by a comma, then the Y value.

AutoCAD draws connected lines on the screen in response to the typed commands just as if the coordinates were being picked using the pointer. AutoCAD creates the line using the exact locations from the coordinate points you type.

But how do you know where your lines are on the screen once you've entered them? How can you keep track of distance on the screen? Where do all those commands on the prompt line go after you're done with them? Is there any way to look back?

KEEPING TRACK — STATUS AND PROMPT LINES

As you work with the AutoCAD program, you'll come to know what it expects from you and how it will react when you do something.

Many AutoCAD commands set up new drawing environments to receive additional commands. To help you keep track of your drawing environment, AutoCAD uses part of the screen to tell you how it's doing.

You have already used the prompt line. The prompt line gives your latest communication with AutoCAD. The Command: prompt is either one or three lines depending on your video hardware. If it is only one line, it will not show your responses — only AutoCAD's prompts to you. If it is three lines, it will show AutoCAD's prompts and your responses. Either way, AutoCAD "keeps track of" its communications with you.

The FLIP SCREEN

AutoCAD sometimes uses a screen full of text instead of the graphics screen to show you information.

Find the FLIP SCREEN function key on your keyboard and press it. (It is usually the **F1** or some times the **HOME** key — check Appendix A for your configuration). The graphics drawing area goes away (along with the screen menu) and a text page appears.

```
Command: LINE
From point: 2,2
To point: 4,2
To point: 4,4
To point: 2,4
To point: 2,2
To point:
Command:
```

FLIP SCREEN showing past Prompt Lines

FLIP SCREEN BETWEEN TEXT AND GRAPHICS

Command: (Use your F1 FLIP SCREEN key.)

(The graphics screen goes away and a page of text appears.)

If you look closely at the text, you will see — in order — all the commands you typed (or picked from the screen menu) when you created the square. The last line of text is what appears on the prompt line.

Using this screen full of information you can look back through prompt lines to see where you've been. If you get interrupted with a phone conversation, using the FLIP SCREEN is an easy way to pick up your place. Some commands (like HELP) automatically FLIP you to the text screen. At other times you can use the FLIP SCREEN just to get information.

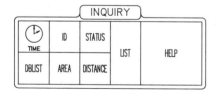

Tablet STATUS Command

The STATUS Command

Another FLIP SCREEN function that gives you information about how AutoCAD is set up is the **STATUS** command. Let's try it now, type STATUS in response to the Command prompt:

```
Command:  STATUS  (RETURN)

(AutoCAD FLIPs to text mode and shows a lot of information.)

Hit the FLIP SCREEN key to get back to graphics.
```

The information in the status text screen will become important to you as you read through this tutorial. For now let's just feel comfortable knowing that we can look at the information and that AutoCAD is keeping track of all that stuff for us.

The Status Line or — "AutoCAD Is Alive and Well and Living Inside the Computer"

Now let's look at the line of text at the top of the graphics screen. This line is called the **status line**. Here you'll find information about how AutoCAD is set up, and how it will react when you issue certain commands.

The status line gives AutoCAD's vital signs. We won't go into all the vital signs, but let's check a few to see how they work.

If you look at the status line area, you will see several numbers to the right. These numbers represent the latest crosshair position:

```
Layer  0                              2.0000,2.0000
```

When you move the pointer around these numbers don't change. They're stuck at the last point that you officially entered with the pointer as part of a command.

Cursor Digital Readout

To make the status line, **X,Y**, readout follow your positions, type ∧**D** (Control key and D at the same time — spoken or read "Control-D"). On many systems the **F6** function key does the same thing. This status command calls for the continuous update and display of the cursor's position — digital readout.

Now move your cursor around the screen. The X,Y readout will keep up with you and always let you know where you are. You can turn off the digital display by hitting ∧**D** (or **F6**) again. It's the COORDS toggle switch.

With the **COORDS** toggled **On**, execute the **LINE** command either by **picking** the screen menu, or typing it from the keyboard. Place your **From point:** at **5,2** and then **drag** the **To point:** around the screen by moving the cursor around — but do not enter the second point:.

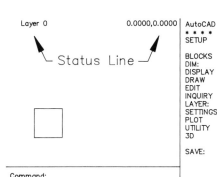

STATUS Line

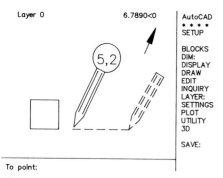

New line and STATUS showing relative coordinate display for 0 degrees

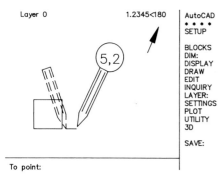

New line and STATUS showing relative coordinate display for 180 degrees

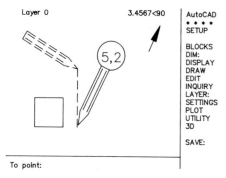

New line and STATUS showing relative coordinate display for 90 degrees

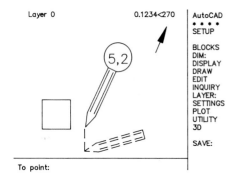

New line and STATUS showing relative coordinate display for 270 degrees

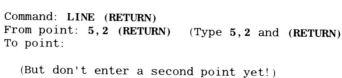

```
Command:  LINE  (RETURN)
From point: 5,2 (RETURN)      (Type 5,2 and (RETURN)
To point:

     (But don't enter a second point yet!)
```

Look at the digital readout now. Instead of an X,Y readout AutoCAD gives you distance and angle of your current cursor position with respect to — the From point:.

This is known as **polar coordinate tracking**. Move the cursor around to get a feel for where the angle = 0 degrees (horizontal to the right of the From point:); where the angle = 180 degrees (to the left); angle = 90 degrees; and angle = 270 degrees (negative 90 degrees). Moving the cursor away from the From point:, you'll see the distance increase in the digital readout.

Move the cursor to the screen point that is **2.0** units to the right of the **From point:** (but still without picking a second LINE point). Your status line will show:

```
     Layer 0                          2.0000<0
```

Do not worry if the distance and angle are not exact. You will soon learn how to lock in exact points and distances using other AutoCAD drawing aids. For now it is enough to know that you can have the digital cursor track your movements.

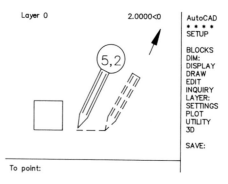

New line and STATUS showing relative coordinate display 2 units to the right

Absolute and Relative Coordinates

So far, playing around with AutoCAD's digital readout, you see you can enter coordinates in two ways: ABSOLUTE from the keyboard, and RELATIVE polar coordinates with the pointer.

You also can enter relative coordinates from the keyboard. It's useful to make this type of entry when you know exactly where you want to place drawing elements in relation to your last drawing point.

The @ Sign for Keyboard Entry

To enter **RELATIVE** coordinates from the keyboard, AutoCAD uses an @ sign before the **X** and **Y** values. AutoCAD understands that the coordinates of the new point you are entering are — relative — to the last point, not exact (ABSOLUTE) coordinates. @ **3,4** entered from the keyboard tells AutoCAD the next point is — 3 units in the positive X direction, and 4 units in the positive Y direction from the last point.

You can draw with either type of coordinate entry. Consider the square already on the screen. You created it using the absolute method. Follow the relative method below to form another square to the right of the first one. Both methods produce the same size square:

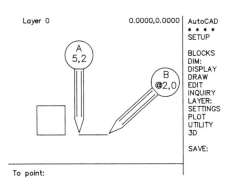

Building a square with relative coordinates — first side

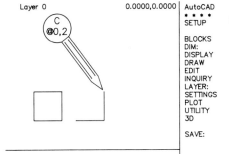

Building a square with relative coordinates—second side

RELATIVE EXAMPLE

When starting the relative square, note that you have already entered the From point:.

Relative Method

Command: **LINE (RETURN)**
From point: **5,2 (RETURN)**
To point: **@2,0 (RETURN)**
To point: **@0,2 (RETURN)**
To point: **@-2,0 (RETURN)**
To point: **@0,-2 (RETURN)**
To point: **(RETURN)**

Absolute Method (Entered)

Command: **LINE (RETURN)**
From point: **2,2 (RETURN)**
To point: **4,2 (RETURN)**
To point: **4,4 (RETURN)**
To point: **2,4 (RETURN)**
To point: **2,2 (RETURN)**
To point: **(RETURN)**

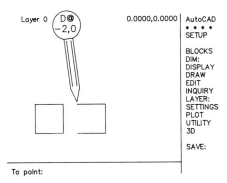

Building a square with relative coordinates—third side

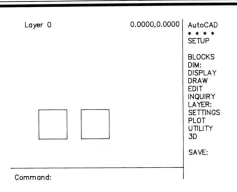

Building a square with relative coordinates—completed square

If you type an incorrect coordinate such as 2.2 instead of 2,2 in response to the From point:, AutoCAD will respond with an **Invalid point**. It will repeat the From point: prompt so that you can type in the correct coordinates.

You can mix and match absolute and relative coordinates to complete the square, but not for the same input point.

If you work in polar coordinates, or have reason to work with angles and distance, you can enter relative coordinates by using a typed input like @ **3<60**. This tells AutoCAD to enter a new point that is—3 units at 60 positive degrees away from the last point. Try another square with relative polar coordinates.

WHAT TO DO ABOUT ERRORS. AND HOW TO GET HELP!

AutoCAD is very forgiving. The worst that happens when you mistype a command name is that AutoCAD warns you that it does not understand what you want to do. It gives you another chance or prompts you to get HELP.

Here are ways to fix errors that haven't gone too far:

Tablet HELP Command

WHAT TO DO ABOUT ERRORS

☐ What if you catch a typing error before you hit (**RETURN**)?

Use the **BS** (backspace) (←) key on the keyboard to erase the wrong characters and continue typing.
also

Control-X (Control key and **X** key pressed together) displays ***Delete***, ignores all previous characters on the line, and gives you a blank new line to enter what you intended.

☐ What if you start the wrong command and it is already showing on the prompt line?

A ^C (hitting the control and **C** keys together) once or twice will cancel commands and return you to the Command: prompt. If you use the tablet menu, the **CANCEL** command will get you out of this jam.

☐ I'm lost, what do I do?

Type **?** (**RETURN**) or **HELP** (**RETURN**). They always gives you more information.

Help!

Help is almost always available in AutoCAD. You can get a complete listing of available commands or more information about a specific command.

If you are at the Command: prompt, you can either type **HELP** or **?** to invoke AutoCAD's friendly help.

Either will prompt you for what you want HELP with. You can get a list of all the available commands, or detailed information about a specific command. HELP on specific commands even refers you to the AutoCAD User Reference for more detail about that particular command. When HELP has shown you all it knows it returns you to the Command: prompt.

TRY GETTING SOME HELP!

Command: **HELP (RETURN)**

or

Command: **? (RETURN)**
Command name (RETURN for list): **(RETURN)**

(Text screen appears:)

Command List (+n = ADE-n feature, ' = transparent command)

APERTUR+2	DELAY	FILL	MEASURE+3	QUIT	SOLID
ARC	DIM+1	FILLET+1	MENU	REDO	STATUS
. . . . .	. . . . .	. . . .	. . . . .	. . . . .	. . . . . .

Press RETURN for further help. **(RETURN)**

   (Another screen of HELP appears)

Command:

(AutoCAD returns you to the Command: prompt line)

Hit the **FLIP SCREEN** function key or tablet **GRAPH SCR TOGL** to get back to the graphics screen.

SETTING UP AND THE AutoCAD PROTOTYPE DRAWING

AutoCAD is a flexible drawing program. Some CAD systems are geared towards specific drafting applications like drafting for printed circuit board layout. AutoCAD is a general purpose program that you tailor for your use. While you can use AutoCAD fresh out of the box, spending some time setting up AutoCAD to fit your own needs will save you hours and make AutoCAD more fun to use.

Tailoring AutoCAD has two sides:

☐ You can set up AutoCAD so that it draws the way you want it to. This means getting the right scale, units, linetype, and text. You can save these settings from drawing to drawing.

☐ You can add special features like your own symbols library and mini-programs that help you do drawing without entering every drafting element.

To get started, we'll concentrate on setting up AutoCAD to work the way you want it to work.

AutoCAD's Assumptions — Defaults

When you first turned on AutoCAD in the beginning of this Chapter, you saw that you could begin drawing as soon as you entered the drawing editor. When you begin a new drawing starting with the Main Menu, AutoCAD makes several assumptions about how you want to draw.

For instance, AutoCAD assumes you want:

- [ ] To enter drawing elements on layer 0.

- [ ] In white, continuous lines.

- [ ] In an X,Y coordinate system that has 12 units in the X direction, and 9 units in the Y direction.

These AutoCAD settings are called **defaults**. (Given the name because—if you don't like the settings the programmers put in AutoCAD—de fault lies with them, not you). Nearly every AutoCAD command that requires your input or setting comes with a default setting.

In fact, fresh out of the box, AutoCAD starts with an entire default prototype drawing. When you started your working session by entering the drawing editor and beginning a new drawing named CHAPTER1, AutoCAD set up many default command settings by reading a prototype drawing stored on your AutoCAD disc.

The AutoCAD standard prototype drawing is called ACAD.DWG and it comes with your AutoCAD software. In ACAD.DWG are factory selected settings for many commands to give you a drawing editor environment in which you can immediately begin drawing without having to bother with a lot of setting up.

If you are interested in the commands that are set up by the ACAD.DWG prototype drawing, see Appendix A. Later in the Book, you will learn how you can set up your own prototype drawing. Every time you begin a new drawing in the drawing editor you can have your drawing files preset with items like your standard drawing title block and symbol libraries.

AutoCAD lets you know what defaults are set up by showing you default values in brackets <default example> in the Command: prompt. You can accept a <default prompt> that AutoCAD offers by just hitting a (**RETURN**). You will see a default prompt in the next example when you set **LIMITS** on the AutoCAD drawing file.

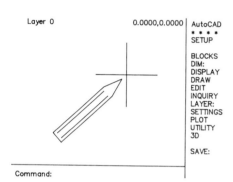

ROOTMENU Showing AutoCAD's Default Setup

SCALE, UNITS AND LIMITS

The squares that we created on the screen are two by two units. Let's take a look at how AutoCAD keeps track of units and scale.

Sizing Up Your Drawing   Utility (1.8 ver)

Use the pointer to pick the **SETTINGS** key from the ROOTMENU. We are looking for the **LIMITS** and **UNITS** commands that will come up on the SETTINGS screen menu. Type or pick **LIMITS**.

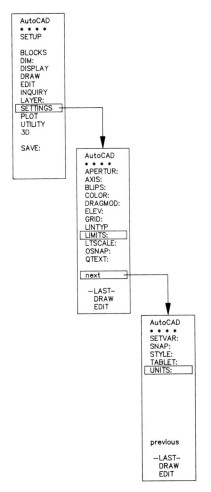

*ROOT to SETTINGS showing
LIMITS and UNITS*

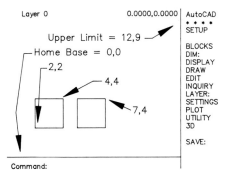

*Cartesian coordinates showing several
screen locations*

```
Command: LIMITS (RETURN)
ON/OFF/<Lower left corner> <0.0000,0.0000>:
```

(You don't need **(RETURN)** if you pick LIMITS from the screen.).

AutoCAD is telling you that the lower leftmost boundary of your drawing file is X = 0,Y = 0 (in Cartesian coordinates). Notice that <0.0000,0.0000> is shown as a default prompt.

Lower Left is Home Base

This is home base, unless you tell AutoCAD otherwise. The colon (:) is asking you where you want the lower leftmost corner limit set. You can enter a new lower left corner by typing new X,Y coordinates. Or, if you're satisfied with the default, hit **(RETURN)** to accept them. For now hit **(RETURN)**:

```
Command: LIMITS (RETURN)
ON/OFF/<Lower left corner> <0.0000,0.0000>:  (RETURN)
Upper right corner: <12.0000,9.0000>:  (RETURN)
Command:
```

AutoCAD can store your drawing data in real world coordinates. In practice, this means whether you're drawing a printed circuit board that is 0.4 meters by 0.5 meters or an office building that is 72′ × 54′ 6″, AutoCAD can track your data in meters, millimeters, feet, inches, fractions, decimals, or just about any unit system that you want.

"The BIGGEST BLOODY THING to get used to is drawing in FULL SCALE all the time — and on a small video screen. A bolt which is two inches looks two feet when it's blown up on the screen, but it's really two inches, no matter how you show it, store it, or plot it."

— Hydraulic Crane Designer

AutoCAD also allows you to store your drawing data in units which are most convenient for you. Rather than drawing your office building at 1/4″ = 1′ to fit 72 feet on a sheet of paper, AutoCAD will store your office building in feet and inches. When you're ready to plot the drawing out, you can decide on the scale you want for presentation.

AutoCAD does not use scale as you do in manual drawing. Inside AutoCAD drawing elements are stored in **real world** coordinates. Only when a human has to look at the drawing does AutoCAD apply scale factors — one to translate real world to screen size for viewing, another to translate real world to plotter sheet size for hardcopy.

One way to keep track of screen scale is to use a ruler.

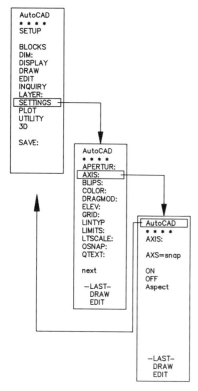

ROOT to SETTINGS to AXIS and Back

The AXIS Command — Making a Ruler

To pick AXIS go back to the ROOTMENU. Pick SETTINGS again. Then pick AXIS. Let's turn it ON.

```
Command: AXIS (RETURN)
Tick spacing(X) or ON/OFF/Aspect <0.0000>: .1 (RETURN)
Command:

(You don't need the first (RETURN) if you pick AXIS
 from the screen.)
```

Notice that the lower and righthand boundaries of the screen now have a built in ruler with tick marks showing. You can use the AXIS to keep track of crosshair movement when you need to. You can turn it OFF now. Since it doesn't get in the way, many users leave it ON so it will be there when needed.

```
Command: AXIS (RETURN)
Tick spacing(X) or ON/OFF/Aspect <0.1000>:  Off (RETURN)
Command:
```

But we still don't know how many units we have or how big they are.

Setting UNITS

Setting **UNITS** does two things for your drawing:

☐ Sets up the input format for entering distances and angles from the keyboard.

☐ Sets up the output format AutoCAD will use when displaying distances and angles.

These formats are not necessarily the same — AutoCAD allows you to short-cut input of distance and angles from the keyboard, but the program will adhere to proper output format according to your instructions. Let's play around with different notations in setting UNITS and LIMITS to see how AutoCAD accepts and displays these values.

Go from the ROOTMENU to SETTINGS and then pick **UNITS** to set up a unit system for the CHAPTER1 drawing file.

Your screen will **FLIP** to non-graphics (alphanumeric) mode. AutoCAD will prompt you for UNITs information:

☐ Which type of UNITS you want: Scientific, Decimal, Engineering, or Architectural.

AutoCAD's AXIS acts like an electronic ruler

☐ The number of decimal places to show when displaying distance (or smallest fraction in the case of Architectural).

☐ How you want angles displayed (decimal degrees, degrees/minutes/and seconds, grads, radians, or surveyor's units.)

☐ How many fractional decimal places you want displayed in your angles.

☐ What direction on your screen will represent the zero angle (usually to the right or "east").

☐ How you want to keep track of angles as you move away from angle = 0, either clockwise or counter-clockwise.

Let's try setting **UNITS** for an ENGINEERING application:

SETTING UNITS FOR ENGINEERING DRAWING

Command: **UNITS (RETURN)**

System of units:

    1. Scientific
    2. Decimal
    3. Engineering
    4. Architectural

Enter choice, 1 to 4 <2:> **3 (RETURN)**
Number of digits to right of decimal point (0 to 8) <4>:
    2 (RETURN)

System of angle measure:

    1. Decimal degrees
    2. Degrees/minutes/seconds
    3. Grads
    4. Radians
    5. Surveyor's units

Enter choice, 1 to 5 <1>: **(RETURN)**
Number of fractional places for display of angles (0 to 8)
<0>: **2 (RETURN)**

Direction for angle 0.00:

    East   3 o'clock =   0.00
    North   12 o'clock =   90.00
    West   9 o'clock = 180.00
    South   6 o'clock = 270.00
Enter direction for angle 0.00 <0.00>: **(RETURN)**

Do you want angles measured clockwise? <N>: **(RETURN)**

Command:

To get back to the graphics screen hit **FLIP SCREEN**

Usually you set up **UNITS** only once for a set of drawings, or, in many cases, forever. You can change UNITS in midstream should the need arise.

USEFUL UNITS

We know of one firm that makes mechanical components for an international clientele. The AutoCAD designer in the firm makes presentation drawings for European customers in DECIMAL, and then replots the shop drawings in ENGINEERING for the U.S. based factory employees. Later when you learn dimensioning, you can see how measurements can be displayed in **both** metric and English at the same time.

Setting LIMITS

Setting LIMITS does two things for your drawing:

☐ Sets up an electronic fence which AutoCAD uses to warn you if you draw outside your boundary. You can turn this feature on and off. The defaults is off.

☐ Gives you a frame of reference for zooming.

When you set drawing file boundaries using the **LIMITS** command, you do not actually limit how big your drawing can be or how many UNITS your "real world coordinate system" is. Using LIMITS simply gives AutoCAD an idea of how big you plan to make your drawing so the program can keep you from "running off the paper". You can always expand by resetting the LIMITS.

Remember, AutoCAD is flexible about scale. When you set an upper right hand boundary for limits, it is like working out a scale on a manual sheet and calculating the largest object that will fit on the paper. (Here's the CAD advantage—if you run out of "room" you can always add more space electronically—just try that with paper!)

Let's set up limits for a schematic to fit on a "D" size sheet (36″ × 24″). Of course, you can just as easily set up a drawing file to handle a one hundred foot building. To get started, pick LIMITS from the SETTINGS screen menu:

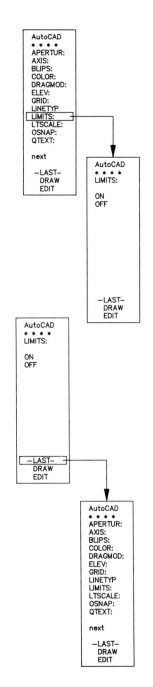

SETTINGS to LIMITS and back

```
        SETTING UP LIMITS FOR "D" SIZE DRAWING

Command: LIMITS (RETURN)
ON/OFF/<Lower left corner> <0'-0.00",0'-0.00">: -1",-1"
   (RETURN)

Upper right corner: <1'-0.00",0'-9.00">: 3'1",2'2" (RETURN)

Command: ZOOM (RETURN)
All/Center/Dynamic/Extents/Left/Previous/Window/<Scale(X)>:
   ALL (RETURN)
Regenerating drawing
Command:
```

NOTE: The exercises generally show "(double quotes) for entry of inches. You do not need to type the " marks; AutoCad will assume inches unless you type ' for feet.

You are going to use this setup later, so save it if you are going to quit or play around.

Here are some practical tips for setting **LIMITS**:

☐ Don't set square limits (for example 100 x 100), unless you have an explicit reason. Your screen and most engineering sheets have an X>Y ratio. You might as well take advantage of the extra drawing area.

☐ Start with an intended plotting scale and sheet size in mind. The sheet size times the plotting scale will be the sheet size in real world drawing units. If you have a 36″ − 24″ sheet at 1″ = 10′, then your electronic sheet will be 360′ − 240′. Make this the extent of your LIMITS.

☐ Make the lower left corner of your drawing file negative. You want 0,0 a little ways away from the edge of your screen drawing area. A setting like lower left corner: **-1″,-1″** gives breathing space. You also will have a border with a width that may depend on your plotter. Allow additional space for the border.

☐ Give your drawing expansion room by setting the upper right corner to more than you need.

Here are some typical settings for **UNITS** and **LIMITS**:

SAMPLE LIST FOR AutoCAD UNITS AND LIMITS

DRAWING TYPE	UNITS Type Decs,System of<,>Decs	LIMITS ** Lower left: Upper right:
Electronic Schematic in millimeters	Decimal 2,1,2	-1.00,-1.00 400.00,300.00
Piping Schematic for "D" size drawing	Engineering 2,1,2	-1.00",-1.00" 3'1.00",2'2.00"
Mechanical in metric	Decimal 3,1,3	-5.000,-5.000 100.000,75.000

400.00,300.00	3'-1.00",2'-2.00"	100.000,75.000
Electronic Schematic	Piping Schematic	Mechanical in Metric
−1.00,−1.00	−0'−1.00",−0'−1.00"	−5.000,−5.000

Electronic Schematic UNITS and LIMITS Setup

Piping Schematic UNITS and LIMITS Setup

Mechanical in Metric UNITS and LIMITS Setup

```
┌─────────────────────────────────────┐
│  3'-1.000",1'-10.000"                │
│                                      │
│                                      │
│        Mechanical in English         │
│                                      │
│  -0'-5.000".-0'-5.000"               │
└─────────────────────────────────────┘
```

Mechanical in English UNITS and
LIMITS Setup

```
┌─────────────────────────────────────┐
│                      140',100'       │
│                                      │
│                                      │
│           Architectural              │
│                                      │
│                                      │
│  -2',-2'                             │
└─────────────────────────────────────┘
```

Architectural UNITS and LIMITS
Setup

```
┌─────────────────────────────────────┐
│  140'-0.0000",100'-0.0000"           │
│                                      │
│                                      │
│            Surveyor's                │
│                                      │
│  -2'-0.0000",-2'-0.0000"             │
└─────────────────────────────────────┘
```

Surveyor's UNITS and LIMITS Setup

Mechanical in English	Engineering 3,1,3	-5.000",-5.000" 37.000",1'10.000"
Architectural	Architectural 4++,1,0	-2',-2' 140',100'
Surveyor's	Engineering 4,5,2	-2',-2' 140',100'

** The numbers listed can be used for keyboard entry. AutoCAD's display may be different.

++ For Architectural, the 4 in this example is the smallest fraction denominator.

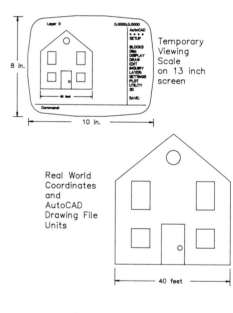

Temporary Viewing Scale on 13 inch screen

Real World Coordinates and AutoCAD Drawing File Units

Temporary Plotting Scale on Plotted "D" Size Sheet

Summary Example of AutoCAD and Scale

AutoCAD's Automatic SETUP

Learning to use AutoCAD's UNITS and LIMITS gives you unlimited flexibility in drawing image size, sheet size, scale and working units. If you have control of your units and limits settings, you will never have to worry about "running off the edge of a sheet" or having to redraw your design at another scale.

However, if you are used to working with "given" sheet sizes and scales, AutoCAD provides a means of running through standard setup calculations with a **SETUP** facility.

If you have a sheet size (say D at 36″ × 24″) and you are used to running a quick calculation to determine scale and the number of units that will fit across a sheet (say 120′ across 30″at 1/4″ = 1′), AutoCAD's SETUP routines will automatically set your units and limits by stepping you through the sheet size and scaling calculations.

If you want to see how SETUP works, try stepping through the setup sequences when you first enter the drawing editor.

When you set units to a scaled setting, you may still find that you "run off" the edge of the drawing file and need to reset your units and limits. For this reason, many users set their own units and limits to draw in real world coordinates and address scale when they plot the drawing. Establishing your standard limits and units setups, saving them in prototype drawings, and calling them up for use is the most efficient method for drawing production.

LAYERS, COLORS AND LINETYPES

As designers and draftspeople tied to the sheet of paper, we often neglect the fact that almost everything we design is separated into layers. Printed circuit boards have layers. Buildings are layered by floors. Even schematic diagrams of piping layouts have layers of information like valves/pumps/connecting pipes/ annotations.

AutoCAD frees drawing from a single two-dimensional sheet and allows natural layer separations. Think of AutoCAD **LAYERS** as clear acetate sheets superimposed one over the other. When looking down through the sheets, you see the whole drawing, but you can pull a single sheet out of the pack to just look at that layer.

"I always use about 20 layers in each drawing, separating interior finishes from store fixtures from architectural and engineering requirements. That way no matter who is calling on the phone at the time I can display just their layer and get the information I need. By the way, I feature the favorite color of each responsible Vice President when I plot out the different layers—I usually get my way when I make presentations!"

— Retail Store Facilities Planner

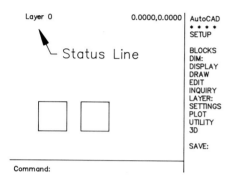

Current LAYER information is shown on the STATUS Line

Sometimes you want to keep information separate. Pulling out text from the graphic section of a sheet is a regular trick many architects and engineers use to save redraw time when a note or a detail needs to be changed.

Other times you want to save redraft time by building one image on top of another. Here AutoCAD layers act as overlays. A "FIRSTFLOOR" layer under a "SECONDFLOOR" layer gives a basis for copying outlines, but not interior details.

Let's think about what having separate layers means operationally. We need a way to let AutoCAD know which layer we want to draw on. We also need a way to turn layers on and off—to see them when we want them, but to get them out of the way when we don't.

LAYERS and Their Logical Properties

AutoCAD is way ahead of you if you are thinking of more layer possibilities. **LAYERS** have the following properties:

- [ ] **ON** or **OFF**. A layer can be visible or temporarily invisible on the screen. If **ON**, you'll see what's stored on the layer on the screen. If **OFF**, you won't see it. But it's still in the drawing file. **OFF** just suppresses the display.

- [ ] **Current** or **Inactive**. Read This One Slowly: You can only draw on one layer at a time, and that is the layer that is **Set** as **Current**. You should keep the current layer **ON** (visible) so you can see what's going on when you draw. You **Set** a LAYER to be Current. A new setting replaces the old current layer with a new one.

- [ ] **Name**. A layer has a name. You can call it anything you want up to 31 letters or digits, or "$", or "-", or "__". Examples are: **first__floor, pin-numbers, piping__1st__floor**. Do not, repeat, DO NOT try to use a space in your layer name—it is not possible.

- [ ] **Color**. A layer has a single default color such that anything drawn directly on that layer will take on this color unless you specifically override the default layer color. A layer has only one default color, but several layers can have the same default color. Color is assigned to layers by names or numbers from among available colors on your microcomputer hardware (up to 256 different colors—limited by your hardware, not AutoCAD).

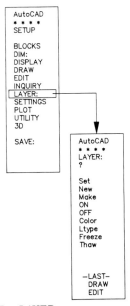

Tablet LAYER Command

ROOT to LAYER

AutoCAD uses the following naming/numbering conventions for seven **standard colors**:

1 - Red   5 - Blue
2 - Yellow   6 - Magenta
3 - Green   7 - White
4 - Cyan

☐ **Linetype**. A layer has a single default Linetype. Lines (and other drawing elements) drawn on a layer will take the linetype assigned to that layer, unless you specifically override the default layer Linetype. As with color, AutoCAD comes with several **standard Linetypes**.

☐ **Frozen** or **Thawed**. Most of the time you want to actively use most layers in your drawing so you would keep them thawed. However, freezing background, setup or other unnecessary layers will increase performance of AutoCAD searches and screen displays. For example, you might freeze a layer that has your title block on it until you are ready to plot your drawing.

You'll find status information about the current layer on the status line of the AutoCAD screen.

Controlling Layers

The first time you enter the drawing editor when you begin a new drawing, AutoCAD sets up a default **LAYER** named **0**. Layer **0** is automatically **Current** (Set), has a default color of **7 white**, and a Linetype of **Continuous**.

Layer **0** is fine for playing around, and it has some special properties that we will see later, but for most drawing work you are going to want to set up your own layers.

The LAYER Command

To set up layers and give them the desired properties, you use the **LAYER** command. You can reach the LAYER command by typing it, or following the screen menu sequence from the ROOTMENU. Either way, your prompt line will show:

```
Command: LAYER (RETURN)
?/Make/Set/New/On/Off/Color/Ltype/Freeze/Thaw:
```

The LAYER command works this way: First you tell AutoCAD which layer property you want to use (like "I want to Set a layer to be Current" or "I want to turn On some layers to be visible"). Then AutoCAD prompts you for the name(s) of the layers you want this property applied to. You can only operate on one property at a time, but you can apply this property to several layers with one swoop of the LAYER command.

Because we have to keep track of the names of different layers when using the LAYER command, AutoCAD provides an aid, a status query ?, which gives you a look at all the relevant layer information. The ? status query plus the layer properties make up the subcommands for the layer command. You see the subcommand options on the prompt line.

Try the ? subcommand now by typing ? in response to the layer prompt. AutoCAD will ask you which layers you want information about. The <*> default prompt is a **wildcard**, meaning—tell me about every layer:

```
Command: LAYER (RETURN)
?/Make/Set/New/On/Off/Color/Ltype/Freeze/Thaw: ? (RETURN)
Layer name(s) for listing <*>: (RETURN)
```

AutoCAD responds by FLIPping to nongraphics mode and displays

Layer name	State	Color	Linetype
0	On	7 (white)	CONTINUOUS

```
Current layer: 0

?/Make/Set/New/On/Off/Color/Ltype/Freeze/Thaw:
```

Since we asked for * or everything and we got only one line of information, this listing tells us that our drawing file has one layer (**layer 0**); it is **On** (visible); it has Color **7 (white)**; and if we were to draw, we would get **CONTINUOUS** lines. Notice, the listing tells us this layer is **Current**. You also can get the current layer name from the status line on the graphics screen.

Right now there is only one layer in the drawing file. Let's put in several more—we'll set them up and then save them for future use. We'll use all of the layer subcommands to get the following layer configuration:

LAYER CONFIGURATION GOAL

Layer name	State	Color	Linetype
0	On	7 (white)	CONTINUOUS
GRAPHIC1	On	1 (red)	CONTINUOUS
GRAPHIC2	On	5 (blue)	CONTINUOUS
TEXT	Off	2 (yellow)	CONTINUOUS
DIMENSION	On	3 (green)	DASHED

```
Current layer: 0
```

Layer 0   0.0000,0.0000

```
AutoCAD
* * * *
LAYER:
?

Set
New
ON
OFF
Color
Ltype
Freeze
Thaw


—LAST—
DRAW
EDIT
```

Command:

LAYER Screen Menu

Creating New Layers

CREATING NEW LAYERS

```
?/Make/Set/New/On/Off/Color/Ltype/Freeze/Thaw: N (RETURN)
New layer name(s): GRAPHIC1,GRAPHIC2,TEXT,DIMENSION
    (RETURN)
?/Make/Set/New/On/Off/Color/Ltype/Freeze/Thaw:
```

Notes on New.

☐ An **N** is enough to initiate the **New** subcommand. In fact, the first (differentiating) character is enough for any of the subcommands except On/Off where you need at least an **On** or an **Of**. AutoCAD tries to save you time.

☐ AutoCAD offers no <default> in **New**—you're on your own thinking up names.

☐ The **Make** subcommand simultaneously creates a new layer and sets it current.

☐ You can (and should) type as many names as you want on the **New layer name(s):** line. Commas , are all you need to separate entries, a **(RETURN)** ends your input. If you put in a space, AutoCAD thinks you are trying to end the input line just like a **(RETURN)**.

☐ Upper and lower case (or mixed) entry is fine. AutoCAD will translate all layer names to caps for storage.

Take a look at the layers status by using the **?** to see how you've done. Use * to get a listing of all the New layers:

DEFAULT PROPERTIES FOR NEW LAYERS

Layer name	State	Color	Linetype
0	On	7 (white)	CONTINUOUS
GRAPHIC1	On	7 (white)	CONTINUOUS
GRAPHIC2	On	7 (white)	CONTINUOUS
TEXT	On	7 (white)	CONTINUOUS
DIMENSION	On	7 (white)	CONTINUOUS

```
Current layer: O
```

Since we didn't invoke any settings for properties for the New layers other than a New name, AutoCAD automatically sets the other properties with defaults. Change them now to get the desired configuration.

Setting LAYER Color

SETTING LAYER COLOR

```
?/Make/Set/New/On/Off/Color/Ltype/Freeze/Thaw:  C  (RETURN)
Color:  1  (RETURN)
Layer name(s) for color 1 (red) <0>:  GRAPHIC1  (RETURN)
?/Make/Set/New/On/Off/Color/Ltype/Freeze/Thaw:  C  (RETURN)
Color:  BLUE  (RETURN)
Layer name(s) for color 5 (blue) <0>:  GRAPHIC2  (RETURN)
?/Make/Set/New/On/Off/Color/Ltype/Freeze/Thaw:  C  (RETURN)
Color:  2  (RETURN)
Layer name(s) for color 2 (yellow) <0>:  TEXT  (RETURN)
?/Make/Set/New/On/Off/Color/Ltype/Freeze/Thaw:  C  (RETURN)
Color:  GREEN  (RETURN)
Layer name(s) for color 3 (green) <0>:  DIMENSION  (RETURN)
?/Make/Set/New/On/Off/Color/Ltype/Freeze/Thaw:
```

Notes on Color.

☐ You can use color number or color name for the standard seven colors—you can interchange them too.

☐ Every different color setting requires that you give a separate execution of the color subcommand.

☐ You can make several layers the same color by giving more than one layer name on the prompt line.

☐ AutoCAD prompts you with the Current layer name as a <default>.

Setting LAYER Visibility (On and Off)

SETTING LAYER VISIBILITY

```
?/Make/Set/New/On/Off/Color/Ltype/Freeze/Thaw:  Off  (RETURN)
Layer name(s) to turn Off:  TEXT  (RETURN)
?/Make/Set/New/On/Off/Color/Ltype/Freeze/Thaw:
```

Notes on On and Off.

☐ Off works the same way as On with one exception: If you try to turn the Current layer **Off**, AutoCAD will ask if you really want to do such a foolish thing.

☐ You can use a wildcard * to turn collections of layer names On or Off. In above example, if you used **GR***, this would include GRAPHIC1 and GRAPHIC2, but not the other names which do not start with **GR**.

Setting the LAYER Linetype

```
DASHED    _ _ _ _ _ _ _
HIDDEN    _ _ _ _ _ _ _ _ _ _ _
CENTER    _ _ _ _ _ _ _
PHANTOM   _ _ _ _ _ _ _
DOT       . . . . . . . . . . . .
DASHDOT   _ . _ . _ . _
BORDER    _ . _ . _ . _ .
DIVIDE    . _ . _ . . _ . . _
CONTINUOUS _ _ _ _ _ _ _
```

Standard LINETYPEs

SETTING LAYER LINETYPE

```
?/Make/Set/New/On/Off/Color/Ltype/Freeze/Thaw: L (RETURN)
Linetype (or ?) <CONTINUOUS>: DASHED (RETURN)
Layer name(s) for linetype DASHED <0>: DIMENSIO (RETURN)
?/Make/Set/New/On/Off/Color/Ltype/Freeze/Thaw:
```

Notes on Linetype.

☐ The **Ltype** subcommand offers you a look at all the linetypes that have been set up in named layers within the drawing file. Use the **?** option to see them.

☐ **<CONTINUOUS>** is always offered as a default as the most common Linetype.

☐ When you type a linetype other than continuous, AutoCAD first looks in its linetype library (ACAD.LIN) to see if it has a linetype definition that matches your request. If it finds your linetype, everything is okay. If not, you have to set up a new one—we cover that in the last Chapter, CUS-TOMIZING AutoCAD.

Setting the CURRENT LAYER

As we have mentioned, you can only draw on one layer at a time. This layer is called the **Current layer**. To tell AutoCAD which layer you want as the Current layer, use the **Set** subcommand of the LAYER command:

```
Layer DIMENSIO    0.0000,0.0000    AutoCAD
                                   * * * *
                                   LAYER:
                                   ?
                                   Make
                                   Set
                                   New
                                   ON
                                   OFF
                                   Color
                                   Ltype
                                   Freeze
                                   Thaw

                                   -LAST-
                                   DRAW
Command:                           EDIT
```

STATUS Line Shows the New Current LAYER

SETTING CURRENT LAYER

```
?/Make/Set/New/On/Off/Color/Ltype/Freeze/Thaw: S (RETURN)
New current layer <0>: DIMENSIO (RETURN)
?/Make/Set/New//On/Off/Color/Ltype/Freeze/Thaw:
```

Notes on Set.

☐ It is a good idea to keep the Current layer **On** (visible) so you can see what's going on when you draw.

☐ AutoCAD always assumes that you do not want to Set a new layer and <default> prompts you with the name of the existing Current layer. This is helpful when you select the **Set** subcommand by mistake. If you want to leave the Current layer alone—just hit a **(RETURN)**.

☐ **Setting** a new Current layer automatically replaces (makes inactive) the old Current layer.

You can now use the LAYER **?** subcommand to see the status of all layers in the drawing file:

Tablet Layer ?

LAYER CONFIGURATION GOAL

```
?/Make/Set/New/On/Off/Color/Ltype/Freeze/Thaw:  ?  (RETURN)
Layer name(s) for listing <*>:  (RETURN).
```

Layer name	State	Color	Linetype
0	On	7 (white)	CONTINUOUS
GRAPHIC1	On	1 (red)	CONTINUOUS
GRAPHIC2	On	5 (blue)	CONTINUOUS
TEXT	Off	2 (yellow)	CONTINUOUS
DIMENSION	On	3 (green)	DASHED

```
Current layer: DIMENSIO

?/Make/Set/New/On/Off/Color/Ltype/Freeze/Thaw:  (RETURN)
Command:
```

If you have altered the properties of layers on the screen (like linetype or color), AutoCAD will regenerate the screen image to reflect these changes when you exit the LAYER command.

ONE MORE UTILITY—SAVING YOUR WORK

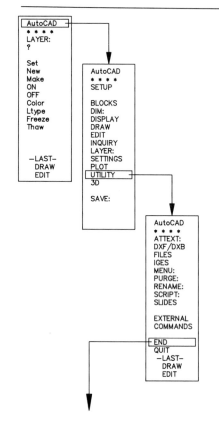

During the last few minutes we have created a working drawing file with real units, limits, and a foundation of layers. Rather than throwing it all away by QUITting and discarding all this useful work, let's SAVE the setup for use in future tutorial sessions.

You have already seen that AutoCAD provides a quick way out of the drawing editor through QUIT. QUIT is fast, but does not SAVE anything.

AutoCAD provides two **SAV**ing commands. Both save your work to a **.DWG** file and secure your work by renaming your previous drawing file on disc with a **.BAK** extension. If you want a backup cushion of old working sessions, think ahead about making copies of old files before entering the drawing editor.

☐ **SAVE** makes a **.DWG** file and returns you to the drawing editor to work on your current file. SAVE gives you the option of saving your current drawing editor session under a file name of your choice.

☐ **END** makes a backup file from your previous (last) file, stores another, up-to-date copy of your file, and exits the drawing editor. END assumes the current drawing file name.

AutoCAD is extremely robust. It is virtually impossible to crash it without a chance to save your work—unless you swap discs or pull the plug.

```
Main Menu

0.  Exit AutoCAD
1.  Begin a NEW drawing
2.  Edit an EXISTING drawing
3.  Plot a drawing
4.  Printer plot a drawing

5.  Configure AutoCAD
6.  File Utilities
7.  Compile shape/font description file
8.  Convert old drawing file

Enter Selection  0

Enter NAME of drawing file (default B:CHAPTER1):
```

C>

LAYERS to ROOT to SETTINGS to
END to Main Menu to MS-DOS

You still should **SAVE** your work frequently. It does not take a lot of time and protects you from a power failure or someone tripping over the power cord. Regular users SAVE several times an hour.

Save your work now using the **END** command:

SAVING THE DRAWING FILE AND EXITING THE DRAWING EDITOR

Command: **END (RETURN)**

You've completed your first AutoCAD session.

Exit AutoCAD with a **0** from the Main Menu.

SUMMING UP

What you've seen so far is typical of AutoCAD setup commands. They are extremely flexible. Other setup commands exist, like the ability to use special text fonts and special scaling conventions to control text and dimension arrow size. We'll provide more detail on these as we work our way through AutoCAD.

Remember, you can always get a detailed listing from AutoCAD with the STATUS command. The status line on the display screen gives you summary status of the important setup commands like Current layer and coordinate values.

We have also had a chance to play around with AutoCAD. Surprise!—It does not bite, and it does not laugh when you make mistakes.

Here's a Setting Up Summary:

☐ AutoCAD is cooperative. It only takes action when you tell it to.

☐ AutoCAD lets you know that it's waiting for your input with the **Command:** or other : prompts on the prompt line.

☐ It is a good idea to look at the screen menus when you are picking a command or key. Then glance at the prompt line to make sure that you and AutoCAD are communicating. Then watch the center of the graphics screen for the action.

☐ You can enter commands from the keyboard or from the screen menu. You also can enter commands through AutoCAD's digitizer tablet menu.

☐ The **LINE** command DRAWs lines (Big News!), using a **From point:** and **To point:**.

☐ AutoCAD tries to save you time by offering <**defaults**> and * **wildcard** options in place of elaborate keyboard entry.

☐ You can **CANCEL** most commands with a **(RETURN)**, by hitting Space bar, by typing ^C, or by picking CANCEL from the tablet menu.

☐ AutoCAD lets you know when it does not understand what you've told it by issuing an error message like **Unknown command** or ***Invalid*** (instead of a Bronx cheer). AutoCAD rings the microcomputer's bell to accompany the error message if you configure it that way.

☐ The **ROOTMENU** is the first menu that AutoCAD puts up on the screen when you turn on the drawing editor. You can get to almost every AutoCAD command through keys and direct commands from the ROOTMENU.

☐ Setting up a drawing file requires setting **UNITS**, **LIMITS**, and a working set of **LAYERS** as a good foundation for future drawing.

☐ If you normally select final sheet size and scale a drawing to fit it, you can use AutoCAD's automatic setup routines found by selecting **SETUP** from the ROOTMENU.

Here's a checklist of Setup Activities. You may want to write your most frequent setting for different setup commands right on the checklist.

SETTING UP CHECKLIST FOR AutoCAD

☐ Disc and File Naming Conventions.

    ☐ Default Drawing Storage Disc is **C:**. (Or **C:\DIR-NAME** if you use a Directory.)

    ☐ File **NAME.DWG.** Extensions (.DWG) is assumed. Name can be characters, numbers, and most symbols, but no spaces.

    ☐ AutoCAD begins new drawings by reading many default settings from a prototype drawing named ACAD.DWG.

☐ Coordinates.

    ☐ Digital Readout ^**D** or **F6 On** or **Off**.

    ☐ Look for ABSOLUTE or RELATIVE Readout.

☐ Units Selection (Real World Coordinates).

    ☐ **SCIENTIFIC** uses scientific decimal notation and a generic whole unit as the smallest drawing unit.

    ☐ **DECIMAL** uses simple decimal notation and a generic whole unit as the smallest drawing unit.

    ☐ **ENGINEERING** uses feet and inches with the inch as the smallest whole unit. Fractions are decimals.

    ☐ **ARCHITECTURAL** uses feet and inches with the inches as the smallest whole unit. Fractions are true fractions.

☐ Limits of Drawing File.

   ☐ Lower Left Hand Corner — set to **0,0** or slightly negative.

   ☐ Upper Right Hand Corner — set to an approximate **4X:3Y** ratio with enough units to cover your largest location or intended sheet size drawing units.

   ☐ **LIMITS** is only an "electronic fence" that helps you keep track of your drawing area. You can draw outside, but AutoCAD will give you a warning to let you know you are outside.

☐ Layer Assignment.

   ☐ Layer **0** is the default layer.

   ☐ Current layer is the active drawing layer.

☐ Color Assignment.

   ☐ **White (Color 7)** is the default color.

   ☐ Color assignment is by standard seven color names or standard seven numbers. Others can be set.

☐ Line Style and Weight.

   ☐ **CONTINUOUS** style is the default.

☐ Drawing Environment — Help, Status and Prompt Lines.

   ☐ Help is always available — type **HELP** or **?** at the Command: prompt.

   ☐ The **status** and **prompt lines** show the latest settings of many setup functions or commands.

   ☐ The **STATUS** command or **FLIP** screen display of the prompt lines gives more detailed listings.

NOTE: Look for more checklists at the end of future Chapters.

HERE WE GO

You've had a chance to set up AutoCAD and play around with the drawing editor by entering a few commands. Now you can move on to learning — How to Get Around in AutoCAD.

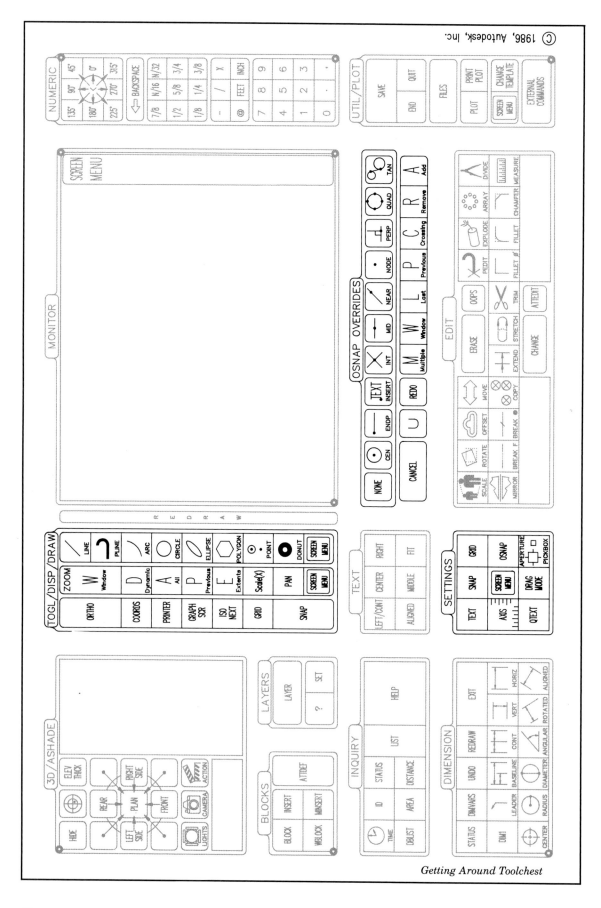

Getting Around Toolchest

CHAPTER 2

GETTING AROUND

MAKING A SMALL DISPLAY SCREEN DO THE WORK OF A BIG PIECE OF PAPER

The Benefits of Getting Around. ▶ A Toolchest for Getting Around. Where Am I? Snap, Grid, and Pick Commands. Ortho—A Special Snap. Snapping to Objects, and the Aperture. ▶ Display Control— Zoom. Naming and Saving Working Displays with View. Pan: Viewing Other Windows while Zoomed-In. ▶ Redraw and Regen. ▶ Summing Up— Checklist For Getting Around.

THE BENEFITS OF GETTING AROUND

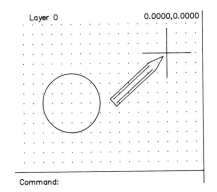

Example of GRID

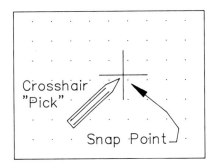

Example of SNAP

Given a straight edge and a rule, a draftsperson can locate a point on a drawing sheet with some degree of accuracy and use that point as a location for graphic elements. At first it's not as easy to get around with a CAD system because there is no tactile feedback similar to a ruler on paper.

In this Chapter you will learn about the electronic tools that replace the draftsperson's manual tools. Some benefits from getting to know AutoCAD's electronic tools immediately stand out: no eraser shavings, always having the "right" scale ruler, never having to borrow your 30-60 triangle back from your neighbor.

But many benefits from electronic tools are not immediately obvious: 100% accurate straight edge and triangles, mathematically defined curves, automatic "blow up" of details, and infinitely flexible graph paper to trace over as a guide.

With the benefits come new commands and new flexibility. In this Chapter you learn how a small display screen and an electronic input device are used to get around "A" size details, "E" size sheets, or 200' schematics. AutoCAD handles all three with ease. You will learn how to use your display as a "window" to "look in" on your drawings and help with your designs.

AutoCAD has its own set of electronic tools to control where you are, where you are going, and how you will get there.

A TOOLCHEST FOR GETTING AROUND

You can type command names or follow the screen menu sequences to get the getting around commands you need. A GETTING AROUND TOOL-CHEST list follows:

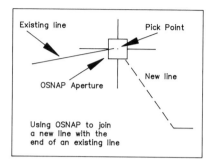

Example of OSNAP

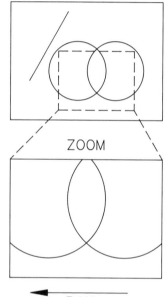

ZOOM

PAN

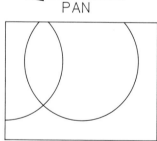

Example of ZOOM and PAN

AutoCAD CROSSHAIR CONTROL COMMANDS

☐ SNAP—Makes the crosshair move in comfortable increments, say every 1/4-inch.

☐ OSNAP—**O**bject **SNAP** allows you to precisely join new lines, arcs, and other drawing elements to exisiting ones.

☐ ORTHO—**ORTHO**gonal allows quick accurate entry of horizontal and vertical lines.

☐ GRID—Gives infinitely flexible graph paper to trace over.

AutoCAD DISPLAY COMMANDS

☐ BLIPMODE—Controls AutoCAD's placement of a small cross on the screen every time you record a point.

☐ PAN—Moves the view screen around the drawing file without changing the viewing scale.

☐ QTEXT**—Displays text on the screen as a box outline so that the screen will regenerate quickly.

☐ REDRAW—Cleans up the display by drawing the screen over.

☐ REGEN—Cleans up the display by recalculating the drawing file database and drawing the screen over.

☐ REGENAUTO—Controls which commands will cause an automatic REGEN.

☐ VIEW—ZOOM or PAN to a particular place in the drawing file.

☐ VIEWRES—Helps AutoCAD keep REGEN and REDRAW time to a minimum by keeping portions of your drawing file active for display, and by limiting the number of individual segments used to draw circles and arcs.

☐ ZOOM—Controls your display view of the drawing file. You can ZOOM-in for a close-up or ZOOM-out.

**QTEXT will not be discussed in this Chapter. You can find a discussion on QTEXT in the next Chapter with TEXT commands.

WHERE AM I

Put your pen point on the period at the end of this sentence. You know where that point is on the page and, with a ruler, you can measure that location to give an X and Y description of where the point is.

Now try that on the screen!

Let's get back into the AutoCAD drawing editor. You will use the drawing file you set up in the last Chapter and stored on disc as **CHAPTER1:**

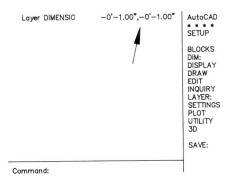

Drawing File CHAPTER1 Showing STATUS Line Digital Readout

```
From the AutoCAD Main Menu:

Enter selection: 2 Edit an EXISTING drawing

Enter NAME of drawing file: chapter1 (RETURN)

Command: LAYER (RETURN)
?/Make/Set/New/On/Off/Color/Ltype/Freeze/Thaw: Off (RETURN)
Layer name(s) to turn OFF: 0 (RETURN)
?/Make/Set/New/On/Off/Color/Ltype/Freeze/Thaw: (RETURN)
Command:
```

Set A Sandbox for Playing Around

When the drawing editor comes up, your screen should look like DRAWING FILE CHAPTER1. Turn off Layer 0 to get the squares out of your way while you use the Current Layer **DIMENSION** as a sandbox for playing around.

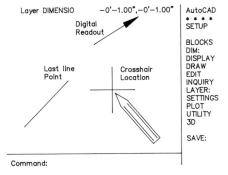

Drawing a line. The last point is different from the crosshair location.

Take a look at the status line and see what the digital readout of coordinates says. Move the pointer around—the coordinates on the status line do not change. Now hit the F6 key or type ^D to turn on coordinate tracking. Did the status line change? What does this mean?

☐ Any time you enter a point by pressing the pointer or entering coordinates from the keyboard, AutoCAD updates the digital readout. When you start a new drawing editor session, the readout shows the lower leftmost limit of the drawing file.

☐ If coordinate tracking is turned On (^D toggle), the status line displays the current location of the crosshairs. AutoCAD remembers the ^D toggle when the drawing is saved.

Keeping track of the last point or crosshair location will soon become second nature.

SNAP, GRID, AND PICK COMMANDS

No these aren't the noisy fellows on the Rice Krispies package!

SNAP, GRID, and the OSNAP group of pick commands help you turn a sea of points into accurate data entry. Try this exercise to see HOW INACCURATE I CAN BE:

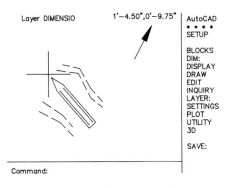

Rumbling trains, heavy feet and wobbly arms contribute to lack of accuracy

```
            HOW INACCURATE I CAN BE

Using the pointer and the coordinate readout, move the
    crosshair to exactly X=1'-4.50", Y=0'-9.25"

Take your hand off the pointer.

Did the coordinates change when you took your hand away?

Now give the pointer a subtle nudge!

Did the coordinates change this time?

Some input devices just have the jitters all the time!
```

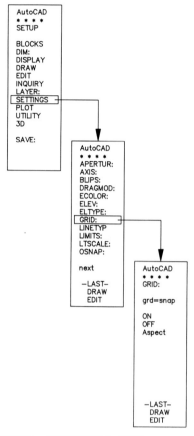

ROOT to SETTINGS to GRID

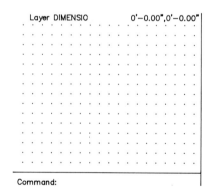

My First Grid

Obviously you need help in pinpointing exact locations. Of course you can type coordinates at the keyboard all the time (remember the absolute and relative brothers?). But you aren't going to remember the exact coordinates of your drawing pieces when you go to **pick** them up and move them.

SNAP, GRID, and the OSNAP group of pick commands help you out. Let's see how these work.

Setting Up a Grid

The **GRID** command creates a frame of reference, a series of construction points that are not part of the drawing file itself. To prove this to yourself, set up a GRID and then move the crosshair around or try the HOW INAC-CURATE I CAN BE exercise again.

Get to the GRID command by selecting the SETTINGS key from the ROOT-MENU and the GRID command on the SETTINGS list of commands.

Turn on a 2″ by 2″ GRID:

SETTING UP A 2-INCH BY 2-INCH GRID

Command: **GRID (RETURN)**
Grid spacing(X) or ON/OFF/Snap/Aspect <0'-0.00">: **2 (RETURN)**
Command:

Your screen should look like MY FIRST GRID. By the way, even though we will not show GRID in all of the drawings in this Book, you should turn on and use a grid to help you get around. The grid helps you "eyeball" distances on the screen and gives you visible indication of your limits.

By now you should recognize the different elements of the prompt line. <0'-0.00"> is a <default> prompt value for this grid execution. The GRID sub-commands are Grid spacing(X) or ON/OFF/Snap/Aspect on the prompt line.

GRID SUBCOMMANDS

☐ **ON/OFF.** Toggle between displaying the grid on the screen or not. **On** or **Of** are enough to switch the toggle. A ^G (Control-G) or (F7) also is a toggle.

☐ **spacing(X).** How far between grid points? If you give a value in response to the prompt, or accept the default with a **(RETURN)**, you will set up a grid with equal X and Y spacing (a square grid). Also, giving a nonzero value will turn **On** the grid.

☐ **Snap.** If you choose Snap or **S** AutoCAD assumes you want the grid to match your snap increment.

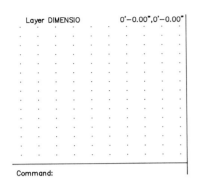

GRID with 2X:1Y Aspect Ratio

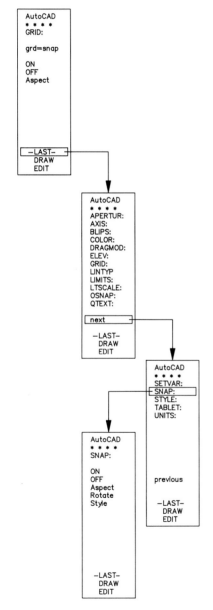

GRID to LASTMENU to SETTINGS to SNAP

☐ **Aspect**. If you choose Aspect or **A**, AutoCAD assumes you want to set up a grid with different X and Y spacing. It will prompt you for different X and Y values and then turns **On** the grid.

This may be the last time you'll see a freely moving crosshair so give the pointer one last whoosh! across the digitizer surface.

Getting Snappy about SNAP

What we need to whip the pointer into shape is **SNAP**. SNAP sets up the smallest increment that AutoCAD will recognize when we move the pointer around.

To get to the SNAP screen menu from the GRID screen menu, select ROOT-MENU (to get back to the SETTINGS menu), and then SNAP.

Let's set up a Standard SNAP at 0.5″ and see what it does to crosshair movements:

TURNING ON SNAP

Command: **SNAP (RETURN)**
Snap spacing or ON/OFF/Aspect/Rotate/Style <0'-1.00">:
   0.5 (RETURN)
Command:

The only thing that should change on your screen as a result of this command is the status line. It should now say **Snap**, indicating that SNAP is **On** and the digital readout should be rounded to half inches. The prompt line will say <**Snap On**>.

Try moving the pointer around. No more smooth movement of the crosshair lines. Why? Because the crosshair is now SNAPpy and jumps to the next snap increment.

Because digitizers are more accurate than wobbly human hands, freehand recording yields points that are off the desired mark. Try the HOW INAC-CURATE I CAN BE exercise one more time.

Could you hit the exact point this time? Still not, huh? But this time for a different reason. You could not get to X = 1'-4.50″, Y = 0'-9.25″ because this is not a current SNAPpable value. Since we set the SNAP to a half-inch (0.5″), we can't get to locations with a finer round-off unless SNAP is changed or turned Off.

SNAP has a toggle (^B) or (F9). You'll find this toggle helpful when you are trying to get a point that is not SNAPpable. Use the ^B in the middle of other commands. This is called an **interrupt** where you take time out from one command to set another parameter or use another command.

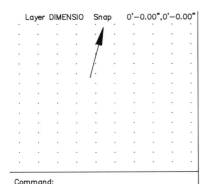

Command:

Setting a SNAP doesn't affect screen display. The word "SNAP" appears on the STATUS Line.

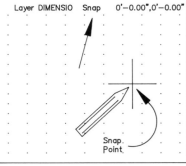

Command:

Crosshair movement and pointer coordinate entry are limited by SNAP

By the way, direct keyboard coordinate entry—either absolute or relative—overrides SNAP control of the pointer. Here are the SNAP subcommands.

SNAP SUBCOMMANDS

☐ **ON/OFF**. A toggle switch again. ^B (Control B) or (F9) does the same toggling.

☐ **spacing**. The SNAP increment—what is the smallest unit you want AutoCAD to recognize? Giving a value automatically sets SNAP **On**.

☐ **Aspect**. As with grid, you can have different X and Y increment values which AutoCAD will prompt you for.

☐ **Rotate**. If you are so inclined—you can rotate the grid and the SNAPping values starting at any point (usually 0,0) and to any angle. AutoCAD will prompt you for input. Using Rotate is like setting a mechanical drafting arm on an angle.

☐ **Style**. Everyone should SNAP with Style. You have two choices:

  ☐ **Standard**. A regular, flat, 2-dimensional SNAP and GRID.

  ☐ **Isometric**. AutoCAD gives you a grid like you would find on ISO-graph paper. You can draw on the top, front, or left "sides" by SNAP-ping to an isometric-style SNAP.

ORTHO—A SPECIAL SNAP

ORTHO limits your pointer movement to right angles from the last point. This means that any lines you enter with the pointer when ORTHO is On will be aligned with grid points, either horizontally or vertically.

To demonstrate the point let's draw a line before and after turning on ORTHO:

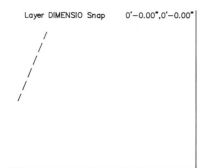

Command:

A line before ORTHO

DRAWING FREEHAND AND ORTHOGONAL LINES WITH ORTHO

```
Command: LINE (RETURN)
From point:    (pick any point with the pointer)
To point:      (pick a point about 3 grid points to the right
  and 5 grid points up)
To point: (RETURN)
Command:
```

Easy, right? Now turn on ORTHO. You can do this by typing ORTHO or by using either ^O or F8, the ORTHO toggle switch. Since ORTHO is either ON or OFF, you might as well get used to just using the toggle—^O (Control-O). Try it now.

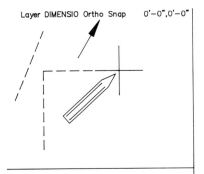

STATUS Line shows "ORTHO" when ORTHO is On

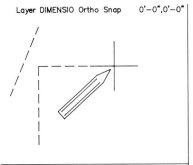

ORTHO limits the next line segment to right angles

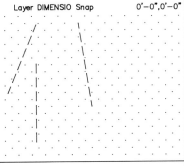

Lines on a Rotated GRID

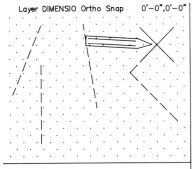

ORTHO constrained line on a Rotated GRID

The only thing that changes on the screen is that **Ortho** appears on the status line and <**Ortho**> shows on the prompt line.

Now try to run through the same line sequence with ORTHO set on.

You can't do it. Pick a **To point:** about 5 grid points to the right of your **From point:** and (RETURN) out of LINE. What happened to the crosshair control? It moves only vertically or horizontally—the effect of the ORTHO setting.

Using the ^O toggle you can use ORTHO as an interrupt just like SNAP. Also like SNAP, keyboard coordinate entry overrides ORTHO pointer control.

Rotating the SNAP Grid

Are you angling for an exercise? Try this one:

ORTHO AND ROTATED SNAP

Use the toggle now to turn ORTHO **Off**

Command: **SNAP (RETURN)**
Snap spacing or ON/OFF/Aspect/Rotate/Style <0'-0.50">:
R (RETURN)
Base point <0'-0.00",0'-0.00">: **(RETURN)**
Rotation angle <0.00>: **45 (RETURN)**
Command:

Now do the line exercise from above again.

Hit ^O

Try the line exercise again. Settle for any **To point:**
Exit the line command with a **(RETURN)**

What did you learn?

☐ Rotated SNAPs also rotate the grid.

☐ The crosshairs follow the angle of rotation.

☐ The grid moves (rotates) but the drawing elements (the first two lines that you drew) stay unchanged.

☐ On a rotated SNAP/GRID, ORTHO still follows a 90-degree angle rule, but the base starting angle is set by the SNAP angle.

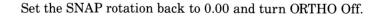

Set the SNAP rotation back to 0.00 and turn ORTHO Off.

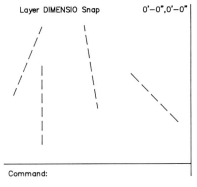

Layer DIMENSIO Snap   0'–0",0'–0"

Command:

ORTHO Practice Screen

```
Command: SNAP (RETURN)
Snap spacing or ON/OFF/Aspect/Rotate/Style <0'-0.50">:
  R  (RETURN)
Base point <0'-0.00",0'-0.00">:  (RETURN)
Rotation angle <45.00>: 0 (RETURN)

  (hit the ^O toggle)

Command: <Ortho off>
```

Your screen should now have four lines on it and look something like the ORTHO PRACTICE SCREEN.

SNAPPING TO OBJECTS AND THE APERTURE

SNAPping to snap increments is great when you want to make original entries for lines, arcs, and text. But when you want to edit existing lines or add graphic elements as extensions to existing elements, you need a way to identify where you want your new or edited versions to "attach" to your existing drawing.

For example, let's say you want to start a new line at the exact endpoint of one of the lines on the screen. Assuming that you haven't changed the snap setting from when you entered the line, (like we did with two of the lines) you probably can pick the endpoint pretty well. But what if you have changed the snap increment? Or what if you want to pick a tangent point to a curve? Or pick the intersection of two lines that doesn't fall on a snap point?

Pinpointing Crosshair Location with OSNAP

AutoCAD's **OSNAP** commands help here. As with SNAP, we can't always trust our shaky hands to accurately locate an exact location. OSNAP commands give us a tolerance or target area for identifying existing locations.

Using an OSNAP command allows you to "get close" without having to get the exact target. Just how close you have to be depends on how large you set the AutoCAD **APERTURE**, an electronic bullseye that homes in on pick points. Let's clear the screen, set up a few objects to OSNAP to, and study the OSNAP commands. You can pick points and commands with either the keyboard or your pointer.

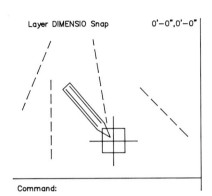

OSNAP turns the crosshair into a tar-get for zeroing in on locations

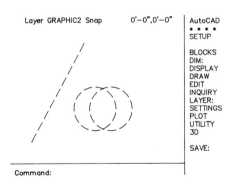

OSNAP Setup Screen

SETTING UP FOR OSNAP

Command: **QUIT (RETURN)**
Really want to discard all changes to the drawing? **y (RETURN)**

(Main Menu appears)

Select **2** Edit an EXISTING drawing

Accept the <CHAPTER1> default prompt with a **(RETURN)**

When you get into the drawing editor, you will not have a GRID or SNAP set because these were not saved during the QUIT process.

Command: **LAYER (RETURN)**
?/Make/Set/New/On/Off/Color/Ltype/Freeze/Thaw: **Off (RETURN)**
Layer name(s) to turn OFF: **0 (RETURN)**
?/Make/Set/New/On/Off/Color/Ltype/Freeze/Thaw: **(RETURN)**
Command:

Turn on a GRID that is 2" x 2".

Turn on SNAP to 0.5".

Command: **ZOOM (RETURN)**
All/Center/Dynamic/Extents/Left/Previous/Window/<Scale(X)>:
 All (RETURN)
Regenerating drawing.
Command: **LINE (RETURN)**
From point: **4",4" (RETURN)**
To point: **1'2",1'10" (RETURN)**
To point: **(RETURN)**
Command: **CIRCLE (RETURN)**
3P/2P/TTR/<Center point>: **1'4",10" (RETURN)**
Diameter/<Radius>: **4" (RETURN)**

Command: **CIRCLE (RETURN)**
3P/2P/TTR/<Center point>: **1'7",10" (RETURN)**
Diameter/<Radius>: **4" (RETURN)**
Command:

Get the coordinate readout to track you with a ^D toggle.

Set Current layer to GRAPHIC2 using the LAYER Set Command.

Your setup screen should look like the OSNAP SETUP SCREEN.

If it doesn't, go back to the **QUIT** line and start again.

We will use this starting base for other INSIDE AutoCAD working sessions, so let's save it and store it so we can use it over and over:

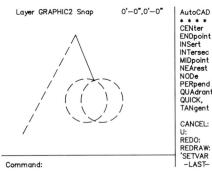

OSNAP Endpoint and Intersec Finished Drawing

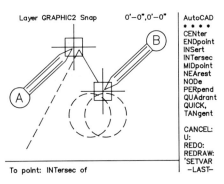

OSNAP Endpoint and Intersec Drawing in Progress

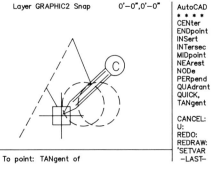

OSNAP Midpoint and Tangent

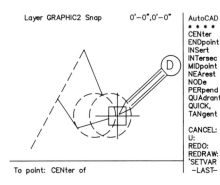

OSNAP Endpoint and Center

```
Command: SAVE  (RETURN)
File name <CHAPTER1>:  chapter2  (RETURN)
Command:
```

This save action stored a copy of the current drawing file (and all included drawing elements and setup parameters) in a new disc file called CHAPTER2. This did not in any way affect the current drawing file called CHAPTER1.

Don't confuse OSNAP with ORTHO (a common mistake).

OSNAP stands for **O**bject **SNAP**. Often you want to SNAP to existing points or drawing elements instead of SNAPping to a GRID point, or an ORTHO constrained grid point. OSNAP lets you do this.

To demonstrate OSNAP **ENDpoint** and OSNAP **INTersec** we'll draw a second line from the upper end of the first line to the upper intersection of the two circles. The resulting drawing will look like OSNAP ENDPOINT AND INTERSEC FINISHED.

GETTING OSNAP TO HELP PICK ENDPOINT AND INTERSEC

```
Get to the LINE command on the screen menu

Command: LINE  (RETURN)
From Point:      (Now type ENDpoint

Command: LINE From Point: endpoint
of

(Now move the crosshair close to the upper endpoint of the
first line. See the aperture bullseye? All you have to do is
get the endpoint inside the aperture bullseye and hit the
pointer. Try it -- you'll see the From point: SNAP to
the endpoint of the line.)

(To prove to yourself that your new line From point: is
tied to the old line endpoint, drag the crosshair around
a bit to see that the new line is firmly anchored to the
old one.)

To point:        (type INTersec)

To point: intersec
of

(Now line the target up on the appropriate intersection of
the two circles and hit the pointer button.)

To point: intersec
of         (pick point)
To point: (RETURN)
Command:
```

Congratulations. You've successfully OSNAPped.

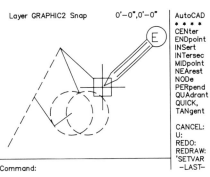

OSNAP Endpoint and Quadrant

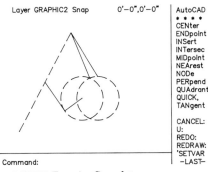

OSNAP Exercise Complete

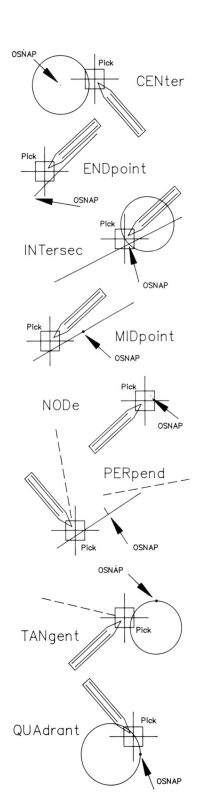

OSNAP Targets and the Points They Pick

Try some more. Use the accompanying OSNAP drawings as guides.

Try a line from the midpoint of the first line tangent to the lower edge of the left circle. Your screen should look like OSNAP MIDPOINT AND TANGENT.

Try moving from that tangent point to the center of the first circle using the **CENter** OSNAP option.

One more. Try moving from the upper endpoint of the first line to the 90-degree **QUAdrant** of the right circle.

Try as many other combinations as you want until you get the hang of the different OSNAP options. Here's a complete list:

OSNAP OPTIONS

☐ CENter—Snaps to the center of an arc or circle.

☐ ENDpoint—Snaps to the nearest endpoint of a line or arc.

☐ INSert—Snaps to the "origin" of a symbol (BLOCK) or text that has been inserted into the drawing file. More about BLOCKS later.

☐ INTersec—Snaps to the nearest intersection of—two— objects in the drawing file.

☐ MIDpoint—Snaps to the midpoint of a line or arc.

☐ NEArest—Snaps to the nearest point on an existing object.

☐ NODe—Snaps to a point object.

☐ PERpendicular—Snaps to a point on the picked object that would form a perpendicular (normal) line from the last point to the picked object.

☐ TANgent—Snaps to a point on a picked arc or circle that forms a tangent to the picked arc or circle from the last point.

☐ QUAdrant—Snaps to the closest 0, 90, 180, or 270-degree point on a picked arc or circle.

☐ QUIck—Forces all other OSNAP options to quickly find the first potential target, not necessarily the best. QUIck finds the potential point that is on the most recent object in the target box.

Setting the Aperture

You can control the size of the crosshair bullseye that OSNAP uses to zero in on target objects. To adjust the size of the aperture use the **APERTUR:** command from the SETTINGS screen menu.

```
Command: APERTUR (RETURN)
Object snap target height (1-50 pixels) <10>: 4 (RETURN)
Command:
```

A pixel is the smallest "dot" that can be displayed on your screen. Four or six pixels (the default value is 10) gives a good target size. Try a few different values to see how comfortable you feel with larger and smaller apertures.

There are advantages and disadvantages to setting large and small APERTUREs.

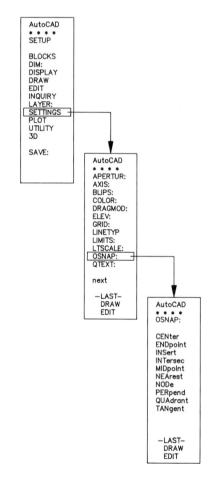

ROOT to SETTINGS to OSNAP List

APERTURE SIZES

APERTURE SIZE	ADVANTAGE	DISADVANTAGE
Small	Finds Point Faster	Hard to Get Crosshairs to Line Up
Large	Easy to Line Up	Slower to Find Point

Optimizing OSNAP

AutoCAD goes through a lot of work trying to find the correct object that you want to OSNAP to when you are using an OSNAP command. In fact, AutoCAD searches every object on the screen that could possibly be a "best" fit to your OSNAP request. This can take a little time when you have a lot of objects in the file.

You can optimize or shorten the OSNAP search process by:

☐ Keeping the aperture reasonably small to keep extraneous objects out of the target.

☐ Using the **QUIck** OSNAP option.

QUIck allows AutoCAD to take the first object that meets your OSNAP criteria instead of doing an exhaustive search. Invoke **quick** by typing it prior to another OSNAP option:

☐ From point: **QUIck,NEArest** to
  or

☐ To point: **QUIck,MIDpoint** of

Quick may sometimes let you down if the first fit that AutoCAD finds is not the one you want. In that case, simply CANCEL what you are doing and start the OSNAP process again, without the **quick** modifier.

Two Ways to Use OSNAP

In the examples above, we have been using OSNAP as an **interrupt** in the middle of the LINE command to fine tune our line endpoints. OSNAP interrupt mode temporarily sets up an OSNAP aperture condition to complete a task at hand. You also can select OSNAP interrupts from the ROOTMENU screen by picking the **** line or by picking the interrupts from the tablet menu.

You can set up OSNAP conditions to be in effect throughout an AutoCAD editing session. This is known as **Running Mode**. To do this you select OSNAP from the SETTINGS screen menu of commands and select OSNAP conditions just as you would in interrupt mode. Running mode OSNAPs remain in effect until replaced by another running mode setting, or temporarily overridden by an interrupt OSNAP option.

Use interrupt mode whenever the need arises. Set up a running OSNAP condition only when you know that you will be spending a good deal of time connecting drawing file elements where OSNAP will be helpful. When a running OSNAP is **On**, the crosshair will always have a bullseye aperture during object or point selection.

A Tip About OSNAP

OSNAP running conditions cannot be **toggled** like SNAP and GRID. Try to plan ahead to get OSNAP help. You can always type the OSNAP interrupt modifiers, but this defeats the purpose of saving time using OSNAP.

If you do type the OSNAP modifier, you just type the first word or first three characters like **END**point or **PER**pend. AutoCAD will fill in the **of** or **to**.

ZOOM

PAN

ZOOM and PAN give you detailed looks at your drawing file

DISPLAY CONTROL—ZOOM

Whether you've set your drawing file limits to represent 2 feet by 3 feet or 2000 feet by 3000 feet, a CAD display screen is not large enough to give you a one-to-one view of your drawing file.

For most professional applications, if you look at your whole drawing file on the screen, you can't make out drawing details accurately. AutoCAD provides the equivalent of binoculars to "zoom in" on part of the drawing file to see the detail. The name of this tool is—remarkably—the **ZOOM** command.

To get a feel for the display control commands, let's use the **CHAPTER2** drawing file saved earlier:

DISPLAY CONTROL SETUP

```
QUIT to get rid of the OSNAP lines and circles

(Main Menu appears)

Select 2 Edit an EXISTING drawing

Enter NAME of drawing (default CHAPTER1): chapter2 (RETURN)
```

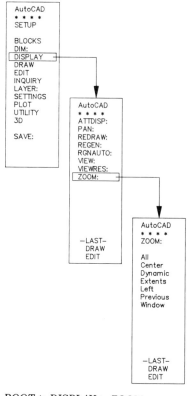

ROOT to DISPLAY to ZOOM

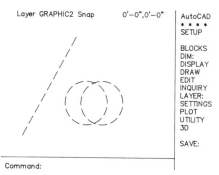

Display Setup Screen

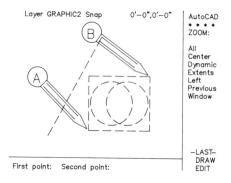

ZOOM Window

Get the Coordinate readout to track you with a ^D toggle.

Your setup screen should look like DISPLAY SETUP SCREEN.

Using ZOOM To Look More Closely

Suppose we want to look more closely at the intersection of the two circles on the screen. To do this we need to "zoom in" on the drawing.

To use the ZOOM command we have to be able to communicate to AutoCAD exactly what part of the current screen we want to see **blown up**. The most common way to tell AutoCAD what we want to see, is to draw a box or **Window** around the area of interest. For this example, you can see the window we want to ZOOM in on in ZOOM Window.

Let's step through a ZOOM Window example. Get to the ZOOM screen menu through the ROOT and DISPLAY menus. Use the ZOOM Window drawing as a guide.

Use the ZOOM window drawing as a guide to picking the corners for a ZOOM window. It is not important to pick exact coordinates—you are just outlining a rough area you want to see in more detail. If you feel uncomfortable picking freehand, use the digital readout to get close to the following lower left (first) and upper right (second) corners:

PICKING A ZOOM WINDOW

Command: **ZOOM (RETURN)**
All/Center/Dynamic/Extents/Left/Previous/Window/<Scale(X)>:
   W (RETURN)
First corner: (pick)   Second corner: (pick)

   (Try to pick the lower left at 11",5"
    and the upper right at 2',1'-3")
Command:

Notice that after you pick the First corner: instead of the normal crosshair, your pointer movements trace out the window for ZOOM control. As soon as you pick the Other corner:, AutoCAD goes to work by repainting the screen and filling it with the desired window.

Don't worry if you don't get exact window corners. The corners that you pick are only guides to AutoCAD in setting up the ZOOMed in display—the next display will not be exactly the same shape as your window because AutoCAD always maintains its screen X and Y ratio, regardless of your corner locations.

You can zoom in further by selecting the ZOOM command again, selecting the **W** subcommand, picking two more window corners and letting AutoCAD redraw the screen. ZOOM in again a few times until you get the hang of the window option.

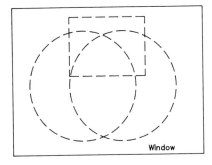

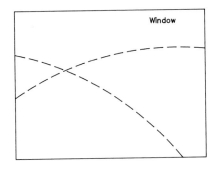

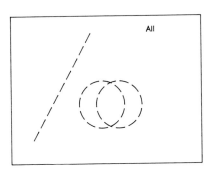

ZOOM, ZOOM, ZOOM, ZOOM All

ZOOM Back Out With ZOOM All

The easiest way to get back to the full display of your drawing file (zoomed out) is to use the ZOOM All subcommand.

ZOOM ALL

```
Command: ZOOM (RETURN)
All/Center/Dynamic/Extents/Left/Previous/Window/<Scale(X)>:
   A (RETURN)
Regenerating drawing.
Command:
```

When AutoCAD sees a ZOOM All, it regenerates and repaints the screen with everything in the drawing file.

Keeping Track of ZOOM Displays

Every time you ZOOM in or out, AutoCAD keeps track of the previous display. In fact, AutoCAD remembers up to five ZOOMs. To get AutoCAD to put the ZOOM-Before-This-One on the screen, use the **Previous** subcommand.

A QUICK SESSION WITH PREVIOUS ZOOM

If you are not already at All, Zoom **All** now.

Zoom in using **W** to an area just surrounding the two circles.

Zoom in again. You can use **Left** and/or **Center** to get to the football-like area created by the overlap of the two circles.

Use the keyboard or pointer to enter the coordinate.

```
Command: ZOOM (RETURN)
All/Center/Dynamic/Extents/Left/Previous/Window/<Scale(X)>:
L (RETURN)
Lower left corner point : 1',6" (RETURN)
Magnification or Height <2'-1.91">: 2X (RETURN)
Command: ZOOM (RETURN)
All/Center/Dynamic/Extents/Left/Previous/Window/<Scale(X)>:
  C (RETURN)
Center point: 1'6,10 (RETURN)
Magnification or Height <1'-0.96">: 10" (RETURN)
```

Zoom **Previous** to go back to the two circles area.

Zoom **Previous** once or twice to get back to All where you started.

Note that Previous does not always ZOOM out. It only ZOOMs to the last ZOOM view setting.

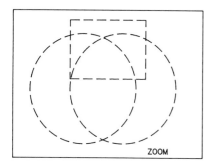

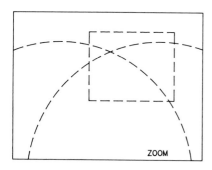

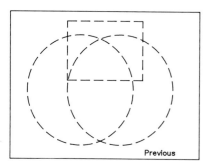

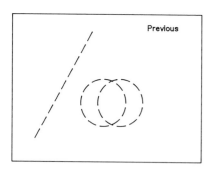

ZOOMing-in to the Circle Overlap

Dynamic ZOOM Gives You More Display Control

There are three subsets in the drawing file. They are:

☐ The entire drawing.

☐ The generated area.

☐ The view screen.

When you use dynamic zoom you can see all three of these areas graphically on the screen before making a decision on what your next screen view will be and how long it will take to appear on the screen.

Take a look at the DYNAMIC ZOOM CONTROL SCREEN. On that diagram you see four rectangular areas outlined. The first three show the entire drawing area (extents), the currently generated area, and the current view screen. The extents will be the limits unless you have drawn beyond the limits.

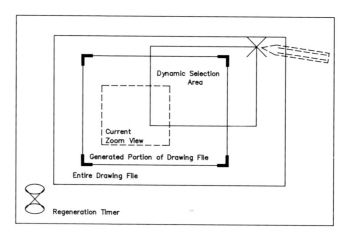

Dynamic ZOOM Control Screen

The fourth rectangular area is a dynamic window under the moveable control of your pointer. You use this dynamic window to select the next screen view you want to see.

If you select your next screen view from within the area bounded by the "generated" data, the next screen view will appear on the screen in REDRAW speed. If you select your next screen view to include data from outside the currently generated data, your zoom will require a regeneration of the entire drawing file as AutoCAD searches for the part of the drawing file you want to see in your next screen view. If you Zoom beyond about 50X, AutoCAD will regenerate the drawing.

Try a ZOOM Dynamic now. First get a zoomed in view on the screen. Then get the ZOOM Dynamic display on the screen. Try to get a feel for how your pointer controls the dynamic zoom window position and size. Finally, select a new screen view and let AutoCAD generate the new screen view:

DYNAMIC ZOOM

Get a zoomed in window on the screen:

Command: **ZOOM (RETURN)**
All/Center/Dynamic/Extents/Left/Previous/Window/<Scale(X)>:
    W (RETURN)
First corner: (pick)   Other corner: (pick)

(Select the top intersection of the circles -- see the diagram as a guide)

Regenerating drawing.   (zoomed in view appears)

Now get the Dynamic Zoom Display on the screen

Command: **ZOOM (RETURN)**
All/Center/Dynamic/Extents/Left/Previous/Window/<Scale(X)>:
    D (RETURN)

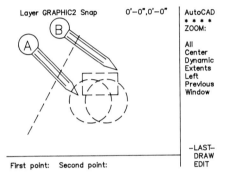

Dynamic ZOOM — Current View

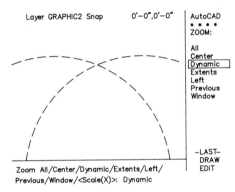

Dynamic ZOOM Sequence

Move your pointer around. Your pointer controls the dynamic viewing window by "dragging" it around the screen. You control the dynamic window as if you held it by a handle (represented by the "X" in the middle of the window).

Notice that when you moved the pointer to outside the "generated" drawing file area a little hourglass appears on the lower left part of the screen. This is AutoCAD's way of telling you that if you select a new screen viewing area that includes data outside the generated portion of the drawing file, AutoCAD will need to regenerate your drawing to give your next screen view.

What if you want to have a next screen view that is larger (more zoomed out) than the current dynamic viewing window? Your pointer also controls the size of the dynamic window.

When you press your pointer button. Notice an "arrow" is at the right side corner of the dynamic window. When you move the pointer to the right, you expand the dynamic window. Move the pointer to the left and the dynamic window contracts.

When you have the dynamic window the **size** you want it, you hit the pointer button again to lock in the size of the dynamic window. Your pointer once again controls the **location** of the dynamic window through the "X" handle in the middle of the window.

You can toggle between controlling the dynamic window size and location by hitting the pointer button and lining up the next viewing screen that you want.

Once you have selected the next viewing screen that you want, get AutoCAD to actually perform the ZOOM by hitting the (RETURN) key while holding the dynamic viewing window in place.

59

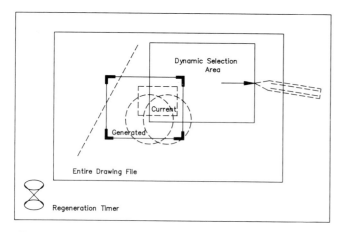

Dynamic ZOOM — Pointer Controls Next View Size

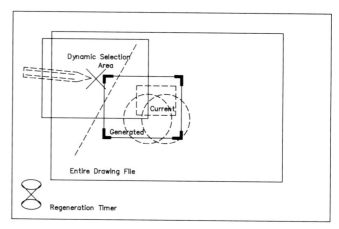

Dynamic ZOOM — Location Control

DYNAMIC ZOOM CONTINUED

All/Center/Dynamic/Extents/Left/Previous/Window/<Scale(X)>:
D (RETURN)

Get a feel for how the pointer controls the dynamic window

Move the dynamic window around with the "X" handle.

Press the pointer button to switch to dynamic window size control.

Stretch or shrink the dynamic window.

Press the pointer button to switch to dynamic window location control.

Line up the dynamic viewing window where you want to see the next screen view.

Hold the pointer in place.

Press the **(RETURN)** key.

Watch the screen regenerate fast.

Command:

If the dynamic window disappears and you see only the arrow or X, you probably have sized it to nothingness. Move and/or hit the pointer to regain control.

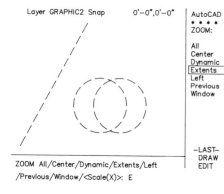

ZOOM Extents

Other ZOOM Options: Center, Extents, and Left

The ZOOM Command: prompt shows many different Zoom subcommands. ZOOM Window, ZOOM All and ZOOM Dynamic are three popular methods for getting ZOOMed in and out of an AutoCAD display. But there are other methods. Here's the complete list:

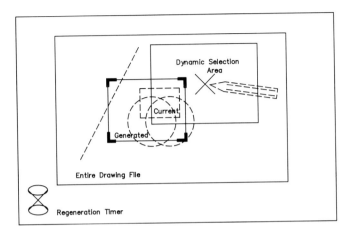

Dynamic ZOOM — Location Control

ZOOM OPTIONS

☐ <Scale(X)>—A numeric ZOOM factor. A magnification factor of 1 displays a view of the drawing limits. A value less than 1 zooms out, and greater than 1 zooms in. A magnification **X** modifier gives zooms relative to your current view. **2X** gives a display twice as large as the last display.

☐ All—ZOOMs out to limits or everything in the drawing file, whichever is inclusive.

☐ Dynamic—Graphically selects any portion of the drawing as your next screen view, but also sees what part of your file is generated and will therefore appear fast.

☐ Center—Pick a center point and a "picture" top and bottom by selecting two endpoints of a "height". Or pick a center point and a magnification.

☐ Extents—Gives the smallest "zoomed-in" view of everything in the drawing file. Extents is similar to All, but ignores limits.

☐ Left—Pick a lower left corner and a height of how much drawing information you want to display to fill up the screen.

☐ Previous—Restores the last ZOOM setting. Previous works with up to 5 previously stored ZOOMs.

☐ Window—Pick two points that define a rectangular window to describe what part of the drawing file will be on the screen.

NAMING AND SAVING WORKING DISPLAYS WITH VIEW

We've tried several ways to generate a ZOOMed display. The one thing all the ZOOM subcommands have in common is the need to specify the boundary of the new screen view. There is another way to keep track of ZOOM displays using the VIEW command.

Suppose that most of your work for the next few hours will be concentrated on the two circles. You will want to periodically ZOOM out to see how the whole drawing is shaping up, but most of the time you will be ZOOMed in to the area of the two circles.

Rather than having to identify a window around the two circles every time you want to fill the screen with just this area, you can store this window, give it a name, and call it up whenever you need it.

A stored window is called a named VIEW.

To store a window, we use the **VIEW** command to name and store it. VIEW can be picked from the DISPLAY screen menu, or can be typed at the keyboard:

SAVING A VIEW

```
ZOOM to an area just surrounding the two circles by any method

Command: VIEW (RETURN)
?/Delete/Restore/Save/Window: SAVE (RETURN)
View name to save: Twocircles (RETURN)
Command:
```

Here's an exercise to test AutoCAD's VIEW command and see that **Twocircles** is recorded as a VIEW:

RESTORING A VIEW

```
Command: ZOOM (RETURN)
All/Center/Dynamic/Extents/Left/Previous/Window/<Scale(X)>:
  A (RETURN)
Regenerating drawing.
Command: VIEW (RETURN)
?/Delete/Restore/Save/Window: R (RETURN)
View name to restore: Twocircles (RETURN)
Command:
```

VIEW has five subcommands.

VIEW SUBCOMMANDS

☐ **?**—Gives a list of all named views, their magnifications and center points.

☐ **Save**—Allows you to name the current display and store it.

☐ **Restore**—Puts the view that you name up on the screen.

☐ **Delete** —Prompts you for the name of a view to delete from the library of named views.

☐ **Window** —Allows you to name and save a view that you specify with a window (not necessarily the current display).

PAN: VIEWING OTHER WINDOWS WHILE ZOOMED-IN

The display list of commands has another item you may want to know about. **PAN** allows you to remain at the current magnification level (ZOOMed-in) and to move around the drawing file.

Think of PAN this way: ZOOM is like putting a pair of binoculars in front of your eyes to look closer. PAN is like moving your eyes and binoculars together to look around.

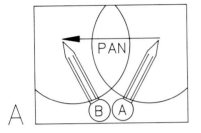

PAN is useful if you are working on a ZOOMed-in area and want to see the part of the drawing file that is "just-a-little-to-the-left" (or up, or down, or to the right).

PAN Needs A Displacement To Get Around

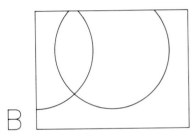

PAN Displacement

The **PAN** command works by getting a **Displacement** from you and applying that displacement to the ZOOMed-in view. You define a displacement by giving two points. These two points determine a vector giving distance and direction. The order you give the points determines the direction of the PAN.

Think of PAN displacements this way: When you give two points to identify a displacement you tell AutoCAD, "I want to pick up the drawing by this point (first displacement point) and put that point over here (second displacement point)". The crosshair trails a line from the first to the second displacement point showing you the path of the PAN.

```
Command: PAN (RETURN)
Displacement:    (pick)    Second point:    (pick)
Command:
```

If you find PAN a little awkward to use, use ZOOM Dynamic.

REDRAW AND REGEN

As your drawing files become larger you will need to control screen size and resolution of your drawing.

When drawing files become large, AutoCAD compensates for the fact that not all the data can be kept **generated** by keeping some data generated around the area you are working, and keeping other data less active (not generated).

Your data is always available. However, instead of asking for data and getting it immediately, AutoCAD and your computer may take many seconds or even a few minutes to get data that is not generated.

Keeping The Right Image Generated

The trick is to have AutoCAD keep just enough and not too much of your drawing active at any one time. This means that you have to be conscious of just what you are asking AutoCAD to keep track of, and how you want it displayed.

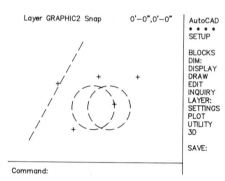

Display Screen before REDRAW

BLIPMODE and REDRAW Keep Screen Clutter To a Minimum

One way to keep a better handle on just what AutoCAD is showing you is to keep screen clutter down.

Here's a simple example. Remember the OSNAP exercises you just did? Every time you enter a point on the screen (either with a pointer or keyboard entry), AutoCAD places a small cross on the screen known as a **BLIP**.

So as you draw, you fill up the screen area with real drawing elements (like lines and circles) and other clutter like construction markers (blips). A construction marker is a point AutoCAD leaves behind when creating drawing elements like the center of a circle or the endpoint of a line.

A few BLIPs are great for keeping an eye on where you've been (or might want to go again), but they become bothersome in quantity when all they seem to do is clutter up the screen.

REDRAW

To clean up the screen and get rid of blips use the **REDRAW** command. This simply clears the screen, and redraws real drawing elements, leaving old blips behind.

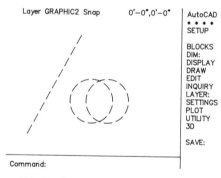

Display Screen after REDRAW

CLEARING UP THE SCREEN WITH A REDRAW

Command: **REDRAW** (RETURN)
Command:

You can also accomplish a REDRAW without typing or picking the command. Toggling GRID on or off with ^G or **F7** causes a REDRAW.

Use BLIPMODE to Control Blips

If you find you just don't need blips, you can use the **BLIPMODE** command to control construction markers. You can keep AutoCAD from drawing these temporary markers by typing BLIPMODE **Off** or selecting BLIPS from the SETTINGS screen menu.

Generated and Non-Generated Data

Beyond screen clutter, the next best way to keep the amount of data that AutoCAD has to work with neat and trim, is to keep an eye on just how much data is **generated**.

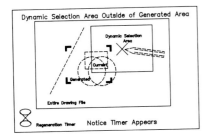

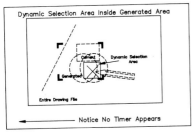

Dynamic ZOOM Shows Generated and Nongenerated areas

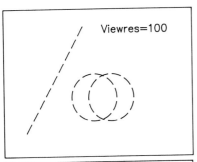

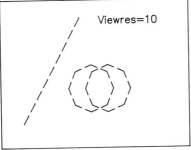

VIEWRES optimizes display generation by trading looks for speed

Think about all of your drawing data in three ZOOM subsets:

☐ The drawing extents. Everything in the drawing file.

☐ Generated data. A portion (up to all) of the drawing file that AutoCAD and your computer can keep "ready active".

☐ The screen view. A portion (up to all) of the generated data that actually appears on the screen.

When a drawing file is small and uncomplicated, all these subsets are one and the same. But as your drawing file gets larger, only portions of the file are generated, and it is more efficient to show only portions on the screen.

Going from one screen view to another within the generated portion of the drawing file with a PAN or ZOOM, is usually performed with REDRAW (fast) speed. However, to call up a screen view that contains non-generated data, requires the generation of a different area data set, and therefore takes more time.

VIEWRES Controls Smooth Curves and Regeneration

When you asked AutoCAD to call up the CHAPTER2 drawing file, AutoCAD performed two important calculations:

☐ How much data to generate as active. In this case, AutoCAD made the entire database active as you wanted a full view upon entering the drawing editor.

☐ How fine to generate curves. When circles or arcs are tiny, AutoCAD needs only a few straight lines on the screen to fool your eye into seeing smooth curves. When arcs are larger, AutoCAD needs more segments to make a smooth arc. AutoCAD determines how many segments to draw depending on what is to be shown on the screen.

The **VIEWRES** (VIEW RESolution) command controls both of these parameters. Let's try altering the "fineness" of the circles on the screen by generating fewer segments. Let's get back to looking at your entire drawing. Select ZOOM ALL from the DISPLAY menu. Then type VIEWRES:

VIEW RESOLUTION

```
Command: ZOOM (RETURN)
All/Center/Dynamic/Extents/Left/Previous/Window/<Scale>(x):
  A (RETURN)
Regenerating drawing.
Command:

Now let's look at VIEWRES.

Command: VIEWRES (RETURN)      (Type VIEWRES.)
Do you want fast zooms? <Y>:  (RETURN)
Enter circle zoom percent (1-20000) <100>: 10 (RETURN)
Regenerating drawing.
Command:
```

Normally you let AutoCAD calculate 100% of the curve edge segments that it wants to. But if you decrease or increase the "circle zoom percent" you can get coarser or finer arcs.

By answering the default <Y> yes to "Do you want fast zooms?" you are telling AutoCAD to minimize the frequency of regeneration by creating as large a generated area as possible when a regeneration occurs.

Controlling Data Generation with REGEN and REGENAUTO

```
AutoCAD
* * * *
SETUP

BLOCKS
DIM:
DISPLAY
DRAW
EDIT
INQUIRY
LAYER:
SETTINGS
PLOT
UTILITY
3D

SAVE:
```

```
AutoCAD
* * * *
ATTDISP:
PAN:
REDRAW:
REGEN:
RGNAUTO:
VIEW:
VIEWRES:
ZOOM:




-LAST-
DRAW
EDIT
```

DISPLAY Menu Showing REGEN and REGNAUTO

Notice that the VIEWRES command caused AutoCAD to regenerate the drawing in order to make the circles coarse or fine. In order to regenerate the drawing, AutoCAD "reads" all the data in the drawing file and calculates the location of each element on the screen. Had the drawing file been full of elements (many lines, arcs, circles, etc.), this regeneration might have taken a long time.

You will see that many commands cause this regeneration including ZOOM, PAN, and VIEW. You can force a regeneration of the screen and drawing file with the REGEN command. Try a REGEN now by typing REGEN or picking it from the DISPLAY menu:

```
Command: REGEN (RETURN)
Regenerating drawing.
Command:
```

Now is a good time to demonstrate the difference between a slow AutoCAD regeneration and a fast one. The REGEN you just did was fast because AutoCAD only had to calculate the line and about a dozen segments for each circle.

Reset VIEWRES now so that we can see how long the REGEN takes with very fine circles.

```
Command: VIEWRES (RETURN)
Do you want fast zooms? <Y>: (RETURN)
Enter circle zoom percent (1-20000) <100>: 20000 (RETURN)
Regenerating drawing.
Command:
```

See how much slower the REGEN was? Try setting VIEWRES back to 100 and once again back to 20000 to see the difference between a slow and a fast REGEN.

Control AutoCAD's Regeneration with REGENAUTO

When you ZOOM, PAN, and VIEW you usually want AutoCAD to make sure that everything in the drawing file is properly represented on the screen. However, since regeneration often takes a long time, sometimes you do not want to have AutoCAD pause to regenerate when you are busy drawing or editing.

You can control how often AutoCAD regenerates the drawing with the REGENAUTO command. When REGENAUTO is OFF, AutoCAD avoids regeneration unless absolutely necessary. When necessary, AutoCAD will first stop and ask you if you really want to regenerate. Of course you can override REGENAUTO by forcing a REGEN with the REGEN command.

Cleaning up and Saving

In this Chapter we altered the CHAPTER2 drawing file by setting VIEWRES and storing away a named VIEW. Make sure VIEWRES is set back to normal and hold onto the named VIEW for use in a later Chapter.

```
Command: VIEWRES (RETURN)

Do you want fast zooms? <Y>: (RETURN)
Enter circle zoom percent (1-20000) <20000>: 100 (RETURN)
Regenerating drawing.
Command: END (RETURN)

(Main Menu Appears)
```

Here is a checklist for Getting Around. You may want to check your most frequent command settings and jot down notes on your display settings right on the checklist.

CHECKLIST FOR GETTING AROUND

☐ Keeping Track of Your Last Point.

    ☐ ^D or (F6) toggles coordinate readout on the status line.

    ☐ The crosshair location is not necessarily the last point.

☐ GRID (and AXIS) Gives a Frame of Reference.

    ☐ GRID spacing can be square or rectangular.

    ☐ ^G or (F7) toggles GRID On and Off. It can also be used for a quick redraw.

☐ SNAP Limits Crosshair Movement to Set Increments.

    ☐ SNAP spacing can be square or rectangular.

    ☐ ^B or (F9) toggles SNAP On and Off.

    ☐ SNAP style can be used to set rotated or isometric GRIDS and SNAP locks.

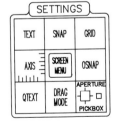

Tablet SETTINGS Commands

☐ ORTHO draws at 90 degree increments.

   ☐ ^O or (F8) toggles ORTHO on.

☐ OSNAP Sets Up a Target for Snapping to Objects.

   ☐ OSNAP cannot be toggled.

   ☐ OSNAP can be invoked temporarily as an interrupt to any Point Selecting command.

   ☐ Running OSNAP mode sets up a full time aperture, which you can override.

   ☐ There is an OSNAP for every occasion.

   ☐ Proper APERTURE setting controls accuracy and the speed of OSNAP searches.

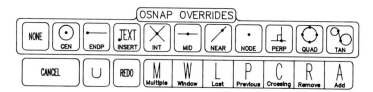

Tablet OSNAP Overrides

There are many ways to get around an AutoCAD display screen. Here are a few tips from experienced users:

Tablet Toggle and Display Commands

TIPS FOR CONTROLLING ZOOM AND REGENERATION

☐ Display Commands Give You a Window On Your Drawing.

   ☐ ZOOM gives you more (or less!) detail.

   ☐ The most common ZOOM-in method is the Window. ZOOM Window is the most intuitive and convenient way to specify what the next screen view will contain.

   ☐ The most common ZOOM-out methods are All and Previous, or Views. When ZOOMing out all the way—A View named ALL or ZOOM Dynamic will get you there in a single step without having to specify ZOOM boundary locations.

   ☐ ZOOM Dynamic allows you to see and control your next ZOOM display screen.

   ☐ ZOOM <Scale(X)> gives you specific or relative magnification.

   ☐ ZOOM Extents gives you the biggest view possible of all of your drawing file. It is a good idea to ZOOM Extents at the end of a drawing session to make sure that you haven't drawn outside your limits.

☐ A PAN displacement gives a nearby ZOOMed view while still ZOOMed-in. When getting from one side of the drawing file to another, use ZOOM Dynamic to get the "whole" view and help you locate your next screen view. ZOOM Dynamic is more intuitive than PAN and gives you feedback on how long it will take to generate your requested image.

☐ VIEW saves and restores ZOOMed-in Windows. A View named All can save extra REGENs. When ZOOMing back to a previous view, take the time to name and store VIEWS for efficiency and to keep your data entry to a minimum. Use ZOOM Previous if you haven't saved a VIEW.

☐ Watch how and how often you regenerate your drawing file.

☐ REDRAW or toggling GRID cleans construction marks off the screen and "refreshes" the image without regenerating the drawing.

☐ VIEWRES optimizes display generation by trading looks for speed.

☐ REGEN gets you the latest look at what's in the drawing file. REGEN-AUTO controls automatic drawing regeneration.

☐ Freezing layers keeps extraneous data from being regenerated. Thaw them when you need them.

It's time to get out of our viewing chairs and climb inside AutoCAD, into the the nitty-gritty of making an electronic drawing. Next we find out how AutoCAD's drafting tools really work, and how they speed up drawing creation.

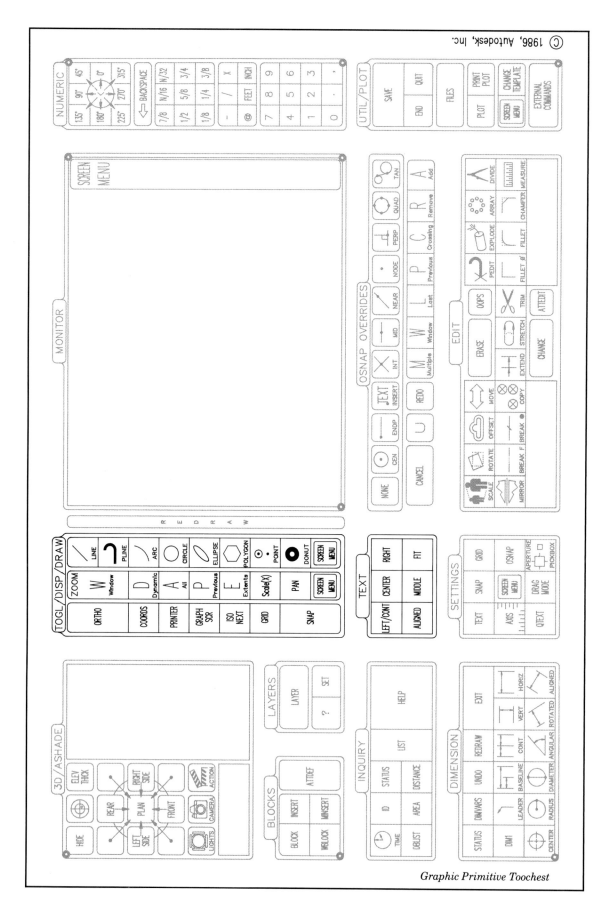

Graphic Primitive Toochest

CHAPTER 3

GRAPHIC PRIMITIVES

LINES AND THE SHAPES THEY MAKE

Lay of The Land—Basic Graphics Functions. ▶ **The Graphic-Primitives Toolchest. Lines and the Shapes They Make. Arcs and Circles.** ▶ **Polylines Are More Sophisticated Lines.** ▶ **A Word About Text.** ▶ **A Few More Not-So-Primitives. Relief for the Disorganized User.** ▶ **Summing Up—Review of Drawing Basics.**

LAY OF THE LAND—BASIC GRAPHICS FUNCTIONS

SETTING UP and GETTING AROUND are really just tools for creating an environment in which to draw. In this Chapter you'll learn about drawing commands—the drawing tools themselves. The **drawing entity** is the most fundamental piece of an AutoCAD drawing. A drawing entity can be a line, an arc, a circle, a string of text, a polyline, a donut, a polygon, an ellipse, a point, a solid, or a shape (symbol). These fundamental drawing elements also are known as **GRAPHIC PRIMITIVES**.

Just as you'll find collections of tools around a manual drafting board for making lines, text, and curves, you will find AutoCAD gives you a collection of electronic tools to perform similar functions.

Why electronic graphic primitives?

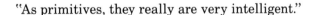

"As primitives, they really are very intelligent."

—CAD Anthropologist

On paper your drawing is static. Inside AutoCAD, graphic primitives are dynamic. An AutoCAD **ARC** has handles for hauling it around. **TEXT** is stored with changeable height, width, slant, and angle information. **LINE**s are defined by two endpoints, but when two lines cross, AutoCAD knows the exact location of the intersection.

Once you know how to use these tools, your drawings will be much more dynamic. You will be able to take advantage of AutoCAD's powerful editing commands (next Chapter) to manipulate drawing elements quickly and easily.

Our goals for this Chapter are two-fold. First, we want to learn about the different graphic primitives and how they're used. Second, we want to begin work on a real drawing by starting with graphic primitives and building a design.

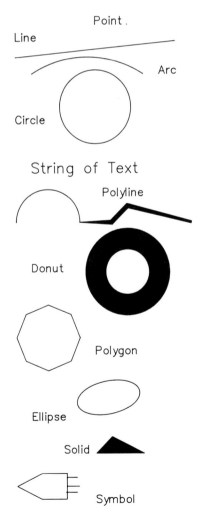

Drawing Elements of Graphics Primitives

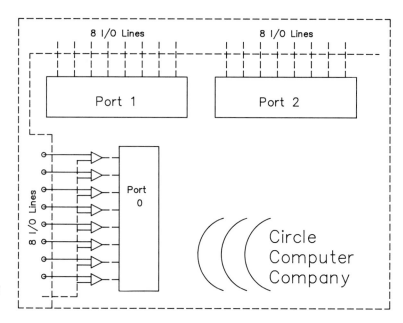

Widget Target Drawing for Using
Graphics Primitives and Editing

By the end of the next Chapter, we would like to have the TARGET DRAW-ING FOR PRIMITIVES AND EDITING on our screen. It is a schematic of a widget showing three simple I/O ports. If you don't know what an I/O port is—don't fret. The drawing we will create is really just a group of graphic primitives properly laid out to illustrate how such a widget might be built.

Build your target widget drawing on the base drawing file stored previously as **CHAPTER1**. You've already seen how the layers for this drawing were set up in the examples of the LAYER command. We will use layer **0** as a playing around and experimentation area, but we will use the named layers (GRAPHIC1, GRAPHIC2, TEXT, and DIMENSION) for placement of elements that are part of the widget drawing.

THE GRAPHIC PRIMITIVES TOOLCHEST

In this Chapter we will focus on commands that **DRAW**. Of course we'll call on old friends like OSNAP and LAYER to help us DRAW properly. If you're not familiar with setup routines and getting around, you may want to review Chapters 1 and 2. From this Chapter forward, INSIDE AutoCAD assumes that you know about LIMITS, GRIDs, AXIS, SNAPping, and all those good setup commands!

You can get to the basic drawing commands by picking the DRAW key on the ROOTMENU. You will notice that the DRAW key also appears as one of two choices at the bottom of most screen menus as a convenience. Of course, you can always execute individual LINE, ARC, CIRCLE, or TEXT commands directly from the keyboard.

The DRAW commands also are shown in the GRAPHIC PRIMITIVES TOOL-CHEST.

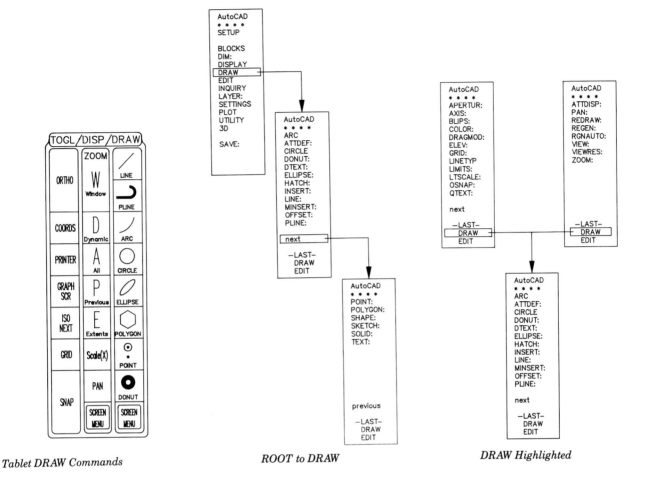

Tablet DRAW Commands　　　　ROOT to DRAW　　　　DRAW Highlighted

LINES AND THE SHAPES THEY MAKE

The **LINE** is the pillar of the drawing community.

You have already played around with the LINE command. Here we will formally introduce the LINE and its properties. Like any outstanding member of a community, the LINE has associates from all walks of life, fat (the TRACE), and thin (the POINT), well-rounded (CIRCLE and ARC), with family connections (POLYLINES), and an all-encompassing buddy—POLYGON.

We will build our target widget drawing on the base drawing file we stored previously as **CHAPTER1**. You've already seen how the layers for this drawing were set up in the examples of the layer command. We will use layer **0** as a playing around and experimentation area, but we will use the named layers (GRAPHIC1, GRAPHIC2, TEXT, and DIMENSION) for placement of elements that are part of the widget drawing.

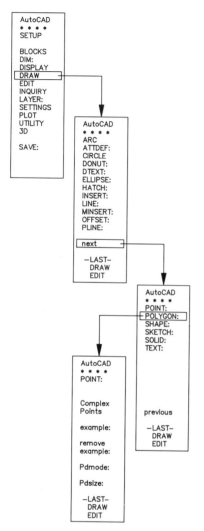

ROOT to DRAW to POINT

A POINT is a Point. That's the Point

Most users have little use for the **POINT**, but it can play a helpful role in building a drawing file. It's simple to use (you just place it where you want it), and it has redeeming qualities.

A POINT WE'D LIKE TO MAKE

Here's the setup:

Enter the drawing editor with **2 Edit an EXISTING Drawing**.

Use **CHAPTER1** for the base drawing. (It has good limits, and units, and it already has the layers we need.)

When you last left your friendly drawing file, you were getting around on layer GRAPHIC2. Grid was 2 inches square, and Snap was 0.5 inches.

Turn layer GRAPHIC2 Off.

Set layer 0 current. 0 is your sandbox layer for playing around.

Set SNAP On to 0.25 inches.

ZOOM All

Select the POINT command by picking the screen menu

Now let's make the POINT

```
Command: POINT (RETURN)
Point: 6.25",9.50" (RETURN)
Command:
```

A white mark at (6.25",9.50") appears on the screen. This mark is actually larger than the point that you placed—it is simply the construction marker (blip) for the point. A REDRAW will clear the construction marker and leave a small, white dot on the screen. That's the point.

Here's why you might want to put points in your file. You can set up a series of markers (points) as reference locations much like the grid. You can't OSNAP to a grid marker, but you can to a point.

Setting up a layer with points or a few reference lines can help organize your drawing file for placement of other elements. When you are all through with your placements, you can turn **OFF** the construction layer with reference points and lines, and leave your desired elements.

Try OSNAPping to the point as a reference:

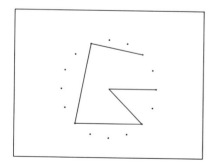

Example of diagram created using Reference Layer Points

USING A POINT AS A REFERENCE FOR OSNAP

```
Command: LINE (RETURN)
From point:  node (RETURN)   (type OSNAP node.)
of
  (Line the point up in the aperture and pick.)


To point:           (pick any other last point.)
To point: (RETURN)
Command:
```

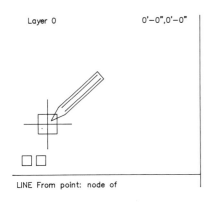

LINE From point: node of

New line begins at OSNAPped Node

OSNAP **node** is the OSNAP modifier that looks specifically for points. In the above exercise you used the point as the **From point:** to locate the line.

PDMODE for Point

The miniscule point can be hard to see. AutoCAD provides for display of "points" as a + (cross), an X, a vertical tic, or about 20 combinations. Point types are set through PDMODE. See the AutoCAD REFERENCE MANUAL for the types and how to set them.

How Two Points Make A Line

You've already used the **LINE** command in SETTING UP (Chapter 1) and GETTING AROUND (Chapter 2). You've seen that AutoCAD's LINE command is simple and straightforward.

Issuing the LINE command to AutoCAD begins a process of recording the two endpoints of a line segment, the **From point:** and the **To point:**. The two points you identify define a line segment.

Once a line is created from two endpoints (however they were entered), AutoCAD assumes that you want to continue drawing lines. Not only that, AutoCAD assumes that you want to continue drawing lines with the last endpoint as the **From point:** for the current segment.

AutoCAD is just trying to help you move along with your line drawing without having you type or issue the LINE command over and over again. This means you can draw line segments one after the other by continuing to enter **To points:**. A **CANCEL**, **(RETURN)**, or a **SPACE** (hitting the space bar) ends the LINE command and returns the Command: prompt.

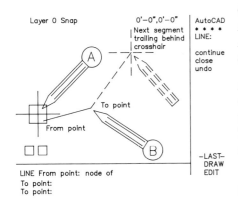

LINE From point: node of
To point:
To point:

DRAWing a line

Check Line Placement With Rubberbanding

Since you can keep on drawing segments every time you see a **To point:** prompt. AutoCAD helps you visualize where the next segment will be located by **rubberbanding** or trailing a segment between your last point and the cursor. You can see how you make a second segment into a line in DRAWING A LINE.

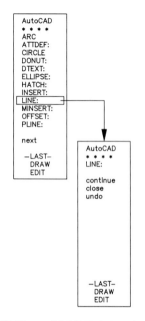

DRAW Menu with LINE Selected

Don't forget there are many ways to enter a new point in response to a **From point:** or **To point:** prompt:

☐ Typing absolute coordinates at the keyboard.

☐ Typing relative coordinates at the keyboard.

☐ Using the pointer and crosshair to select points interactively.

☐ Using SNAP, ORTHO, and OSNAP commands to control the crosshair selection process.

☐ Any combination of the above.

A LINE has a From Point and a To Point. It's that simple.

Here's a little LINE exercise:

A LITTLE LINE EXERCISE

```
Command: LINE (RETURN)     (Use the screen menu to get LINE.)
From point: 4.50",4.50" (RETURN)
To point: @8" <90 (RETURN)
To point: @15",6" (RETURN)
To point:
```

Continue, Close and Undo

At this point, the next segment should be trailing from your crosshair. Instead of ending the segment entry process let's see what else we can do with LINE. Look at the screen menu, where you see the following options:

☐ **continue**—Starts a new segment from the last point that was used as a line endpoint. (Not necessarily the crosshair location.)

☐ **close**—Uses the **From point** of the first line segment in the current LINE command as the next **To point**. This makes a **closed** polygon out of the connected segments you are working with and ends the command.

☐ **undo**—A wonderful command! It lets you wipe out mistakes without leaving the LINE command. If you make a mistake with a **To point**, you can **undo** the last point by picking the screen **undo**, or typing **U** at the keyboard then, re-issue your next **To point**.

Let's try the **close** option. Your prompt should still read To point:. Instead of picking or typing a new To point:, use your pointer to pick **close** from the screen menu:

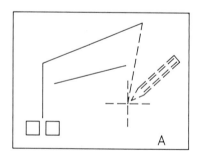

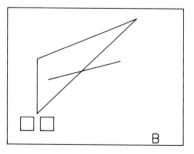

CLOSE makes a polygon out of continuous lines

THE LINE EXERCISE CONTINUED
USING CLOSE TO COMPLETE A POLYGON

```
To point: close          (type C(RETURN) or pick close.)
Command:
```

Your screen should look like CLOSE MAKES A POLYGON OUT OF CONTINUOUS LINES. Notice that you are no longer in the LINE command, but that the Command: prompt is showing. Any time you have drawn a few line segments and want to make them into a polygon, you can **close** the figure. A **c (RETURN)** is all you need from the keyboard in response to the To point:.

Picking Up the Last Point With Continue

Let's try **continue**. Continue will pick up the last point used in the most recent LINE command as a From point: and begin trailing a new segment behind the crosshair. Pick **continue** from the screen menu, or type **LINE (RETURN)(RETURN)**, or even just **(RETURN)(RETURN)**. Remember, a (RETURN) or (SPACE) at the Command: prompt will repeat the previous command. The second (RETURN) or (SPACE) at the To point: prompt makes AutoCAD continue lines from the previous endpoint. Your screen should look like CONTINUE BEGINS A NEW LINE SERIES FROM AN OLD ONE.

Give a To point: to put in another segment, put in another, and then take out the last segment with an **undo**.

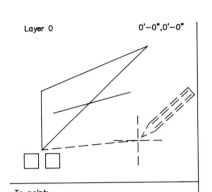

CONTINUe begins a new line series from an old one

CONTINUE AND UNDO PICK UP WHERE YOU LEFT OFF

```
Command: LINE (RETURN)
From point:                    (pick continue.)
To point: 1'10",1' (RETURN)
To point: 2'4",8" (RETURN)
To point: u (RETURN)           (or pick undo.)
To point:
```

Undo eliminates the last segment and backs up one To point: to let you try the line segment again.

You can keep **undo**ing as long as you are in the same LINE command and have not exited with a **(RETURN)**, **Space Bar**, or **CANCEL**. Get rid of the last segment with another **undo**. You will not be able to back up any further, because the previous segment was created as part of another LINEcommand execution. Get out of LINE with a **(RETURN)**.

Creating the Widget for the Target Drawing

Let's use what we've learned to create part of our widget drawing. The following exercise will get you onto the right drawing layer and store the lines that make up one of the widgets in the target drawing. Our goal for this exercise is shown in WIDGET LINES:

Layer GRAPHIC2 Snap   0'-0",0'-0"

Command:

Widget Lines

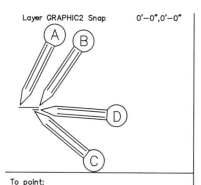

Layer GRAPHIC2 Snap   0'–0",0'–0"

To point:

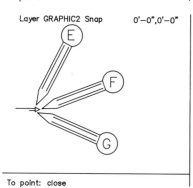

Layer GRAPHIC2 Snap   0'–0",0'–0"

To point: close

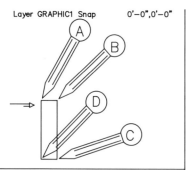

Layer GRAPHIC1 Snap   0'–0",0'–0"

To point: close

*Widget Creation Working Session
Progress Screens*

Layer GRAPHIC1 Snap   0'–0",0'–0"

Command:

Target Drawing with Port "O"

CREATING THE WIDGET FOR THE TARGET DRAWING

Widgets go on layer GRAPHIC2.

Set layer Graphic2 current.

Turn layer 0 Off.

```
Command: LAYER (RETURN)
?/Make/Set/New/On/Off/Color/Ltype/Freeze/Thaw: S (RETURN)
New current layer <0>: GRAPHIC2 (RETURN)
?/Make/Set/New/On/Off/Color/Ltype/Freeze/Thaw: Off (RETURN)
Layer name(s) to turn OFF: 0 (RETURN)
?/Make/Set/New/On/Off/Color/Ltype/Freeze/Thaw: (RETURN)
Command:


Command: LINE (RETURN)
From point: 2.66",1'1.22" (RETURN)
To point: 6.74",1'1.22" (RETURN)
To point: (RETURN)
Command: (RETURN)
LINE From point: 5.54",1'0.74" (RETURN)
To point: 6.74",1'0.74" (RETURN)
To point: (RETURN)
Command: (RETURN)
LINE From point: 6.74",1'1.46" (RETURN)
To point: 7.70",1'0.98" (RETURN)
To point: 6.74",1'0.50" (RETURN)
To point: c (RETURN)
Command:
```

You now have all of the lines of the widget; the only thing missing is the little circle on the end of the long line. We'll come back and put in the circle when we have covered those commands. Your screen should look like WIDGET LINES.

Now let's put in **Port 0**, one of the three rectangles we need for the widget drawing. We'll use keyboard entry to get the rectangle placement just right:

PLACING PORT 0

Port 0 goes on the GRAPHIC1 layer.

Set layer GRAPHIC1 Current.

```
Command: LINE (RETURN)
From point: 9.14",1'1.94" (RETURN)
To point: 1'0.50",1'1.94" (RETURN)
To point: 1'0.50",1.94" (RETURN)
To point: 9.14",1.94" (RETURN)
To point: c (RETURN)
Command:
```

Your screen should now look like the TARGET DRAWING WITH PORT "0". We'll leave the other Ports for the next Chapter when we can COPY and MOVE, instead of creating.

What about the little circle that belongs on the widget tail? It must be time for...

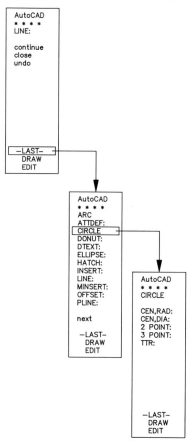

LASTMENU to DRAW to CIRCLE

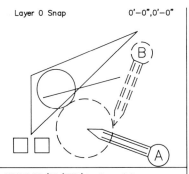

CIRCLE 3P/2P/TTR/<center point>:
Diameter/<Radius>:

Use the Sandbox to play around with CIRCLEs

ARCS AND CIRCLES

The next class of graphic primitives to consider is **ARCS** and **CIRCLES**. Unlike lines, these elements require more than two simple endpoints. Also unlike lines, ARCs and CIRCLEs can be created in at least a dozen different ways.

Inside AutoCAD arcs and circles are stored by the parameters you enter at the time of creation (like endpoints, angles, directions, or chords). Using this geometric information, AutoCAD can REGENerate curves at the best possible resolution and smoothness regardless of viewing or plotting scale.

Let's make some circles and see how AutoCAD's CIRCLE options work. Then we'll move on to arcs.

Getting To Know CIRCLES

Let's execute the CIRCLE command from the screen menu. Notice the prompt line still reads: **Command:** and does not register a CIRCLE prompt. **CIRCLE** is the screen menu key that gets you to yet another screen menu listing five separate CIRCLE creation commands.

Why so many? Different drafting tasks provide different information about where circles should go. For example, if you're designing a round patio to touch (tangentially) to a house corner and one or more site lot boundaries, you would like to have a 2 POINT or 3 POINT circle definition to help you get the touch points. Most often you know the CENTER point and the RADIUS or DIAMETER. In these cases, you use this information to create the circle:

CIRCLE EXERCISES

Set Layer 0 Current to play around. Turn GRAPHIC1, and GRAPHIC2 Off.

Try a few of the CIRCLE options, creating a circle with points, a radius, and a diameter. Use OSNAP interrupts to see how these modifiers affect circle creation. Notice how AutoCAD automatically Drags the circle.

Here are AutoCAD's CIRCLE possibilities:

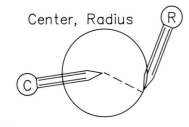

Center, Radius

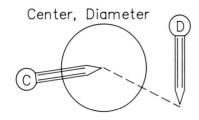

Center, Diameter

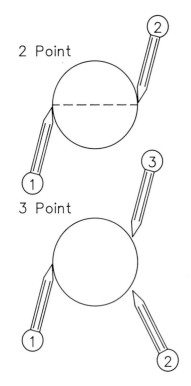

2 Point

3 Point

CIRCLE Options

AutoCAD CIRCLE CREATION OPTIONS

☐ 2 POINT—(2P) allows you to pick the two endpoints of the circle's diameter.

☐ 3 POINT—(3P) allows you to pick any three points randomly, then AutoCAD fits a circle to the points.

☐ TTR or Tangent, Tangent, Radius.—Allows you to pick two tangent points and a radius. If a circle exists through these three points, AutoCAD will generate it for you.

☐ CENTER,RADIUS—This is the default. It creates a circle using a digitized center point (or keyboard coordinate). Then AutoCAD **drags** the Radius according to your pointer movement.

☐ CENTER,DIAMETER—Works like CEN,RAD with a twist. You create a diameter distance, using the first point as the circle center point and another point you choose. The diameter distance is evenly split over the first (center) point.

Make sure you understand the difference between CENTER,DIAMETER and 2 POINT. Most often readers think of diameter as a distance between two points. When you pick two points, you want to see a circle appear between those two points. The command that does this is 2 POINT. Not CENTER,DIAMETER.

You now know that you can create a circle in at least five ways. Which one do you choose? If you know ahead of time whether you have a radius, diameter, or points, you can pick the correct option from the screen menu. For those of us who don't think that far ahead, AutoCAD allows you to pick your options in midstream if you use keyboard entry.

```
Command: CIRCLE (RETURN)
3P/2P/TTR/<Center point>:
```

At this point you can enter a Center point (keyboard, screen or tablet pick), or you can select the 3 POINT, 2 POINT, or TTR method. Typing **2P**, **3P**, or **TTR (RETURN)** will get you one or the other of those options, and AutoCAD will prompt you for the necessary points.

If you pick a Center point, you will get a circle through the CENTER,RADIUS method. A **D (RETURN)** response will get the Diameter prompt. Then a pick will give you a circle through the CENTER,DIAMETER method.

One last note about circles. You can use OSNAP commands to help you create the circle. OSNAP commands are valid anytime AutoCAD prompts you for coordinate input. AutoCAD automatically **drags** everything it can, and the drag will help you visualize what your circle will look like.

Layer GRAPHIC2 Snap   0'-0",0'-0"

Command:

Widget, Port "0" and Circle Drawing

Use CIRCLE to Pin the Tail on the Widget

Now follow this example to pin the little circle on the end of the widget. We'll use the **endpoint of** the existing line as our center, and a typed radius:

WIDGET CIRCLE

Set layer GRAPHIC2 Current.

Turn layer 0 Off.

Zoom in on the widget with ZOOM Window.

Command: **CIRCLE (RETURN)**   (type **END.**)
3P/2P/TTR/<Center point>: endpoint of:

(pick the endpoint of the longer line by lining it up
in the aperture.)

Diameter/<Radius>: **0.19"** (RETURN)
Command:

ZOOM All to get a full view.

Your widget drawing is coming along. It should now look like PORT "0", WIDGET AND CIRCLE.

Getting To Know ARCs with 3-point

There are two ways to classify the different 3ARC options, **The Whole ARC Catalog** and simple ARCs. We'll start with the simple ARCs.

The most straightforward way to enter arcs is with the default 3-point ARC command.

To get to 3-point ARC, select DRAW from the ROOTMENU and then select ARC. The ten options are shown in the ARC OPTION TREE.

3-point ARC works just about the same way as 3 POINT CIRCLE. The first point is the arc's beginning, the second and third points define the arc's curvature. The last point and first point define the chord of the arc.

```
AutoCAD
* * * *
CIRCLE

CEN,RAD:
CEN,DIA:
2 POINT:
3 POINT:
TTR:




-LAST-
 DRAW
 EDIT
```

```
AutoCAD
* * * *
ARC
ATTDEF:
CIRCLE
DONUT:
DTEXT:
ELLIPSE:
HATCH:
INSERT:
LINE:
MINSERT:
OFFSET:
PLINE:

next

-LAST-
 DRAW
 EDIT
```

```
AutoCAD
* * * *
ARC

3-point:
S,C,E:
S,C,A:
S,C,L:
S,E,A:
S,E,R:
S,E,D:
C,S,E:
C,S,A:
C,S,L:
CONTIN:

-LAST-
 DRAW
 EDIT
```

LASTMENU to DRAW to ARC

Set layer 0 Current.

Turn all other layers Off.

Command:

Try an arc by picking the 3-point option from the ARC menu.

Command: ARC Center/<Start point>:   (pick a point.)
Center/End/<Second point>:   (pick another point.)
End point: (DRAG automatically comes on.)

(Drag the curve around until satisfied, then pick a point.)

Command:

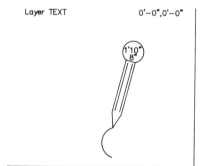

3-point ARC placement using DRAG

Make sure you feel comfortable with the way AutoCAD uses **drag** to help you decide where the 3-point arc is going to fall. After the first two points are entered, DRAG is automatically turned on. Do you understand why the arc can flip around depending on the third point's placement? Push the pointer around enough until you do.

CREATING AN ARC LOGO FOR THE WIDGET DRAWING

Set layer TEXT Current.

Turn all other layers Off.

Command: (pick 3-point.)
Command: ARC Center/<Start point>: **1'10",2"** **(RETURN)**
Center/End/<Second point>: **1'8",4"** **(RETURN)**
End point: **1'10",8"** **(RETURN)**
Command:

First Logo Arc

Some Brief ARC Examples

Most of the time, you'll find that the 3-point or arcs created with a START and CENTER method will satisfy your arc needs. Here's an exercise to help show you some of the ARC options. Remember, you have to type the '(quote) for feet, but can omit the "(double quote) for inches.

ARCS EXAMPLE

Set layer 0 Current and turn layer TEXT Off.

Start, Center, Angle S,C,A

Command: (pick S,C,A)
Command: ARC Center/<Start point>: **2',1'4"** **(RETURN)**
Center/End/<Second point>: C Center: **2',1'2"** **(RETURN)**

```
Angle/Length of chord/<End point>: A Included angle: DRAG
  240 (RETURN)
Command:
```

Using Center, Start, Length of Chord and **continue**

```
Command:              (pick C,S,L)
Command: ARC Center/<Start point>: C Center: 2'2",1'10"
  (RETURN)
Start Point: 2'2",1'6" (RETURN)
Angle/Length of chord/<End point>: L Length of chord: DRAG
  7 (RETURN)
Command:              (pick CONTIN:)
Command: ARC Center/<Start point>:
End point: DRAG 2'4",1'10" (RETURN)
Command:
```

Layer DIMENSION   0'-0",0'-0"

Command:

ARC Drawing

Your screen should look like ARC DRAWING.

The Whole ARC Catalog

Here are the ten options for ARC grouped by common functions:

AutoCAD ARC OPTIONS

☐ **Class 1—3-point.** Creates an arc that passes through any three selected points.

☐ **Class 2—Start, Center—and—end, angle, or chord.** These arc commands require an arc starting point, and the center of the circle that would be created if the arc were complete (360 degrees). The third parameter determines the arc by specifying an endpoint, an angle, or a chord length.

☐ **Class 3—Start, End—and—radius, angle, or direction.** This class of arc commands allows you to define the starting and ending points of the arc first, followed by how you draw the arc. You select the shape of the arc curve with a radius, angle, or tangent direction.

☐ **Class 4—Center, Start, DRAG—and end, angle, or chord.** This arc class allows you to first pin down the center of the arc, then determine the arc length and direction by positioning a drag line to determine the included angle or length of chord.

3-POINT

S,C,E   S,C,A   S,C,L

S,E,-270   S,E,R   S,E,D

C,S,E   C,S,A   C,S,L

3-point ARC Options

Other Notes on ARCs

Just as with lines, you can CONTIN: all of the ARC commands, making use of the previous point and direction as the beginning point of the next ARC command.

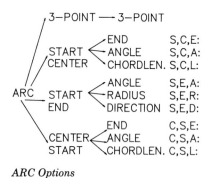

ARC Options

Don't forget you can always use OSNAP modifiers to interrupt and refine an ARC command.

AutoCAD allows you to select any of the ten arc options from the screen arc or tablet menu. The options are abbreviated by mnemonic letters. If you're keying arc commands from the keyboard, you'll find the commands have common beginnings according to their class (Start, Center; Start, End, etc).

You can choose your options midstream and select one arc creation over another by entering the ARC command and prompt letters from the keyboard. A pick point will move down the start branch of ARC, a **C** will move you to the center branch.

POLYLINES ARE MORE SOPHISTICATED LINES

You now know how to create the most common graphic primitives, the LINE, the ARC, and the CIRCLE. In the next several Chapters, and throughout your AutoCAD career, you will find infinite combinations of these basic primitives as you put together whole drawings.

Given what you already know about primitives, how would you create lines that are thicker than the ones you put on the screen with the LINE command? How would you attach a LINE to an ARC? Can you make a closed polygon with three straight sides (lines) and one curved side?

Polylines

You might want to try these exercises on your own to see if you can make these figures. But before you spend too much time on making basic graphic primitives work too hard, you should consider the POLYLINE or **PLINE**.

Instead of having to create multiple lines to get a thick one, or having to independently create arcs and then connect them to lines, AutoCAD provides the **PLINE**. PLINEs are different than independent line segments joined with **continue**. PLINE segments are treated by AutoCAD as a **single** drawing entity that includes some line-like and curve-like features.

For example, the "Port 0" rectangle in the widget drawing is now made of four separate line segments. Later if we wanted to copy this rectangle we would have to make sure that AutoCAD knew that all four segments were to be copied. Selecting any segment of a PLINE, selects all segments.

Let's try creating the next widget rectangle, "Port 1" using PLINE. PLINE is available from the DRAW key list of commands.

PLINEs can have many shapes and sizes

ENTERING PORT 1

Set layer GRAPHIC1 Current.

Turn layer 0 Off and turn SNAP Off.

Turn On the other widget layers, if you wish.

Insert another Port -- **Port 1**

```
Command: PLINE (RETURN)
From point: 2.90",16.34" (RETURN)
Current line-width is 0'0.00"
Arc/Close/Halfwidth/Length/Undo/Width/<Endpoint of line>:
   14.90",16.34" (RETURN)
Arc/Close/Halfwidth/Length/Undo/Width/<Endpoint of line>:
   14.90",19.70" (RETURN)
Arc/Close/Halfwidth/Length/Undo/Width/<Endpoint of line>:
   2.90",19.70" (RETURN)
Arc/Close/Halfwidth/Length/Undo/Width/<Endpoint of line>:
   c (RETURN)
Command:
```

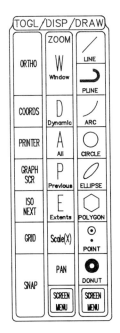

PLINE can make a rectangle in the Widget Drawing

What were all of those other possibilities on the PLINE prompt line? Let's find out.

PLINE has the capability of drawing two basic kinds of segments — straight ones and curved ones. When drawing straight segments you get prompts similar to the LINE command like Endpoint, Close, and Undo. When drawing curved segments you get the prompt:

```
Angle/CEnter/CLose/Direction/Halfwidth/Line/Radius/Second
pt/Undo/Width/<Endpoint of arc>:
```

This includes now familiar ARC prompts like Angle/CEnter/Radius as well as Second pt, and Endpoint of arc.

So drawing LINES and ARCS with PLINE is very similar to drawing the equivalent elements with the basic LINE and ARC commands.

But notice several important differences. First, you get all the prompts every time you enter a new PLINE vertex. Second, there are additional prompts that control the width of the segment you draw like **Halfwidth** and **Width**. When a polyline has width, you can control line fill by turning **FILL** On or Off. And third, you will see that you can switch back and forth from straight segments to curved segments, all the time adding additional segments to your growing PLINE.

Try a PLINE that uses several of these features. As you saw in the "Port 1" example, the prompt line that PLINE first issues, is one for drawing straight segments. Create the series of segments shown in the PLAYING WITH PLINE DRAWING. First create straight segments, then use the PLINE Arc mode to connect arc and line segments.

PLINE is with Tablet DRAW Commands

PLAYING WITH PLINE

Set layer 0 Current.

Turn all other layers Off.

Command: **PLINE (RETURN)**   (Let's pick PLINE from DRAW menu.)

From point: **20",6" (RETURN)**
Current line-width is 0'-0.00"
Arc/Close/Halfwidth/Length/Undo/Width/<Endpoint of line>:
  24",4" (RETURN)
Arc/Close/Halfwidth/Length/Undo/Width/<Endpoint of line>:
  30",6" (RETURN)
Arc/Close/Halfwidth/Length/Undo/Width/<Endpoint of line>:
  32",10" (RETURN)

Now the arc.

Arc/Close/Halfwidth/Length/Undo/Width/<Endpoint of line>:
  A (RETURN)
Angle/CEnter/CLose/Direction/Halfwidth/Line/Radius/Second
  pt/Undo/Width/<Endpoint of arc>: **30",16" (RETURN)**
Angle/CEnter/CLose/Direction/Halfwidth/Line/Radius/Second
  pt/Undo/Width/<Endpoint of arc>: **22",14" (RETURN)**
Angle/CEnter/CLose/Direction/Halfwidth/Line/Radius/Second
  pt/Undo/Width/<Endpoint of arc>: **S (RETURN)**
Second point: **26",14" (RETURN)**
End point: **26",10" (RETURN)**

Line again.

Angle/CEnter/CLose/Direction/Halfwidth/Line/Radius/Second
  pt/Undo/Width/<Endpoint of arc>: **L (RETURN)**
Arc/Close/Halfwidth/Length/Undo/Width/<Endpoint of line>:
  W (RETURN)
Starting width <0'-0.00">: **(RETURN)**
Ending width <0'-0.00">: **0.5" (RETURN)**
Arc/Close/Halfwidth/Length/Undo/Width/<Endpoint of line>:
  20",12" (RETURN)
Arc/Close/Halfwidth/Length/Undo/Width/<Endpoint of line>:
  12",8" (RETURN)
Arc/Close/Halfwidth/Length/Undo/Width/<Endpoint of line>:
  W (RETURN)
Starting width <0'-0.50">: **1.5" (RETURN)**
Ending width <0'-1.50">: **0.0" (RETURN)**

Back to arc.

Arc/Close/Halfwidth/Length/Undo/Width/<Endpoint of line>:
  A (RETURN)
Angle/CEnter/CLose/Direction/Halfwidth/Line/Radius/Second
  pt/Undo/Width/<Endpoint of arc>: **CL (RETURN)**
Command:

Let's undo the pline to clear the working screen.

Command: **undo**   (pick or type **undo**)
Auto/Back/Control/End/Group/Mark <number>: **(RETURN)**
PLINE
Command:

Layer 0   0'-0",0'-0"

Arc/Close/Halfwidth/Length/Undo/Width/
<Endpoint of line>: A

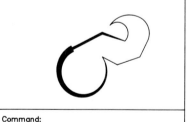

Layer 0   0'-0",0'-0"

Command:

PLINE Playing Around Sequence

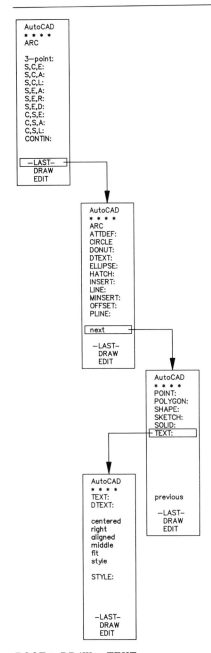

ROOT to DRAW to TEXT

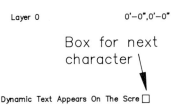

Text: Dynamic Text Appears On The Scre

A WORD ABOUT TEXT

Just like LINEs and ARCs, AutoCAD's **TEXT** has a set of parameters that define how text is placed and stored. You have to select a beginning and ending point for your TEXT block, a height for the characters, and/or how the text is to be justified (like a wordprocessor). Finally, you must key in the text characters. Typically, you do this from the keyboard.

Dynamic Text and Regular Text

AutoCAD has two text commands, **DTEXT** and **TEXT**. Either command allows you to create and place text—the only difference is that DTEXT (you might have guessed it) does it dynamically.

If you use TEXT, AutoCAD waits for all your text characters, as well as information about character height, width and placement. When you are through giving AutoCAD instructions and you exit the TEXT command, your text then appears on the screen.

With DTEXT, your text appears on the screen, character-by-character, as you type at the keyboard. DTEXT helps you check text parameters (size, style, and placement). If you are prone to spelling errors, DTEXT also helps you catch your spelling errors since characters are generated as you type.

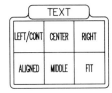

Tablet TEXT Commands

Getting Started with DTEXT

To get started with the text, let's pick DTEXT from the DRAW key menu list to get the following prompts:

PLAYING AROUND WITH TEXT

Set layer 0 (the "sandbox") Current.

Command: **DTEXT (RETURN)**
Start point or Align/Center/Fit/Middle/Right/Style:

Dynamic TEXT appearing on Screen

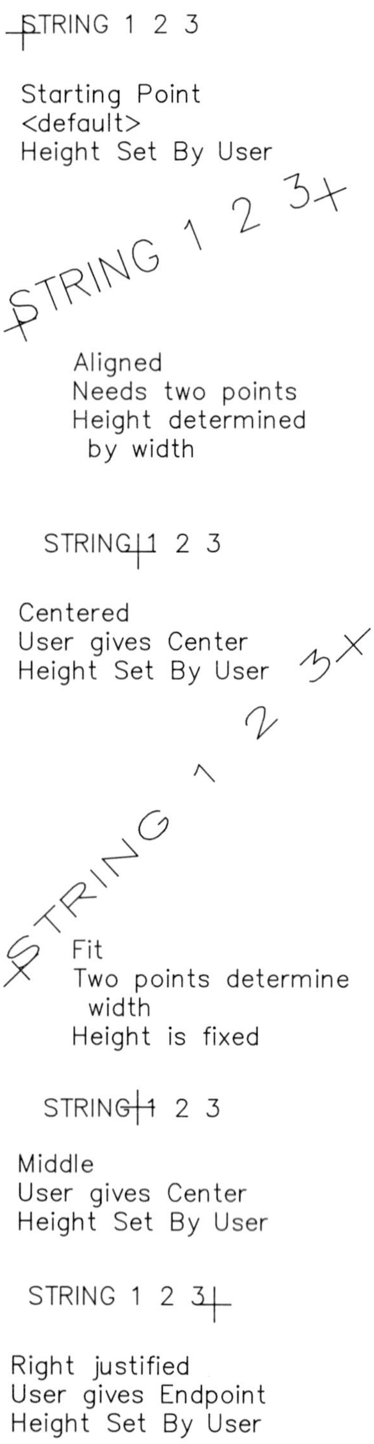

STRING 1 2 3

Starting Point
<default>
Height Set By User

STRING 1 2 3+

Aligned
Needs two points
Height determined
by width

STRING 1 2 3

Centered
User gives Center
Height Set By User

3+

2

STRING 1

Fit
Two points determine
width
Height is fixed

STRING 1 2 3

Middle
User gives Center
Height Set By User

STRING 1 2 3+

Right justified
User gives Endpoint
Height Set By User

TEXT Options

The first thing AutoCAD wants to know about your text is where you want to place it. You have—couldn't you guess—several options to determine where to put text. Here they are:

TEXT OPTIONS

☐ **Starting Point**—Left Justified is the default setting. Just respond to the prompt by picking a point. Left justified needs a height and angle to complete where the text will go.

☐ **Aligned**—You give the start and endpoint of the text location. AutoCAD determines the height and baseline angle from your points and the length of the text string you type in.

☐ **Centered**—You give the centerpoint of the base line of the text along with height and angle. AutoCAD does the centering.

☐ **Fit**—Like Aligned, you give the starting point and endpoint of the text string, AutoCAD uses the text height you specify and stretches text in the x-direction to fit.

☐ **Middle**—Like Centered, you give the centerpoint of an imaginary rectangle around the text. AutoCAD fits the text neatly centered around this point.

☐ **Right Justified**—Like left, except that the text abuts the point that you give from the right.

☐ **Style**—An **S** typed from the keyboard, or picking style from the menu, allows you to select from various styles you have previously set up.

☐ **Style**—Typing **STYLE** at the Command: prompt, or selecting STYLE from the menu, allows you to set up a new style of text for future text definition and placement.

These options are shown in the drawing TEXT OPTIONS. Try using a starting point and <defaults> for other DTEXT parameters to play around.

Let's proceed with **Left Justified** (the default) by entering a starting point and either typing or dragging answers to the height and angle prompts. We will enter the text annotations for the widget target drawing. We'll also try a few other ways to enter text.

The goal of all of these text exercises is the partial widget drawing shown in TARGET DRAWING WITH TEXT:

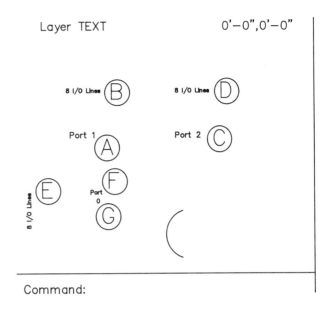

Layer TEXT
0'-0",0'-0"

8 I/O Lines Ⓑ   8 I/O Lines Ⓓ

Port 1 Ⓐ   Port 2 Ⓒ

Ⓔ   Port Ⓕ
8 I/O Lines   0

Ⓖ

Command:

Widget Target Drawing with Text

ANNOTATING THE WIDGET DRAWING WITH TEXT

Set layer TEXT Current.

Turn other layers Off

Command: **DTEXT (RETURN)**
Start point or Align/Center/Fit/Middle/Right/Style:
   7.22",1'5.30" (RETURN)
Height <0'-0.20">: **0.72" (RETURN)**
Rotation angle <0.00>: **(RETURN)**
Text: **Port 1(RETURN)**
Text: **(RETURN)**
Command: **(RETURN)**

(A **(RETURN)** puts you back into Dtext.)

DTEXT Start point or Align/Center/Fit/Middle/Right/Style:
   6.74",1'11.06" (RETURN)
Height <0'-0.72">: **0.51" (RETURN)**
Rotation angle <0.00>: **(RETURN)**
Text: **8 I/O Lines(RETURN)**
Text: **(RETURN)**
Command:

Now try these next two as aligned text.

Command: **(RETURN)**
DTEXT Start point or Align/Center/Fit/Middle/Right/Style:
   a (RETURN)
First text line point: **1'9.14",1'5.30" (RETURN)**
Second text line point: **2'0.98",1'5.30" (RETURN)**
Text: **Port 2(RETURN)**
Text: **(RETURN)**
Command:

```
Command: (RETURN)
DTEXT Start point or Align/Center/Fit/Middle/Right/Style:
  a (RETURN)
First text line point: 1'9.14",1'11.06" (RETURN)
Second text line point: 2'1.94",1'11.06" (RETURN)
Text: 8 I/O Lines (RETURN)
Text: (RETURN)
Command:

Next try rotated text from a Starting Point:

Command: (RETURN)
DTEXT Start point or Align/Center/Fit/Middle/Right/Style:
  1.94",5.78" (RETURN)
Height <0'-0.51">: 0.51" (RETURN)
Rotation angle <0.00>: 90 (RETURN)     (DRAG or type 90)
Text: 8 I/O Lines (RETURN)
Text: (RETURN)
Command:

Last try Centered:

Command: (RETURN)
DTEXT Start point or Align/Center/Fit/Middle/Right/Style:
  c (RETURN)
Center point: 10.82",10.10" (RETURN)
Height <0'-0.51">: (RETURN)
Rotation angle <90.00>: 0 (RETURN)          (get back to 0)
Text: Port (RETURN)
Text: (RETURN)
Command:

Command: (RETURN)
DTEXT Start point or Align/Center/Fit/Middle/Right/Style:
  c (RETURN)
Center point: 10.82",9.00" (RETURN)
Height <0'-0.51">: (RETURN)
Rotation angle <0.00>: (RETURN)
Text: 0 (RETURN)
Text: (RETURN)
Command:

Clean up your screen to get rid of construction markers.

Command: REDRAW (RETURN)
Command:
```

Another Word About The Word "Text"

AutoCAD uses the word "Text" in two command prompts. DTEXT (or TEXT) initiates the text command—this shows on the prompt line when you pick DTEXT from the screen menu. Text: also appears on the prompt line as a prompt to enter a string of characters, numbers, or symbols from the keyboard.

After you enter text characters, you hit (RETURN) to end your text input. AutoCAD uses your placement parameters to actually put the text string in the drawing file, and draw it for you on the screen.

After AutoCAD draws your text string, you will get the Command: prompt. If you give a (RETURN), AutoCAD will put you back in the DTEXT command and reissue the DTEXT prompt (Starting point or Align/Center/Fit/ Middle/Right/Style:). Remember that a **(RETURN)** after the completion of most commands will put you back in the same command to continue working.

To demonstrate continuous successive lines of text, put a company name on the widget drawing. The words "Circle" "Computer" "Company" will line up under one another:

CONTINUOUS LINES OF TEXT

Make sure layer TEXT is still Current.

```
Command: DTEXT (RETURN)
Start point or Align/Center/Fit/Middle/Right/Style:
   1'10",6" (RETURN)
Height <0'-0.51">: 1.00" (RETURN)
Rotation angle <0.00>: (RETURN)
Text: Circle (RETURN)
Text: Computer (RETURN)
Text: Company (RETURN)
Text: (RETURN)
Command:
```

Layer TEXT   0'-0",0'-0"

8 I/O Lines   8 I/O Lines

Port 1   Port 2

8 I/O Lines   Port 0

Circle
Computer   Ⓐ
Company   Ⓑ
             Ⓒ

Command:

Continuous TEXT

IMPORTANT NOTE

This is the last time in this Chapter that we will enter drawing elements into our drawing file for the widget target drawing. Use END to save your work.

Command: **END** (**RETURN**)

If you want another file to play around with for the rest of the Chapter, re-enter the drawing editor using the CHAPTER2 file that you saved last Chapter. When you are through playing around with CHAPTER2, QUIT (do not save your doodles) so we can keep this file clean for future work.

Here are some tips on TEXT entry:

TIPS ON TEXT ENTRY

☐ You can enter text upside down by using an angle definition to the left of the starting point.

☐ You can use OSNAP, ORTHO, and SNAP to help set TEXT parameters.

☐ AutoCAD never forgets. Its <default> prompts during the TEXT command show your last parameter settings. You can speed parameter entry by (**RETURN**)ing to signify that you accept height and rotation angle defaults.

☐ Often you can set height and angle once (say when you are setting up your drawing file), and simply use these <defaults> for all future text use.

☐ What happens if you make a mistake entering text? With TEXT if you catch your mistake before hitting (**RETURN**) to enter the text, you can correct the text entry on the prompt line by using the Backspace or the Delete key. If you use DTEXT, you can correct your errors as you type, backspacing back to previous lines. (If you do not realize that you have a mistaken text entry until you see it on the screen, don't panic—all is repairable. But for now, let's leave editing text to the EDITing Chapter.)

%%d ˙ ˙ 35°F
%%p ± ± 35±
%%c ⌀ ⌀ 35⌀
%%u 35
%%o 35
Underscored Overscored

Special TEXT Options

Special Text

Underscores, superscripts and special symbols are used regularly in text strings on drawings. Normally, you will not find these symbols on standard keyboards.

In the illustration, TEXT OPTIONS, the underscored and overscored text was typed into the TEXT command as follows:

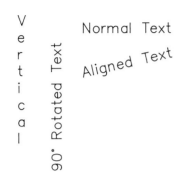

Vertical Text Font Example

Characters — RAW Text

| A |
| B |
| C |
| D |
| . |
| . |
| . |

Fonts — STYLE: Command

| Txt |
| Simplex |
| Complex |
| Italic |
| . |
| . |
| . |

Orientation — STYLE: Command

| Name |
| Font |
| Height |
| Width |
| Obliquing |
| Upside–down |
| Backwards |
| Vertical |

Placement — TEXT: Command

| Aligned |
| Centered |
| Right |
| Style |
| Height |
| Angle |
| Starting Point |

Drawing File

Diagram for TEXT Filters

TEXT UNDERSCORE AND OVERSCORE EXAMPLE

`Text: %%uUnderlined%%u %%oOverscored%%o`

You can enter the special character (%% notations) and underlined and over-scored switches at any time while you are typing a text string in response to the **Text:** prompt.

Angled vs. Vertical Text

Most text that appears on drawings reads horizontally from left to right. Sometimes, however, you may want text which is not horizontal.

You have two options. First, you can use normal TEXT or DTEXT parameters to Rotate or Align your text at any angle. Second, if you know you want your text to read vertically, you can create a style and give it a vertical orientation. Vertical orientations align characters one below another. All standard AutoCAD fonts can be given a vertical orientation. Examples are shown in VERTICAL TEXT FONT EXAMPLES.

"S" Is For Style

By now you may be wondering what the **S**tyle option is when it appears in the DTEXT Command: prompt.

S is for Style and AutoCAD has Style. So can you if you get to know how AutoCAD does it!

Think about this: If you had to draw the letter "A", you would need 7-19 line strokes, depending on the font. AutoCAD stores characters in a compact code reflecting these strokes.

In translating text from the compact code to your screen or plotter, AutoCAD passes the text through several "filters" to get it to come out the way you want. These are shown in the DIAGRAM FOR TEXT FILTERS.

Rather than forcing you to go through the whole process of defining text fonts, styles, and other command parameters, AutoCAD supplies you with several default settings. When you get going in the drawing editor for the first time, you are automatically equipped with a simple font and style, as well as standard height, angle, and orientation.

The Style filter is one of the filters that AutoCAD uses in preparing text for display on the screen. Style is a collection of instructions about how text will be translated from compact code into strokes on the plotter or characters on the screen.

T
X
T

V
e
r
t
i
c
a
l

This is TXT text
This is SIMPLEX text
This is COMPLEX text
This is ITALIC text
Simplex Skinny
Simplex Normal
Simplex Wide
Oblique = 0
Oblique = 10
Oblique = 15
Oblique = 20
Oblique = 45
Upside-down
Backwards

Text Examples showing: TXT, SIM-
PLEX, COMPLEX, ITALIC, Skinny,
Medium, Wide, Slant Examples (0, 10,
15, 20, 45 degrees), Upside-down and
Backwards

Creating and Maintaining TEXT Styles

If you use the **STYLE** commands to create new styles, you have a nearly unlimited combination of options for creating different type styles for drawing text.

All of the type used in the figures of this tutorial comes from a style we created. The text in your screen drawings does not look like the Book's drawings, because you are using the TXT font in a default style called STANDARD.

Next time you are in the drawing editor, you can redefine your standard style to look like ours using the following example with a SIMPLEX font. When you are through with the redefinition, AutoCAD will REGEN your screen and replace all the old standard TXT with standard SIMPLEX.

CREATING A TEXT STYLE

Get chapter2 file.

Set layer TEXT Current.

Turn other layers Off.

```
Command: STYLE (RETURN)      (Pick or type STYLE.)
Text Style name (or ?): Standard (RETURN)
Font file <TXT>: Simplex (RETURN)
Height <0'-0.00" >: (RETURN)
Width factor <1.00>: (RETURN)
Obliquing angle <0.00>: (RETURN)
Backwards? <N>: (RETURN)
Upside-down? <N>: (RETURN)
Vertical ? <N>: (RETURN)
STANDARD is now the current text style.
Command:
```

Here are the text style parameters:

TEXT STYLE PARAMETERS

☐ Name—Just a name for this collection of style parameters to help you remember how text drawn in this style will look.

☐ Font—The name of the character set that defines how the text will look. AutoCAD provides four Standard fonts: TXT, Simplex, Complex, or Italic.

☐ Height— Normally this is zero and does not affect the way characters appear on the screen. However, if you set style height to be greater than zero, text placed using this style will always have the height you give.

☐ Width—A multiplier, normally set to **1**, that augments the "width" of characters and how they appear on the screen. With a style width greater than one, you will have "squat" looking characters. With a style width less than one, the type will look "tall".

☐ Slant—Normally characters are upright with a slant angle = 0. But you can oblique your characters making them lean forward with a positive slant or backwards with a negative one. Be careful: a small angle like 15 or 20 degrees causes a dramatic slant.

☐ Upside-down and backwards settings—If you like mirror writing or need to annotate the bottom of something, you can set up a style with upside-down or backwards writing. This also is useful for transparencies or the backs of printed circuit boards. Or just for fun!

☐ Vertical—Any of the four standard fonts can be styled vertically.

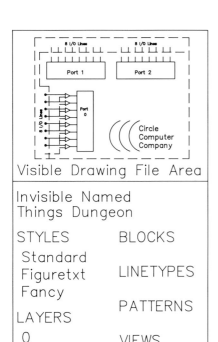

Visible Drawing File Area

Invisible Named
Things Dungeon

STYLES   BLOCKS
  Standard
  Figuretxt   LINETYPES
  Fancy
                PATTERNS
LAYERS
  0   VIEWS
  Graphic1
  Graphic2   FONTS
  Text
  Dimension

*Named Things Are Stored Invisibly
Inside AutoCAD*

Notes on STYLE

☐ Inside AutoCAD style definitions are maintained in an invisible part of the drawing file. You can store many styles in a single drawing file.

☐ When using the STYLE command, a **? (RETURN)** in response to the **Text style name (or ?):** prompt will give you a list of the styles currently defined and stored in the drawing file.

☐ When you give a new name in response to the **Text style name (or ?):** prompt, AutoCAD creates a new style in the style library.

☐ When you give an existing style name in response to the **Text style name (or ?):** prompt, AutoCAD assumes you want to change or edit the existing style. It prompts you for all the style parameters using the old settings as <default> prompts. It **does not warn** you that you are redefining a style.

☐ When you change the font (or horizontal/vertical orientation) of a style of text that is currently in the drawing file or showing on the screen, AutoCAD REGENs the screen, and updates the text in the drawing file with the new style definition.

Quick vs. Fancy Text

As your drawing file fills up with drawing elements, every time you ZOOM or ask AutoCAD to REDRAW or REGEN the screen, it takes longer and longer to put all these elements on the screen. Sooner or later you're going to want to cut down on the REGEN time or screen clutter. One way to cut clutter is to store your entities intelligently on layers, and only display those layers needed for your immediate work.

AutoCAD offers two other options for speeding up text handling.

First, you can do all your text work in a simple style (say using the TXT font) while you are creating the drawing. When it comes time for presentation, you can enhance the drawing by replacing the simple font with a more elegant one. You save time when you are doing initial drawing editor work, but your drawings still come out "pretty" with the last-minute font change.

If you try this trick, make sure you leave all other style parameters the same when you substitute one font for another in editing your style. If your Height, or Obliquing Angles change, you may find the new "fancy" text will not fit where you had placed the old text. Font character definitions differ, you also may have to adjust width to get a close fit.

The QTEXT Option

A second option (and the one we recommend) is to use AutoCAD's **QTEXT** command. The QTEXT (for Quick TEXT) command allows you to temporarily replace text with a rectangle. This is shown in the QTEXT DRAWING. Compare this drawing to our widget drawing—it is the same except for QTEXT.

The QTEXT command is available from the keyboard or from the SETTINGS screen menu. When QTEXT is On, new text is displayed normally until a regeneration occurs.

QTEXT—Drawing showing Widget Text in QTEXT Mode

A FEW MORE NOT-SO-PRIMITIVES

A fun little primitive is the **DONUT** (or DOUGHNUT for you old work enthusiasts). As you might imagine, the DONUT creates a donut-looking primitive, filled or unfilled. In fact, a donut with a 0 inside diameter is a filled in circle.

Get a cup of coffee and try the Donut:

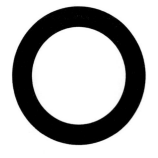

DONUT Example—DONUT is really a fat, closed PLINE

DONUT

```
Use layer 0 for playing around with donuts.!

Command: DONUT (RETURN)
Inside diameter <0.00>:        (enter a value or pick two points to
  show the distance)
Outside diameter <0.00>:       (enter a value or pick two points to
  show the distance)
Center of doughnut:            (enter a value or pick a point)
Command:

It keeps on prompting Center of doughnut until you hit
(RETURN)!
```

The donut that AutoCAD contructs is actually a PLINE that has the following three PLINE properties: It is Curve Fit. It has Width (you set the widths by entering the inside and outside diameter). And it is Closed.

Drawing Regular Polygons with POLYGON

Anyone for equilateral triangles? How about a hexagon? A dodecagon you say?

If you want multi-segmented polygons with irregular segment lengths, use closed LINES or PLINES. But if you want nice, regular polygons, take a look at the POLYGON command.

POLYGON gives you two ways to define the size of your figure, by defining a circle to inscribe or circumscribe the polygon, or by showing the length of one of the edges. Try one of each way:

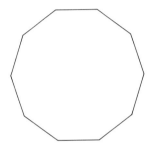

POLYGONs are PLINEs with 0 width, sides and angles

POLYGONS

```
Use Layer 0 Current to play around on.

Select Polygon from the Draw menu.

Command: POLYGON (RETURN)

Use the circle inscribed/circumscribed method.

Number of sides: 10 (RETURN)  (or any number from 3 to 1024)
Edge/<Center of polygon>:        (pick a center point)
Inscribed in circle/Circumscribed about circle (I/C):
  I (RETURN)
Radius of circle:          (enter a value or show with pointer)
Command:

Now use the edge method.

Command: POLYGON (RETURN)
Number of sides: 10 (RETURN)  (or any number from 3 to 1024)
Edge/<Center of polygon>: E (RETURN)
First endpoint of edge:         (pick a point)
Second endpoint of edge:        (pick another point)
Command:
```

Notice that POLYGON Edge method always generates a polygon going counterclockwise according to the two edge endpoints you select. The POLYGON generated is actually a PLINE with 0 width segments. If you want to see a slow "circle", just do a POLYGON with 1000 edges.

Last—But Not Least—The Ellipse

The **ELLIPSE** is another command on the DRAW screen menu. To define an ELLIPSE, follow AutoCAD prompts for major and minor axis entry or rotation. Use the ELLIPSE DRAWING as a guide.

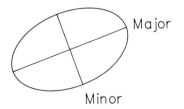

Define an ELLIPSE with a Major and Minor Axis

For the ELLIPSE command, when you drag the cursor, you define the major and minor axis and angle of rotation of the ELLIPSE. Try playing around with ELLIPSE. You will use it later on to help create your own ergonomic chair. The ELLIPSE also is a polyline in disguise.

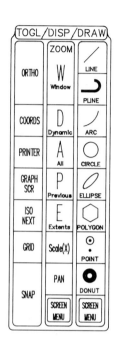

Tablet Menu Toggles

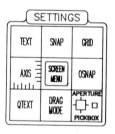

RELIEF FOR THE DISORGANIZED USER

As you learn AutoCAD, you'll find that you have neither the time to sit down and work with all the commands nor the inclination to commit them all to memory. Instead you will read through these pages (and portions of the AutoCAD ReferenceManual),playing around with the command descriptions that seem useful.

You may put aside learning additional commands and options until you need them, or have some extra time to explore AutoCAD further. When you do try to make new (or even familiar) commands work, you will find that AutoCAD is helpful.

Default Settings

AutoCAD is patient about how little you use the different commands, and how little you may remember from one working session to the next when you are starting out. It provides default settings and prompts to help you get your drawing work done.

Remember to look for <default> prompts or /(suggested responses)/ on the prompt line. Usually, the default setting is:

☐ The last setting that you used in the command. In this case, the prompt is as good as your last parameterized setting.

☐ A setting provided by AutoCAD which, in most cases, will help you muddle through. If a default setting makes no sense, you need to reset it.

Interrupts or Modes

AutoCAD is tolerant in other ways. The OSNAP command is your friend along with keyboard toggle switches for SNAP and ORTHO. They will save you countless bottles of aspirin. The QTEXT command and LAYER control will help you save REDRAW time.

Nobody, but nobody can think far enough ahead about how their drawings will come together, entity by entity, to set a complex command like OSNAP. AutoCAD anticipates this need by allowing you to **interrupt** DRAWing commands with OSNAP modes.

OSNAP overrides are available from the * * * * line of the screen menu and from the third digitizer button on your puck.

In the next few Chapters you will see how the drawing editor helps you to revise existing drawings. In EDITing you will need to interrupt commands constantly. So before we move on to EDITing, it is important that you make sure you are comfortable with interrupts.

When creating simple lines, you saw that you can tie a **To point:** to another object using the OSNAP interrupt. Similarly, ORTHO or SNAP can be turned **On** and **Off** in the middle of entity draw commands for precision control of your pointer.

Here are the major interrupt commands that will make your life in the drawing editor easy:

MAJOR INTERRUPT COMMANDS

☐ ^C—The best interrupt of all. If you are completely flustered, a ^C (Control-C), or at most two ^Cs, will get you back to the Command: prompt.

☐ HELP—The next-to-best interrupt. Help is almost always available. The **?** is a shortcut to help.'**?** or '**HELP** gets you help in the middle of a command.

☐ SNAP—You can toggle SNAP **On** and **Off** using ^B, or execute the SNAP command from the keyboard, or the pick SNAP command from the SETTINGS menu (available from the ROOTMENU).

☐ ORTHO—Remember ORTHO, when active, affects all coordinate entry from the pointer, including work in ARC, CIRCLE, etc. You can toggle ORTHO **On** and **Off**, using the ^O from the keyboard, or type the ORTHO command from the keyboard.

☐ OSNAP—OSNAP either temporarily or permanently turns the cursor into a **target** so you can zero in on objects that already exist, and use them as points for DRAWing or EDITing elements. You override a DRAW command and select a mode by typing the modifier on the prompt line.

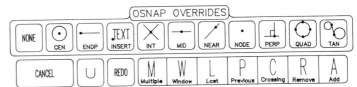

Remember OSNAP Overrides

While we are reviewing toggles, don't forget that you can control the X,Y digital readout on the status line with ^**D** and GRID on and off with a ^**G**.

SUMMING UP—REVIEW OF DRAWING BASICS

In this Chapter we've covered a lot of material. Congratulate yourself on a whirlwind tour of graphic primitives.

Screen and tablet menus are becoming our friends, like road signs in a new town. While the number of side streets we can traverse seems endless, we're beginning to understand how the primary DRAWing commands, like major highways, will get us almost all the way to our destination.

If you like Sunday drives into the country, AutoCAD allows you to wander through some of the less frequently used commands without letting you go too far astray. You can always get HELP or return to the **Command:** prompt with a ^C. (If you like getting lost on back roads in rural areas, we invite you to master the ten different ways to create an arc!)

Here's a checklist for using graphic primitives:

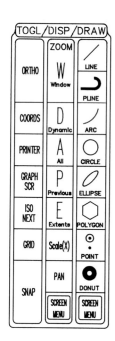

Tablet DRAW Commands

GRAPHICS PRIMITIVE CHECKLIST

☐ POINTS are useful reference locators for later OSNAP links. They can be displayed in various sizes and styles (PDMODE).

☐ LINES are the pillars of the drawing community.

    ☐ Connected lines are the norm, CANCEL, (RETURN), or a space stops a connected line run.

    ☐ Continue starts a line at the last point.

    ☐ Close makes a polygon by tying together lines in a connected line series.

☐ CIRCLE creation flexibility requires minimal information to generate full circles. Center,Radius is the most common circle creation method.

☐ A 3-point ARC is the most convenient to create. The START, CENTER series is also useful.

☐ AutoCAD automatically DRAGs entities to help you put your drawing elements together.

☐ PLINEs allow you to create single graphic elements composed of linear and curved segments.

    ☐ DONUT, and POLYGON, and ELLIPSE are made up from PLINEs.

☐ TEXT gets to the screen through a filtering process that controls:

    ☐ TEXT Justification.

    ☐ TEXT Style.

    ☐ TEXT Height.

    ☐ Rotation.

☐ DTEXT dynamically places text as you key characters at the keyboard.

☐ STYLE gives you flexibility in creating typestyles that are tailored to your needs.

☐ Keeping text on its own layer and/or using QTEXT keeps REDRAW/ REGEN times to a minimum as drawing files expand.

☐ Interrupts like SNAP, GRID, OSNAP or just plain ^C can keep your working sessions running smoothly, even if you are organized.

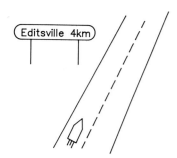

The Road Ahead

Onward

In this Chapter we began earnest work on a real drawing. While widgets may not be your thing, you have already mastered setting layers, drawing lines and circles, and inserting text. By the end of the next Chapter, this drawing will be complete: a four layer, full color widget schematic.

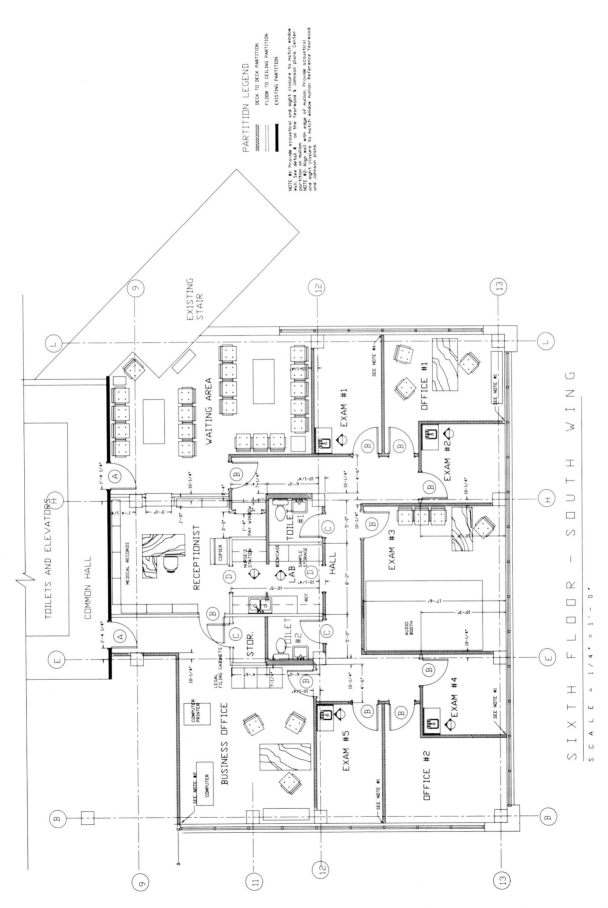

Architect's Plan Drawn With AutoCAD (Richard A. Barron, Architect)
Courtesy of Autodesk, Inc.

101

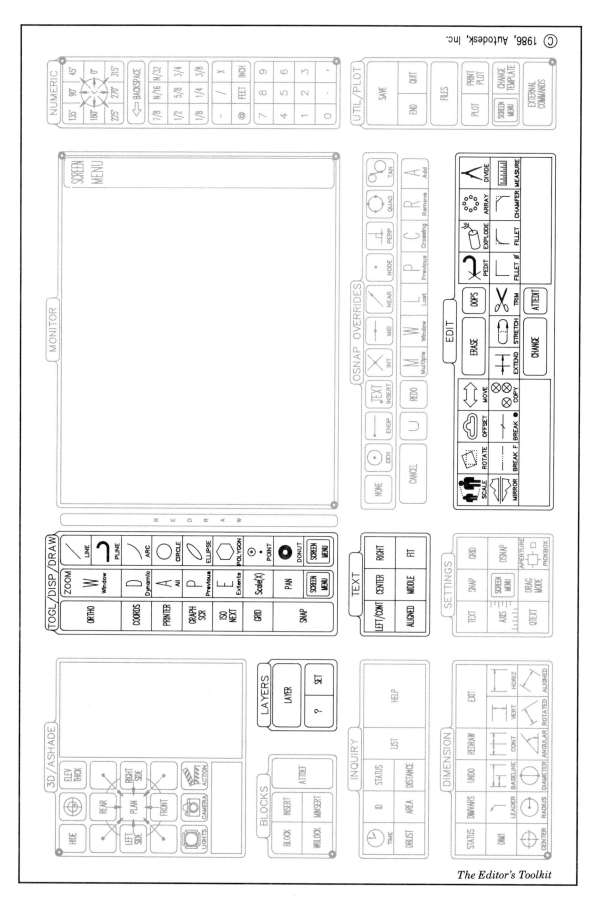

The Editor's Toolkit

CHAPTER 4

INTRODUCTION TO EDITING

IF AT FIRST YOU DON'T SUCCEED, TRY EDITING

You Edit More Than You Create. ▶ The Editor's Toolkit. Some Quick MOVEs. The Editing Buffer. Displacement—Another Editing Feature. The COPY Command. Arrays—Multiple Copies with One Command. MIRROR Imaging. ERASE and Its Sidekick, OOPS. You Can Undo Too. Going Through Changes. Using Break to Cut Objects. ▶ ROTATE and SCALE Commands. ▶ Changing Color and Linetype of Existing Elements. ▶ Editing Polylines. Creating a Drawing With Edits. ▶ Summing Up—Tips on Edit.

YOU EDIT MORE THAN YOU CREATE

As you go through the Book's examples you may have a nagging feeling saying, "give me a drafting board, a straight edge, and a compass, and I can beat this CAD system in a flash!".

It just isn't so. While some draftspeople may be able to create original linework faster than AutoCAD, it is safe to say that no human can revise and print new clean drawing sets faster than AutoCAD (and an organized user).

The one certainty in the drawing business is—change. Change this! Change that! Drawing revision numbers keep mounting! Becoming familiar with the AutoCAD EDITing functions is critical to your successful use of AutoCAD.

So far you have spent most of your tutorial time creating new drawing entities and storing them in the drawing file. Beginning with this Chapter, you'll see how AutoCAD's commands easily adjust drawing file contents. In time, you will find yourself spending more time editing existing drawings than creating new ones.

The benefits of editing are pure and simple. Editing allows you to stay on top of changes and create multiple images from minimal original entry.

EDITing Activities—Changing, Copying, and Erasing

What type of activities will you encounter in EDITing a drawing? Three areas stand out:

- ☐ Changing—existing elements. You can change all sorts of properties of existing elements: location, size, color, linetype, endpoints, layer, and more.

- ☐ Copying. You can make one or more copies of existing elements either one at a time or in a swoop (ARRAY) of creation.

- ☐ Erasing. Yes, you can get rid of all those mistakes, too.

A fourth major area crosses between drawing creation and editing. We'll call this area "Construction Tools" and cover them in the next Chapter.

In this Chapter we'll cover the basics of editing. We'll change both the spatial (location) and appearance (color, linetype) properties of existing elements. In addition, we'll learn simple copying, multiple copying and how to erase.

MOVE, COPY, and ERASE Commands

These three functions are the most common editing functions, and their operations are straightforward. Take a look at the SIMPLE EDITING EXAMPLES as you read the next few paragraphs.

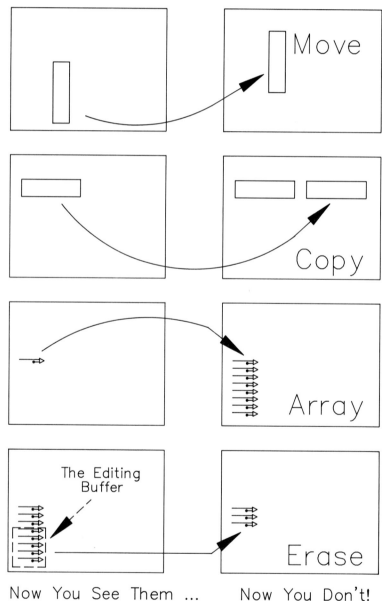

Simple Editing Examples   Now You See Them ...   Now You Don't!

THE EDITOR'S TOOLKIT

While most of the EDIT commands are gathered on the EDIT menus available from the ROOTMENU, you will find that AutoCAD has many editing tools, not limited to just the menu lists. EDIT commands work this way:

☐ **What** kind of edit do you want to do?

☐ **Which** objects do you want to edit?

☐ **How** do you want to edit them?

☐ The **edit** then occurs.

The Editor's Toolkit has tools for helping with the **What?** and with the **Which?**:

WHAT = EDITING TOOLS
Spatial Changes to Existing Elements

☐ ARRAY —Places multiple copies of objects with a single command.

☐ BREAK —Cuts existing objects and/or erases portions of objects.

☐ COPY —Makes copies of objects.

☐ ERASE —Allows you to select objects in the drawing file, and then do the evil deed of wiping them out.

☐ CHANGE—Changes spatial properties of some objects like location, text height, circle radius or line endpoint location.

☐ MIRROR—Creates a mirror image of objects.

☐ MOVE —Picks up existing objects and puts them down in another part of the drawing file.

☐ ROTATE—Turns existing objects to your angular specification.

☐ SCALE —Scales objects up or down to your specification.

Visual Changes To Elements

☐ COLOR—Allows you to enter subsequent elements in a color you select.

☐ LINETYPE—Allows you to enter subsequent elements in a linetype you select.

☐ CHANGE—Also allows you to change a number of properties including color, linetype, and layer of existing elements.

☐ LAYER —Default element appearance is tied to certain LAYER properties like linetype and color.

To establish **which** objects to edit, AutoCAD asks you to form a group or **selection set** of one or more objects. We call this set the Editing Buffer.

BASIC SELECTION SET TOOLS

☐ object—The default selects a set by picking individual objects.

☐ Window—Selects a set by herding objects together in a window.

☐ Last—Uses only the last object created as a selection set.

☐ Crossing—Works like Window, except it also includes any object which is partially within (or **Crossing**) the window.

☐ Remove—Switches to Remove mode, so you may select objects to be removed from the Selection Set (not from the drawing).

☐ Add—Switches from Remove back to normal, so you may again add to the Selection Set.

☐ Multiple—Allows you to pick multiple objects in close proximity, and/or speed up selection by allowing multiple selections without highlighting or prompting.

☐ Previous—Adds (or removes) the entire Previous Selection Set (from a previous command) to the current Selection Set.

☐ Undo—Undoes or reverses the last Selection operation. Each U undoes one selection operation.

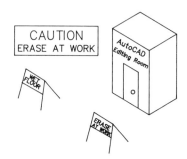

ERASE Command at Work

CAUTION: ERASE Command at Work

Neither AutoCAD nor any other computer system can read between the digitizer lines or your fingers on the keyboard. Be careful using ERASE on any files that are valuable to you.

If you make a mistake, you have **Undo** and **OOPS** to get you back to where you were.

Layer DIMENSIO   0'–0",0'–0"

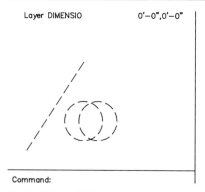

Command:

Setting Up for Editing

SOME QUICK MOVES WITH AutoCAD

For exercise, let's get into the drawing editor and edit the existing file **CHAPTER2**. When you load the file, your screen should look like SETTING UP FOR EDITING.

Get to the MOVE screen menu by picking EDIT from the ROOTMENU, and picking MOVE from the EDIT menu or pick MOVE from your tablet menu.

Let's **MOVE** the line to the right of the circles. Use the **Window** option to select the line. When you select the line in your editing buffer window, your screen will look like TRAPPING THE LINE. This is like trapping a lion, but it's only a line:

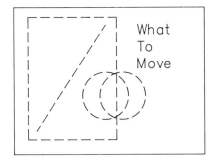 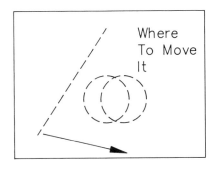 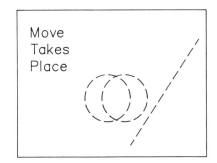

Moving Logic Flow: Selection, Displacement, and Move

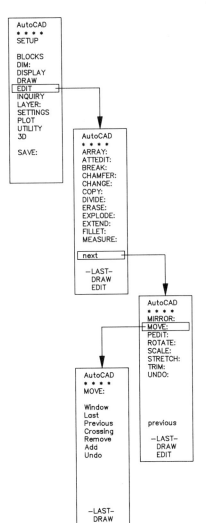

ROOT to EDIT to MOVE

TRAPPING A LINE

Get the CHAPTER2 drawing.

Set layer DIMENSION Current.

Use the crosshair to trap the line in an editing window.

Command: **MOVE (RETURN)**
Select objects: **W (RETURN)**   (pick window from the
  screen menu)
First corner: (pick) Other corner: (pick) 1 found.

Select objects: **(RETURN)**   (This (RETURN) tells
  AutoCAD you are through selecting).

Base point or displacement: **4",4" (RETURN)**
Second point of displacement: **1'8",2" (RETURN)**
    (The move takes place.)
Command:

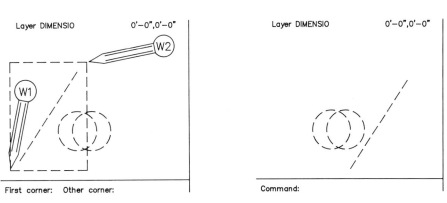

Creating an Editing Buffer with Window, and Trapping the Line

A Tamed (MOVEd) Line

When you finish, your screen should look like A TAMED (MOVED) LINE.

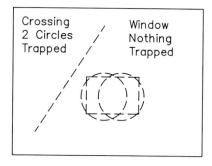

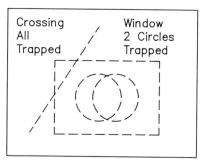

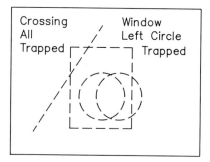

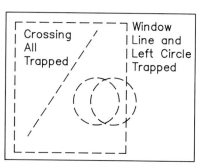

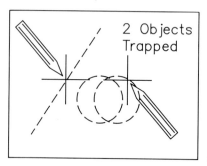

THE EDITING BUFFER

In the MOVE command, AutoCAD asked you to "Select objects" that you wanted to move. There are three basic ways to collect objects to be moved: individual objects, Window, and Last. In all three cases, AutoCAD sets up a temporary **Editing Buffer**. The editing buffer is a collection of object(s) that is operated on by EDITing commands. MOVE, COPY, ERASE, and other edit commands make use of this Selection Set.

As you select objects to edit, AutoCAD highlights them on the screen by temporarily turning their linetypes to dotted. This way you can see what you've selected to edit.

In Add mode you get the prompt, **Select objects:**. When you first begin an edit buffer, AutoCAD assumes you want to **add** objects to the buffer. You can use the pointer (which turns into an aperture bullseye) to individually pick objects or use a **W** (Window) or **L** (Last) from the keyboard or screen menu. With a **W** AutoCAD prompts for window corners (like a ZOOM) and with **L** AutoCAD puts the last object created into the editing buffer.

In response to the add mode prompt **Select objects:**, you can type an **R** or **Remove** to get the prompt **Remove objects**. You can remove objects from the buffer by going into the Remove mode and using any type of object selection.

ADD AND REMOVE MODES

```
Command: MOVE (RETURN)     (or any edit command.)
Select objects:            (add to the buffer.)

or

Command: MOVE (RETURN)     (or any edit command.)
Select objects: R (RETURN)
Remove objects:     (remove from the buffer.)
```

The first example uses the selection process to add objects to the buffer, the second uses the same process to remove objects from the buffer. An **A** gets you back to **Add** mode from **Remove** mode.

Ways to Add or Remove Objects From the Editing Buffer

You can use any of the three basic methods alone or in combination for adding or removing objects from the editing buffer.

Filling the Editing Buffer with Window Selections

```
Command: MOVE (RETURN)    (or any edit command.)
Select objects:   (pick a few objects, then (RETURN)
Select objects: W (RETURN)

(Use a window to get a few more)

Select objects: (RETURN)    (finish selection with a (RETURN))

(The edit command continues by reporting its findings.)
```

AutoCAD Lets You Know What's In The Editing Buffer

While you've been selecting, AutoCAD has been searching through the drawing file for drawing elements that qualify for the editing buffer.

Every time you select more elements for the editing buffer, AutoCAD let's you know how many you've selected, and how many it actually found. These numbers are not always the same for two reasons:

☐ You can select objects that do not qualify for editing, or

☐ You may have already selected that element. In the latter case, AutoCAD lets you know it found a duplicate. In all cases, except multiple selections, AutoCAD uses the highlighting feature to show you what is currently in the editing buffer.

☐ When you've finished picking objects for the editing buffer, you tell AutoCAD you're through by hitting a **(RETURN)** in response to a final **Select objects:** or **Remove objects:** prompt. When you are through selecting, AutoCAD continues with whatever edit command is in progress.

Let's Try an Object Selection to Fill the Buffer

Let's MOVE the line back where it was (to the left of the circles) using the objects option for filling the editing buffer.

```
          FILLING THE EDITING BUFFER WITH OBJECTS

Command: MOVE (RETURN)
Select objects:   (pick point on line)  1 selected, 1 found.
Select objects: (RETURN)

Base point or displacement: endpoint
of  (pick line lower endpoint)
Second point of displacement: 4",4" (RETURN)

(The move takes place.)

Command:
```

DISPLACEMENT IS ANOTHER EDITING FEATURE

Let's MOVE the line back to the right to demonstrate displacement.

DISPLACEMENT EXAMPLE

```
Command: MOVE (RETURN)
Select objects: (pick line )  1 selected, 1 found.
Select objects: (RETURN)

Base point or displacement: 4",4" (RETURN)
Second point of displacement: 1'8",2" (RETURN)

(The move takes place.)

Command:
```

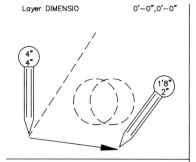

Layer DIMENSIO   0'-0",0'-0"

Second point of displacement:

MOVE Displacement

Here's a way to think about displacement: Imagine the line we want to move has a handle on it (say at the bottom endpoint). We are going to pick up the line by that handle and carry it to the right of the circles and put the handle down. The displacement is a line from the original handle location to its moved location.

AutoCAD does not actually draw a displacement line, it gets the information it needs from the displacement points. If you are picking displacement points on the screen, AutoCAD will show you a temporary displacement line trailing behind the crosshair from the first point you pick until you pick the second. You can see how this works by looking at MOVE DISPLACEMENT.

DRAGMODE Controls When AutoCAD Turns Drag On or Off

The default for DRAGMODE is Auto, which causes AutoCAD to drag everything that makes sense. If you want to be selective about what you drag, you can turn DRAGMODE ON.

With DRAGMODE On you must tell AutoCAD you want to turn on drag in the middle of a command. To do so, you simply type **DRAG (RETURN)** before picking the point that you wish to drag. This is built into many of the standard AutoCAD Menu items. Off turns DRAGMODE off entirely. You may wish to control DRAGMODE when editing very large Selection Sets. You can do this by using the DRAGMODE command. Turn it On.

CONTROLLING DRAG

```
Command: DRAGMODE (RETURN)
On/Off/Auto <Auto: On (RETURN)
Command:
```

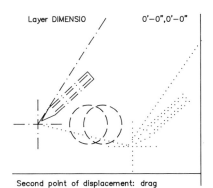

Layer DIMENSIO   0'-0",0'-0"

Second point of displacement: drag

Dragging an Editing Buffer before Placement (Dashed Lines represent Moving Buffer)

Instead of entering two points to set up the displacement for the MOVE command, you may enter one coordinate point as a starting point, and then pick the second point. If you type **drag**, AutoCAD makes the move in drag mode. You see the contents of the editing buffer moving around the screen before you commit to a placement of the second point.

Let's MOVE the line (one more time!) back to the left of the circles using **drag**. The prompt sequence looks like this:

DRAGGING THE MOVE

```
Command: MOVE (RETURN)
Select objects:   (pick point on line)  1 selected, 1 found.
Select objects: (RETURN)

Base point or displacement: endpoint (type endpoint.)
of   (pick line lower endpoint)
Second point of displacement: drag (RETURN)

(Edit buffer contents drag with the crosshair.)

(Pick 4",4" by keeping an eye on the status line readout
or type 4",4" (RETURN).)

(The move takes place.)

Command:

When you are done set DRAGMODE back to Auto.
```

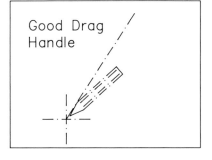

Good Drag Handle

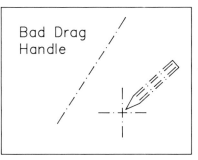

Bad Drag Handle

Bad and Good Handles on a Dragged Editing Buffer

Getting a Handle on Drag

When setting up an editing buffer for drag, the first displacement point you pick will be the point by which the buffer gets dragged around by the crosshair. This first point is the **handle** you use to carry the editing buffer around.

If this point is not in, on, or near the contents of the editing buffer, it will appear that you are carrying the buffer around magically without "touching" it. It's a good idea to make this drag anchor (first displacement point) a reference point you will use to **put down** the buffer once you have dragged it.

If you happen to have a slow computer that does not support DRAG efficiently, you might want to turn DRAGMODE off altogether.

COPY COMMAND

The basic **COPY** command is similar to the MOVE command. The only difference between the COPY command and MOVE is that COPY leaves the original to-be-copied objects intact.

Let's try an example using the two circles in the drawing. Make a copy of the circles and place them 10 inches directly above the existing circles. See COPYING CIRCLES for the location of the COPY Window corners:

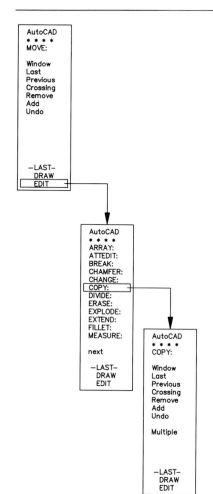

MOVE to EDIT to COPY

COPYING CIRCLES

```
Command: COPY (RETURN)
Select objects: W (RETURN)
First corner:    (pick)  Other corner:    (pick)  2 found.
Select objects: (RETURN)

<Base point or displacement>/Multiple: 16",10" (RETURN)
Second point of displacement: 16",20" (RETURN)

(The copy takes place)

Command:
```

When you've completed the exercise, your screen should look like COPIED CIRCLES.

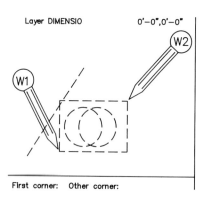

COPYing Circles

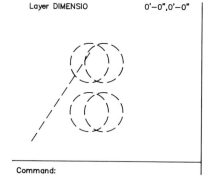

Copied Circles

COPY Command Options

The COPY command options are similar to the MOVE command options: displacement points identification, object selection options, and a new one—**Multiple**. You can always use OSNAP, SNAP, and ORTHO functions during the COPY command as modifiers to help you get an exact displacement location, or select the correct objects for the editing buffer.

Multiple Copy

Selecting the **Multiple** option of the COPY command lets you copy the contents of your selection set several times with having to respecify the selection set. If you pick or type **M** in response to the ..../Multiple: prompt, AutoCAD will continue to promot you for a <Second point of displacement> after each COPY operation. A simple (**RETURN**) response gets you out of the Multiple COPY loop.

If you want to fill up your screen, try a few Multiple copies and then see how AutoCAD can organize these multiples by copying again with the ARRAY command.

Try the new Multiple Copy option.

ARRAYS—MULTIPLE COPIES WITH ONE COMMAND

Often you want to make multiple copies of an object or group of objects. For example, suppose you have a rectangle that represents a table in a cafeteria. It would be useful if AutoCAD had some way of placing that table repeatedly every 9 feet in the X direction and every 14 feet in the Y direction to make— say 5 rows by 8 columns of tables.

Never fear, **ARRAY** is here. An ARRAY is a regular pattern of entities. The ARRAY command works just like the COPY command. However, instead of making one COPY of the editing buffer contents the ARRAY command makes many. To make ARRAY work, you determine the number of copies and the repetition pattern.

Looking In On Rectangular ARRAYS

Let's try a rectangular ARRAY example. We will place a line seven more times for a total of eight lines. While you can make a rectangular ARRAY have both rows and columns of repeated objects, we'll just have a single row with eight columns in this example. The target drawing is shown in REC-TANGULAR ARRAY WITH LINE.

RECTANGULAR ARRAY

```
Command: ARRAY (RETURN)
Select objects:   (pick the line)  1 selected,  1 found.
Select objects: (RETURN)

Rectangular/Polar array  (R/P): R (RETURN)
Number of rows (---) <1>: (RETURN)
Number of columns (|||) <1>: 8 (RETURN)
Distance between columns (|||): 2"   (RETURN)

(The copying takes place)

Command:
```

Rectangular ARRAY with Line

AutoCAD
* * * *
COPY:

Window
Last
Previous
Crossing
Remove
Add
Undo

Multiple

—LAST—
DRAW
EDIT

AutoCAD
* * * *
ARRAY:
ATTEDIT:
BREAK:
CHAMFER:
CHANGE:
COPY:
DIVIDE:
ERASE:
EXPLODE:
EXTEND:
FILLET:
MEASURE:

next

—LAST—
DRAW
EDIT

AutoCAD
* * * *
ARRAY:

Window
Last
Previous
Crossing
Remove
Add
Undo

Rectang
Polar
—
Yes

—LAST—
DRAW
EDIT

COPY to EDIT to ARRAY Rectangular

Layer DIMENSIO   0'-0",0'-0"

Command:

113

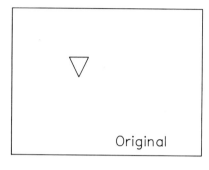

Original

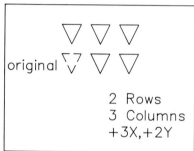

original

2 Rows
3 Columns
+3X,+2Y

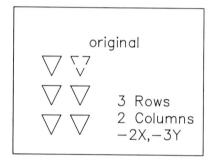

original

3 Rows
2 Columns
−2X,−3Y

Positive and Negative ARRAY Offsets

Notes on Rectangular Array.

☐ You can show the displacement between rows or columns by picking two points with or without drag.

☐ If you set up a big array (many rows and columns), AutoCAD will ask you if you really want to repeat the editing buffer so many times. If it gets out of hand, you can stop it with a ^C and then reverse it with a **U** for Undo.

☐ You can use positive as well as negative offset distances. The offset distance is the X and Y direction from the original:

+ X gives columns to the right.

− X gives columns to the left.

+ Y gives rows up.

− Y gives rows down.

Looking In On Polar Arrays

In addition to rectangular arrays, AutoCAD supports polar or circular arrays. The contents of editing buffer are placed around the circumference of a circle or along an arc which you specify.

Examples of a regular and a rotated circular arrays are shown in POLAR ARRAYS.

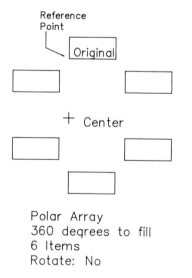

Reference
Point

Original

+ Center

Polar Array
360 degrees to fill
6 Items
Rotate: No

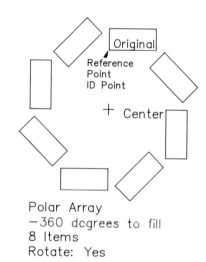

Original

Reference
Point
ID Point

+ Center

Polar Array
−360 degrees to fill
8 Items
Rotate: Yes

Polar ARRAYs

MIRROR IMAGING

Using the **MIRROR** command, you can mirror the contents of an editing buffer. AutoCAD can mirror at any angle.

To operate the MIRROR command, select MIRROR directly from the EDIT list of commands, type **MIRROR** at the keyboard, or pick MIRROR from your tablet menu. MIRROR asks you to identify a Selection Set in the usual manner (objects, Window, Last, etc.).

Then comes the mirror twist. AutoCAD prompts you for the beginning and endpoint of a mirror line. The line can be any direction—if you want a straight 180-degree flip, be sure to use ORTHO to help you get a straight mirror line. If you want mirroring at a precise angle, use relative polar coordinates (for example, @8<60, or use a rotated SNAP.

Finally, AutoCAD asks if you want to keep the original object(s) in place or erase them as the mirroring takes place. (MOVE or COPY the contents of the editing buffer through the mirror).

Take a look at the MIRROR EXAMPLE to get a feel for how this works. Try it. You can always **U** to undo your experiment.

Once you specify a MIRROR command, sit back and watch all those lovely lines, arcs, circles, and text cross the mirror line and come out on the other side.

TEXT!! Did you say that TEXT goes through the mirror too? Look closely at the MIRROR EXAMPLE. AutoCAD's mirror function does not discriminate against drawing entities of any type. Sometimes mirrored text is a desired effect. But if you do not want text mirrored, you can tell AutoCAD not to invert text.

AutoCAD provides another way to MIRROR that allows graphics to be mirror-inverted, but text to come out the way it goes in. Look for MIRRTEXT in the Chapter on CUSTOMIZATION.

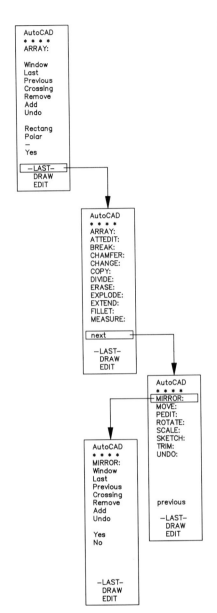

ARRAY to EDIT to MIRROR

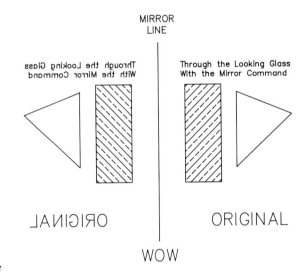

MIRROR Example

ERASE AND ITS SIDEKICK, OOPS

ERASE, like a hammer, can be a constructive tool. But, as with a hammer, watch out! ERASE has been the scourge of many a good drawing file.

Let's get rid of the upper pair of circles we copied. Take a look at the ERASE EDITING BUFFER WINDOW to see how the editing buffer window should look.

To start, select ERASE from the EDIT list, type ERASE from your keyboard, or select it from your tablet menu:

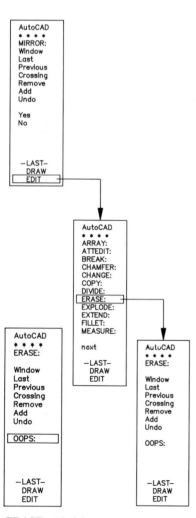

Erase Editing Buffer

ERASE EXAMPLE TO DELETE TWO UPPER CIRCLES

Command: **ERASE (RETURN)**
Select objects: **W (RETURN)**
First corner: (pick)   Other corner: (pick)   2 found.
Select objects: **(RETURN)**

(The deletion takes place)

Command:

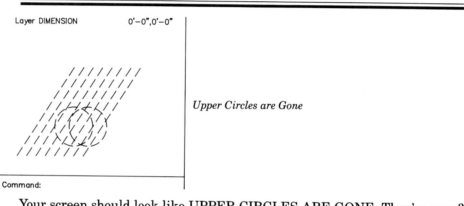

Upper Circles are Gone

Your screen should look like UPPER CIRCLES ARE GONE. They're gone?

Oops!.... I Didn't Really Mean It

Prominently displayed on the ERASE screen menu (and also available by typing) is a good friend, the **OOPS** command. OOPS asks no questions—it just goes about its business of restoring whatever you just obliterated.

Every time you execute an ERASE command, AutoCAD keeps a copy of what you ERASEd in case you want to OOPS it back into the file. But only the most recent ERASE is kept OOPS ready!

OOPS allows you to do the unthinkable—after you have mistakenly deleted an object from the file, you can recover the last deletion (under most circumstances) with the OOPS command.

Try an OOPS now:

OOPS ON BACK YOUR LAST ERASE

Command: **OOPS (RETURN)**

(Here come the two circles)

Command:

ERASE with OOPS Highlighted

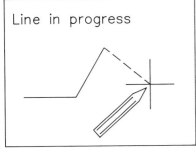

Line in progress

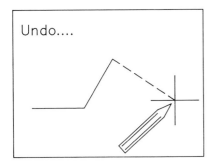

Next segment

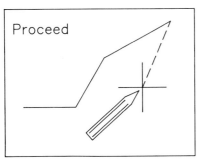

Undo....

Proceed

Three Steps Forward and One Step Back. (Using the LINE Undo Option to Help Fix Errors.)

YOU CAN UNDO TOO

You also have seen how **U** (for undo) helps out in the LINE command.

AutoCAD, when it receives the **undo** command, first mutters under its breath, then obediently steps back to see what you did last. Then it sets about **undoing** your last effort.

In LINE, for example, you can **undo** all the way back to the beginning of the LINE command—eradicating all the line segments since you last invoked the command. Each hit on the **undo** command erases another segment.

You might think, "Why not just ERASE the last segment and enter a new one?"

When you invoke ERASE you stop all the current command's activity in order to execute the ERASE command. **Undo** acts only as a temporary interrupt, returning control to the LINE command immediately after **undoing** the last line segment. You do not have to restart the LINE command and you pick up at the end of the last segment.

U and UNDO

In additon to the Undo function in some commands (LINE, PLINE, for example) there are two additional Undo commands: **U** and **UNDO**. **U** just undoes any one command (or menu item) at a time, but can step backwards through your drawing, to the beginning of the session in most cases. **UNDO** controls UNDO settings as well as allowing large UNDOs in one step.

Later you will see how undo is helpful in dimensioning and PEDIT. In the next Chapter on advanced editing and construction, you will see how AutoCAD's UNDO and REDO features help you recover from big mistakes.

GOING THROUGH CHANGES

CHANGE allows you to selectively edit one or more of the parameters that give a drawing element its identity, location, and appearance in the drawing file. Different entities have different parameters that you can change. When you select objects to change, AutoCAD prompts you for the appropriate parameters to edit.

To demonstrate, let's CHANGE two items on the screen. Change the location of the upper endpoint of the leftmost line and increase the diameter of the left circle.

Here's the prompt sequence to make the changes happen:

CHANGING LINE ENDPOINT LOCATION

Command: **CHANGE (RETURN)**
Select objects: (pick leftmost line) 1 selected, 1 found.
Select objects: **(RETURN)**

Properties/<Change point>: **2",22"** **(RETURN)**

(The line endpoint changes, realigning the line)

Command:

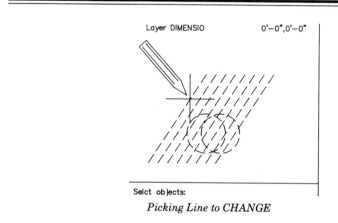

Picking Line to CHANGE

INCREASING THE CIRCLE DIAMETER WITH CHANGE

Command: **CHANGE (RETURN)**
Select objects: (pick any point on the left circle)
   1 selected, 1 found.
Select objects: **(RETURN)**
Properties/<Change point>:
   (pick a point about 1 unit to the left of the left circle.
   The new circumference passes through this point. The
   circle size increases.)

Command:

ERASE to EDIT to CHANGE

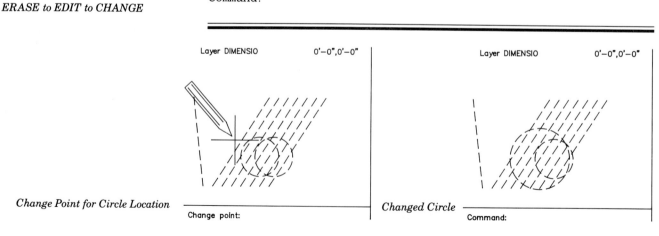

Change Point for Circle Location

Changed Circle

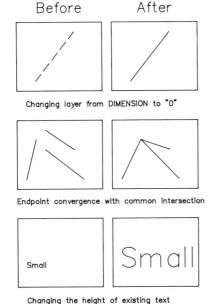

Before   After

Changing layer from DIMENSION to "0"

Endpoint convergence with common intersection

Small   Small

Changing the height of existing text

CHANGE has dozens of other applications. Here's list of change possibilities:

HOW CHANGE CAN AFFECT DIFFERENT ENTITIES

☐ Lines—CHANGE endpoints. You can make several non-coincident endpoints **come together** with one CHANGE command by picking many lines, but only one one **Change point**.

☐ Circles—CHANGE circle forces the circumference of an existing circle to pass through a new **Change point** keeping the same circle.

☐ Text—CHANGE location, rotation angle, height, style, and text string. For text, CHANGE acts as a second chance to set all the text parameters correctly. You also can use the STYLE command to change a text style throughout the drawing at one time.

Possible CHANGEs

USING BREAK TO CUT OR PARTIALLY ERASE OBJECTS

To use the **BREAK** command you have to let AutoCAD know which element you want to BREAK, where you want to BREAK it, and how big a chunk you want to BREAK off.

To let AutoCAD know which element you want to break, use any of the standard fill-the-edit-buffer techniques. Picking is the safest way to get the object you want.

AutoCAD uses this first pick point as the start of the break and prompts you for another point. This second point is the end of the break segment. If you pick the same point again, AutoCAD breaks your object at the selected point, but does not delete any of it.

Here's the prompt sequence for BREAKing off a few inches from the top of the rightmost line on your screen. You can see the end result in BREAK EXAMPLE. Use the BREAK EXAMPLE drawing as a guide to locate the correct first point:.

```
AutoCAD
* * * *
CHANGE:

Window
Last
Previous
Crossing
Remove
Add
Undo

Color
Elev
LAyer
LType
Thickness
—LAST—
 DRAW
 EDIT
```

```
AutoCAD
* * * *
ARRAY:
ATTEDIT:
BREAK:
CHAMFER:
CHANGE:
COPY:
DIVIDE:
ERASE:
EXPLODE:
EXTEND:
FILLET:
MEASURE:

next

—LAST—
 DRAW
 EDIT
```

```
AutoCAD
* * * *
BREAK:

First
⊕


—LAST—
 DRAW
 EDIT
```

CHANGE to EDIT to BREAK

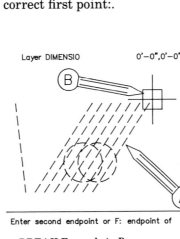

Layer DIMENSIO   0'-0",0'-0"

Enter second endpoint or F: endpoint of

BREAK Example in Progress

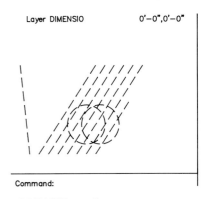

Layer DIMENSIO   0'-0",0'-0"

Command:

BREAK Example

Before   After

BREAK activity is dependent on the sequence of break point identification

Before   After

BREAK EXAMPLE

```
Command: BREAK (RETURN)
Select object:   (pick the rightmost line near midpoint)

Enter second point or F:    (pick the line upper endpoint)

   (The break occurs, the end is erased.)

Command:
```

A note on BREAK. At complicated intersections of multiple elements you have to think ahead about breaking. AutoCAD can be confused if you select an intersection as a first break point. The way to approach the problem is to first pick the object to be broken, then specify two break points. To get a **First point:** prompt, use **F**.

Right and Wrong BREAK sequence at busy intersections. (You may need two or three steps to get the right sequence.)

ROTATE AND SCALE—TWO QUICK EDITING COMMANDS

Several other AutoCAD commands act on the spatial appearance of elements already in place. Two are obvious: ROTATE and SCALE.

Use ROTATE to Turn Objects About a Base Point

Why don't you just try ROTATing the right line about its midpoint:

```
Layer DIMENSIO        0'-0",0'-0"
```

```
Command:
```

ROTATE Line

ROTATION EXERCISE

```
Command: ROTATE (RETURN)
Select objects:   (pick the line)   1 selected, 1 found.
Select objects:   (RETURN)
Base point:  midpoint   (type)
of (pick the line again.)
<Rotation angle>/Reference: -30 (RETURN)

   (Rotation takes place.)

Command:
```

When you're satisfied it is rotated, rotate it back.

```
Command: ROTATE (RETURN)
Select objects:   (pick the line) 1 selected, 1 found.
Base point:  midpoint   (type)
of (pick the line again.)
<Rotation angle>/Reference: 30 (RETURN)
```

(Rotation takes place again.)

Command:

Here are some notes on ROTATE:

☐ The rotation base point needn't be on the object that you are rotating. You can put it anywhere and AutoCAD will figure out how to turn your selected objects relative to the base point. But be careful, just like with "bad drag handles", you can become confused with rotation base points that are not on the object(s) you intend to rotate.

☐ Notice the first ROTATE you did above used a negative angle value. Negative angles produce clockwise rotation, positive counterclockwise, just like in setting UNITS.

☐ The **Reference** part of the ROTATE prompt, is useful. You can change the angle of an object by giving AutoCAD a reference angle that should be set equal to a new angle. In effect you say, "Put a handle on 237 (for example) and turn it to 165." This is often easier than calculating the difference (72 degrees clockwise) and typing that number at the prompt.

SCALE Shrinks or Enlarges Objects in Place

Try growing the right circle:

Layer DIMENSIO   0'-0",0'-0"

Command:

SCALE Right Circle

SCALE THE CIRCLE

```
Command: SCALE (RETURN)
Select objects:   (pick the right circle)  1 selected, 1 found.
Select objects: (RETURN)
Base point:  center (type)
of  (pick the circle again.)
<Scale factor>/Reference: 2 (RETURN)
```

(Circle grows 100%)

Command:

Return the circle to its original size with a 0.5 scale factor.

Some notes on SCALE:

☐ The base point you choose remains constant in space— everything around it grows or shrinks by your scale factor. If you had selected a base point on the circle circumference, the circle would have grown from that point, or shrunk to that point.

☐ Just as with ROTATE, you can specify an original "Reference" length and a new length rather than giving an explicit scale multiplier.

CHANGING THE COLOR AND LINETYPE APPEARANCE OF EXISTING ELEMENTS

So far the kinds of edits you have done change the location, size or shape of elements already in place. There are two additional properties of existing elements that are important to edit. These are COLOR and LINETYPE.

In order to edit the properties of an existing element, it helps to know just what kinds of properties an element can have. Although you may not have thought about it, the edits (like MOVE) actually change a property of the element.

For example, in the case of MOVE, you are changing a "location" property. You change location by a Displacement. When you first created the line on the screen, you gave it a location property by fixing its endpoints.

Similarly, when you created the line you gave it a color and linetype. You might not have thought about it at the time, because color and linetype are usually assigned automatically, according to default color and linetypes you've already put in place.

The line and circles on the screen were created on layer DIMENSION. Back in Chapter 1 you set up layer DIMENSION to have a green default color and a dashed default linetype. Check LAYER ? to refresh your memory about layer color and linetype settings.

```
Command: LAYER (RETURN)
?/Make/Set/New/On/Off/Color/Ltype/Freeze/Thaw: ?  (RETRUN)
Layer name(s) for listing <*>:  (RETURN)

(AutoCAD flips to nongraphics mode and displays layer list.)

Current layer: DIMENSION

?/Make/Set/New/On/Off/Color/Ltype/Freeze/Thaw:
```

So when you created the line and two circles, these elements picked up their characteristics from the default layer settings.While you were editing these lines on layer GRAPHIC2 they retained their color and linetype.

Elements need not only follow the default color and linetype settings of the layer they were created on. In fact, an element can have any color or linetype, independent of any layer or other element. You set what color or linetype an element will get with the LAYER, COLOR, and LINETYPE commands. You can change the color or linetype of existing elements with the LAYER and CHANGE commands.

Entity Color Logic

1. COLOR Setting

   if COLOR = BYBLOCK...

2. Block COLOR Setting

   if Block has no COLOR

   or

   if COLOR = BYLAYER

3. Layer Color Setting

Entity Color Logic

How an Element Gets its Color: COLOR

The **COLOR** command is in charge of making sure an element gets the color you want. When a new entity is created, AutoCAD checks the current setting of COLOR, finds out what COLOR says, and then assigns whatever color COLOR says to the newly formed entity.

COLOR can be set to any valid color name or number (remember you can have 1—255 colors, they needn't be named). In addition, COLOR can be set BYLAYER or BYBLOCK.

So while COLOR is set, say, to blue, then any new entities formed will be blue.

Why, then, did the line and circles come out green? You might have guessed:

The standard default COLOR is BYLAYER.

When COLOR is set to BYLAYER, it doesn't give new entities a specific color. Instead, it gives new entities the default color property of whatever default layer the entity is created on. This means that new entities will take on the current layer color, and, should you later change that layer's color with the LAYER C option, all entities on that layer with a BYLAYER COLOR will change accordingly.

The BYBLOCK COLOR setting is only appropriate for elements that will be herded into BLOCKS, something we'll cover when we talk about making symbols.

Take a look at the COLOR setting right now, to show yourself that COLOR really is set to BYLAYER:

```
Command: COLOR (RETURN)
New entity color <BYLAYER>: (RETURN)
Command:
```

How an Element Gets its Linetype: LINETYPE

After the COLOR discussion, you might have guessed that linetype default and entity setting has a similar control. You're right! Take a look at LINETYPE:

```
Command: LINETYPE (RETURN)
?/Create/Load/Set: S (RETURN)
New entity linetype <BYLAYER>: (RETURN)
Command:
```

CHANGE P and LAYER Change the Color and Linetype Appearance of Existing Elements

As entities are created, AutoCAD checks the COLOR, LINETYPE, and LAYER default settings to give the new entities a color and a linetype. But what do you do if you want to change the color or linetype of entities already in place?

You have three options:

☐ Use LAYER. If the entities you want to change were originally created with a BYLAYER COLOR or LINETYPE setting (the default setting for these two parameters), you can change the color and linetype of entities by changing the default settings of the layers the entities are on. Use the Color and Ltype subcommands in the LAYER prompt.

☐ Use CHANGE. The **CHANGE** command with the **P**roperties subcommand individually changes many appearance properties of entities already in place.

☐ Change the LAYER of the entity. If an entity was created by using the BYLAYER COLOR or LINETYPE setting, changing the LAYER of the entity to a layer with different color and/or linetype will change the appearance of the entity.

Try changing the color and linetype of the left circle on the screen:

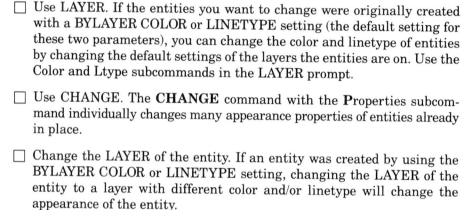

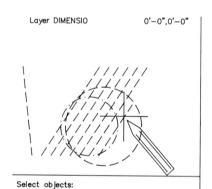

CHANGE P to Change the Left Circle Color and Linetype

CHANGE P CHANGES PROPERTIES OF EXISTING ELEMENTS

```
Command: CHANGE (RETURN)
Select objects:    (pick the left circle)  1 selected, 1 found.
Select objects: (RETURN)
Properties/<Change point>:  P (RETURN)
Change what property (Color/Elevation/LAyer/LType/Thickness)?
   C (RETURN)
New color <bylayer>: CYAN (RETURN)
Change what property (Color/Elevation/LAyer/LType/Thickness)?
   LT (RETURN)
New linetype <bylayer>: dashdot (RETURN)
Change what property (Color/Elevation/LAyer/LType/Thickness)?
   (RETURN)
Command:
```

Picked Line to Change

Notice three other possibilities in CHANGE P: change LAyer, Elevation, and Thickness. Elevation and Thickness are properties associated with 3-D.

Let's change the appearance of the line's color and linetype by changing its LAyer. Right now the much abused line on the screen is dashed, green, and on the DIMENSION layer. The line was originally created using the BYLAYER setting for COLOR and LINETYPE. By changing it from DIMENSION to GRAPHIC2, it will take on the default color and linetype characteristics from its new layer assignment.

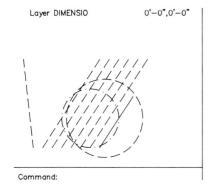

Layer DIMENSIO   0'-0",0'-0"

Command:

Changed Line Layer

Command: **(RETURN)**   (restarts last command)
Change: Select objects: (pick the line) 1 selected, 1 found.
Select objects: **(RETURN)**
Properties/<change point>: **P (RETURN)**

Change what property (Color/Elevation/LAyer/LType/Thickness)?
  LA (RETURN)
New layer <DIMENSION>: **GRAPHIC2 (RETURN)**
Change what property (Color/Elevation/LAyer/LType/Thickness)?
  (RETURN)
Command:

  (The line should turn blue and continuous from the new
   layer's color and linetype assignments.)

Command:

PEDIT GIVES ULTIMATE CONTROL OVER POLYLINES

So far you have used COPY and MOVE to change the location of graphic
entities, and CHANGE to alter entity properties. What about POLYLINES?
Since polylines have many properties, AutoCAD provides a command called—
PEDIT—just for editing polylines.

As you think about PLINE properties you are probably already imagining
the list of PEDIT subcommands. To manage the list, PEDIT is divided into
two groups of editing functions. One group of functions works on the whole
PLINE you are editing. The second group of editing functions works on
connecting vertices of individual segments within the PLINE.

Try drawing a PLINE on your sandbox LAYER 0, then get the PEDITprompt
on the screen by selecting PEDIT from the EDIT screen menu, tablet menu,
or by typing **PEDIT**.

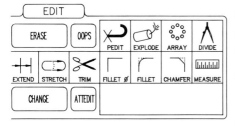

Tablet PEDIT Command

Command: **PLINE (RETURN)**
From point: (Enter any from point.)
Current line-width is 0'-0.00"
Arc/Close/Halfwidth/Length/Undo/Width/<Endpoint of line>:
  (Enter several PLINE segments including lines and arcs.)
Arc/Close/Halfwidth/Length/Undo/Width/<Endpoint of line>:
  (RETURN)   (To end.)
Command: **PEDIT (RETURN)**   (To get PEDIT prompts.)
Select polyline:
  (Use any selection method to pick a polyline.)
Close/Join/Width/Edit vertex/Fit curve/Uncurve/eXit <X>:

With the exception of **Edit vertex**, all the PEDIT subcommands shown on the prompt line affect the overall characteristics of the polyline.

PEDIT
Before   After

Fit Curve

Break

Straighten

Width

PEDIT Examples

OVERALL POLYLINE EDITING

☐ **Close.** If you did not close the polyline at the time it was created, use Close. If the selected polyline is already closed, you will get an Open prompt, allowing you to remove the last segment created with the Close subcommand.

☐ **Join.** Join lets you add non-polyline arcs and lines to an existing polyline.

☐ **Width.** Sets a single width for all segments of a PLINE, overriding any individual widths already stored.

☐ **Fit curve.** Creates a smooth curve through the PLINE vertices.

☐ **Uncurve.** Undoes a Fit curve by replacing curve segments with straight ones.

☐ **eXit.** As you might imagine, the default <X> gets you out of PEDIT and returns you to the Command: prompt.

Try a few PEDITs, especially the Fit curve option. It is fun to watch AutoCAD do the curve smoothing. PEDIT Join is useful for connecting segments into a continuous PLINE entity that can be edited (MOVEd, COPied, MIRRORed, ect.) as a single entity.

Once you have played around with PEDIT functions and tried to fit a few curves, you may want to look at how PEDIT lets you edit individual segments or vertices within your selected polyline.

EDITING VERTICES IN A PLINE

```
Close/Join/Width/Edit vertex /Fit curve/Uncurve/eXit <X>:
  E (RETURN)    (To Edit vertex.)
Next/Previous/Break/Insert/Move/Regen/Straighten/Tangent/
Width/eXit<N>:
```

When you Edit a vertex, the first vertex of the PLINE you are editing is marked with an **X**. This **X** shows you what vertex you are editing with the Edit vertex subcommands.

INDIVIDUAL PLINE VERTEX EDITING

☐ **Next/Previous.** Edit vertex operates on individual vertices. Next/Previous gets you from one vertex to another.

☐ **Break.** Splits a PLINE into two PLINEs. The first break point is the vertex where you invoke the Break option. You use Next/Previous to get to another break point. **Go** performs the break.

☐ **Insert.** Adds a vertex at a point you specify after the vertex currently marked with an **X**. Remember, a PLINE has a direction, from first to last vertices.

☐ **Move.** Changes the location of the current (X-marked) vertex to a point you specify.

☐ **Regen.** Forces a regeneration of the PLINE so you can see the effects (like width changes) of your vertex editing.

☐ **Straighten.** Removes all intervening vertices from between the two vertices you select, replacing them with one straight segment. It also uses the Next/Previous and Go options, like BREAK.

☐ **Tangent.** Allows you to specify a tangent direction at each vertex to control curve fitting. The Tangent is shown at the vertex with an arrow, and can be dragged or controlled numerically from the keyboard.

☐ **Width.** Controls the starting and ending width of an individual PLINE segment.

☐ **eXit.** The default <X> gets you out of vertex editing and back to the main PEDIT editing.

Play around with vertex editing. Try a few tangents, refit your curves, and then exit from PEDIT.

EXITING FROM PEDIT

```
Next/Previous/Break/Insert/Move/Regen/Straighten/Tangent/
Width/eXit<N>: X (RETURN)   (To get to main PEDIT.)
Close/Join/Width/Edit vertex/Fit curve/Uncurve/eXit <X>:
  X (RETURN)     (To exit.)
Command:
```

CREATING A DRAWING WITH EDITS

It's time to put the editing commands to work. When we last left our widget drawing (CHAPTER1) we had stored many sandbox and real drawing components in the file. To check its state, compare your screen to the CURRENT STATE OF CHAPTER1 FILE.

You can ignore the sandbox (layer **0**) because this layer is not used in the widget drawing. GRAPHIC1, GRAPHIC2, and TEXT layers have useful pieces of the widget drawing already on them.

If your DIMENSION layer has some sandbox clutter, you will have to ERASE its contents. You will also need this layer for the widget drawing.

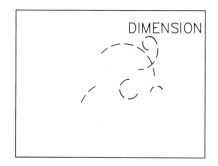

DIMENSION

The Current State of CHAPTER1 File

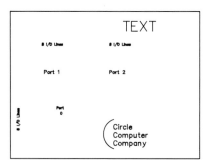

TEXT

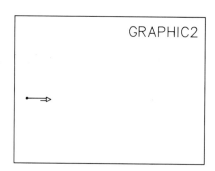

GRAPHIC2

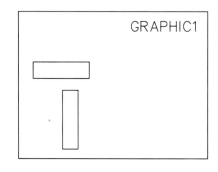

GRAPHIC1

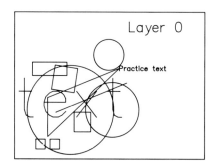

Layer 0

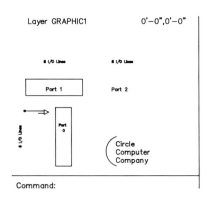

Layer DIMENSIO   0'–0",0'–0"

First corner: Other corner:

*ERASE Window Deletes All Layer
DIMENSION Doodles*

GETTING READY TO COMPLETE THE WIDGET DRAWING

END the CHAPTER2 file.

Select Main Menu **2 Edit an EXISTING Drawing**

Get **CHAPTER1**

Set layer GRAPHIC1 Current.

Turn all other layers Off.

Turn layers GR* On.

Your screen should look like the TARGET DRAWING WITH TEXT.

You already have created and stored many of the raw elements you need to complete the target widget drawing. With some editing commands now under your belt, you should be able to breeze through the remainder!

The widget editing working session does not contain an explanation about commands and how they work. The drawing points are given as X,Y coordinate points. (After you complete the drawing this way, you may want to go back and create the drawing using a grid and snap.)

Follow the instructions and keep an eye on the WIDGET TARGET DRAWING and interim TARGET drawings. Good luck!

Layer GRAPHIC1   0'–0",0'–0"

Command:

Widget Drawing with Text — Target A

128

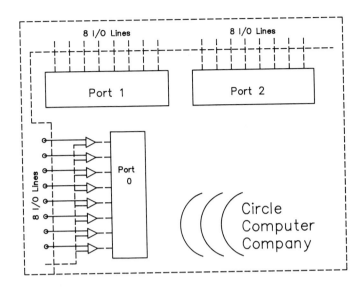

Widget Target Drawing

COMPLETING THE WIDGET DRAWING

See the WIDGET TARGET-(A) for the starting Drawing

We'll leave layer TEXT Off for now so the "Port 1" text is not copied when the Port 1 rectangle is window copied.

1. Make a copy of **Port 1** for **Port 2**

Command: **COPY (RETURN)**
Select objects: **W (RETURN)**

First corner: (pick) Other corner: (pick)   1 found.
Select objects: **(RETURN)**

<Base point or displacement>/Multiple: **2.90",16.34" (RETURN)**
Second point of displacement: **17.30",16.34" (RETURN)**
Command:

Compare your drawing to WIDGET TARGET-B

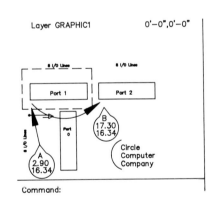

Layer GRAPHIC1   0'-0",0'-0"

Widget Target—B

2. Use LINE to create the first Widget Leader

Set layer **DIMENSION** Current
Turn layer TEXT On.

Command: **LINE (RETURN)**
From point: **7.70",12.98" (RETURN)**
To point: **9.14",12.98" (RETURN)**
To point: **(RETURN)**
Command:

Compare your drawing to WIDGET TARGET-C

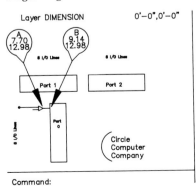

Layer DIMENSION   0'-0",0'-0"

Widget Target—C

3. Use a rectangular ARRAY to make seven more Widgets
(with their leaders attached)

Set layer **GRAPHIC2** Current

Command: **ARRAY** **(RETURN)**
Select objects: **W** **(RETURN)**
First corner: (pick)   Other corner: (pick)   7 found.
Select objects: **(RETURN)**

Rectangular/Polar array (R/P): **R** **(RETURN)**
Number of rows (---) <1>: **8** **(RETURN)**
Number of columns (|||) <1>: **(RETURN)**
Unit cell or distance between rows (---): **-1.44"**
   (RETURN)

   (ARRAY goes to work)
Command:

   Compare your drawing to WIDGET TARGET-D

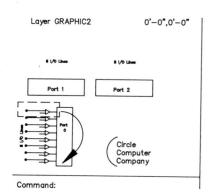

Layer GRAPHIC2   0'-0",0'-0"

Command:

Widget Target—D

4. Use a rectangular ARRAY to make 2 more arcs.

Set layer **TEXT** Current.

Command: **ARRAY** **(RETURN)**
Select objects: **W** **(RETURN)**
First corner: (pick)   Other corner: (pick)   1 found.
Select objects: **(RETURN)**

Rectangular/Polar array (R/P): **R** **(RETURN)**
Number of rows (---) <1>: **(RETURN)**
Number of columns (|||) <1>: **3** **(RETURN)**
Unit cell or distance between columns (|||): **-2.0"**
   (RETURN)

   (ARRAY goes to work)

Command:

   Compare your drawing to WIDGET TARGET-E

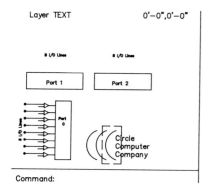

Layer TEXT   0'-0",0'-0"

Command:

Widget Target—E

5. Set up Port 1 I/O line

Set layer **DIMENSION** On

Command: **LINE** **(RETURN)**
From point: **3.86",22.58"** **(RETURN)**
To point: **3.86",19.70"** **(RETURN)**
To point: **(RETURN)**
Command:

   Compare your drawing to WIDGET TARGET-F

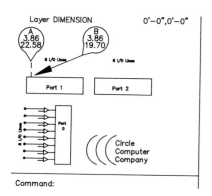

Layer DIMENSION   0'-0",0'-0"

Command:

Widget Target—F

6. Use a rectangular ARRAY to make seven more I/O lines

Command: **ARRAY** **(RETURN)**
Select objects: **L** **(RETURN)**
1 found.
Select objects: **(RETURN)**

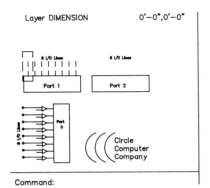

Widget Target—G

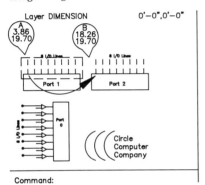

Widget Target—H

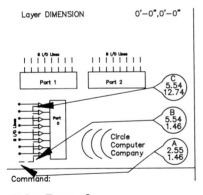

Widget Target—I

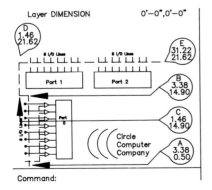

Widget Target—J

Rectangular/Polar array (R/P): **R (RETURN)**
Number of rows (---) <1>: **(RETURN)**
Number of columns (|||) <1>: **8 (RETURN)**
Unit cell or distance between columns (|||): **1.44" (RETURN)**

   (ARRAY goes to work)

Command:

   Compare your drawing to WIDGET TARGET-G

7. Use COPY to mimic **Port 1**'s I/O lines on **Port 2**

Command: **COPY (RETURN)**
Select objects: **W (RETURN)**
First corner: (pick)   Other corner: (pick)   8 found.
Select objects: **(RETURN)**

<Base point or displacement>/Multiple: **3.86",19.70" (RETURN)**
Second point of displacement: **18.26",19.70" (RETURN)**

   (COPY takes place)

Command:

   Compare your drawing to WIDGET TARGET-H

8. Draw a positive line

Command: **LINE (RETURN)**
From point: **2.55",1.46" (RETURN)**
To point: **5.54",1.46" (RETURN)**
To point: **5.54",12.74" (RETURN)**
To point: **(RETURN)**
Command:

   Compare your drawing to WIDGET TARGET-I

9. Draw a ground line

Command: **PLINE (RETURN)**
From point: **3.38",0.5" (RETURN)**
Current line-width is 0'-0.00"
Arc/Close/Halfwidth/Length/Undo/Width/<Endpoint of line>:
   3.38",14.90" (RETURN)
Arc/Close/Halfwidth/Length/Undo/Width/<Endpoint of line>:
   1.46",14.90" (RETURN)
Arc/Close/Halfwidth/Length/Undo/Width/<Endpoint of line>:
   1.46",21.62" (RETURN)
Arc/Close/Halfwidth/Length/Undo/Width/<Endpoint of line>:
   31.22",21.62" (RETURN)
Arc/Close/Halfwidth/Length/Undo/Width/<Endpoint of line>:
   (RETURN)
Command:

   Compare your drawing to WIDGET TARGET-J

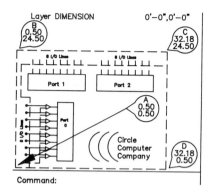

Widget Target—K

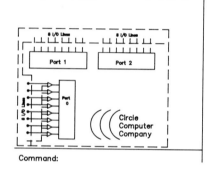

Widget Target Drawing

10. Finish with a boundary

```
Command: LINE (RETURN)
From point: 0.5",0.5" (RETURN)
To point: 0.5",24.5" (RETURN)
To point: 32.18",24.5" (RETURN)
To point: 32.18",0.5" (RETURN)
To point: c (RETURN)
Command:
```

    Compare your drawing to WIDGET TARGET K

11. You're almost done: SAVE

```
Command: SAVE (RETURN)
File name <CHAPTER1>: WIDGET (RETURN)
Command: END (RETURN)
```

    (You now have CHAPTER1.DWG and WIDGET.DWG with identical contents.)

12. Congratulations!

SUMMING UP AND TIPS ON EDIT

Now you can now see how important editing is in constructing a drawing. In the beginning of the Chapter on GRAPHICS PRIMITIVES we said the primitives are intelligent and drawings are dynamic. Now, with a first course in editing under your belt, you can see just how dynamic a drawing file is.

Are you prepared for the next Engineering Change Order?

Here's an EDITOR'S GUIDE TO EDITING to keep you prepared:

EDITOR'S GUIDE TO EDITING

☐ Plan ahead for editing. As you first set up a drawing think ahead about:

    ☐ Layers. Everything on one layer complicates editing. Plan to use multiple layers.

    ☐ Repetitive Features. Draw it once, copy it forever.

    ☐ Building Blocks. Start by defining your basic components and building up from there.

    ☐ Set up a Reference (Construction) Layer. A reference layer with a few schematic pointers helps with OSNAP placement. Make the reference layer visible only when you need it.

☐ You should not have a favorite EDIT command. Use all the EDIT commands:

    ☐ Use SNAP, ORTHO, and OSNAPs to set up MOVE and COPY displacements.

    ☐ MIRROR and ARRAY can fill up a repetitive drawing in a hurry.

    ☐ Be careful with ERASE—learn to use all of the object selection options, including the Remove option to avoid disasters. There's always OOPS and Undo.

☐ All the fill-the-selection-set techniques have their roles.

    ☐ Last is used all the time when you realize that AutoCAD did what you said, not what you meant.

    ☐ The object method is best for detail work, especially with OSNAP.

    ☐ Window is powerful, but it does not do it all. Remember what you see in the window is what goes into the buffer.

☐ Think ahead about individual edits:

    ☐ Use display control to keep your field of view small and your concentration level high.

    ☐ Don't get caught setting up the first point of a displacement only to find that the second point is off the screen (CANCEL ZOOM and try again).

☐ Don't underestimate the power of CHANGE. Use CHANGE, it really is an effective tool.

    ☐ A one-step CHANGE endpoint avoids a two-step ERASE, LINE.

    ☐ Extending lines by changing endpoint instead of creating an additional segment helps keep your drawing file organized.

    ☐ CHANGing text is almost always easier than redoing text. AutoCAD prompts you for every change.

☐ CHANGE Properties is even more powerful. It allows you to change the layer, color, and linetype properties of existing elements.

☐ Stay informed about what AutoCAD is up to.

    ☐ Watch the current layer name on the status line—create entities in the layers you intend to.

    ☐ Watch the prompt line for EDIT prompts—it is easy to start creating an edit buffer window while the prompt line is waiting for you to select **W**indow to initiate the selection.

    ☐ Use FLIP SCREEN to see what's gone down.

So far we have looked at some of AutoCAD's basic editing commands. Let's move on to more advanced editing commands and see how you can combine editing commands with CAD drafting techniques to get more productivity out of editing your drawings.

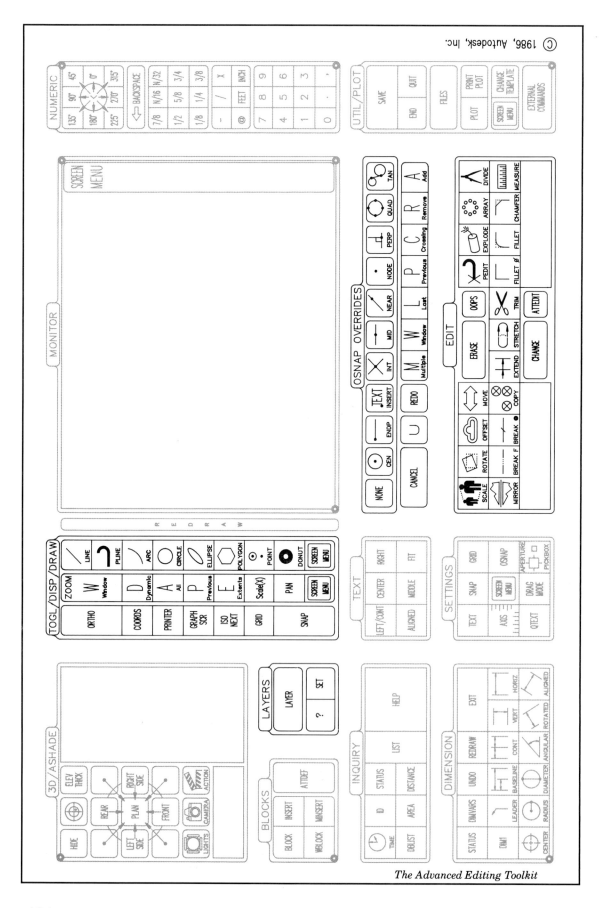

The Advanced Editing Toolkit

CHAPTER 5

DRAWING CONSTRUCTION TECHNIQUES

QUICK WAYS TO BUILD WHOLE DRAWINGS WITH ADVANCED EDITING

▶ Putting Drawings Together — CAD Style. ▶ The Advanced Editing Toolkit. Joining Lines with FILLET and CHAMFER. ▶ Two Steps Forward and One Step Back — Controlling the AutoCAD UNDO File. ▶ Power Drawing with EXTEND, STRETCH, and TRIM Commands. ▶ Constructing Whole Drawings. ▶ Using Construction Techniques with the Mockup Exercise. ▶ Making the Most of OFFSET, MEASURE, and DIVIDE. ▶ Summing Up — Tips for Power Drawing.

PUTTING DRAWINGS TOGETHER—CAD STYLE

To take full advantage of the power of CAD, you need to combine AutoCAD commands with CAD drafting techniques. AutoCAD has many more editing commands to help you create drawings than you have learned so far.

While the commands you learned in the last Chapter on Editing help you speed up your drafting, the tools you learn in this Chapter will begin to change the way you think about creating drawings.

Take, for example, AutoCAD's STRETCH command. Consider the WIDGET drawing from last Chapter. Suppose the part called Port 2 had to be moved down so that it sits right on top of the title area as shown in EDITED WIDGET DRAWING. Moving the rectangle itself is easy with the MOVE command, but you need to have the 8 I/O Lines elongated so they start at the same place and end at the new location for Port 2.

If you were adept at cut and paste drawing, you might do this manually. But if you are familar with the STRETCH command, you can stretch all the I/O lines and move Port 2 in one step!

Benefits and Cautions

Don't expect AutoCAD to do all the work for you after you master this Chapter. However, you will begin to think ahead about a division of drafting labor—you will do the thinking and setting up, AutoCAD will do the bulk of the carrying out.

As you use these more powerful editing commands, you must be aware that you can botch up your whole drawing with a single command that deposits hundreds of entities into the drawing file or worse still, erases them.

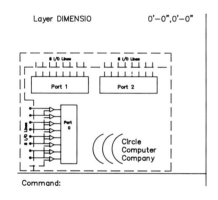

Widget Target Drawing

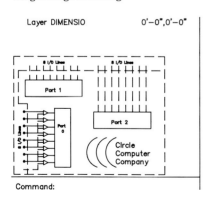

Edited Widget Drawing

We will show you how to undo mistakes by **backing up** a few commands. And think about this — if you can back up a few commands, why not try working out a drawing one way, and, if you don't like the way it comes out, back up and try another way. AutoCAD will allow you to place a marker in a drawing sequence so that you can back up to it and try again.

Try a few exercises to become familiar with advanced editing commands. Next take a look at tools you will use on background layers, like "electronic" construction lines, to help you work out major sections of a drawing. Then learn about the back up feature and how to control AutoCAD's UNDO/History File.

Finally you can put it all together by constructing a completely new drawing exercise — the MOCKUP.

THE ADVANCED EDITING TOOLKIT

There are three general classes of advanced editing tools. You will find most of these tools on the EDIT screen menus, but some are found in the SETTINGS and DRAW menus as well.

☐ Advanced Editing Commands—tools that go beyond moving and copying to take advantage of just how much information AutoCAD knows about the not-so-primitive graphic primitives that you have drawn.

☐ Drawing Construction Tools—tricks of the trade that save time by setting up information rich "underlayers" like construction line grids, parallel rules, and accurate drawing tracing masters.

☐ UNDO File Control—every time you execute a command, AutoCAD writes down what you did in a temporary UNDO/History file to disc. You can play back, UNDO, or if you UNDO too much, REDO parts of your past command sequence.

ADVANCED EDITING COMMANDS

☐ CHAMFER and FILLET — are ways to join two lines.

☐ EXTEND — elongates existing drawing entities like lines, polylines, and arcs until they meet a boundary you specify.

☐ STRETCH—moves a window-full of entities, stretches most entities which cross the window, but leaves any entities hanging outside the window in place.

☐ TRIM — breaks off and deletes any overhangs beyond a cutting edge you specify.

☐ DIVIDE — marks a line, polyline, circle or other entity into the number of equal sections you specify. It places a point or marker at each section point.

☐ MEASURE — marks a line, polyline, circle, or other entity into equal length sections which you specify. It places a point or marker at each section point.

Before   After

Radius=6

Fillet

Extend

Stretch

Trim

Advanced Editing Examples

□ OFFSET—makes a copy of a line, polyline, or other entity parallel to the existing entity, but away from it by a distance you specify.

Before	After
	Divide
	Measure
	Offset

More Advanced Editing Examples

DRAWING CONSTRUCTION TOOLS

□ Construction Layer — not an AutoCAD command, but a concept — a layer or group of layers you create to hold background or "underlayer" construction lines, grids, and partial drawings to trace.

□ OSNAP: Permanent — a running OSNAP mode that always looks for one or several of the OSNAPs you set like endpoint or intersection. With permanent OSNAP you can quickly pick out construction line points by tracing over a Construction Layer grid.

□ Temporary Drawing Worksheet—also not a command, but a way to set up part of your drawing file as a "doodle" area for working out drawing pieces before you set them into place in the production drawing area.

UNDO FILE HANDLING

□ Undo within LINE or PLINE — gets rid of the most recently created segment when you are creating a multiple segment LINE or PLINE.

□ U — from the Command: prompt, U will step back a single command, wiping out what you just did. This is similar to the OOPS command. You can recover a U with a REDO. You can reverse an OOPS with a U.

□ UNDO Command — from the Command: prompt, UNDO allows you to step back through a number of commands you have recently entered — in reverse order, undoing their effects and restoring the drawing to its previous condition. It extends the U feature.

□ REDO — if you U or UNDO by mistake, you can REDO to undo the last undo.

□ OOPS — we have covered OOPS. Make sure you understand the difference between U and OOPS. You can UNDO an OOPS.

To try out the advanced editing commands, use drawing files that you already have created and stored on disc.

Call up CHAPTER2 with its lines and circles to test CHAMFER and FILLET commands. Then switch to a copy of the WIDGET drawing to learn about EXTEND, STRETCH, and TRIM.

Layer DIMENSIO   0'-0",0'-0"

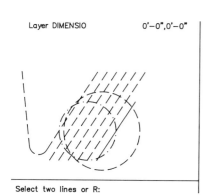

Select two lines or R:

FILLET Example

Layer DIMENSIO   0'-0",0'-0"

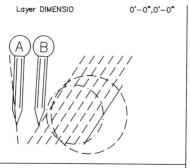

Select two lines or R:

FILLET Example in Progress

Before   After

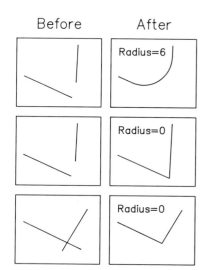

Radius=6

Radius=0

Radius=0

FILLET Examples

JOINING LINES WITH FILLET AND CHAMFER

A **FILLET** is an arc swung between two lines to create a round corner. The command sequence for FILLET is different from other EDITing commands, and simpler.

AutoCAD asks you to identify two lines that you would like joined. You do so by picking the lines. Keep in mind that FILLET works only on two non-parallel lines, polylines, or lines and curves. AutoCAD uses an ARC for the FILLET corner, then wants to know "how rounded" the corner should be. You give the RADIUS of the arc.

Here's an example joining the two leftmost lines in the CHAPTER2 drawing file. You can see the pick points used and the result in the FILLET EXAMPLE. Use the FILLET EXAMPLE drawing to help you locate your pick points.

JOINING LINES WITH A FILLET

Open the CHAPTER2 file:

Select Main Menu 2.   Edit Existing Drawing   CHAPTER2.

```
Command: FILLET (RETURN)
Polyline/Radius/<Select two objects>: R (RETURN)
Enter fillet radius <0'-0.00">: 2" (RETURN)
Command: (RETURN)
FILLET Radius/<Select two lines>:    (pick two lines near end.)
```

(The fillet is created.)

Command:

The default Radius for FILLET is <0.00">. It shows in the fillet prompt sequence when you select Radius. Once you set a new fillet Radius that becomes the new default.

A FILLET with Radius = 0 is useful for cleaning up under- or over-lapping drawing lines. See the FILLET EXAMPLES.

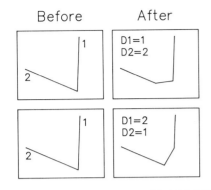

Before   After

D1=1
D2=2

D1=2
D2=1

CHAMFER is another way to join two lines. See the CHAMFER EXAMPLES.

Try playing around with FILLET and CHAMFER using the CHAPTER2 drawing file. When you are through, END to clear the decks for more exercises.

CHAMFER Examples

TWO STEPS FORWARD AND ONE STEP BACK—CONTROLLING THE AutoCAD UNDO FILE

"If I could just back up three commands and try that again."

A familiar refrain that we all find ourselves thinking. But, there is something that you can do about it.

AutoCAD keeps track of every command UNDO entry that you issue in a temporary file called an UNDO file. The UNDO file is active whenever you are in the drawing editor—recording all of your moves. You won't find this file on disc when you're done with an editing session, because it's a hidden file, and at the end of a session AutoCAD wipes it out and cleans up the disc. A PLOT or PRPLOT also wipes out the UNDO file.

This establishes the first rule of UNDO.

You can't UNDO back beyond the beginning of the current editing session.

—The First Rule of UNDO

ERASING vs. UNDOING

You might be thinking, "I already know how to delete the last entity that I drew using the ERASE Last command." You can erase your last entry with ERASE Last quickly and easily after virtually all entity draw commands.

You can even decide that you really didn't want to ERASE your last entry and OOPS it on back. Remember, OOPS restores the last item that you ERASEd, and nothing more.

But ERASing the last item you drew is only part of going back in time through your drawing file. Most of the time when you decide you want to go back, it is not just to erase the last item, but to undo a whole sequence of draw and edit commands.

Here is where U and the UNDO set of commands come in handy. UNDO gives you complete control over stepping back through your past commands, one at a time or in groups.

To really see how U, UNDO, and REDO work, you need to do something. As you step through the exercises for advanced editing commands (EXTEND, STRETCH, and TRIM) you will use the UNDO commands as part of the exercises.

The U Command

The U Command backs up the UNDO file by one command. This means that whatever you did immediately before issuing the U command will be UNDone when you type U (RETURN).

Like the OOPS command, U undoes just the last item. But unlike the OOPS command, U works to undo the last command any number of times, stepping back through each previous "last" command, one-by-one. This means you can even U an OOPS or U an ERASE.

The UNDO Command

The UNDO command can go further (or further back!) than U. You can UNDO N, where N equals a number of steps you want to return. Or you can group a series of commands together, and then, if what you are working on doesn't work out, you can UNDO the whole group at once. Actually UNDO has six different subcommands, here they are:

```
Command:  UNDO  (RETURN)
Auto/Back/Control/End/Group/Mark/<Number>:  (RETURN)
Command:
```

UNDO OPTIONS

☐ <Number>—if you type a number here, AutoCAD will step back through the UNDO file by that many steps.

☐ Auto—requires an ON/OFF answer. You can set UNDO Auto On or Off at any time. Sometimes a single menu item creates or edits many entities. Everything done by one command is one backstep in UNDO. Auto affects menu items only?

☐ Back and Mark—An UNDO Back will make AutoCAD step back through the UNDO file, UNDOing along the way, until it comes to a MARK in the UNDO file. If no Mark has been placed, you get a warning, "This will undo everything. OK <Y>". You say Yes or No. You leave a Mark simply by executing the UNDO command with the **Mark** option. You may Mark as many times as you like, each time setting a stop for the next UNDO Back.

☐ Control—creating an UNDO file and storing all the command sequences takes a lot of disc space. Control lets you control how active the UNDO file will be with three options — All/None/One.

    ☐ All—is the default.

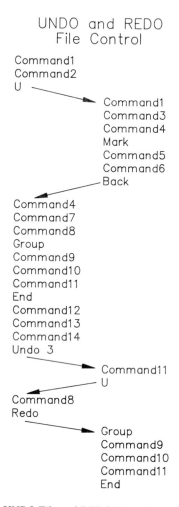

UNDO and REDO File Control

```
Command1
Command2
U
              Command1
              Command3
              Command4
              Mark
              Command5
              Command6
            Back
Command4
Command7
Command8
Group
Command9
Command10
Command11
End
Command12
Command13
Command14
Undo 3
              Command11
            U
Command8
Redo
            Group
              Command9
              Command10
              Command11
              End
```

UNDO File and REDO Example

☐ None—If you do not want to use the UNDO file feature at all you can turn it off with None.

☐ One—If you want to keep a limited UNDO just to go back one command, One keeps just the last command item in the Index file. When Control is set to One, none of the other UNDO subcommands are available. All restores Control to its full functionality.

☐ Group and End—are advanced control features. Like Mark and Back, Group and End put boundaries on series of commands in the UNDO file so that you can UNDO the series in one sweep. Unlike Back, however, you can begin a group with the Group option, end the group with the End option, and continue doing work. Later you step back with U or UNDO <Number>. When the backstep gets to an End, the next UNDO step will wipe out everything between the End and Group markers as if it were a single command.

REDO Gives an Extra Measure of Safety

Let's say you UNDid more than you planned. If you issue a REDO immediately after an UNDO type command (U, UNDO Back, or UNDO <Number>), the REDO will undo the UNDO.

This means you can be daring if you are not sure how far back you want to go—do something drastic like UNDO BACK or UNDO 20 —and then recover with a REDO and try something more conservative like an UNDO 5.

Be careful—UNDO has the power to wipe out your entire drawing in one step, but if you catch it immediately with REDO, you can save it.

Let's Pretend

You really have to try all this UNDOing and REDOing to get a feel for it. **QUIT** your drawing and get ready to do some fancy editing. In the following exercises showing UNDO and REDO, just pretend you have your boss looking over your shoulder and making changes on the screen.

POWER DRAWING WITH EXTEND, STRETCH AND TRIM

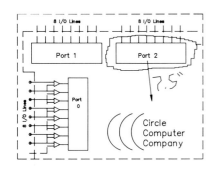

Marked Up Widget Drawing

In the beginning of the Chapter we suggested that Port 2 of the widget might have to be moved down. Sure enough, the senior engineer at Circle Computer Company redlined our beginner's attempt at a widget and sent back the MARKED UP WIDGET DRAWING indicating the need to drop PORT 2 down 7.50".

Well, you might be new enough not to know how to create a widget, but have been around enough to know that this is probably the first of many changes the boss wants to make. To protect the original drawing and to be able to go back at any point, make a copy of the original WIDGET and use UNDO File Control to make sure you can go back to your intermediate solutions.

STRETCH to Move One Side, But Not All of an Entity

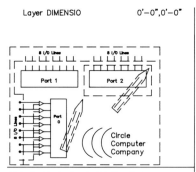

Layer DIMENSIO   0'-0",0'-0"

Select objects to stretch by window...
Select objects: Crossing
First corner: Other corner:

STRETCH Window

Layer DIMENSIO   0'-0",0'-0"

Command:

Port 2 Moved

MOVING PORT 2 WITH STRETCH

Main Menu

1. Begin a new drawing.

Select item 1.

Enter NAME of Drawing (default CHAPTER2):
     WIDGEDIT=WIDGET (RETURN)

Setting WIDGEDIT equal to WIDGET starts a new drawing, but uses the existing WIDGET as its prototype. WIDGEDIT starts out identical to WIDGET.

Make sure all Layers are On, and DIMENSION is Current.

Command: **STRETCH (RETURN)**
Select objects to stretch by window   (Use Crossing.)
Select objects: **Crossing (RETURN)** (a C is enough.)
First corner: (pick)   Other corner: (pick)   10 found

(Look at STRETCH WINDOW for window corners.)

Select objects: **(RETURN)**
Base point: **2'2",1'6" (RETURN)**
New point: **@0,-7.5" (RETURN)**

(Note: 0 in X, negative 7.5" in Y)

(Watch the show!)

Command:

Your drawing should now look like PORT 2 MOVED.

See what we mean by Power Drawing!

Just what happened in the **STRETCH** Command? You selected a group of objects, some you wanted moved, others you wanted stretched — using a new object selection set option named **Crossing**. You told AutoCAD where to move/stretch your selected objects. Then everything inside the window you selected (the POLYLINE making up the rectangle and the TEXT 'Port 2') was moved, and everything Crossing the window (the 8 I/O lines) was STRETCHed.

NOTE: STRETCH won't accept absolute displacements, like MOVE and COPY do. Picking **any** point for the Base point, and then typing relative coordinates, such as **@0, − 7.5 (RETURN)** is equivalent to the absolute displacement 0, − 7.5.

Filling The Editing Buffer With Crossing and Previous

When we introduced the notion of filling the editing buffer with object selection options in the previous Chapter, we mentioned two extra options named **Crossing** and **Previous** beyond the regular Object, Window and Last options. We said Crossing and Previous are especially helpful for advanced editing techniques. You've already seen Crossing in action.

☐ Crossing — selects everything that either falls within your selection window or crosses the boundary of the window. With some advanced editing commands (like STRETCH) the objects selected in the window are treated differently than those that cross the window boundary.

☐ Previous — if you have previously done an object selection, a Previous object selection will fill the editing buffer with whatever was done in the last selection set you selected. Previous is different from Last, which selects the last created object that is visible on the screen.

Previous reselects the last object(s) that you selected the last time you were in object selection mode. Previous is helpful for editing a group of objects, then realizing that you made a slight mistake. It allows you to edit the Previous set without having to select them individually again. Previous does not work with some editing commands (like STRETCH) where a Window or Crossing is specifically required.

Selections made in FILLET, CHAMFER, and entities selected to be TRIMmed or EXTENDED do not affect Previous.

Crossing Examples

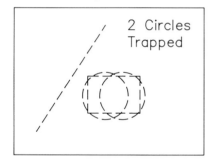

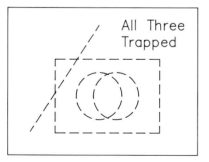

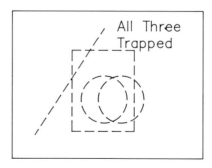

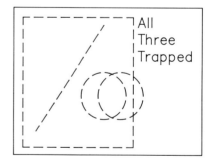

Crossing Selection Set Examples

STRETCH Works In Reverse, Too — Shrinking

Sure enough, you showed PORT 2 MOVED on-screen to the boss and she didn't like it. She wants Port 2 moved back up an inch.

But your draftperson's intuition tells you that PORT 2 MOVED is the way the drawing is going to end up, and moving Port 2 back up an inch is really a waste of time. To appease the boss you'll do it, but **Mark** the UNDO file first so you can later UNDO the 1-inch move and go back to the way the drawing is now.

You can use STRETCH to "unSTRETCH" or shrink.

STRETCH EXERCISE WITH PREVIOUS AND MARK

First put a Mark in the index file.

```
Command: UNDO (RETURN)
Auto/Back/Control/End/Group/Mark/<Number>: Mark (RETURN)
Command:
```

Now unSTRETCH the Port.

```
Command: STRETCH (RETURN)
Select objects to stretch by window...
Select objects: Crossing (RETURN)   (gather the Port in
  the window and I/O Lines across the window boundary)
10 found.
Select objects: (RETURN)
Base point: 2'2",1'6" (RETURN)
New point: @0,1 (RETURN)    (Note: 0 in X,
  and a positive 1 in Y.)
```

(Watch the show!)

```
Command:
```

Your drawing should now look like PORT 2 MOVED UP AN INCH.

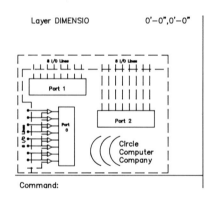

Layer DIMENSIO   0'-0",0'-0"

Command:

Port 2 Moved Up an Inch

You might want to play around with STRETCH to find out some of its quirks. Remember, only lines, arcs, traces, solids, and polylines will STRETCH. Although it may seem to act funny with some types of entities that cross the Crossing window, STRETCH will do what you expect. PLINES, ARCS, and CIRCLES act differently depending on what segment, endpoint, or center-point rests inside or outside the Crossing window.

We could tell you about all of these variations until the cows come home, but they won't make any sense until you try them for yourself. Any new entities that you create here with STRETCH will be UNDOne in the next series of exercises, so try away until you are satisfied you have mastered the command.

UNDO Back To Start Again

Sure enough, the boss liked the Port where it had been. While she was looking at the screen, she noticed that the Port 2 I/O Lines need to be EXTENDed up to the drawing border. She also wanted the Port 1 I/O Lines trimmed on the ground line. (See PORT 2 MOVED UP AN INCH.)

First, restore Port 2 to its proper position, then tackle EXTEND and TRIM.

Layer DIMENSION   0'–0",0'–0"

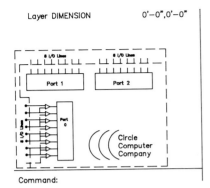

Command:

Port 2 Moved (Again)

Layer DIMENSIO   0'–0",0'–0"

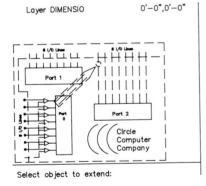

Select boundary edge(s)...
Select objects:

EXTEND Boundary Pick

Layer DIMENSIO   0'–0",0'–0"

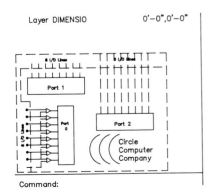

Select object to extend:

First I/O Line to EXTEND

Layer DIMENSIO   0'–0",0'–0"

Command:

UNDO BACK

```
Command:  UNDO  (RETURN)
Auto/Back/Control/End/Group/Mark/<Number>:  Back  (RETURN)
STRETCH:
Mark encountered
Command:
```

Using EXTEND to Stretch Objects to a Boundary

Although you could STRETCH the Port 2 I/O lines to meet the boundary, try it with the EXTEND Command. EXTEND allows you to select objects to elongate until they meet the edge(s) you specify.

Do you think the boss may change her mind again? You had better set up a GROUP in the Index file, just in case.

EXTENDING PORT 2 I/O LINES

```
Command:  UNDO  (RETURN)
Auto/Back/Control/End/Group/Mark/<Number>:  Group  (RETURN)
Command:  EXTEND  (RETURN)
Select boundary edges(s)...
Select objects:  1 selected, 1 found.

(Pick the top boundary -- see EXTEND BOUNDARY PICK.
Use the point method of object selection.)

Select objects:  (RETURN)    (That's all we need for now,
  but you can use more than one object as a boundary.)

Select object to extend: (Pick the FIRST I/O LINE TO EXTEND.)
Select object to extend: (Pick the next one.)
Select object to extend: (And four more.)
Select object to extend: (Then pick the last one)
Select object to extend:  (RETURN)    (To end extension.)
Command:
```

Now mark the **END** of the Group in the UNDO file so we can treat all of the extensions as one UNDO step.

```
Command:  UNDO  (RETURN)
Auto/Back/Control/End/Group/Mark/<Number>:  End  (RETURN)
Command:
```

```
Your drawing should now look like WIDGEDIT WITH
PORT 2 I/O LINES EXTENDED.
```

Widgedit with Port 2 I/O Lines Extended

Notice that the extended I/O Lines run right through the Port 2 "8 1/0 Lines" text. It's a good thing you **Grouped** the extensions in the UNDO file — the boss is almost surely going to want the I/O Lines unEXTENDED and you'll be able to UNDO them all in one step.

With EXTEND you have to individually select each object to extend. You cannot fill a Selection Set full of objects that you want EXTENDed, and then extend them all at once. EXTEND also cannot shorten objects.

Use TRIM to Cut the Port 1 I/O Lines

In case you have to go back to this point, put a Mark in the UNDO file to protect your work.

USING TRIM TO CUT PORT 1 I/O LINES

```
Command: UNDO (RETURN)
Auto/Back/Control/End/Group/Mark/<Number>: Mark (RETURN)
Command: TRIM (RETURN)
Select cutting edge(s)...
Select objects:  1 selected, 1 found.
  (Pick the ground line.)
Select objects: (RETURN)     (One trim boundary is
  enough for now.)
Select object to trim:  (Pick the FIRST I/O LINE TO TRIM.)
Select object to trim:  (Pick the next one.)
Select object to trim:  (And four more.)
Select object to trim:  (Then, pick the last one.)
Select object to trim: (RETURN)    (To end trimming.)
Command:
```

Your drawing should now look like WIDGEDIT WITH PORT 1 I/O LINES TRIMMED.

Select cutting edge(s)...
Select objects:

TRIM to the Ground Line

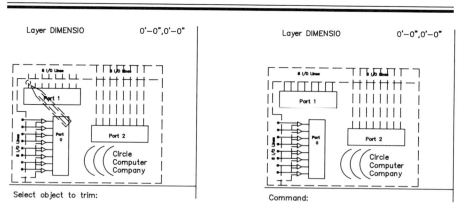

Select object to trim:

First I/O Line to TRIM

Command:

Widgedit with Port I/O Lines Trimmed

Like EXTEND, TRIM forces you to identify each trim item individually.

Satisfying the Boss With Quick UNDO's and REDO's

The day of reckoning has come and the WIDGEDIT drawing must be finished. The boss takes a fateful next-to-final look at the screen and...

USING UNDO AND REDO TO GO BACK IN THE UNDO FILE

First UNDO the TRIM.

```
Command:  UNDO (RETURN)
Auto/Back/Control/End/Group/Mark/<Number>: 1 (RETURN)
TRIM
Command:
```

(Presto! Chango!   Now try REDO!)

```
Command: REDO (RETURN)    (The TRIM happens again.)
Command:
```

Now go back one step with U.   (A **U** is the same as UNDO 1.)

```
Command: U (RETURN)
TRIM
Command:
```

How about going back through the Group/End EXTEND in one whole step.

```
Command: UNDO (RETURN)
Auto/Back/Control/End/Group/Mark/<Number>: 1 (RETURN)
GROUP
Command:
```

Now show the boss how smart you were by Backing until the Mark before the last Port 2 STRETCH.

```
Command: UNDO (RETURN)
Auto/Back/Control/End/Group/Mark/<Number>: Back (RETURN)
STRETCH
Mark encountered
Command:
```

Good. Another Back will go all the way:

```
Command: UNDO (RETURN)
Auto/Back/Control/End/Group/Mark/<Number>: Back (RETURN)
This will undo everything. OK? <Y> (RETURN)
STRETCH (and whatever other commands you used.)
Command:
```

Play around with STRETCH, TRIM, EXTEND, and the UNDO sequences and then...

SAVE or END as you please.

CONSTRUCTING WHOLE DRAWINGS WITH CAD CONSTRUCTION TOOLS

AutoCAD's drawing construction tools are as much a frame of mind as a framework of commands and options. Under the heading "Drawing Construction Tools" we have included several specific commands that get used more in the background of constructing a drawing than in the foreground of placing drawing entities in the file for permanent display.

DIVIDE, MEASURE, and OFFSET are new commands to study and understand. Besides these new commands, you will learn the CAD concepts of: "Dropping construction lines", "building drawing modules and putting them together", "using underlayers", and "tracing over construction lines".

To refresh your memory about drawing construction commands and concepts, here is the list again from the Toolkit at the beginning of the Chapter.

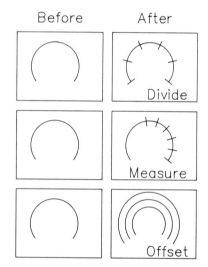

More Advanced Editing Commands

DRAWING CONSTRUCTION TOOLS

☐ DIVIDE — Marks a line, polyline, circle or other entity at the number of equal sections you specify. It places a point or marker at each section.

☐ MEASURE — Marks a line, polyline, circle, or other entity at equal lengths, which you specify. It places a point or marker at each section point.

☐ OFFSET — Make a copy of a line, polyline, or other entity parallel to the existing entity, but away from it by a distance you specify.

☐ Construction Layer — Not a specific command, but a concept — layer or group of layers you create to hold background or "underlayer" construction lines, grids, and partial drawings to trace.

☐ OSNAP: "Permanent" — A way to have the cursor always look for one or several of the OSNAPs you set like endpoint or intersection. With a permanent SNAP you can quickly pick out construction line points by tracing over a Construction Layer grid.

☐ Temporary Drawing Worksheet—Also not a specific command, but a way to set up part of your drawing file as a "doodle" area for working out parts of drawings before you set them into place in the production drawing area.

You will see in the next exercise that there are many more techniques and commands that you will use regularly as part of your drawing construction process. There is never only one way to build an AutoCAD drawing. In fact the opposite is more often true — there are many ways to build the same drawing. The trick is to find the methodology that works most intuitively and efficiently for you.

To demonstrate drawing construction techniques you will go through a new exercise to build "The MockUp" (a sister product to the Widget). The MOCKUP is actually two section drawing details of the top of a storage tank. Like the Widget exercise, if you don't know or care about storage tanks, this exercise is still for you—you will learn the concepts of drawing construction techniques.

We will show you how to handle the new commands that are introduced here, but after that, you will get only limited commentary on how to create the drawing. Chances are you will be thinking of other ways to draw the image, and you are welcome to try them. All of the dimensions you need to create the drawing are on the MOCKUP TARGET DRAWING.

Why don't you get up and STRETCH to OFFSET all that reading. When you are feeling TRIM, come back and we'll try to EXTEND your working knowledge of advanced editing and construction techniques with a new drawing exercise.

Feel free to use any technique at any time—you will need to improvise and use ZOOM. Use REDRAW and REGEN when you need to.

USING CONSTRUCTION TECHNIQUES WITH THE MOCKUP EXERCISE

Complete The MOCKUP drawing in a series of continuous steps. For convenience we have broken the exercise into **5** steps. First read the description of each step, then carry out the exercises in the boxes.

Step 1. Set up the MOCKUP drawing using UNITS, LIMITS, LAYERS, GRID, and SNAP. Draw construction lines to aid in creating the drawing objects.

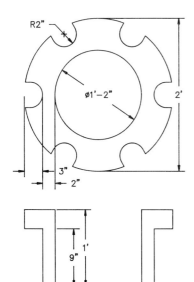

Mockup Target Drawing

STEP 1. SETTING UP THE MOCKUP DRAWING WITH SET UP, UNITS, AND LAYERS

Use Main Menu 1. Edit a New Drawing to begin the MOCKUP.

Use UNITS to get architectural units, default (1/2 fraction denominator), and default for all other settings.

Use LIMITS to get a working area 30" wide by 50" high. This leaves a boundary around the active drawing area.

Turn on GRID. Set SNAP to 1".

ZOOM All

Use LAYER to get the following collection:

Layer name	State	Color	Linetype
0	On	7 (white)	CONTINUOUS
CONSTRUC	On	1 (red)	CONTINUOUS
PARTS	On	3 (green)	CONTINUOUS
DIMENSIO	On	2 (yellow)	CONTINUOUS

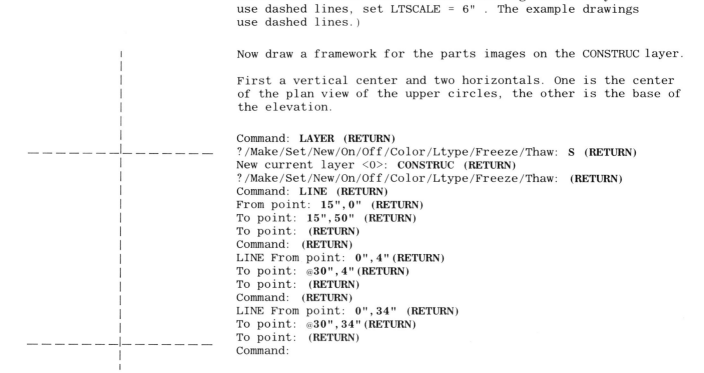

(If you have a monochrome system you should try dashed
construction lines and continuous drawing lines. If you
use dashed lines, set LTSCALE = 6" . The example drawings
use dashed lines.)

Now draw a framework for the parts images on the CONSTRUC layer.

First a vertical center and two horizontals. One is the center
of the plan view of the upper circles, the other is the base of
the elevation.

```
Command: LAYER (RETURN)
?/Make/Set/New/On/Off/Color/Ltype/Freeze/Thaw: S (RETURN)
New current layer <0>: CONSTRUC (RETURN)
?/Make/Set/New/On/Off/Color/Ltype/Freeze/Thaw: (RETURN)
Command: LINE (RETURN)
From point: 15",0" (RETURN)
To point: 15",50" (RETURN)
To point: (RETURN)
Command: (RETURN)
LINE From point: 0",4" (RETURN)
To point: @30",4" (RETURN)
To point: (RETURN)
Command: (RETURN)
LINE From point: 0",34" (RETURN)
To point: @30",34" (RETURN)
To point: (RETURN)
Command:
```

Construction Frame Work Lines

Step 2. Draw The Three Circles, and two Horizontal Construction Lines on
the CONSTRUC Layer. The inner circle (14″ in diameter) is the center of the
tank top opening. The outer two circles (18″ and 24″ in diameter) are the
inner and outer construction line guides for the flange cut outs. Set up a
running OSNAP intersec mode to help pick points off the construction lines.

STEP 2. DRAWING CIRCLES AND CONSTRUCTION LINES

```
Command: OSNAP (RETURN)
Snap object modes: INT (RETURN)
Command: CIRCLE (RETURN)
3P/2P/TTR/<Center>: (Pick the CIRCLE CENTER at intersection.)
Diameter/<Radius>: D (RETURN)
Diameter: 14" (RETURN)
Command: OFFSET (RETURN)
Offset distance or Through <Through>: 2" (RETURN)
Select object to offset:  (Pick the circle.)
Side to offset?   (Pick any point outside the circle.)
Select object to offset: (RETURN)  (To end the
  OFFSET command.)
Command: (RETURN)   (To begin OFFSET again for a
  different distance.)
Offset distance or Through <0'-2">: 5" (RETURN)
Select object to offset:   (Pick inner circle carefully.)
Side to offset?   (Pick any point outside the circles.)
Select object to offset: (RETURN)
Command:
```

Now create two horizontal construction lines as guides for the flange cut itself. The flange cut is 4 inches in diameter, you need one construction line 2 inches above the top red line, one 2 inches below.

Create the first construction line with OFFSET <distance 0'-2">

Mirror to get the construction line.

Your drawing should now look like SECTION A-A READY FOR PARTS

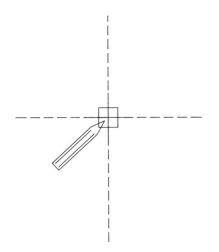

Running OSNAP INTersec Mode

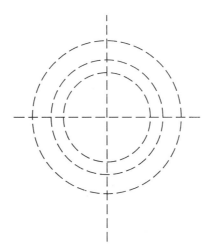

Horizontal Lines for Flange

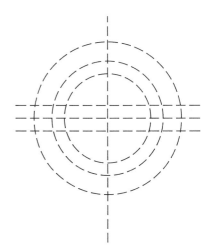

Section A-A Ready for Parts

Step 3. Creating the Section A-A Plan Drawing. Your first task is to convert the inner circle to green on the CONSTRUCTION layer using CHANGE. Then create half a flange cut. Mirror image to get two halves. ARRAY the whole cut to get a full circle of flange cuts.

There are six flange cuts in the outer circle of the MOCKUP Section A-A Drawing. Create one. Associate an arc portion (one sixth) of the whole circle with the cut. Then use a Polar ARRAY to create a whole set arrayed (six times) around the circle.

To make the semi-circle "bottom" of the flange cut, use an ARC. The pick points of this arc lie on the intersection of existing construction lines.

Draw a line connecting the arc to the outer red circle. You can depend on OSNAPS to get the line the right length. To get the arc length, use the DIVIDE command to mark the outer circle with points. Once you have the right flange line and arc section, you can MIRROR and ARRAY.

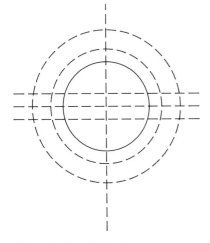

Changed PARTS Circle

STEP 3. CREATING THE MOCKUP SECTION A-A FLANGE CUT

Set Layer to PARTS.

Convert the inner circle from the CONSTRUCTION layer to the PARTS layer.

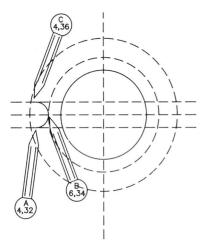

Flange ARC Points

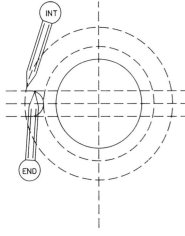

Flange Indentation

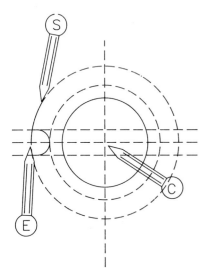

Flange ARC for DIVIDE

Command: **CHANGE (RETURN)**
Select objects: (pick the inner circle) 1 selected, 1 found.
Select objects: **(RETURN)** (To end selection)
Properties/<Change point>: **PROP (RETURN)**
Change what property (Color/Elev/LAyer/LType/Thickness) ?
LA (RETURN)
New layer <Construc>: **Parts (RETURN)**
Change what property (Color/Elev/LAyer/LType/Thickness) ?
(RETURN)
Command:

Create the curved flange bottom with a 3-point ARC
using the intersections shown in FLANGE ARC POINTS . If you
want to type the coordinates, they are listed.

Command: ARC Center/<Start point>: **4",32" (RETURN)**
Center/End/<Second point>: **6",36" (RETURN)**
End point: **4",36" (RETURN)**

Draw the top side of the flange cut by first OSNAPping to the
end of the top of the arc. Use ORTHO as a guide to OSNAP
intersection with the outer (red) circle.

Command: **LINE (RETURN)**
From point: end of (pick the upper, left facing arc edge)
To point: (pick the circle and construction line intersection)
To point: *Cancel*
Command:

You now have the flange indentation which should look like
FLANGE INDENTATION.

_____

Next you need to create a small arc piece out of the circle on top and bottom
of the flange indentation. The total arc distance you need is 1/6th of the circle
circumference. Use DIVIDE to mark the circumference in 12 equal parts.
Pick one of these divisions to get half the proper arc length. Then use MIR-
ROR to get the bottom half.

_____

USING DIVIDE TO GET A PIECE OF THE FLANGE CIRCLE

Command: **DIVIDE (RETURN)**
Select object to divide: (Pick the outer circle)
Divide into how many parts / Block: **12 (RETURN)**
   (12 points appear in green equidistant around the red circle,
    starting at angle = 0.)
Command:

Use a start-center-end ARC to get the correct arc piece.

Command: **ARC** **(RETURN)**
Center/<Start point>: **Node** **(RETURN)**   (To override
    the running OSNAP intersec to pick the divide point.)
of   (Pick the node one node above the flange cut.)
Center/End/<Second point>:   **Center** **(RETURN)**
Center: CENTER of (Pick OSNAP center to use the circle center
  as the arc center. Pick the inner circle to get the center.)
End point: **Node RETURN**
of   (Pick the divide point in the center of the flange cut.)
Command:

Now erase all those points in one step with the Previous
Selection Set.

Command: **ERASE** **(RETURN)**
Select objects: **Previous** **(RETURN)**
12 found.
Select objects: **(RETURN)**   (To end selection.)

    (ERASure takes place.)

Command:

Now TRIM the arc where it covers half the flange opening.

Command: **TRIM** **(RETURN)**
Select cutting edge(s)...
Select objects: (Pick little flange horizontal.)
1 selected, 1 found.
Select objects: **(RETURN)** (To end selection.)
Select object to trim: (pick the arc where it dangles in front
  of the flange opening.)
Select object to trim: **(RETURN)** (To end trimming.)
Command:

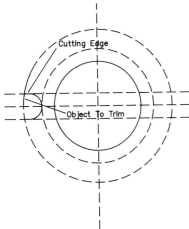

Flange TRIM

To complete the single flange cut, MIRROR the small horizontal and arc
piece using the center construction line as the mirror line.

Command **MIRROR** **(RETURN)**
Select objects: (pick the little horizontal)
1 selected, 1 found.
Select objects: (pick the arc piece) 1 selected, 1 found.
Select objects: **(RETURN)** (To end selection.)
First point of mirror line: (Pick the circles' center)
Second point: (Pick another point on the center horizontal
  construction line.)
Delete old objects? <N> **(RETURN)**
Command:

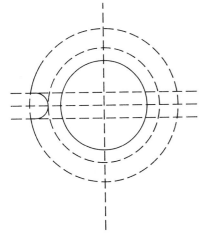

MIRRORed Flange Cut

To complete the ring of flange cuts, use a polar ARRAY to copy the flange
cut construction all the way around the circle.

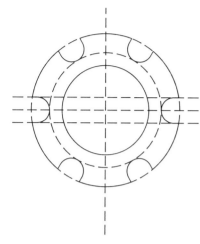

ARRAYed Mockup Section A-A

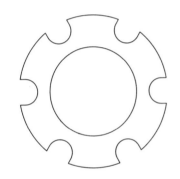

Section A-A Complete

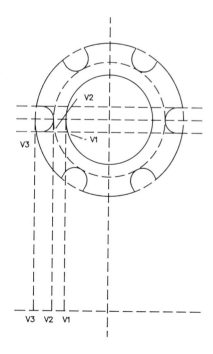

Construction Lines for Section B-B

FINISHING MOCKUP SECTION A-A WITH ARRAY

ARRAY we go! Copy the flange cut and arc pieces around the outer (red) circle.

Command: **ARRAY (RETURN)**
Select objects: **Window (RETURN)**
First corner: Other corner: 5 found.
  (Pick a window to include the PARTS flange cut pieces, but nothing else.)
Select objects: **(RETURN)**   **(To end selection.)**
Rectangular or Polar array (R/P): Polar (RETURN)
Center point of array: (Pick the circles' center)
Number of items: **6 (RETURN)**
Angle to fill (+=CCW, -=CW) <360>:   **(RETURN)**
  (To accept the 360 default.)
Rotate objects as they are copied? <Y> **(RETURN)**

  (ARRAY they go!)

Command:

Now clean up your drawing with a REDRAW and take a good look.

ZOOM all. Then, turn off the CONSTRUCTION layer.

Command: **LAYER (RETURN)**
?/Make/Set/New/On/Off/Color/Ltype/Freeze/Thaw: **Off (RETURN)**
Layer name(s) to turn Off: **CONSTRUC (RETURN)**
?/Make/Set/New/On/Off/Color/Ltype/Freeze/Thaw: **(RETURN)**
Command:

Good work! Your drawing should look like SECTION A-A Complete.

This is a good time to SAVE.

Section B-B Uses Construction Lines To Trace the Elevation View

Step 4. Setting up Construction Lines for the B-B Section.

Most of the geometry necessary to create the B-B Section drawing already exists in the A-A drawing. Using the intersection of the three flange circles and the center, upper horizontal construction line you can drop three vertical construction lines down into the B-B area. Two more horizontal construction lines, offset 9″ and 12″ from the bottom act as upper and lower guides for the flange lip profile.

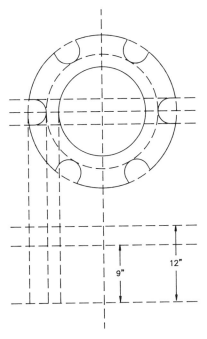

Section B-B Ready for Parts

SECTION B-B CONSTRUCTION LINES

Turn All Layers On.
Set CONSTRUC Layer Current.

ZOOM All to get a full view of both the Section A-A and
B-B areas.

Turn ORTHO On.

Command: **LINE (RETURN)**
From point: (Pick the V1 intersection of the inner circle
  and the middle (red) horizontal.)
To point: (Pick a point on the lower (red) horizontal.)
To point: **(RETURN)**
Command: **(RETURN)**
LINE From point: (Pick the V2 intersection of the middle
  circle and the middle (red) horizontal.)
To point: (Pick a point on the lower (red) horizontal.)
To point: **(RETURN)**
Command: **(RETURN)**
LINE From point: (Pick the V3 intersection of the outer
  circle and the middle (red) horizontal)
To point: (Pick a point on the lower (red) horizontal.)
To point: **(RETURN)**
Command:

Now OFFSET the lower red horizontal construction line
up 9 inches and 12 inches.

Your drawing should now look like SECTION B-B READY FOR PARTS.

Step 5. Finish MOCKUP By Tracing Straight Lines.

Use PLINE to trace the PARTS lines on the left side of the B-B Section by
OSNAPping to the appropriate intersections on the construction lines. Then
MIRROR this collection of lines over to the right side.

TRACING SECTION B-B STRAIGHT LINES

Set Layer PARTS Current.

Use PLINE to trace over the proper construction line
intersections. Use B-B SECTION LINES as a guide.

When you have completed the left B-B side, use MIRROR to
complete the drawing by mirroring the left B-B section to
the right. The center vertical construction line is the
mirror line.

Congratulations!

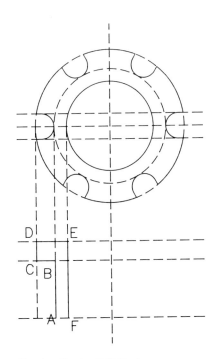

Tracing Section B-B Parts

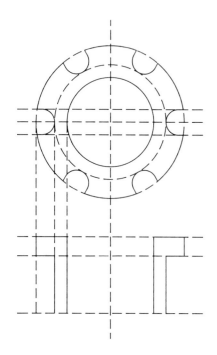

ZOOM out to see the entire MOCKUP drawing.
If you like, turn off all layers except PARTS.

When you are through admiring, END.

MIRRORed Parts

MAKING THE MOST OF OFFSET, MEASURE AND DIVIDE

Now that you've had a chance to use some advanced editing Commands and techniques, you should know some more about them. Here are a few pointers on OFFSET, MEASURE, and DIVIDE.

Finished MOCKUP Drawing

☐ OFFSET distances cannot be negative. Offset direction is "shown" with coordinates or a pick, not with a negative or positive value.

☐ If OFFSET cannot figure out a logical offset (say you show AutoCAD a negative radius Through point), it will tell you and let you try again.

☐ Some types of primitives cannot be offset. The legal list is LINE, ARC, CIRCLE, and POLYLINE.

☐ The new object that is created with the OFFSET command has the same linetype, color, and layer settings as the original object that it was copied from.

☐ Only Lines, Arcs, Circles, and Polylines can be DIVIDEd and MEASUREd.

☐ When you learn how to create and store symbols, you can replace the standard point in DIVIDE and MEASURE with a symbol. You also can make the point more visible with PDMODE and/or PDSIZE.

☐ If you use a symbol in DIVIDE and MEASURE you can align it with a line or the curvature of an arc, circle, or polyline.

☐ All of the markers (points or symbols) that are inserted by DIVIDE and MEASURE into a drawing are part of the Last Selection Set. This means they can all be ERASEd using a Previous Selection Set if no other objects have been selected.

SUMMING UP CHECKLIST FOR DRAWING CONSTRUCTION TECHNIQUES

☐ Use Construction Lines to Line Up Your Drawing Entities.

    ☐ Set up one or more layers for your construction lines.

    ☐ Construction lines needn't be linear—use ARCS and CIRCLES for angular or curved tracing.

    ☐ MEASURE and DIVIDE help align new entities at specified distances.

    ☐ Running OSNAP modes help fast tracing over construction lines.

    ☐ OFFSET is great for parallel entity creation—it both creates and measures as it goes.

☐ Use The Extra Room On Your Drawing Sheet For Background Construction.

    ☐ A far off corner on a construction layer is great for putting together pieces of a drawing that will later be MOVED, COPIED or ARRAYED into place.

☐ Use UNDO File Control To Protect Work Sequences.

    ☐ REDO to the rescue—but only immediately after a U, UNDO Back, or UNDO <number>. Marks and Groups help control UNDOs and make going back easier.

    ☐ Going Back to a Mark is no substitute for SAVEing regularly—this is still the best way to protect your drawing file.

☐ Be Daring With Construction Techniques.

    ☐ Use UNDO controls to go back in case you make mistakes.

    ☐ It never hurts to put a few extra construction lines in —and it could help make your drawing life easier.

☐ Training and Tracking with a printer.

    ☐ If you have a printer hooked up to your system you can get a copy of all of your command prompt lines on paper, as they go by. Just type control-Q (^Q) to start your printer printing —(or pick the PRINTER TOGL) on the tablet menu. It will write all your prompts. Another ^Q turns off printing.

    ☐ Getting a printed listing of your efforts, helps to learn AutoCAD. When you are teaching someone else, you can show the listings or "play back" with REDO to show them how it is done.

Wouldn't it be useful if you could save the contents of the editing buffer and use it as a rubber stamp whenever you need it? It's time to herd objects into symbols.

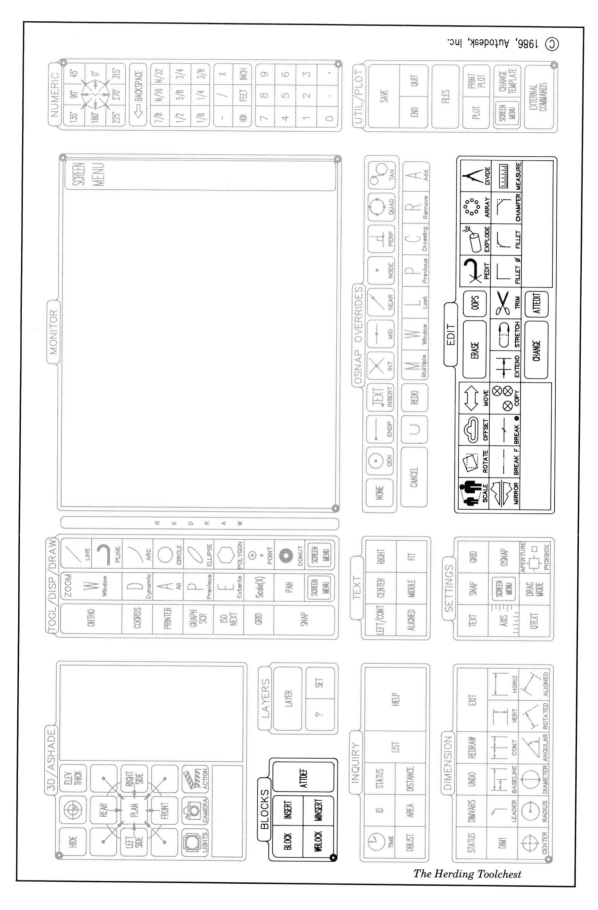

The Herding Toolchest

CHAPTER 6

HERDING OBJECTS INTO SYMBOLS

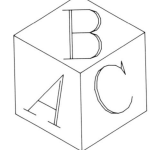

Door
2 Objects

Table
4 Objects

Chair
2 Objects

Window
4 Objects

14 — Pin Chip
22 Objects

Spaceship
6 Objects

"O" Ring
2 Objects

Pointer
9 Objects

Common Symbols

Authors' First Block

Formal, Temporary and Permanent Symbols. The Herding Toolchest. BLOCK and INSERT Commands. ▶ INSERT With Changes. ▶ Making Symbols Permanent. The Power of BLOCKs. Global Symbol Replacements. AutoTown—A BLOCK Exercise. ▶ Summing Up and Tips For Riding Herd.

FORMAL, TEMPORARY AND PERMANENT SYMBOLS

Up to now you have edited with MOVE, COPY, ERASE and some more advanced commands, depending on the **editing buffer** to collect a series of objects to edit.

To make repetitive drawing tasks easier you need a way to capture the contents of an editing buffer, give it a name, save it, and make it available later in the drawing or for use in other drawings.

Symbols

A collection of individual objects that belong together is known as a symbol. AutoCAD calls symbols **BLOCKS**. Users typically build up libraries of frequently used symbols to speed drawing creation.

If you were merely moving or copying the symbol objects, you could collect the individual drawing elements into a Selection Set and make the appropriate edits.

However, as drawings become crowded, it becomes more difficult to get just the correct objects into the editing buffer. It is much easier to group the elements together as a symbol, give the symbol a name, and then MOVE or COPY the symbol as a single entity.

AutoCAD lets you do just that: group objects, give the group a name, and then operate on the group as a whole.

What's the catch? Entities in BLOCKed symbols stick together: MOVE one part of the block and the whole moves. You can, of course, break up a block. You'll see how, when, and why.

"To BLOCK or not to BLOCK, that is the question."
—Hamlet at his Workstation

In this Chapter you will learn how to create, store and use symbols to build drawing files efficiently. You benefit from BLOCKing graphic primitives into more formal associations.

Once blocked, symbols can be used for convenience within a drawing file or made into permanent symbols as parts of a library of symbols for use within one or more different drawing files.

One benefit of symbols is the ability to insert them in your drawing file at any scale and rotation, allowing a quick and easy buildup of a drawing file from simple symbols. Another benefit is being able to globally replace one symbol with another and revise entire drawings with a single command.

THE HERDING TOOLCHEST

The herding commands you will learn about in this Chapter can be seen in THE HERDING TOOLCHEST Tablet Menu. All are available from screen menus, but as always, you are welcome to type the command names from the keyboard.

AutoCAD has a second type of symbol creation called **SHAPES**. Text is a special form of the Shape feature. When we refer to symbols in this Chapter, we mean BLOCKS.

Herding symbols is really very simple. BLOCK creates 'em, INSERT places 'em, and WBLOCK makes 'em permanent.

Tablet BLOCKS Commands

BLOCK AND INSERT COMMANDS

Let's follow the execution of a BLOCK command. First, you'll create two concentric circles on the screen similar to the "o" ring symbol in the COMMON SYMBOL EXAMPLES.

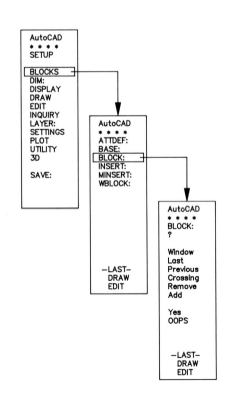

ROOT to BLOCKS to BLOCK

SETTING UP FOR BLOCK

Get into the drawing editor to edit an EXISTING Drawing:

Get CHAPTER2

Use the familiar ERASE Window to delete the all-too-familiar single line and two circles and any other tidbits you may have left there. Turn Snap Off.

Set layer GRAPHIC2 Current.

Turn all other layers Off.

Create the "O" ring:

```
Command: CIRCLE (RETURN)
3P/2P/TTR/<Center point>: 15,15 (RETURN)
Diameter/<Radius>: 4 (RETURN)
Command:  (RETURN)
CIRCLE 3P/2P/TTR/<Center point>: 15,15 (RETURN)
Diameter/<Radius>: 3 (RETURN)
Command:
```

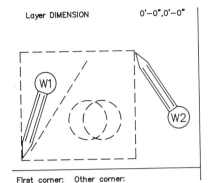

Layer DIMENSION 　　　　0'-0",0'-0"

First corner: Other corner:

ERASE Window to Delete Clutter

Layer GRAPHIC2 　　　　0'-0",0'-0"

Command:

BLOCK Setup Screen

Layer GRAPHIC2 　　　　0'-0",0'-0"

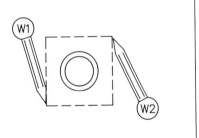

First corner: Other corner:

BLOCK Selection Window

Layer GRAPHIC2 　　　　0'-0",0'-0"

Command:

Circles Disappear

Your screen should look like BLOCK SETUP SCREEN.

Now let's turn the two circles into a single block. When AutoCAD asks you to select the items to be included in the block, use a window editing buffer surrounding the two circles. Select BLOCKS from the ROOTMENU and the BLOCK command from the the BLOCKS menu.

CREATING YOUR FIRST BLOCK

```
Command: BLOCK (RETURN)
BLOCK Block name (or ?): Doorknob (RETURN)
Insertion base point: center   (type center)
of   (pick center of either circle.)
Select objects: W (RETURN)
First corner:   (pick)  Other corner:   (pick)  2 found.
Select objects: (RETURN)

(And they're gone!)

Command:
```

First, AutoCAD asks you what you want to name the group of objects you have selected in the window to store as a block. Use **Doorknob** to give the circles a name.

Insertion Base Point

Next AutoCAD wants to know an **Insertion base point**. An insertion base point is the **handle** you use to carry a block around. When you later place the block, AutoCAD will ask you where the Insertion base point goes. This is the reference point for placing a block in its new setting. Use the center point of the circles.

Next you identify what goes in the block. What happens when you finish selecting? Right—all the window contents disappear. But all is not lost. The objects are now safely stored away as a block called **Doorknob**.

Where is the **Doorknob**? AutoCAD keeps track of all blocks in an invisible part of the drawing file. For you to use the **Doorknob**, the block definition must be in the block storage area of the drawing file. Using the BLOCK command creates a definition of **Doorknob** and stores it in the BLOCKS area of the current drawing file.

The drawing BLOCK AND INSERT WITH "INVISIBLE" BLOCK STORAGE AREA shows how the block storage area is set up and how the BLOCK command stored your **Doorknob** symbol.

The INSERT Command

To get the **Doorknob** back, you need to INSERT it from the block storage area into the active part of the drawing file.

INSERT is a great command! Not only does INSERT place a copy of the block in the active drawing area, but it allows you to modify the block as it is placed.

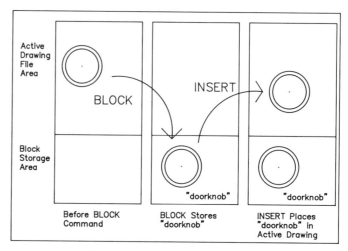

BLOCK and INSERT with "Invisible" Block Storage Area

INSERT does four things:

☐ Makes a reference to the BLOCK definition.

☐ Leaves the original BLOCK definition in the block storage area.

☐ Applies modifications like scale or rotation to the symbol.

☐ Places the new (modified) symbol in the drawing.

The INSERT command requires you to specify which block you wish to INSERT, where the block is to go, and its scale and rotation factor(s).

First, AutoCAD wants to know which block you want to INSERT. If you respond with **?**, AutoCAD will give you a list of the names for all **defined blocks** that are currently in the storage area of your drawing.

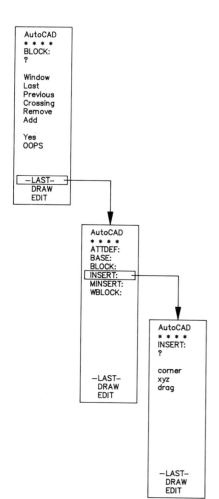

BLOCK to BLOCKS to INSERT

GETTING A LIST OF BLOCK NAMES WITH INSERT ?

Command: **INSERT (RETURN)**
Block name (or ?): **? (RETURN)**

   (Screen FLIPs to character mode and displays:)

Defined blocks.
   DOORKNOB
1 user blocks, 0 unnamed blocks.

Command:

(When you've seen the list, hit FLIP SCREEN or (F1).

Layer GRAPHIC2   0'–0",0'–0"

Command:

INSERT Doorknob Target Drawing

Layer GRAPHIC2   0'–0",0'–0"

Insertion point: drag

DRAGging the Doorknob

INSERT your **Doorknob**. You want to place the the Doorknob in the file so that it looks like the INSERT DOORKNOB TARGET DRAWING. You can **drag** the block upon insertion or just give the coordinates of the **Insertion point:**. The drawing DRAGGING THE DOORKNOB shows what your screen will look like when you use drag.

Here's the prompt sequence for INSERTing the Doorknob:

INSERT THE DOORKNOB BLOCK

```
Command: INSERT (RETURN)
Block name (or ?): Doorknob (RETURN)
Insertion point:

(Use coords readout and drag it where you want it, or a
 coordinate to get it exactly where you want it.)

Insertion point: 18,12 (RETURN)
X scale factor <1>/Corner/XYZ: (RETURN)
Y scale factor <default=X>: (RETURN)
Rotation angle <0>: (RETURN)
Command:
```

INSERT WITH CHANGES

Now INSERT your Doorknob, using different X and Y scales. Here the circles are turned into ellipses (like the porcelain doorknobs in old houses!). Here's the prompt sequence you can use to create the SCALED PORCELAIN DOORKNOB TARGET DRAWING.

Layer GRAPHIC2   0'–0",0'–0"

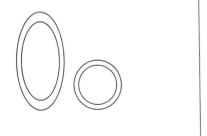

Command:

Scaled Porcelain Doorknob Target Drawing

INSERT WITH SCALE CHANGE

```
Command: INSERT Block name (or ?) <DOORKNOB>: (RETURN)
Insertion point: 6,17 (RETURN)
X scale factor <1>/Corner/XYZ: (RETURN)
Y scale factor <default=X>: 2 (RETURN)
Rotation angle <0>: (RETURN)
Command:
```

Note that after you have used the INSERT command the first time in a drawing editor session, AutoCAD will prompt you with the name of the last inserted block inside a default bracket <blockname>. You can accept the prompt with a **(RETURN)** or type the name of another block.

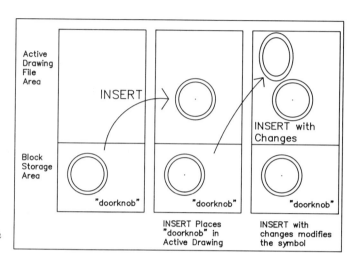

Doorknob Drawing—INSERT with Changes

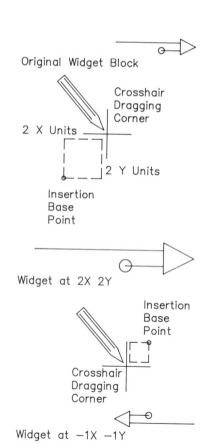

Original Widget Block

Widget at 2X 2Y

Widget at −1X −1Y

Corner Insertion Scale

Insertion X and Y Scale Factors

You can define scale in two ways. The first asks for an X and Y multiplier from the keyboard. AutoCAD will give you the same <default> prompt for the Y factor as the X factor to try to keep your drawing symbol in a 1:1 ratio. You can use different X and Y scales by typing a different response.

The second way to create an insert scale factor is to use the **Corner** option. Here the **Insertion point:** is the lower left hand corner of a rubberband rectangle and AutoCAD asks you to **drag** the upper right hand corner to determine scale.

The drawing CORNER INSERTION SCALE shows a few ways of using corner.

When you pick the upper right hand corner, AutoCAD uses the width of the rectangle as X-scale and the height as Y-scale. The width and height are measured in drawing file units.

You have to be careful with corner! The dragged scale is relative to one unit square. If your screen width represents many drawing file units, even a small rectangle will give a large scale factor. Instead of dragging the corner, you can, of course, type relative corner coordinates at the keyboard, @2,3 gives a scale of 2X and 3Y.

Whether you use keyboard entry or Corner, you can specify negative scale factors to mirror the block's insertion or turn it upside-down (or both). With **Corner**, just enter the second rectangle point to the left and/or below the **Insertion point**.

Insertion Rotation Angle

The last step in inserting a block is to give AutoCAD an angle of rotation. Again you can accept the default prompt <0> or type an angle, or pick a rotation by dragging the crosshair.

A handy trick for inserting objects that are normally horizontal or vertical is to use your pointer to pick a rotation angle with ORTHO (^O) turned On. This limits the rotation angle to 0, 90, 180, or 270 degrees.

After you give the rotation angle, AutoCAD goes ahead and makes a copy of the block with your changes and places the block in your active drawing file.

Try placing **Doorknob** in the active drawing file as shown in the ANGLE DOORKNOB DRAWING. (Hint: the scale is the same as for the elliptical doorknob, the angle is 45).

If you make a mistake, you can Undo or ERASE Last to remove the entire block that you just inserted.

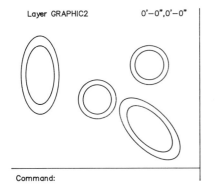

Layer GRAPHIC2 0'-0",0'-0"

Command:

Angle Doorknob with Insertion

A NOTE ABOUT BLOCKS

A BLOCK is a BLOCK is a BLOCK. Once you use the BLOCK command to identify collected objects as a single symbol, those objects act collectively as one object when INSERTed in a drawing file. When you ERASE a BLOCK, the whole BLOCK but not its stored definition is ERASEd. The same holds for MOVing and COPYing BLOCKs.

—Authors of the First Edition

When is a BLOCK not a BLOCK?

A Block is not a Block when It is *Inserted

Sometimes you want to be able to indvidually edit different elements that make up a block after you insert them. In your Doorknob example, the two concentric circles that make up the Doorknob lose their individual identity when stored as a block.

What if you wanted to take the inner circle and move it independently from the outer circle?

If you want to edit individual pieces of a block after insertion, AutoCAD provides an asterisk option * for the INSERT command. By placing an * in front of a block name at time of insertion, you instruct AutoCAD to break the block back into its individual elements as it is inserted.

Here's the prompt sequence for * INSERTion:

---

*INSERTION TO BREAK BLOCKS INTO COMPONENTS

```
Command: INSERT Block name (or ?) <DOORKNOB>: *DOORKNOB (RETURN)
Insertion point: 29,19 (RETURN)
Scale factor <1>/Corner/XYZ:  (RETURN)
Rotation angle <0>:  (RETURN)
Command:
```

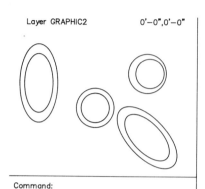

Layer GRAPHIC2   0'−0",0'−0"

Command:

Angle Doorknob with Displaced Circle

The newest **Doorknob** is really two separate circles. Don't believe it? Prove it to yourself by moving the inner circle to the right:

---

*INSERTED BLOCK ELEMENTS HAVE SEPARATE IDENTITIES

```
Use the screen menus to execute the MOVE command.

Select the circle with a single object pick.

Drag the displacement of one snap point to the right.

The inner circle moves, the outer stays.


Now do you believe it?
```

AN UNFORTUNATE NOTE ABOUT * INSERTION

When using the * option to insert a block, AutoCAD restricts your flexibility in rescaling the objects as they are placed in the active drawing file. You can only specify a single, positive scale factor in the * mode. No negative scales, or X not equal to Y.

You often can accomplish your "rescaling" with the STRETCH, SCALE, EXTEND and other editing commannds.

A Block is More Than a Block When It is MINSERTed

Suppose you wanted to put a whole bunch of doorknobs in your drawing (or desks, or printed circuit board drill locations, or any other symbol you might have blocked away). You could first INSERT one copy of the block and then use the ARRAY command to make several columns and rows.

MINSERTion is another option. Think of MINSERTion (Multiple **INSER-**
Tion) as a single command combining insertion and rectangular arrays (no
polar arrays with MINSERT).

There is one major difference, however. With ARRAY, every element that
the ARRAY command generates is an individual element in the drawing
file—it can be edited, deleted, copied or even arrayed individually. With
MINSERT, every occurence of the BLOCK that MINSERT generates is part
of a single MINSERTED BLOCK. The individual component blocks that
result cannot be operated on individually by AutoCAD commands. They also
cannot be * MINSERTed.

Even with this limitation, MINSERT is an efficient way to place multiple
copies of a block in a drawing file. With ARRAY, every occurence takes up
disc space and must be edited individually. With MINSERT, the block reference occurs only once in the drawing file along with information about the
number of rows, columns, and spacing of elements. This way you can delete
all MINSERTed blocks with one delete command, and save drawing file disc
space.

Try a MINSERT, the prompts are just like INSERT and ARRAY:

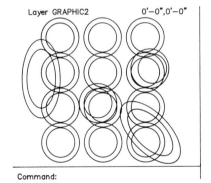

Layer GRAPHIC2   0'-0",0'-0"

Command:

MINSERT of Doorknobs

MINSERT A BLOCK

```
Command: MINSERT Block name (or ?) <*DOORKNOB>:
  Doorknob (RETURN)
Insertion point: 10,4 (RETURN)
X Scale factor <1>/Corner/XYZ:  (RETURN)
Y Scale factor <default=X>:  (RETURN)
Rotation angle <0>:  (RETURN)
Number of rows  (---):  4 (RETURN)
Number of columns (||||):  3 (RETURN)
Unit cell or distance between rows (---):

(pick two points to make a positive 6X, and
 positive 6Y unit cell)

Command:

(Multiple doorknobs appear.)

Prove to yourself that all of these are tied to one another by
erasing them with a one object selection erase command.
```

When you specify a rotation in MINSERT the array is rotated, as well the
individual blocks within it.

A Block is not a Block when it is EXPLODED

*Insertion is great when you want to bring the individual elements of a
block into the drawing file so that you may edit each component individually.
But what do you do when you want to edit individual components of a block
that is already inserted?

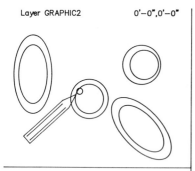

Layer GRAPHIC2   0'-0",0'-0"

Select block reference or polyline.

Picking a Doorknob to EXPLODE

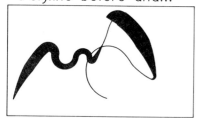

Polyline before and...

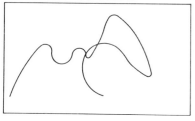

...after EXPLODE

Polyline—Before and After Explosion

You could find out the insertion point, scale and rotation, write it down, delete the block, and reinsert it using *Insertion at the same place, but that seems like a lot of work.

Or you could EXPLODE it! Yes, as you might imagine, EXPLODE blows up a block back to bits and pieces. The pieces left over are identical to the image before explosion with the exception of BYBLOCK, color, linetype, and layer assignments that might come undone. If an exploded block included nested blocks, only the outer level of nesting is broken up by EXPLODE.

Try EXPLODing the round doorknob in the middle of the screen with EXPLODE. Select EXPLODE from the EDIT menu.

TRY EXPLODING

```
Command: EXPLODE (RETURN)
Select block reference or polyline.  (A single object pick is
    safest. The one you select will be redrawn as it explodes.)

(Explosion takes place!)

Command:
```

Things You Can't EXPLODE

You cannot EXPLODE an *INSERTed BLOCK because it already is exploded. You cannot EXPLODE a MINSERTed BLOCK. And you cannot EXPLODE a block with different X and Y (and Z) scale factors—just straight BLOCKS.

As you may have gathered from the prompt, EXPLODE may be used to break a PLINE into its individual segments. Be careful with this one, however, EXPLODEd PLINEs lose all their width and tangent information and come out looking like a shaved poodle — with only centerlines.

MAKING SYMBOLS PERMANENT

So far the blocks you have identified and stored in the block storage area have been self-contained in the current drawing file. As long as you work in the current drawing file, these block definitions will be there. However, sooner or later you will want to use the symbols created in this drawing file in another drawing file.

WBLOCK—The Write BLOCK Command

AutoCAD provides for permanent blocks through the use of the **Write BLOCK** command, **WBLOCK**. The WBLOCK command creates a permanent copy of a block on disc with its own file name. In this way, independently named block files can be called into any drawing file from disc.

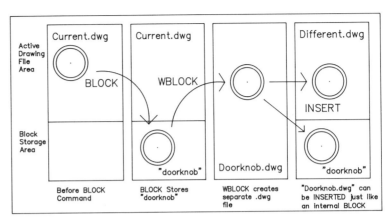

WBLOCK and INSERTion

Try storing **Doorknob** as a separate file on disc called DOORKNOB.DWG. Later you can insert this Doorknob block into another drawing file. Once INSERTed or *INSERTed, this block will act like any other.

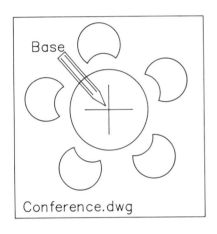

Conference.dwg

WBLOCK EXAMPLE

To write Doorknob to **DOORKNOB.DWG**, WBLOCK it.

```
Command: WBLOCK (RETURN)
File name: Doorknob (RETURN)

(AutoCAD automatically adds the .DWG.)

Block name: = (RETURN)     (Responding to Block name with
   = tells AutoCAD the Block name equals the file name.
   If you WBLOCK to a different File name, just type out the
   Block name.)

Command:
```

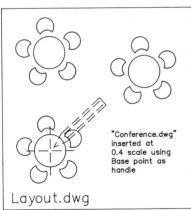

"Conference.dwg" inserted at 0.4 scale using Base point as handle

Layout.dwg

Insertion Base Point Sequence: Creating an Insertion base point, and inserting a whole drawing into another drawing file.

To later insert DOORKNOB.DWG into another drawing file you use the INSERT command, and call the file from disc using its disc File name, DOORKNOB.

Here's a neat trick for the bold ones. A group of elements does not have to be blocked to be WBLOCKed. If you enter a (RETURN) instead of giving an existing block name in response to the Block name: prompt, you will be prompted for an INSERTION base point and object selection. You can use any of the standard object selection techniques (Window, Last, or pick) to select items to be WBLOCKed. When you finish selecting with a final (RETURN), the elements are copied to the disc file you specified and are defined as Blocks in the current drawing.

Creating A Block Called RECTANG

Blocks don't have to be complex. You will find it convenient to have a simple 1 unit by 1 unit rectangle as a block in your symbol library. Using INSERT you can drag and stretch the rectangle with INSERT's scale factors.

Note: If you have an older version of AutoCAD, you may already have a rectangle drawing as RECTANG.DWG in your drawing files. If you do, use a different file name for the WBLOCK in the following exercise.

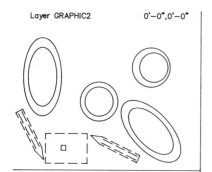

Layer GRAPHIC2   0'−0",0'−0"

Select objects: W
First corner: Other corner:

Creating a Single-unit Rectangle Block

CREATING A BLOCK CALLED RECTANG

Zoom-in to the lower left corner of your drawing.

Create the rectangle with PLINE.

```
Command: PLINE (RETURN)
From point: 10,4 (RETURN)
Arc/Close/Halfwidth/Length/Undo/Width/<Endpoint of line>:
    11,4 (RETURN)
Arc/Close/Halfwidth/Length/Undo/Width/<Endpoint of line>:
    11,5 (RETURN)
Arc/Close/Halfwidth/Length/Undo/Width/<Endpoint of line>:
    10,5 (RETURN)
Arc/Close/Halfwidth/Length/Undo/Width/<Endpoint of line>:
    close (RETURN)
Command:
```

Now WBLOCK into RECTANG.DWG

```
Command: WBLOCK (RETURN)
File name: Rectang (RETURN)
Blockname: (RETURN)
Insertion base point: 10,4 (RETURN)
Select objects: w (RETURN)
First corner: (pick)  Other corner:   (pick)   1 found
Select objects: (RETURN)

Command:
```

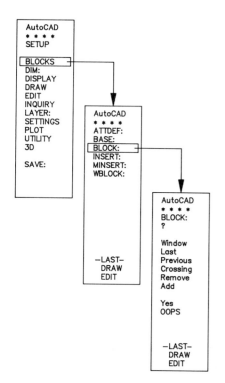

AutoCAD
* * * *
SETUP

BLOCKS
DIM:
DISPLAY
DRAW
EDIT
INQUIRY
LAYER:
SETTINGS
PLOT
UTILITY
3D

SAVE:

AutoCAD
* * * *
ATTDEF:
BASE:
BLOCK:
INSERT:
MINSERT:
WBLOCK:

−LAST−
DRAW
EDIT

AutoCAD
* * * *
BLOCK:
?

Window
Last
Previous
Crossing
Remove
Add

Yes
OOPS

−LAST−
DRAW
EDIT

BASE is on BLOCKS Menu

Try inserting RECTANG.DWG using various scales and rotation angles. Use drag as a visual aid for sizing and alignment. We will use REC-TANG.DWG later in this Chapter.

The drawing file created by WBLOCK is just like any other drawing file. You can INSERT any drawing file as a BLOCK into any drawing.

The BASE Command

The **BASE** command creates an **Insertion base point** in a drawing file so you can later call this whole drawing file into another file. The BASE point is an INSERTion **handle** just like the **Insertion base point** on a regular block.

If you make a drawing, store it on disc, and later INSERT it in another drawing, it defaults to 0,0 as the Insertion base point, unless you specify the base point.

You get to BASE through the BLOCK key screen menu. BASE simply prompts you for a base point location, just like POINT. The base point is not an entity or visible point.

Unit Scale Trick for Efficient Block Placement

At first you may think that you will use scale and rotation only occasionally for block insertions.

Nothing could be further from the truth! Scaling and rotating symbols during insertion are invaluable tools. (Besides, you will impress your colleagues and friends.) Here's a trick:

Create your symbols in a 1 × 1 unit cell—just like you created REC-TANG.DWG.Then, when you insert the block, you can **stretch** or **shrink** it to fit. The block is good at any scale with an insertion scale factor.

For example, you can store a resistor symbol so that the symbol endpoints are on the left and right edges of the unit cell. Then insert the symbol with appropriate scale factors to fill the area you need. To see how this works, see the drawing, A UNIT SCALE RESISTOR IS SIZED TO FIT USING SCALED INSERTION.

If you get handy with the insert scale corner option and store your blocks in unit cell, you can get symbol edges to connect to existing elements. Drag mode will help you line up blocks when scaling and rotating.

Take a look at USING A UNIT BLOCK FOR FLEXIBLE SCALE INSERTION to get an idea how unit scale works.

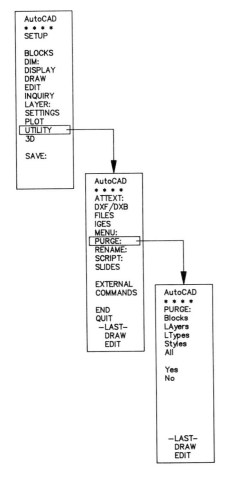

A Unit Scale Resistor is sized to fit using Scaled Insertion

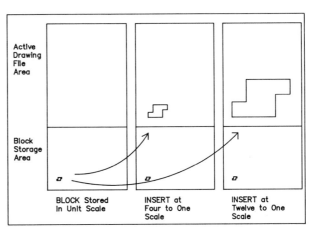

Using a Unit BLOCK for flexible Scale Insertion

The PURGE Command

The **PURGE** command removes unused block definitions from the block storage of the current drawing file. You can build up extraneous blocks in the storage area by inserting them and later deleting them. PURGE helps keep the storage name list neat and helps keep disc space in check.

PURGE only works immediately after entering the drawing editor.This means that as soon as your drawing file appears on the screen after **Edit an EXISTING Drawing**, you can use the PURGE command. Any other time is too late.

ROOT to UTILITY to PURGE

You get to the PURGE command by picking UTILITY from the screen ROOT-MENU or by typing PURGE at the keyboard. PURGE is selective and prompts you extensively, giving you information about what blocks are stored in the block storage area and asking you explicitly if you want to clean them out.

By the way—PURGE works on all named entities in the drawing file. You can use PURGE to clean out unused layers or views or styles—anything that you gave a name at any time during a drawing editor session.

THE POWER OF BLOCKS

The intelligent placement of blocks can make your drawing easy. You should be aware that AutoCAD allows nesting of blocks, and allows blocks to be ARRAYed like any other entity. Blocks can include elements on different layers.

A block can be made up of blocks. This is called **nesting**. You can place a block inside a block inside a block. There is no limit to the number of block nesting levels in AutoCAD, although it can get confusing if you go more than a few levels deep.

To include a block in another block, simply include the first in the editing buffer when you BLOCK the second.

Nesting can be very useful. There is no reason that a whole drawing file can't be INSERTed as a Block into yet another drawing file.

You can use edit commands like ARRAY, COPY and MOVE on a block, just like a regular object.

BLOCKS can be ARRAYed: Polar "chairs" around a round conference table

Nested BLOCK Example

Blocks and Layers

A block can be made up of elements stored on many layers. For example, you can place the graphics parts of your symbols on layer GRAPHICX and annotations on layer TEXTY at the time of block creation.

As long as the elements to be included are visible, AutoCAD will store them inside the block on their appropriate layers. The only rule is:

THE LAYERED BLOCK DEFINITION RULE

Objects must be visible at the time of BLOCK definition.

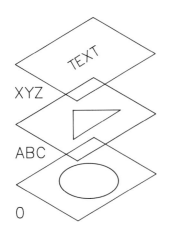

A BLOCK can have objects on many Layers

Later, when you insert a multiple-layers block, AutoCAD places the elements into their original layers (except Layer 0). To lessen confusion, the layer names in the block and the current drawing file should be the same. If the receiving file does not have all of the block's layers, insertion will create the appropriate layers in the current file.

When you give AutoCAD an INSERTION BASE POINT, that invisible reference point is defined along with the block at the time of creation. The reference point anchors the block into the drawing file at the insertion point coordinates at the time of insertion. When you INSERT a block, AutoCAD does not actually insert all the information that makes up the block at this point, but only a Block Reference back to the invisibly stored Block Definitions. This means that whatever layer you use to insert the block will contain the block reference at this Insertion point.

If you insert a block on a layer and later LAYER Freeze that layer, you will suppress display of that block, even if the block has elements on other layers.

When you insert multiple-layer blocks, the elements you insert retain their color and linetype parameters as set at the time of block creation. Remember that elements included in the block at the time of block creation can have color or linetype specification set by default (BYLAYER) or by specific COLOR or LINETYPE settings.

The color and linetype of elements included in a block will normally retain these properties at the time of insertion. However, there is one exception to how block element color and linetype will appear upon block insertion.

Block Properties—Layer 0 and BYBLOCK are Special Block Properties

If you would like your blocks to take on the color or linetype of the layer that you insert them on, you can create the elements that go into the block in "neutral" color and/or linetype. Then, upon insertion of the block, these elements will take on the color and/or linetype of the layer into which you are inserting the block.

If you create objects on layer 0 (with COLOR and LINETYPE set BYLAYER) and store them in a block, when you go to insert this block on a different active layer the objects will take on the color and linetype of the receiving layer. Blocks made from layer 0 elements act like chameleons.

This is not true for an *Insertion. Any elements that were on layer 0 at the time of block creation will go back to layer 0 with *Insertion. Similarly, when

EXPLODED, individual elements will return to their original color and linetype or COLOR and LINETYPE settings after explosion.

BYBLOCK for When You're not on Layer 0

If you do not happen to be on layer 0 at the time of block creation, you can create elements to go into your block (or edit existing ones with CHANGE) to have the BYBLOCK property. Then, like layer 0 elements, these elements will take on the color and linetype settings of either COLOR or LINETYPE settings at the time of block creation, or the respective default layer color and linetype setting at the time of insertion if these parameters are set BYLAYER at the time of block creation.

An example of a multiple-layer block insertion is shown in the LAYER INSERTION DRAWING. An example of a color insertion is shown in the COLOR LAYER INSERTION DRAWING.

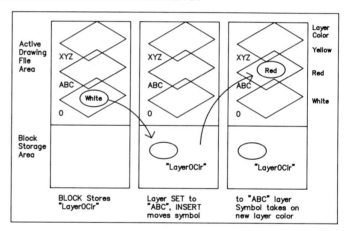

Layer Insertion Example

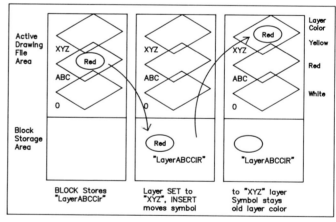

Color Layer Insertion Example

GLOBAL SYMBOL REPLACEMENT

You can globally replace blocks in your drawing file. You probably already feel the power behind those words — anything global has to be important. What do we mean by global replacement?

To demonstrate global replacement and review all the Block grouping tools, let's do an exercise.

The goal for the exercise is to create a simple drawing with simple blocks. Then replace the simple blocks with more complex ones to show how you can replace blocks in a drawing.

The two target drawings are shown in AutoTOWN WITH SIMPLE FIGURES and AutoTOWN WITH COMPLEX FIGURES.

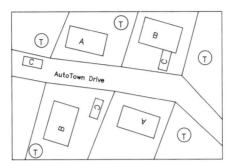

AutoTown with Simple Figures

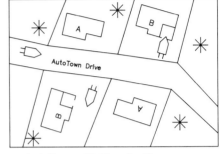

AutoTown with Complex Figures

AutoTOWN—A BLOCK EXERCISE

To create the drawing of the simple subdivision called **AutoTown**, you insert a house model (type A or B) in every building lot, along with a tree, and a car in the driveway.

To get going you have to do some setting up. First you need to create the subdivision layout. Then you have to draw a version of each symbol (block) in the **simple** drawing: (House Type A, House Type B, Car, Tree) and group them into blocks. Finally you have to create the more complex versions of each block so you can replace the simple version with the more complex blocks.

Give the blocks simple names to save typing time. Make sure that the insertion base point of the simple and complex blocks coincide so you won't have to adjust the location of each symbol upon replacement. The replacement blocks will use the same insertion base point, scale, and rotation as the simple symbols. Coordinate points are given as X,Y values.

The simple and complex blocks and their names are shown in the SIMPLE AND COMPLEX SYMBOLS DRAWING.

Simple and Complex Symbols Drawing

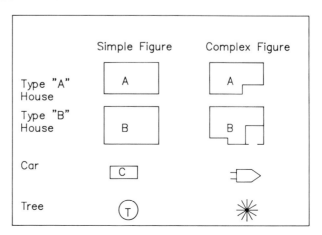

Here's the prompt sequence to set up and create these eight figures:

SETTING UP THE FIGURES

QUIT the CHAPTER2 drawing file. You will need it one more time.

Begin a NEW drawing file called: **AutoTown**

Leave UNITS at <default> and set SNAP to 0.5

Set LIMITS to -2,-2 and 50,38

ZOOM All.

1. Creating A1

```
Command: INSERT (RETURN)
Block name (or ?): RECTANG (RETURN)
Insertion point: 14,22 (RETURN)    (If you can't find RECTANG,
  create it with LINE or PLINE. It is a one-inch square box
  with its Insertion base point at the lower left corner.)
X scale factor <1>/Corner/XYZ: 9 (RETURN)
Y scale factor <default=X>: 5 (RETURN)
Rotation angle <0>: (RETURN)
Command: TEXT (RETURN)
Start point or Align/Center/Fit/Middle/Right/Style:
  17,23.5 (RETURN)
Height <0.2000>: 1.2 (RETURN)
Rotation angle <0>: (RETURN)
Text: A (RETURN)
Command:
```

A1

2. Creating B1

```
Command: INSERT (RETURN)
Block name (or ?) <RECTANG>: (RETURN)
Insertion point: 14,14 (RETURN)
X scale factor <1>/Corner/XYZ: 9 (RETURN)
Y scale factor <default=X>: 6 (RETURN)
Rotation angle <0>: (RETURN)
Command: TEXT (RETURN)
Start point or Align/Center/Fit/Middle/Right/Style:
  17,16 (RETURN)
Height <1.2000>: (RETURN)
Rotation angle <0>: (RETURN)
Text: B (RETURN)
Command:
```

B1

3. Creating C1

```
Command: INSERT (RETURN)
Block name (or ?) <RECTANG>: (RETURN)
Insertion point: 15,8.5 (RETURN)
X scale factor <1>/Corner/XYZ: 4.5 (RETURN)
Y scale factor <default=X>: 2 (RETURN)
Rotation angle <0>: (RETURN)
Command: TEXT (RETURN)
Start point or Align/Center/Fit/Middle/Right/Style:
  16.5,9 (RETURN)
```

C1

```
Height <1.2000>:  (RETURN)
Rotation angle <0>:  (RETURN)
Text: C  (RETURN)
Command:
```

T1

4. Creating T1

```
Command: CIRCLE  (RETURN)
3P/2P/TTR/<Center point>:  18,3.5  (RETURN)
Diameter/<Radius>:  1.58  (RETURN)
Command: TEXT  (RETURN)
Start point or Align/Center/Fit/Middle/Right/Style:
   17.5,2.5  (RETURN)
Height <1.2000>:  (RETURN)
Rotation angle <0>:  (RETURN)
Text: T  (RETURN)
Command:
```

A2

5. Creating A2

```
Command: LINE  (RETURN)
From point:  31.5,22  (RETURN)
To point:  31.5,27  (RETURN)
To point:  40.5,27  (RETURN)
To point:  40.5,23.5  (RETURN)
To point:  37,23.5  (RETURN)
To point:  37,22  (RETURN)
To point:  c  (RETURN)
Command: TEXT  (RETURN)
Start point or Align/Center/Fit/Middle/Right/Style:
   34.5,23.5  (RETURN)
Height <1.2000>:  (RETURN)
Rotation angle <0>:  (RETURN)
Text: A  (RETURN)
Command:
```

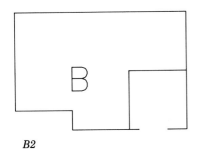

B2

6. Creating B2

```
Command: LINE  (RETURN)
From point:  38,14  (RETURN)
To point:  34.5,14  (RETURN)
To point:  34.5,15  (RETURN)
To point:  31.5,15  (RETURN)
To point:  31.5,20  (RETURN)
To point:  40.5,20  (RETURN)
To point:  40.5,14  (RETURN)
To point:  39.5,14  (RETURN)
To point:  (RETURN)
Command: LINE  (RETURN)
From point:  40.5,17  (RETURN)
To point:  37.5,17  (RETURN)
To point:  37.5,14  (RETURN)
To point:  (RETURN)
Command: TEXT  (RETURN)
Start point or Align/Center/Fit/Middle/Right/Style:
   34.5,16  (RETURN)
Height <1.2000>:  (RETURN)
Rotation angle <0>:  (RETURN)
Text: B  (RETURN)
Command:
```

7. Creating C2

C2

```
Command: LINE (RETURN)
From point: 40,9 (RETURN)
To point: 38.5,10 (RETURN)
To point: 36,10 (RETURN)
To point: 36,8 (RETURN)
To point: 38.5,8 (RETURN)
To point: c (RETURN)
Command: LINE (RETURN)
From point: 36,8.5 (RETURN)
To point: 35,8.5 (RETURN)
To point: (RETURN)
Command: LINE (RETURN)
From point: 36,9.5 (RETURN)
To point: 35,9.5 (RETURN)
To point: (RETURN)
Command:
```

8. Creating T2

T2

```
Command: LINE (RETURN)
From point: 39.5,3.5 (RETURN)
To point: 36,3.5 (RETURN)
To point: (RETURN)
Command: ARRAY (RETURN)
Select objects: L (RETURN)
Select objects: (RETURN)
Rectangular/Polar array (R/P): P (RETURN)
Center point of array: 37.75,3.5 (RETURN)
Number of items: (RETURN)
Degrees to fill (+=CCW,-=CW)<360>: -180 (RETURN)
Angle between items: 45 (RETURN)
Rotate objects as they are copied? <N>: Y (RETURN)
Command:
```

Your screen should now have all eight figures displayed. If not, figure out where you made an error, UNDO and create the offending figure over again.

Now you want to turn these figures into blocks using the BLOCK command:

TURNING AutoTOWN FIGURES INTO BLOCKS

```
Command: BLOCK (RETURN)
Block name (or ?): A1 (RETURN)
Insertion base point:    (pick rectangle lower left corner)
Select objects: W (RETURN)
First corner:    (pick)  Other corner:    (pick) 5 found.
```

   (Just get the A1 symbol with the Window.)

```
Select objects: (RETURN)
```

   (The figure will disappear.)

Repeat for each figure. Here are the insertion base points:

```
B1 rectangle lower left corner
C1 rectangle lower left corner
T1 circle center
A2 lower left corner
B2 31.5,14
C2 35,8.5
T2 37.75,3.5
```

All of the figures should be cleared from the screen. Now lay out the subdivision road and plot boundaries:

SUBDIVISION MAP BOUNDARIES

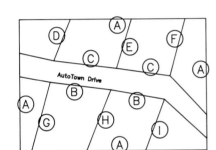

Subdivision Map Boundaries Labelled as a Guide

First create a new layer for the drawing boundary.

```
Command: LAYER (RETURN)
?/Make/Set/New/On/Off/Color/Ltype/Freeze/Thaw: MAKE (RETURN)
New current layer : Boundary (RETURN)
?/Make/Set/New/On/Off/Color/Ltype/Freeze/Thaw: Color (RETURN)
Color: Blue (RETURN)
Layer name(s) for color 5 blue <BOUNDARY>: (RETURN)
?/Make/Set/New/On/Off/Color/Ltype/Freeze/Thaw: (RETURN)
Command:
```

Now create boundary A

```
Command: LINE (RETURN)
From point: -1,1 (RETURN)
To point: -1,34.5 (RETURN)
To point: 48,34.5 (RETURN)
To point: 48,1 (RETURN)
To point: c (RETURN)
Command:
```

Put the rest of the subdivision boundaries on layer 0.

```
Command: LAYER (RETURN)
?/Make/Set/New/On/Off/Color/Ltype/Freeze/Thaw: Set (RETURN)
New current layer <BOUNDARY>: 0 (RETURN)
?/Make/Set/New/On/Off/Color/Ltype/Freeze/Thaw: (RETURN)
Command:
```

Boundary B

```
Command: LINE (RETURN)
From point: -1,20 (RETURN)
To point: 7,18.5 (RETURN)
To point: 23,16.5 (RETURN)
To point: 37,14 (RETURN)
To point: 48,4 (RETURN)
To point: (RETURN)
Command:
```

179

Boundary C

Command: **LINE (RETURN)**
From point: **-1,26 (RETURN)**
To point: **8,24 (RETURN)**
To point: **24.5,22 (RETURN)**
To point: **38.5,20 (RETURN)**
To point: **48,10 (RETURN)**
To point: **(RETURN)**
Command:

Boundary D

Command: **LINE (RETURN)**
From point: **12.5,34.5 (RETURN)**
To point: **8,24 (RETURN)**
To point: **(RETURN)**
Command:

Boundary E

Command: **LINE (RETURN)**
From point: **28.5,34.5 (RETURN)**
To point: **24.5,22 (RETURN)**
To point: **(RETURN)**
Command:

Boundary F

Command: **LINE (RETURN)**
From point: **42.5,34.5 (RETURN)**
To point: **38.5,20 (RETURN)**
To point: **(RETURN)**
Command:

Boundary G

Command: **LINE (RETURN)**
From point: **2,1 (RETURN)**
To point: **7,18.5 (RETURN)**
To point: **(RETURN)**
Command:

Boundary H

Command: **LINE (RETURN)**
From point: **16.5,1 (RETURN)**
To point: **23,16.5 (RETURN)**
To point: **(RETURN)**
Command:

Boundary I

Command: **LINE (RETURN)**
From point: **32,1 (RETURN)**
To point: **37,14 (RETURN)**
To point: **(RETURN)**
Command:

Naming AutoTown Drive

Command: **TEXT (RETURN)**
Start point or Align/Center/Fit/Middle/Right/Style:
 9,20 (RETURN)
Height <1.2000>: **1.0 (RETURN)**
Rotation angle <0>: **352 (RETURN)**
Text: **AutoTown Drive (RETURN)**
Command:

Let's insert the simple figures. Here is a list to show you where they go:

FIGURE INSERTION LOCATIONS

Command: **INSERT (RETURN)**
Block name (or ?): **A1 (RETURN)**
Insertion point: **11.5,26.5 (RETURN)**
X scale factor <1>/Corner/XYZ: **(RETURN)**
Y scale factor <default=X>: **(RETURN)**
Rotation angle <0>: **347 (RETURN)**
Command:

Here are the parameters for the others:

Block name	Insertion point	X Scale	Y Scale	Rotation angle
A1	33.5,10.5	1	1	162
B1	28.5,27.5	1	1	344
B1	12.0, 4.0	1	1	73
C1	1.5,22.5	1	1	349
C1	35.0,21.0	1	1	75
C1	18.5,15.0	1	1	250
T1	6.0,28.0	1	1	0
T1	24.5,32.0	1	1	0
T1	44.0,24.0	1	1	0
T1	39.0, 6.5	1	1	0
T1	4.5, 3.0	1	1	0

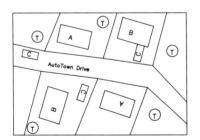

AutoTown with Simple Figures

Your drawing should now look like AutoTOWN WITH SIMPLE FIGURES.

Now comes the tricky part. You want to replace the block definitions of **A1**, **B1**, **C1**, and **T1** in the block storage area with **A2**, **B2**, **C2**, and **T2** respectively.

In response to the INSERT or BLOCK **?** option you get:

BLOCKS DEFINED IN THE BLOCK STORAGE AREA

Command: **INSERT (RETURN)**
Block name (or ?): **? (RETURN)**

```
                (FLIP SCREEN)

        Defined blocks.
           RECTANG
           A1
           B1
           C1
           T1
           A2
           B2
           C2
           T2

        9 user blocks, 0 unnamed blocks.
```

What AutoCAD tells you is that, although only some of the blocks are inserted in the active drawing file, all nine block definitions are stored in the block storage area.

You have to get the complex figures out onto the disc as .DWG files before you can perform a global replace.

To temporarily get rid of the complex figures write them as independent drawing files, using the block names as the drawing file names:

WBLOCK COMPLEX FIGURES

```
Command: WBLOCK (RETURN)
File name: A2 (RETURN)
Block name: A2 (RETURN)
Command:
```

Do the same for B2, C2, and T2.

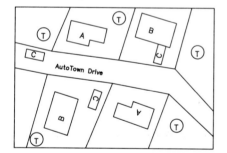

House Type Figure A1 Replaced by A2

Now you can do the replacement. The AutoCAD INSERT command does replace as well as insert. We told you it was a remarkable command.

A special option of INSERT is the = or **redefinition** option. Here's how it works:

REPLACING A SIMPLE FIGURE WITH A COMPLEX ONE

```
Command: INSERT (RETURN)
INSERT Block name (or ?): A1=A2 (RETURN)
Block A1 redefined
Regenerating drawing.
Insertion point: ^C   (control-C)
   *Cancel*
Command:
```

By typing **A1 = A2 (RETURN)**, you tell AutoCAD that you want to do a redefinition. Essentially you are saying: "You know the old block named **A1**? Let's give it a facelift by redefining what it looks like." But keep the name **A1** because that's how the drawing file knows the block location, scale, and rotation.

You are changing the block definition in the storage area, but you are leaving the name the same. When you do an = INSERT, AutoCAD performs an automatic REGEN.

Continue the exercise until you have replaced all four blocks in the example. Your finished drawing will look like the AutoTOWN COMPLEX SYMBOL DRAWING:

REPLACING THE REST OF THE SIMPLE FIGURES

```
Command: INSERT (RETURN)
INSERT Block name (or ?): B1=B2 (RETURN)
Block B1 redefined
Regenerating drawing.
Insertion point: ^C    (control-C)
  *Cancel*
Command:
```

Replace C1 with C2 and T1 with T2

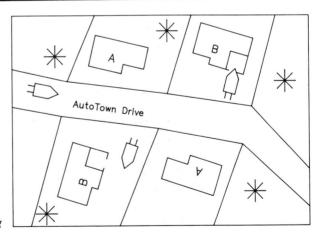

AutoTown Complex Symbol Drawing

If you no longer need them, you may wish to PURGE the unused original Block definitions. You also can **WBLOCK** * your entire drawing to its own file name, and then QUIT. Or you can PURGE the next time you load the file.

Recall that PURGE erases all unused extraneous blocks, or other named objects from the storage part of the drawing file. Also recall that PURGE only works immediately after entering the drawing editor.

PURGING THE COMPLEX BLOCKS

Command: **END (RETURN)**

Main Menu appears

Select 2 Edit EXISTING Drawing: **AutoTown**

Command: **PURGE (RETURN)**
Purge unused Blocks/LAyers/LTypes/SHapes/STyles/All:
  All (RETURN)
Purge block A2 <N>: **Y (RETURN)**
Purge block B2 <N>: **Y (RETURN)**
Purge block C2 <N>: **Y (RETURN)**
Purge block T2 <N>: **Y (RETURN)**
No unreferenced linetypes found.
No unreferenced text styles found.
No unreferenced shapes found.
Command:

After purging, your **INSERT Block name (or ?):** option will look like this:

Command: **INSERT (RETURN)**
Block name (or ?): **? (RETURN)**

   (FLIP SCREEN)

Defined blocks.
   RECTANG
   A1
   B1
   C1
   T1

5 user blocks, 0 unnamed blocks.

Why go through all the work of a global replacement?

Block redefinition can speed regen and redraw time in a complex drawing. If you have a number of complex blocks in your drawing, you can temporarily represent them with simple outlines to improve regen and redraw time. Then redefine them back to complex blocks prior to plotting.

If you are satisfied with a part of a drawing (or a part on a layer) and you won't be working on that part for a while, BLOCKit and replace it with a simple BLOCK to improve REDRAW speed and reduce screen clutter.

When you are ready you can =INSERT to put the drawing back together again.

SUMMING UP AND TIPS FOR RIDING THE HERD

Did you realize that the Simple AutoTown Subdivision map you just created has over 100 individual entities in it? In the next Chapter, when you add a little shading to the picture, the number can climb to over 1,000 entities.

Without blocks you would not be able to keep track of all the individual components that make up even a simple drawing. Blocks help you organize your drawing by herding useful collections of drawing elements together.

But that's not all blocks do. Here's a set of TIPS FOR RIDING HERD:

TIPS FOR RIDING HERD

☐ Naming Conventions for Blocks.

    ☐ Give your symbols useful names. CAR1 and CAR2 are better than C1 and C2 but not as good as BUG and PORSCHE.

    ☐ Keep an alphabetical log of symbol names in a LITTLE BLACK BOOK next to your workstation. This way you won't accidently call the wrong one or duplicate symbol names.

    ☐ Try to plan ahead to INSERT many of the same BLOCKs at the same time. This way you can use AutoCAD's Insertion <default prompts> instead of typing BLOCK names over and over. If all the insertions are identical in Scale and rotation, COPY Multiple is efficient for duplicating blocks.

    ☐ You might want to create BLOCKs in a separate "library" file so you don't have to purge them to keep the BLOCK storage name list clean.

☐ Create Blocks When You Need Them.

    ☐ It usually does not pay to just sit down and create a number of BLOCKS. As you form new symbols while drawing, use the regular edit commands like COPY and MOVE to manipulate these unBLOCKed symbols.

    ☐ If you find that you are COPYing the same group of unBLOCKed objects all the time, BLOCK them (setting appropriate colors and layers).

    ☐ If the BLOCK is really useful, WBLOCK it to a separate disc file. Periodically collect all your WBLOCKed symbols into a library and update your little black book (or print out lists).

☐ Insertion Made Easy.

    ☐ DRAG mode with Insertion is recommended. Before you dump a BLOCK into your drawing file you really want to know how it's going to look.

    ☐ This is especially true with an *INSERTed BLOCK. If you place a complex *INSERTed BLOCK in the wrong place in a layer with lots of other entities, use UNDO to get rid of all the pieces.

185

☐ Creating Many Blocks or Many Pieces With One Command.

  ☐ MINSERT combines INSERT with rectangular ARRAY to give you multiple occurrences of your inserted blocks. Remember all blocks inserted with MINSERT act as a single entity.

  ☐ When you EXPLODE a block you free the individual entities that make up the block from the block reference, just like *INSERT.

  ☐ Redefinitions. Redefining simple/complex blocks can save redraw time. Redefining obsolete blocks can globally update your drawing. If you need a new block similar to an existing block, EXPLODE or *INSERT the old block, edit it, and BLOCK it to a new name.

☐ AutoCAD Keeps Track of Many Named-Things.

  ☐ All the following are inside AutoCAD's named-things library inside your drawing file:

    ☐ Blocks   ☐ Linetypes
    ☐ Styles   ☐ Views
    ☐ Layers   ☐ Fonts

  ☐ Use **?** Options for all named-things commands to periodically see what is in the dungeon.

  ☐ Use PURGE to keep the Invisible-Named-Things-Dungeon clear. Or you can use WBLOCK * QUIT to keep your drawing file clean. If you respond to the Block name prompt of WBLOCK with an asterisk *, WBLOCK will write out the entire drawing file. It will not write out unused named entities, Layers, Styles, etc. Unlike PURGE, it wipes them all out if they are unused.

  ☐ AutoCAD's RENAME command can be used to change the name of named-things.

  ☐ Use the Main Menu **5. File Utility** to get a listing of all separate .DWG files on your disc.

☐ Be Careful When INSERTing From a Separate Disc File.

  ☐ Existing named-things and their parameters take precedence over incoming named-things.

  ☐ When you do an insertion from a disc file, all named things in the outside file get copied into the receiving file. If the STYLE/LAYER already exists in the receiving drawing, it takes precedence. This may change text styles in the newly inserted parts, or add layers to the current drawing file.

Visible Drawing File Area

Invisible Named
Things Dungeon

STYLES   BLOCKS
Standard   A1
           A2
           B1
           B2
LAYERS   C1
0   C2
Boundary   T1
           T2

▼ PURGE ▼

Visible Drawing File Area

Invisible Named
Things Dungeon

STYLES   BLOCKS
Standard   A1
           B1
           C1
           T1
LAYERS
0
Boundary

Purging Invisible Named-Things from the Named-Things Dungeon

Preformed symbols speed production drawing. But what about just sketching and coloring in a few ideas? In the next Chapter we bring out the artist in you.

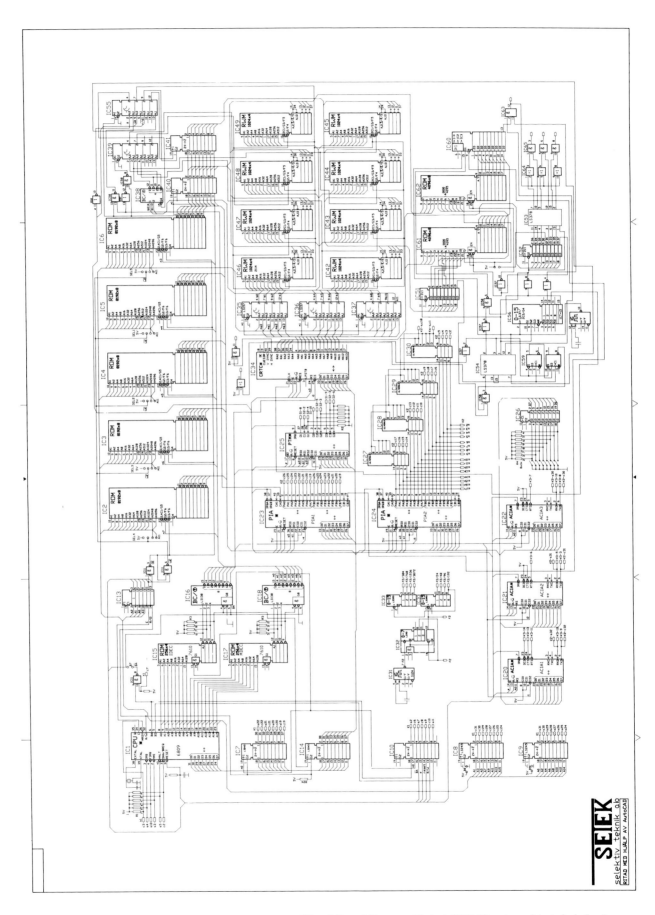

Circuit Board Drawn with AutoCAD (Courtesy of Autodesk, Inc.)

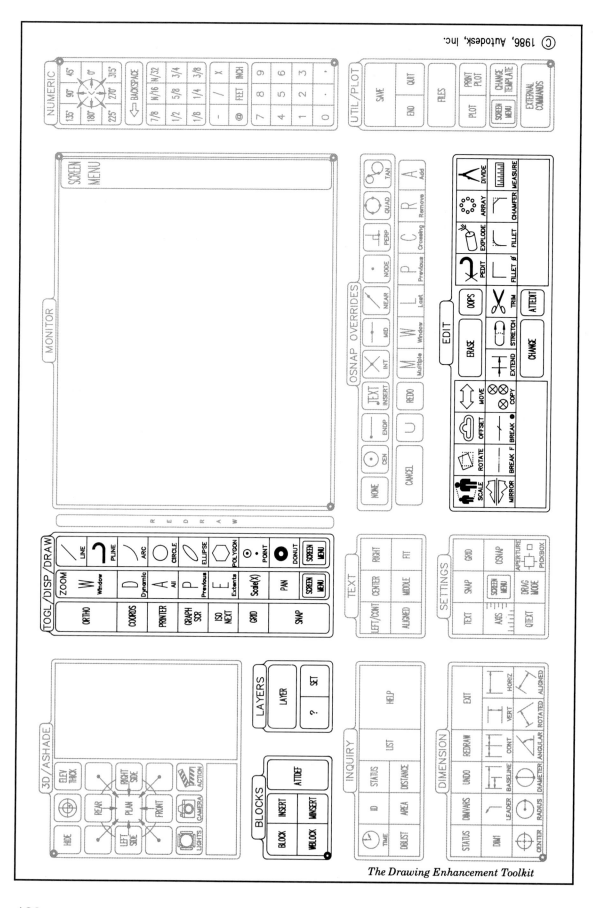

The Drawing Enhancement Toolkit

© 1986, Autodesk, Inc.

CHAPTER 7

DRAWING ENHANCEMENTS

MAKING DRAWINGS MORE PRESENTABLE

Making Drawings More Impressive. The Drawing Enhancement Toolkit. Trace is a Fat Line. Freehand Drawing With Sketch. Creating Patterns. Hatching and Hatch Boundaries. ▶ Layering Tricks for Enhanced Images. ▶ Playing With Hatch and Linetype. A Solid is a Polygon Filled with Ink. Solids and Fill. A Title Block Example. ▶ Summing Up and Tips.

MAKING DRAWINGS MORE IMPRESSIVE

All the drawings you have tried up to this point have been simple. We wouldn't go so far as to say they are "ugly" — let's just say they are not very interesting. As professionals who are frequently drawn to embellishment, you want to be able to add that special something to your drawings to give them design presentation quality. Drawing enhancement makes your drawings more impressive.

In this Chapter you will look at traces and sketching and you will make use of color and layer separation to keep your drawing enhancements in order. In addition, you will learn how to create and place shading or pocheing in your drawing and how to effectively use linetype as a drawing enhancement tool.

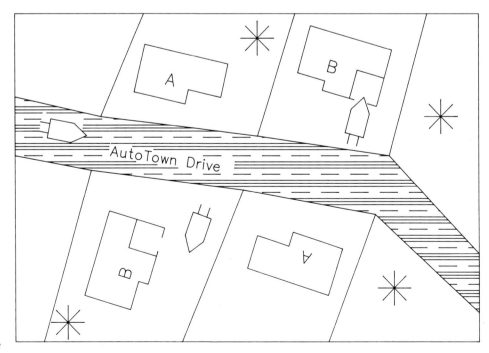

Shading Example: Paving AutoTown Drive

THE DRAWING ENHANCEMENT TOOLKIT

In this Chapter you will explore the basic drawing enhancement techniques that AutoCAD provides. You will make use of the commands listed in DRAWING ENHANCEMENT COMMANDS:

DRAWING ENHANCEMENT COMMANDS

☐ TRACE—Acts like fancy ketchup. It makes lines that are thick.

☐ SKETCH—Provides freehand line entry for everything from doodles to rendering.

☐ HATCH—Gives a way to fill a polygon with a pattern.

☐ LINETYPE—Is a way to select or create different line styles.

☐ SOLIDS—Creates a polygon that is completely filled with the current color.

TRACE IS A FAT LINE

TRACE is a big, fat line. You can also think of TRACEs as unconnected PEDIT segments with no continuity. You draw TRACEs just like you draw lines, with a **From point:** and a **To point:**. But AutoCAD asks you how wide you want the TRACE. You can create TRACE as wide as you want. When drawing TRACEs, AutoCAD lags one segment behind in displaying the TRACE, calculating the "bevel" angle between the first TRACE segment and the next.

TRACE A FAT LINE

Begin a NEW drawing file called **Envelope**

Set LIMITS from 0,0 to 16,12. (Leave UNITS to default.)

For convenience give yourself a GRID of 1 unit and SNAP value of 1 unit.

Create a layer called **Doodles**. (Set it Current.)

Try a fat line using TRACE. (Type **TRACE**.)

Pick a width of 2 (inches)

TRACE a few segments. Use CANCEL to end continuous segments.

Try another one.

Erase Last a few times to see the trace bevel edge.

Here are some observations about traces.

☐ You can't **curve** a trace.

☐ You can't **close** a trace.

☐ You can't **continue** a trace.

☐ You can't **undo** a trace segment.

☐ You end a trace sequence with a **(RETURN)**, Space, or CANCEL.

Okay, so TRACE is only kind of like a line. But you get the idea. Don't forget that you can get somewhat thick lines just by using colors and a thick technical pen when you go to plot a drawing. Of course, you can also create thick lines with PLINE. PLINE can do anything TRACE can do, and a lot more.

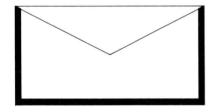

Sequence for Making Envelope

Because traces have thickness, AutoCAD likes to give the trace end a **beveled edge**. This bevel depends on the direction of the next trace. Sometimes this **bevel** can give a desired effect as shown in the ENVELOPE EXAMPLE.

HOW TO CREATE THE ENVELOPE EXAMPLE

```
Set layer 0 Current.

Turn layer DOODLES Off.

Command: TRACE (RETURN)
Width: .25 (RETURN)
From point: 6,9 (RETURN)
To point: 2,6 (RETURN)
To point: 2,2 (RETURN)
To point: 10,2 (RETURN)
To point: 10,6 (RETURN)
To point: 6,9 (RETURN)
To point: (RETURN)
Command:

Erase the two upper, triangle segments. REDRAW. Then add
new flap lines.

Command: LINE (RETURN)
From point: 1.875,6.05 (RETURN)
To point: 6,4 (RETURN)
To point: 10.125,6.05 (RETURN)
To point: c (RETURN)
Command:
```

Envelope Example

FREEHAND DRAWING WITH SKETCH

If you want to create the envelope clasp and learn about SKETCHing continue with the following text. If you would prefer to go directly to creating patterns, skip to CREATING PATTERNS.

In a few more exercises you are going to open the envelope to see the safety pattern printed on the inside. When you do that you will not want the clasp showing. Set up a new layer for the clasp so that you can later turn it off:

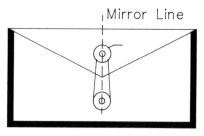

Using MIRROR to save time creating the envelope clasp

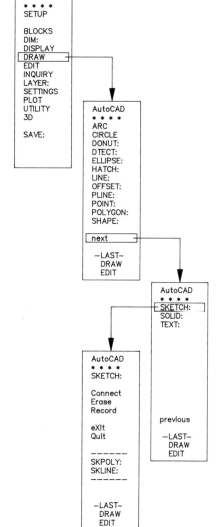

ROOT to DRAW to SKETCH

CREATING THE ENVELOPE CLASP

Create a new layer named CLASP. Set it Current. Turn SNAP Off.

First draw the top circles and copy them down. Draw the lefthand taut string using OSNAP NEArest to the circles.

Then use the MIRROR command to duplicate the string left to right.

Try adding the loose end with SKETCH which follows below.

SKETCH Brings Out the Artist In You

SKETCH gives you the opportunity to draw lines freehand, without being bothered by from points and to points, (**RETURN**)s, and other alignment or input parameters.

AutoCAD provides the sketch facility to trace contours or capture freehand drawing much the same way you would doodle or draw on a piece of paper. Keep in mind that sketching, without clearly thinking ahead about where line segment **endpoints** are going to be pinned down, is contrary to almost all other methods for entering graphic primitives in AutoCAD. Just about every other command asks you to define location — SKETCH allows you to just roam.

AutoCAD stores sketches in the drawing file database as successive short line or polyline segments. Because AutoCAD doesn't know where your sketching may lead you, both you and the program have to take precautions not to let the amount of sketch information get out of hand. Just a few quick passes pointing in sketch mode can create a huge number of short segments in the database.

To help AutoCAD keep sketch information in control, you have to tell the program how short a line segment it can use to store your sketch data. This is known as the **Record Increment**. From then on, AutoCAD will store a new segment every time your pointer moves more than the Record Increment away from the last stored segment endpoint. Try to keep the Record Increment as large as possible to minimize the number of lines.

Do your sketching on a separate layer to keep it separate from CLASP and ENVELOPE and so you can later turn your doodles off.

Here's how you get into sketch:

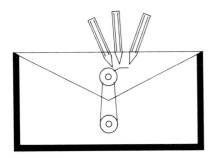

SKETCHing the Loose End

SKETCHING THE LOOSE STRING ON THE ENVELOPE CLASP

Set layer DOODLES Current, and ERASE any trash here.

Turn SNAP Off to get a freely moving crosshair.

Command: **SKETCH (RETURN)**
Record increment <0.1000>: **0.5 (RETURN)**   (example increment)
Sketch.   Pen eXit Quit Record Erase Connect.

The Record Increment is given in current units. For example, if the width of your screen currently represents 30 inches, and the screen pointing area on your digitizer is 6″ wide, the **0.5** Increment means your sketch segments will be one half-inch, and that AutoCAD will record a new segment every time you move the input device about one-tenth-inch (6 inches divided by 30 inches divided by 0.5 inches.

You also have to let AutoCAD know when you consider the sketching pointer **up** (off the paper) or **down** (sketching). AutoCAD keeps all sketch input in a temporary state until you specifically ask that all the sketch lines be entered into the drawing file database. You can E (Erase) sketched lines before you R (Record) them. In addition to normal SNAP and ORTHO toggles available in sketch, the following commands, entered without a **(RETURN)**, control sketch mode:

SKETCH MODE CONTROLS

☐ Pen or **P** is a toggle that tells AutoCAD the pointer is up or down. You just type **P**, without a (RETURN), or hit the pointer pick button, to change the toggle.

☐ eXit or **X** stores the sketch segments you have been creating in the drawing file and gets you back to Command: prompt. A **SPACE** or **(RETURN)** will do the same thing.

☐ Quit or **Q** leaves sketch mode without storing the segments you have been creating. A ^C will do the same thing.

☐ Record or **R** keeps you in sketch mode, but stores the segments you have been creating so far in the drawing file. It is just like a **SAVE**, but once you **Record**, segments that get stored are not available for Erase from within sketch.

☐ **Erase** is somewhat like **undo** but erases any unrecorded segment from a point you pick to the last segment drawn.

☐ Connect or **C** within sketch mode connects the pen to the end of the last endpoint of an active sketch chain. It is like Continue. You can always use normal AutoCAD editing techniques to connect sketch chains to other elements.

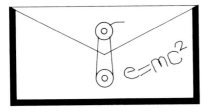

Notes on the Back of the Envelope

Play around with sketch to draw the loose string on the end of the envelope clasp. You may also want to add a wax seal or other doodles on this layer.

Serious Sketching With SKPOLY

If you need to trace in existing contours or other maps, you will find SKETCH truly useful. To get good smooth curves with SKETCH you need to SKETCH with polylines by setting SKPOLY. You can set SKPOLY from the Screen Menu, or with the SETVAR Command. If it is 0, SKETCH will draw lines, but if it is 1, SKETCH will draw Polylines, which can be STRETCHed, and edited easily. The big advantage is that you can Curve Fit the polyline and get a smooth curve.

CREATING PATTERNS

Remember the AutoTown Subdivision drawing we created in the last Chapter? Wouldn't that drawing look better if the road looked like a road?

Let's take a crack at fixing up the road. We'll do so first by way of learning the HATCH command.

The HATCH Command and ACAD.PAT

AutoCAD comes complete with at least 41 patterns. These are stored in a disc file labelled **ACAD.PAT**. You can find out the names of these patterns by executing the **HATCH** Command from the DRAW Menu. Then ask for a listing of pattern names and descriptions by picking or typing **?** **(RETURN)** in response to the prompt.

```
Command: HATCH (RETURN)
Pattern (? or name/U,style) <U>: ? (RETURN)
```

A FLIP SCREEN will appear with a listing. (You get past the **More** break in the listing by hitting any key). Part of the listing is shown in ACAD.PAT.

Hit the FLIP SCREEN key when you are through looking.

A HATCH Example

Here's the chance you have been waiting for. Everyone knows that a houndstooth check pattern is what appears inside "safety" envelopes so the postman cannot read who is sending you checks. Let's "open" the envelope and see the pattern inside:

OPEN ENVELOPE WITH HOUNDSTOOTH PATTERN

Use the envelope on your screen.

Set layer 0 Current.

If you created the clasp, turn layer CLASP Off.

If you doodled, turn layer DOODLES Off.

AutoCAD PATTERNS

ANGLE	Angle Steel
ANSI31	ANSI Iron
ANSI32	ANSI Steel
ANSI33	ANSI Bronze
ANSI34	ANSI Plastic
ANSI35	ANSI Fire brick
ANSI36	ANSI Marble
ANSI37	ANSI Lead
ANSI38	ANSI Aluminium
BOX	Box steel
BRASS	Brass
BRICK	Brick
CLAY	Clay
CORK	Cork
CROSS	Crosses
DASH	Dashed lines
DOLMIT	Rock layering
DOTS	Dots
EARTH	Earth (ground)
-- More --	
ESCHER	Escher pattern
FLEX	Flexible material
GRASS	Grass area
GRATE	Grated area
HEX	Hexagons
HONEY	Honeycomb pattern
HOUND	Houndstooth check
INSUL	Insulation material
LINE	Parallel horiz. lines
MUDST	Mud and sand
NET	Horizontal/vert. grid
NET3	Network 0-60-120
PLAST	Plastic material
PLASTI	Plastic material
SACNRC	Concrete
SQUARE	Small squares
STARS	Star of David
STEEL	Steel material
SWAMP	Swampy area
TRANS	Heat transfer matrl.
-- More --	
TRIANG	Equilateral triangles
ZIGZAG	Staircase effect

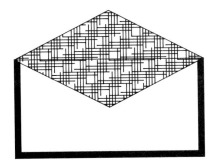

Open Envelope with Houndstooth Pattern

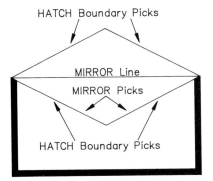

Open Envelope with Boundary Pick Points

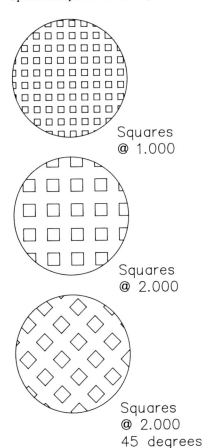

Squares
@ 1.000

Squares
@ 2.000

Squares
@ 2.000
45 degrees

HATCH Parameter Examples

MIRROR the flap pieces open by picking the two angled flap lines for MIRROR. Use the top of the envelope as the MIRROR line.

Your open envelope should look like the OPEN ENVELOPE.

Make sure SNAP is Off so you can pick freehand.

```
Command: HATCH (RETURN)
Pattern (? or name/U, style): Hound (RETURN)
Scale for pattern <1.0000>: 2 (RETURN)
Angle for pattern <0>: (RETURN)
Select objects: W (RETURN)    (pick four angled lines and
  mirror line)
First corner: (pick)  Other corner: (pick)  5 found.
Select objects:  R (RETURN)
Remove objects:  (Pick mirror line)  1 selected,  1 found,
1 removed
Select objects:    (RETURN)

(The pattern fill takes place.)

Command:    (Toggle GRID for a REDRAW.)

Command: END (RETURN)
```

The HATCH command needs several parameters to work.

☐ **Pattern.** Here AutoCAD wants to know what type of shading you want to use to fill an area. Responding with one of the names from ACAD.PAT will call up that pattern and get it ready for use. A **U** allows you to define your own simple pattern using angled lines: you set the angle and spacing between lines by answering a few easy prompts. A **?** gives you a list of the available pattern names stored in ACAD.PAT.

☐ **Scale for pattern.** Here AutoCAD wants to know how big you want the pattern elements. Pattern insertion is just like block insertion. AutoCAD allows you to scale the pattern as you insert it. Almost all AutoCAD standard patterns are scaled to look good in one unit value of space. This means that you almost always will scale the pattern when you bring it into a drawing. If you leave the pattern at the default value (<**1.0000**>), you will usually find the pattern too dense for your requirements.

☐ **Angle for pattern.** AutoCAD standard patterns have a horizontal orientation. If you want to slant your patterns, adjust the angle.

☐ **Select objects** or Window or Last. Here is where AutoCAD wants to know what you want to fill in with a pattern. If you select something as simple as a circle or rectangle, AutoCAD will fill it in, stopping the pattern at the edges. If you want to fill in a more extensive boundary, you have to identify the boundary area explicitly so that AutoCAD does not let the pattern **spill out** of the boundary area.

195

Patterns are BLOCKS

AutoCAD keeps all the objects that make up a pattern as a block. An Erase Last will wipe out all segments in a pattern after an insertion. Similarly, MOVE, COPY, and other edit operations will operate on the pattern as a whole.

Like *Insertion with blocks, if you want to operate on individual objects within a pattern, use the asterisk option, *, before the pattern name (*CLAY, for example).

If you insert a pattern that has the wrong scale or angle, you can always erase Last or Undo to get rid of it and try again. A ^C will stop a pattern fill in progress just like ^C stops a REGEN in progress.

HATCHING AND HATCH BOUNDARIES

It's time to pave AutoTown Drive. The trick here will be to correctly define the boundary for the paving pattern.

In order to use the HATCH command to fill an irregular area (or one not bounded by a simple rectangle or circle), you must completely define the fill area boundaries. You have to watch out for open-ended polygons with one or more edges "hanging off the side". Closed polylines make excellent, safe boundaries. Some guidelines are shown in the HATCH BOUNDARY DIAGRAM.

You create a boundary for a hatch pattern by OSNAPping the lines, circles, or arcs that surround the target hatch area. You also can Window an area to include all objects for hatching, Removing or Adding objects if required.

For AutoTown Drive, you want to outline just the road boundary for pattern display. You could pick the various line segments that separate the building lots from the road. But you run into a problem where the road meets the edge of the drawing.

If you BREAK the rectangle boundary, you can hatch within the line segments that you want. If you select the drawing boundary itself, you would have an overhang situation like that pictured in IMPROPER HATCH BOUNDARY. You are unlikely to get good results if AutoCAD tried to use these overhangs as hatch boundaries.

There are two ways around this problem:

☐ You can BREAK the exterior lines, at the intersections, separating the segments you want, identify them while picking the hatch boundary, and proceed to fill with the pattern. (See BREAKING EXISTING ELEMENTS FOR HATCHING BOUNDARY.)

☐ Another way is to use another layer. You can trace over the boundary you want with a closed polyline on a layer that will not affect the current drawing. When you have the boundary defined, you can use that boundary as the constraint for the fill pattern. (See BUILDING A SEPARATE LAYER FOR HATCHING BOUNDARY.)

HATCH Boundary Diagram

Improper HATCH Boundary

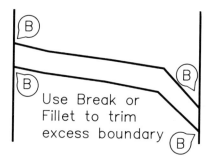
Breaking Existing Elements for HATCHing Boundary

196

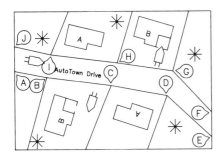

*Step-by-Step Building a Separate Layer
for HATCHing Boundary*

LAYERING TRICKS FOR ENHANCED IMAGES

Creating a separate layer for hatching is a good idea anyway. In most cases, you want to Freeze and Thaw HATCH to control regen/redraw speed and screen clutter. Keep in mind that, if Thawed, all the elements that make a hatch are regenerated along with the rest of the drawing.

Let's set up a layer called **Shading**, use OSNAP to create a proper boundary, and then give the road a paving:

PAVING AutoTOWN DRIVE

Get the EXISTING file AUTOTOWN.

Create a New layer called Shading.

Give it a CONTINUOUS linetype with your favorite color.

Set layer SHADING Current.

Set a running OSNAP mode to **ENDpoint**.

Use PLINE to trace the road paving boundary by picking the
endpoints **in order** around the boundary.
Use C to close the last line segment to the first.

```
Command: HATCH (RETURN)
Pattern (? or name/U, style)<HOUND>: CLAY (RETURN)
Scale for pattern <2.0000>: 10 (RETURN)
Angle for pattern <0>: (RETURN)
Select objects: L (RETURN)  1 selected,1 found

Select objects: (RETURN)

Command:
```

When AutoCAD gets down hatching, turn all layers On.

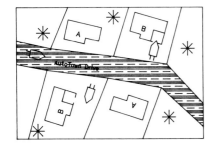

AutoTown Shaded Drive

Your drawing will look like AutoTOWN SHADED DRIVE.

But look closely at your SHADED DRIVE. What's wrong with it?

The hatch pattern drew directly over the text and car symbol in the road. This will never do.

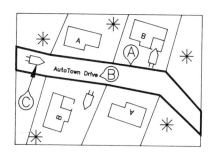

Using a separate boundary in conjunction with individual objects to get a complete donut-and-hole boundary

The Donut and the Hole

With a little prodding, AutoCAD can hatch around objects like text and the block **C2** (car). If you select these objects in the hatch command when you are outlining the boundary, AutoCAD (with HATCH style Normal) will decide what is the donut and what is the hole when figuring out where to hatch. But to do this, you have to select all of the boundary and interior objects.

Let's do it again. This time, select the text, car, and polyline boundary.

PAVING AutoTOWN DRIVE AGAIN

ERASE Last or Undo to get rid of the previous hatching.

Turn OSNAP End off.

```
Command: HATCH (RETURN)
Pattern (? or name/U, style)<CLAY>: (RETURN)
Scale for pattern <10.0000>: (RETURN)
Angle for pattern <0>: (RETURN)
Select objects:
```

Now pick the polyline boundary, car and text.

```
Select objects: L (RETURN)   1 selected, 1 found.
Pick Beginning point of the text.
Select objects: 1 selected, 1 found.
Pick Any point on the Car block.
Select objects: 1 selected, 1 found.

Select objects: (RETURN)
Command:
```

Erase the polyline boundary.

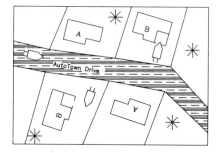

AutoTown Properly Shaded Drive

Your screen should finally look like the AutoTOWN PROPERLY SHADED DRIVE.

Save your AutoTown drawing so you can plot it out in the next Chapter. Before you use **END** you also need to set up a VIEW of AutoTOWN for use in the next Chapter:

ROADTURN VIEW

```
Command: VIEW (RETURN)
?/Delete/Restore/Save/Window: W (RETURN)
View Name to save: Roadturn (RETURN)
First corner: 32.50,11.00 (RETURN)
Other corner: 46.00,21.00 (RETURN)
Command:
```

Use an END.

```
Command: END (RETURN)
```

PLINE and PEDIT Help With Hatch Boundaries

In the last example we spent a lot of energy in order to create a boundary PLINE for hatching. The method we used to set up a separate layer, individually specifying the segments for the boundary, will always get you out of a jam. Here are two other methods that will also work:

☐ Use PLINE to create the street and lot-lines in the first place. Plan ahead if you are going to HATCH something.

☐ Use PEDIT to join individual segments (LINES or PLINES) together into one continuous new PLINE as the boundary for hatching. If you create these boundaries on a separate layer, you can set up overlapping PLINES for shading different details different ways.

Use PLINE and PEDIT to Place Fire Hydrants on AutoTown Drive

Let's try an exercise that will take advantage of PLINE and PEDIT features to help you make a single entity boundary.

We will use AutoCAD's **DIVIDE** command to place the hydrants on the street boundary.

USE PEDIT TO PAVE AGAIN

Use AutoCAD to start a new drawing for the file.

Call it **Atown=Autotown**

Zoom All.

Erase the Hatch (and polyline, if you didn't already) on layer SHADING

While on layer SHADING, use LINE to trace over the two line segments at the ends of the street where they hit the drawing file boundary.

Use PEDIT to Join the first of these new lines with adjacent line/street edge segments. Start with the left line.

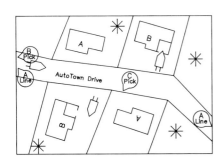

Using PEDIT to join 10 line segments into a Boundary

```
Command: PEDIT (RETURN)
Select polyline:   (pick left line.)
Entity selected is not a polyline
Do you want to turn it into one? <Y>   (RETURN)
Close/Join/Width/Edit vertex/Fit curve/Decurve/
  Undo/eXit/ <X>: join (RETURN)
Select objects:   (pick lines clockwise around the boundary.)
```

(You will get nine segments to join the polyline.)

```
Select objects: (RETURN)
9 segments added to polyline.
Close/Join/Width/Edit vertex/Fit curve/Decurve/
  Undo/eXit <X>: (RETURN)
Command:
```

(The polyline is complete.)

199

Hatch the boundary as you did before.

```
Command: hatch (RETURN)
Pattern (? or name/U, style) <CLAY>: (RETURN)
Scale for pattern <10.0000>: (RETURN)
Angle for pattern <0>: (RETURN)
Select objects: L (RETURN)
1 found.
Select objects:   (pick text)      1 selected 1 found.
Select objects:   (pick car)       1 selected 1 found.
Select objects: (RETURN)

(Hatching occurs.)

Command:
```

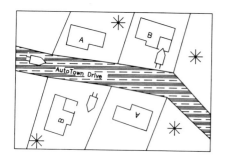

HATCHing with PLINE

If you want to put in some hydrants, try the DIVIDE AND HYDRANT EXERCISE:

DIVIDE AND HYDRANT EXERCISE

Turn off layer BOUNDARY.

Create a circle for the hydrant. Work next to the tree in Lot B where you have the space.

```
Command:   CIRCLE (RETURN)
3P/2P/TTR/<Center point>:   (pick a center.)
Diameter/<Radius>:   (pick a small radius.)
Command:
```

Make it red.

```
Command: CHANGE (RETURN)
Select objects:   (pick the circle.) 1 selected 1 found.
Select objects:   (RETURN)
Property/<Change point>: P (RETURN)
Change what property (Color/Elev/LAyer/LType/Thickness)?
   color (RETURN)
New color <BYLAYER>: red (RETURN)
Change what property (Color/Elev/LAyer/LType/Thickness) ?
   (RETURN)
Command:
```

Turn it into hydrant block.

```
Command: BLOCK (RETURN)
Black name (or ?): hydrant (RETURN)
Insertion base point:   (pick a point just above the circle.)
Select objects:   (pick the circle.)   1 selected 1 found.
Select objects: (RETURN)
Command:
```

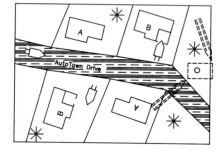

Creating the Hydrant Circle

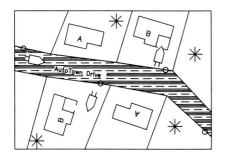

Four Hydrants Divided into Place

Now insert it with the DIVIDE command.

Command: **DIVIDE (RETURN)**
Select objects to divide: (pick the polyline at the upper
  left boundary corner where it is free from the hatching.
Divide into how many parts / Block: **block (RETURN)**
Block name to insert: **hydrant (RETURN)**
Align block with object? <Y> **(RETURN)**
Divide into how many parts: **4 (RETURN)**

Command:

    (In go the hydrants. If your insertion base was right, they
      went on the lots and not in the street or houses!

Command: **END (RETURN)**

PLAYING WITH HATCH AND LINETYPE

Hatch has one more trick up its sleeve. Let's say that you want to use some
simple parallel lines as a pattern to fill a boundary. Immediately after invoking the hatch command, you can screen pick, tablet pick or type **U (RETURN)**.

U stands for "U design it". This hatch option allows you to create parallel
lines or a 90-degree cross pattern. Let's try one:

HATCH "U" (Gezundheit) PATTERN

Begin a NEW drawing named **Uplay**

Leave UNITS and LIMITS to default.

Create a new layer called UHATCH. Give it your favorite
color. Set it Current.

Command: **CIRCLE (RETURN)**
3P/2P/TTR/<Center point>: **2,5 (RETURN)**
Diameter/<Radius>: **1.5 (RETURN)**
Command: **HATCH (RETURN)**
Pattern (? or name/U, style) <CLAY>: **U (RETURN)**
Angle for crosshatch lines <0>: **45 (RETURN)**
Spacing between lines <1.0000>: **.2 (RETURN)**
Double hatch area? <N>: **(RETURN)**
Select objects: **L (RETURN)**
1 found.
Select objects: **(RETURN)**
Command:

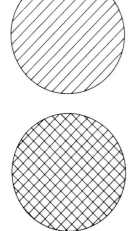

UNHATCH Examples

Your screen should look like the single hatch in UHATCH EXAMPLES.

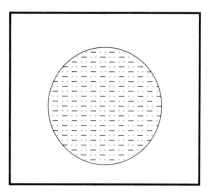

Mud Pattern

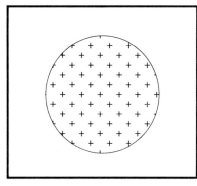

Cross Pattern

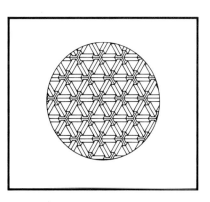

Escher Pattern

If you respond **Y** to **Double hatch area?**, you get the double hatch example shown in UHATCH EXAMPLES.

Rest for the Eyes

Let's look at some AutoCAD standard hatch patterns to wind up hatching:

```
                           REST  YOUR  EYES

Create a layer. Call it Scenery. Set it Current.
Turn all other layers Off.

Command: CIRCLE (RETURN)
3P/2P/TTR/<Center point>: 6,5 (RETURN)
Diameter/<Radius>: 3 (RETURN)
Command: HATCH (RETURN)
Pattern (? or name/U, style) <U>: (your choice here) (RETURN)
Scale for pattern <10.0000>: 1 (RETURN)
Angle for pattern <45>: 0 (RETURN)
Select objects: L (RETURN)
1 found.
Select objects: (RETURN)
Command:

If you are frustrated, try slinging mud on the screen with
the MUDST pattern.

If you require a little faith, try the CROSS pattern.

If you just want to give your eyes some respite from
AutoTown Drive, try the ESCHER pattern.

When you are through resting your eyes, END.

Command: END (RETURN)
```

Playing With LINETYPE

We have already seen that AutoCAD comes from the factory with eight standard linetypes. AutoCAD provides a mechanism for creating additional linetypes or playing around with the original ones.

The **LINETYPE** and **LTSCALE** commands give this capability. LINETYP and LTSCALE are found on the SETTINGS Menu. LINETYPE affects only LINES, ARCS, CIRCLES, and PLINES.

Every Linetype is made up of a pattern of short line segments or dots. You can control the overall length of these patterns with LTSCALE. You create your own patterns using LINETYP.

Using LTSCALE to Control Line Pattern Spacing

The LTSCALE command is straightforward. Each line pattern is defined to look good in a single unit length at LTSCALE = 1. By adjusting the LTSCALE you can condense or stretch the pattern.

Create a new layer to play with linetypes. Then get the LTSCALE command from the SETTINGS menu. Here's what a prompt sequence looks like:

```
Create a new layer called LINES. Set it On.
Turn all other layers Off.

Command: LTSCALE (RETURN)
New scale factor <1.0000>:
```

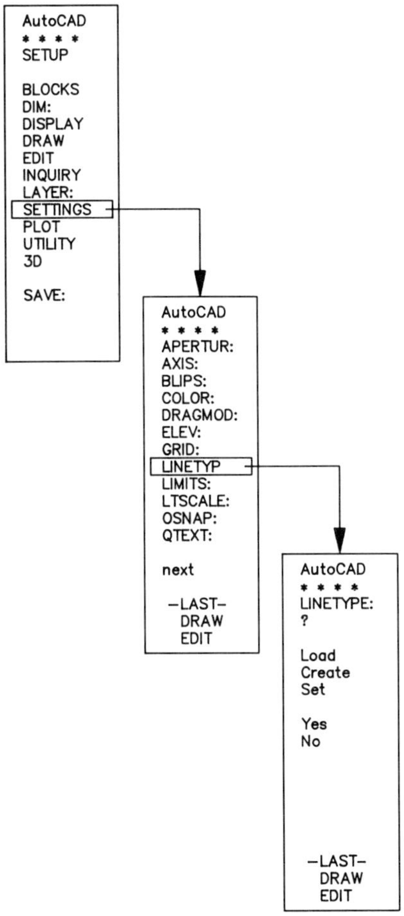

You simply put in a number other than 1 to change the LTSCALE.

The LTSCALE session shows how several of the standard linetypes look at different LTSCALEs:

LTSCALE

LTSCALE

```
Dashed
1   — — — — — — — — — — — — — — — — —
2   —  —  —  —  —  —  —  —  —  —  —  —
4   —   —   —   —   —   —   —   —

Dashdot
1   — . — . — . — . — . — . — . — . —
2   —  .  —  .  —  .  —  .  —  .  —  .
4   —   .   —   .   —   .   —

Divide
1   — . — . — . — . — . — . — . — . —
2   —  .  —  .  —  .  —  .  —  .  —  .
4   —   .    .    —    .    .    —
```

Creating Your Own Linetypes

The LINETYPE command allows you to define your own **dots and dashes** pattern and store that pattern away as a linetype. AutoCAD's standard line-types are stored in a file on your ACAD disc named **ACAD.LIN**. You can create your own files for linetypes. Here's how:

CREATING LINETYPES

```
Command: LINETYPE (RETURN)
?/Load/Create: C (RETURN)
Name of linetype to create: Myline (RETURN)
File for storage of linetype <ACAD>: Mylines (RETURN)
Creating new file
Descriptive text: Myline _____ ..... _____ ..... (RETURN)
Enter pattern (on next line):
```

Menu diagram (left margin):

```
AutoCAD
* * * *
SETUP

BLOCKS
DIM:
DISPLAY
DRAW
EDIT
INQUIRY
LAYER:
SETTINGS
PLOT
UTILITY
3D

SAVE:
```

```
AutoCAD
* * * *
APERTUR:
AXIS:
BLIPS:
COLOR:
DRAGMOD:
ELEV:
GRID:
LINETYP
LIMITS:
LTSCALE:
OSNAP:
QTEXT:

next

—LAST—
DRAW
EDIT
```

```
AutoCAD
* * * *
LINETYPE:
?

Load
Create
Set

Yes
No

—LAST—
DRAW
EDIT
```

ROOT to SETTINGS to LINETYP

```
      A, .4, -.1, 0, -.1, 0, -.1, 0, -.1, 0, -.1, 0, -.1   (RETURN)
New definition written to file.
?/Load/Create:   (RETURN)
Command:
```

Instead of **C** for create, you can get a listing of available linetypes with a **?**. The linetype FLIP SCREEN shows names and decriptive text for a **?** query.

This is what's going on in the linetype definition:

☐ Name of linetype to create. This is the name of the linetype you want to create.

☐ File for storage of linetype. This is the name of the disc file where the definition of the linetype will be stored. It is not a good idea to use **ACAD** because this is where AutoCAD's standard linetypes are. Think up your own names.

☐ Descriptive text. This is what you will see when you issue a **?** in response to the **?/Load/Create** prompt. It is a dot and dash represention of the linetype that shows on a FLIP (alphanumeric) screen. Just type **dashed — underscores_____** and **periods . . .** to get descriptive text.

☐ Enter pattern (on next line). Here AutoCAD is asking for the actual definition of the linetype. Here's how you make one:

  ☐ A positive number like **.4** gives the unit length of a **pen down** stroke — in other words, a length line that will appear as the first segment.

  ☐ A negative number like **−.1** gives the unit length of a **pen up** stroke — in other words the length of the blank space.

  ☐ A **0** is a dot.

  ☐ Separate values with commas.

Once you have stored one or more linetypes in a **name.lin** file, you can load these linetypes for use. After you do a number of drawings you may find that you build up a library of linetypes in a **name.lin** file. You can call these linetypes up for active duty with the Load option of the LINETYPE command:

LOADING A LINETYPE

Create a new file.

```
Command: LINETYPE (RETURN)
?/Load/Create: L (RETURN)
Name of linetype to load: Myline (RETURN)
File to search <ACAD>: Myline (RETURN)
Linetype MYLINE loaded.
?/Load/Create:   (RETURN)
Command:
```

```
File to list <ACAD>: (RETURN)

Linetypes defined in file A: ACAD.LIN:

   Name        Description
DASHED      _ _ _ _ _ _ _
HIDDEN      _ _ _ _ _ _ _ _
CENTER      ___ _ ___ _ ___
PHANTOM     ___ _ _ ___ _ _
DOT         . . . . . . . . . . .
DASHDOT     _ . _ . _ . _ .
BORDER      ___ ___ . ___ ___ .
DIVIDE      ___ . . ___ . . ___
CONTINUOUS  _____

?/Load/Create:
```

LINETYPE Flip Screen Shows Names and Descriptive Text

```
Replace CONTINUOUS with MYLINE.

Command: LAYER (RETURN)
?/Make/Set/New/On/Off/Color/Ltype/Freeze/Thaw: L (RETURN)
Linetype (or ?) <CONTINUOUS>: Myline (RETURN)
Layer name(s) for Linetype MYLINE <0>: (RETURN)
?/Make/Set/New/On/Off/Color/Ltype/Freeze/Thaw: (RETURN)
Command:

Take a look at it.

Command: CIRCLE (RETURN)
3P/2P/TTR/<Center point>: 6,5 (RETURN)
Diameter/<Radius>: 3 (RETURN)
Command:

When you are done playing around with linetypes,
END the file.

Command: END (RETURN)
```

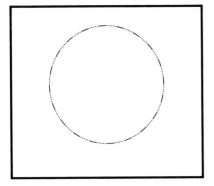

Rest Your Eyes with Myline

You can create and store as many linetypes as you desire. If you use the Set option of the LINETYPE Command to set MYLINE Current instead of BYLAYER, all **new** entities will be drawn with MYLINE, overriding the layer default Linetype.

Creating HATCH Patterns

AutoCAD provides a mechanism for creating your own hatch patterns in a fashion similar to linetype creation. Hatch patterns are more complex — creation is not covered in this tutorial, but can be found in the AutoCAD User Reference. There you can also get more information about hatching donuts and holes.

A SOLID IS A POLYGON FILLED WITH INK

It's that simple, using **SOLID** is a way to create a polygon that is filled with ink. In AutoCAD, a SOLID is a 2-dimensional boundary filled with color.

Creating Solids

The SOLID command allows you to create a solid **filled** area. This area is defined by three or four points forming either a triangular or quadrilateral shape. More complex shapes can be constructed by **continuing**—adding more vertices.

The order in which you enter solid vertices, and the spatial relationship between these points, determines what the solid will look like. You have to be careful not to get a **Bow Tie** shape from four points when you really want a quadrilateral. Nine times out of ten, users first create bowties and butterflies instead of quadrilaterals.

Here's how a few solid prompt sequences look. The drawings that might be created as a result of these sequences are shown in the SOLID SHAPE EXAMPLES.

205

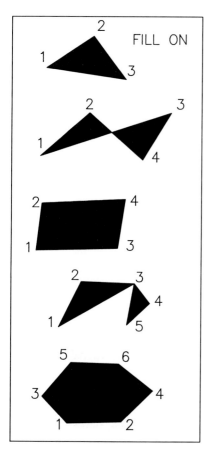

FILL ON

*Solid Polygons Come in all Shapes
and Sizes*

If you want to play around with solids, begin a NEW drawing file for practice and try the following examples and a few of your own:

SOLID SHAPE EXAMPLES

Begin a NEW drawing named **Bowties**

Leave default settings for UNITS and LIMITS.

3-Points creates a triangle

```
Command: SOLID (RETURN)
First point:        (pick a point)
Second point:       (pick a point)
Third point:        (pick a point)
Fourth point: (RETURN)
Third point: (RETURN)
Command:
```

(RETURN) if you want to skip the fourth point)

4-Points, creates a quadrilateral or a Bowtie

```
Command: SOLID (RETURN)
First point:        (pick a point)
Second point:       (pick a point)
Third point:        (pick a point)
Fourth point:       (pick a point)
Third point: (RETURN)
Command:
```

5-Points, creates two adjacent triangles (sharing a single vertex) or two overlapping triangles (sharing a single vertex). See what else you can make with five points or more.

```
Command: SOLID (RETURN)
First point:        (pick a point)
Second point:       (pick a point)
Third point:        (pick a point)
Fourth point: (RETURN)
Third point:        (pick a point)
Fourth point:       (pick a point)
Third point: (RETURN)
Command:
```

It may be easier to get a handle on the spatial relationships between your vertices if you turn FILL off. REGEN, when you turn it OFF or back ON, to see the hollow or filled Solids.

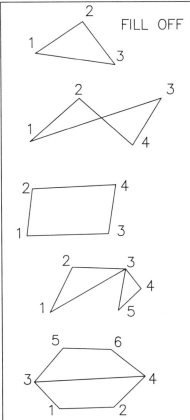

Fill Off

FILL 'er Up!

FILL temporarily reduces solids, wide polylines, donuts, and traces to their boundary. When FILL is **ON**, solids and traces are **filled in** or shaded on the screen and at plotting time. When FILL is **OFF**, solids and traces appear as single-line outlines of their shapes.

You will notice the **FILL ON** and **FILL OFF** keys on the SOLID screen menu. FILL is a toggle—it is either on or off. You can use the screen menu to pick either setting. Here's the prompt sequence for FILL:

```
Command: FILL (RETURN)
ON/OFF <current setting>: OFF (RETURN)

Put away your bowties.

Command: REGEN (RETURN)

Command: END (RETURN)
```

A TITLE BLOCK EXAMPLE

In the next Chapter you are going to begin plotting out drawings on sheets of paper. To give these drawings a proper look, you need a Title Block. Here's a simple one that you can use.

Title BLOCK

TITLE BLOCK EXAMPLE

Begin a NEW drawing named **Titleblk**

Set LIMITS to -1,-1 and 37,25

Set UNITS to ENGINEERING with two decimals all around

Set GRID to 1. Set SNAP to 1

ZOOM All

1. PLINE the boundary

```
Command: PLINE (RETURN)
From point: 0,0 (RETURN)
Current line-width is 0'-0.00"
Arc/Close/Halfwidth/Length/Undo/Width/<Endpoint of line>:
Width (RETURN)
Starting width<0'-00">: .0625 (RETURN)
Ending width<0'-0.06">: (RETURN)
Arc/Close/Halfwidth/Length/Undo/Width/<Endpoint of line>:
  36,0 (RETURN)
Arc/Close/Halfwidth/Length/Undo/Width/<Endpoint of line>:
  36,24 (RETURN)
Arc/Close/Halfwidth/Length/Undo/Width/<Endpoint of line>:
  0,24 (RETURN)
Arc/Close/Halfwidth/Length/Undo/Width/<Endpoint of line>:
  C (RETURN)
Command:
```

2. Set up the Title Area lines

```
Command: LINE (RETURN)
From point: 31,0 (RETURN)
To point: 31,24 (RETURN)
To point: (RETURN)
Command:
Command: (RETURN)    (Try SPACE or (RETURN) to restart LINE.)
LINE From point: 31,7 (RETURN)
To point: 36,7 (RETURN)
To point: (RETURN)
Command: (RETURN)
LINE From point: 31,6 (RETURN)
To point: 36,6 (RETURN)
To point: (RETURN)
Command: (RETURN)
LINE From point: 31,5 (RETURN)
To point: 36,5 (RETURN)
To point: (RETURN)
Command: (RETURN)
LINE From point: 31,4 (RETURN)
To point: 36,4 (RETURN)
To point: (RETURN)
Command: (RETURN)
LINE From point: 31,3 (RETURN)
To point: 36,3 (RETURN)
To point: (RETURN)
Command:
```

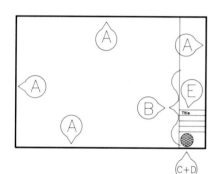

Title Block Construction Sequence

3. Create the Logo boundary

```
Command: CIRCLE (RETURN)
3P/2P/TTR/<Center point>: 32.5,1.5 (RETURN)
Diameter/<Radius>: 1.2 (RETURN)
Command:
```

4. Fill in the Logo

```
Command: HATCH (RETURN)
Pattern (? or name/U,style): Hex (RETURN)
Scale for pattern <1.0000>: (RETURN)
Angle for pattern <0>: (RETURN)
Select objects: L (RETURN)
1 found.
```

```
Select objects: (RETURN)
Command:
```

5. Fill in Your Own Title

```
Command: DTEXT (RETURN)
Start point or Align/Center/Fit/Middle/Right/Style:
  31.5,6.2 (RETURN)
Height: .5 (RETURN)
Rotation angle <0>: (RETURN)
Text: (Give Your Title Here with < 10 characters) (RETURN)
Text: (RETURN)
Command:
Save the Title Block for plotting.
```

Command: **END** **(RETURN)**

TITLE BLOCK

SUMMING UP AND TIPS

AutoCAD provides nearly limitless possibilities for creating fancy drawings. This Chapter covers the essentials. We can only invite you to experiment with the many options you will encounter in each drawing enhancement command.

Here are some parting tips:

DRAWING ENHANCEMENT TIPS

☐ Hatching Tips.

　☐ AutoCAD needs a fully closed boundary for hatching.

　☐ You need to identify objects within objects (**donut holes**) with Window or OSNAP when you define the hatch boundary.

　☐ Use PLINE to create closed continuous boundaries for hatching.

　☐ If you already have individual LINEs or PLINEs bounding an area, use PEDIT to join them to get a continuous boundary.

　☐ A Control-C (^C) will terminate hatching in progress. What you have already drawn will remain in the drawing file.

☐ Standard AutoCAD patterns are unit scale and usually require further scaling for use. Don't use *HATCH until you know what scale will work.

☐ An ERASE Last or **U**ndo will get rid of hatch patterns as a block. An Undo will undo a *HATCH

☐ HATCH U is handy when you just want a quick shade.

☐ Here are some tips for linetypes.

☐ Like replacement of blocks and styles, loading a new definition of an existing linetype will cause a REGEN and replace old linetypes with new.

☐ Use a good descriptive name to label any linetype you create so that later you can figure out what it is.

☐ If your lines "draw" very slow, or if all of your lines look solid no matter which linetype you are using, you may need to adjust LTSCALE.

☐ You can think ahead about the sequence for entering SOLID vertices. But we bet you'll get a bowtie anyway!

☐ You can take advantage of the bevel edge in TRACE to get angled ends for fat lines. Otherwise, you will find PLINE superior to TRACE for most purposes.

☐ Be careful with SKETCH. It's fun to play around with, but before you turn the pointer over to your kids, make sure you understand your disc capacity limitations. Use it with a large increment, SKPLOY = 1, and Curve Fit with PEDIT for smooth efficient curves.

If you have been doing all the exercises in this book, you now have ten or more full drawing files on disc (AutoTown, Bowties, Chapter1, Chapter2, Envelope, Mockup, Titleblk, Uplay, Widget, and Widgedit) and a few separate WBLOCKS and linetypes. You can call them up on the screen, but what good are they if you can't carry them around to show them off?

Let's learn how to plot.

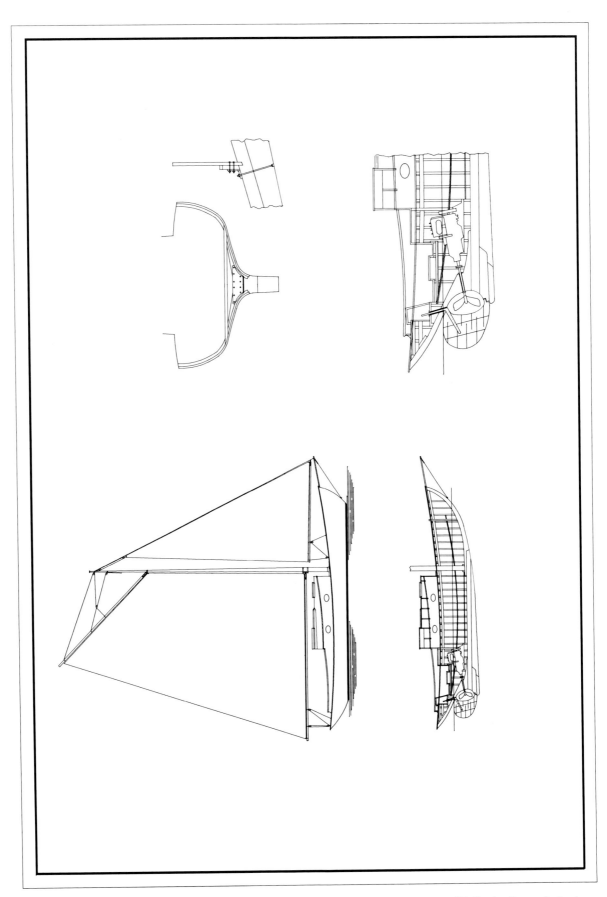

Sailboat Drawn with AutoCAD (Courtesy of Palisades Research, Inc.)

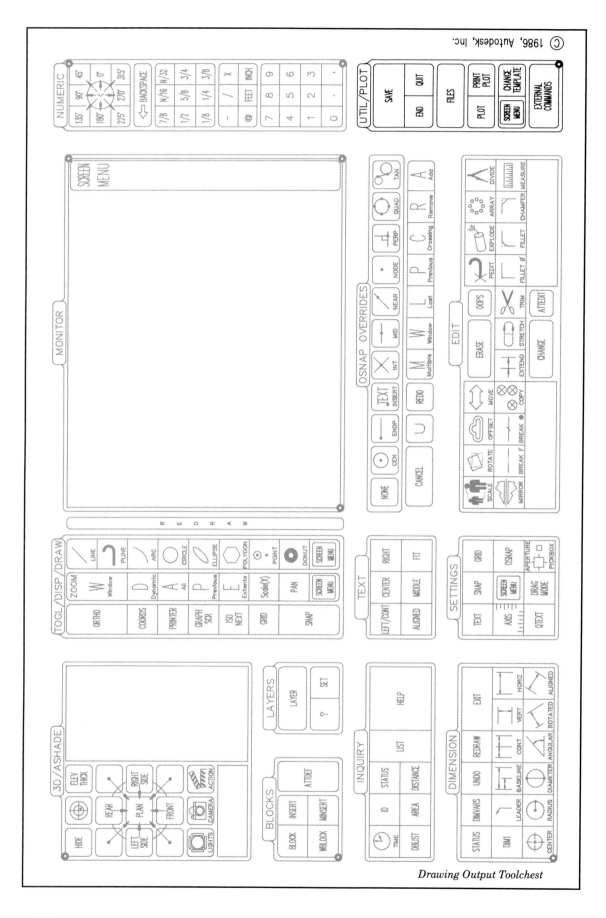

Drawing Output Toolchest

CHAPTER 8

DRAWING OUTPUT

The Steps from Disc to Plotter. Drawing Output Toolchest. Getting Ready. Plot AutoTown Drive. The Logic Behind Plotting. Setting the Plotting Scale. Changing the Plotting Area. Changing Physical Plotting Parameters— Plotter Linetype. Plotting in Color. ▶ Titles, Setups and Regular Formats. Creating Detail or Multiple Sheet Drawing. ▶ Summing Up—Tips for Plotting.

THE STEPS FROM DISC TO PLOTTER

As you create a drawing file, AutoCAD stores your drawing information in a compacted form. A line is stored as two endpoints. A circle becomes a center point and radius. A PLINE is stored as vertices with tangent, curve, and width information. When it is time to make a picture, AutoCAD translates this cryptic compact code into visible images that make sense to you.

Each time AutoCAD displays a screen or makes a plot, this translation process occurs. In order to make a plot, AutoCAD takes the drawing information out of its database, turns it into plot instructions, and scales the drawing to fit the plotter paper size.

The information flow from disc to plotter is shown in the DISC-TO-PLOT INFORMATION FLOW DIAGRAM.

As you can see from the diagram, a lot of **Getting Ready** occurs well before a plotter begins to draw an image on paper. You have to compose what will go into the final image. You have to make sure the plot parameters are correctly set. You have to physically get the plotter ready for action.

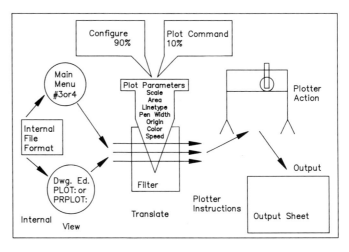

Disc-to-Plot Information Flow Diagram

When you install AutoCAD on your computer, you automatically set up the flow shown in the PLOT FLOW DIAGRAM. You set 90% of the flow controls for your plot translation when you configure your system by telling AutoCAD what type of plotter you have. If you have not already configured your plotter, you should do so now using the setup guide in Appendix C.

When you're ready to plot, creating a paper hardcopy from the drawing file, AutoCAD wants to know such details as how to handle scale, color, layers, plotter linestyles, and pen speed. These plot parameters can be changed for most plotters.

For discussion, this Book uses a Houston Instrument (HI) Model DMP 52 pen plotter. This is a single pen plotter which plots on **D** size paper (36″ × 24″) with an approximate maximum image size of 34″ × 21.5″.

A NOTE ABOUT DEFAULT PLOTTER SETUP

This Book assumes that this Chapter is the first time your AutoCAD installation and configuration will be used for plotting. This means that the Book assumes certain default settings for plotter pen assignment, pen speed, and plotter linetypes.

If your AutoCAD installation has been used for plotting before now, there is a good chance that some of these default settings shown in this Chapter will be different. If this is the case and you wish to follow the exercises, you should reconfigure your plotter parameters. Use Main Menu Task 5, and specify you want a new plotter configuration. Then select your plotter and take all the defaults for prompts.

AutoCAD can also produce drawings on printer plotters—like dot matrix and laser printers. The discussion in this Chapter is generic for all plotting device-types, printer plotters or pen plotters, with the exception of plot parameters specific to the DMP 52. You use virtually the same setup and run features to get images from the drawing file to another pen plotter or a printer plotter.

Wherever you see pen **PLOT** command sequence, you can substitute an equivalent printer plotter **PRPLOT** sequence.

DRAWING OUTPUT TOOLCHEST

Drawing output commands can be found at the Main Menu Level or from within the drawing editor on the ROOTMENU. The Tablet Menu Commands are shown in the DRAWING OUTPUT TOOLCHEST at the start of the Chapter.

GETTING READY

You get ready for plotting in two stages—readying the plotter for action; and readying your drawing file with AutoCAD. Readying the plotter requires a one-time internal plotter setup and a once-a-plot setup of the paper and pen.

Getting The Plotter Ready

Here's a checklist for getting the plotter ready:

PLOTTER READY CHECKLIST

☐ First Time Check.

   ☐ Is the plotter plugged in and turned on?

   ☐ Is the plotter data cable plugged into the computer port? If you use the same port for your digitizer, make sure you've switched data cables from digitizer to plotter.

   ☐ Is the paper movement path clear? No obstacles?

   ☐ Are the internal plotter settings correct? (To check these settings for the HI DMP 52, see the list labelled CHECKING THE DMP 52 INTERNAL PLOTTER SETTINGS in Appendix C.)

   ☐ Run the plotter self-test. Does the example drawing look okay? Any pen skips? Paper misalignments? (To run the plotter self-test for the HI DMP 52, see the list labelled RUNNING THE HI DMP SELF-TEST in Appendix C.)

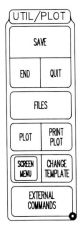

Tablet PLOT Commands

PLOT AutoTOWN DRIVE

AutoCAD's **PLOT** or **PRPLOT** Commands are where you set your drawing scale and other drawing parameters. There are several ways to initiate plotting: Using the PLOT command from the ROOTMENU typing PLOT or PRPLOT; using the Tablet Menu; or selecting options **3** or **4** from the Main Menu.

Plotting a Whole Drawing File

We'll use the AutoTOWN SUBDIVISION DRAWING as a sample file for plotting. You saved this file on disc as **AUTOTOWN**. If you didn't save the file, you can use any file that you think will work, and follow along with the explanations and examples.

Getting the AutoTown Drawing to Fit the Maximum Plotting Area

Select option number **3 Plot a drawing** from the Main Menu:

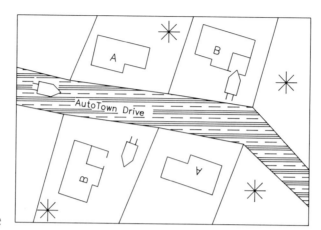

AutoTOWN First Plot

WHOLE FILE PLOT EXAMPLE

Main Menu

0. Exit AutoCAD
1. Begin a NEW drawing
2. Edit an EXISTING drawing
3. Plot a drawing
4. Printer plot a drawing

5. Configure AutoCAD
6. File Utilities
7. Compile shape/font description file
8. Convert old drawing file

Enter selection: **3 (RETURN)**

Enter NAME of drawing <default>: **AUTOTOWN (RETURN)**

Specify the part of the drawing to be plotted by entering:
Display, Extents, Limits, View, or Window <L>: **E (RETURN)**

Plot will NOT be written to a selected file
Sizes are in Inches
Plot origin is at (0.00,0.00)
Plotting area is 34.00 wide by 21.50 (MAX size)
Plot is NOT rotated 90 degrees
Pen width is 0.010
Area fill will NOT be adjusted for pen width
Hidden lines will NOT be removed
Plot will be scaled to fit available area

Do you want to change anything? <N> **(RETURN)**
Effective plotting area: 30.54 wide by 21.50 high
Press RETURN to continue or S to Stop for hardware setup

(Set up a sheet of paper in the plotter.
 Make sure your plotter is ready, then hit (RETURN).)

(RETURN)

```
Processing vector: nn        (cycles through all vectors)

Install pen number 1, color 7 (white)
Press RETURN to continue:  (RETURN)

(Plotting takes place.)

Plot complete.
Press RETURN to continue:

(RETURN)

(Main Menu reappears.)
```

Take your first plot out of the plotter and show it off. When you get done parading around the office, reset the plotter and put in another sheet of paper for the next example.

THE LOGIC BEHIND PLOTTING

In the plot you just completed, AutoCAD used all <default> plotter parameters to set up the plotter, viewing area, and scale. These <defaults> were set up at the time AutoCAD was configured.

Here are the four key steps you have to go through every time you set up a plot:

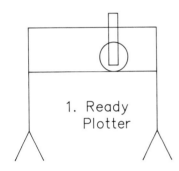

1. Ready Plotter

FOUR STEPS TO PLOTTING

☐ **Ready the Plotter.** You have already done this: turning the plotter on, running the self-test, and aligning the paper and pen. Use the PLOTTER READY CHECKLIST as a handy reminder.

☐ **Size the Plotting Area.** Pick the size of the paper area for the plot. This can be any size you specify, making use of part or all of the plotting paper. The lower left corner of the plot will be placed at the **plot origin**

☐ **Pick the Part of the Drawing to Plot.** You can pick all or part of the drawing you want to plot by specifying the part the same way you specify ZOOM. You have the choice of plotting just the screen display (whatever magnification), drawing extents or limits, a named view, or a window you specify.

☐ **Set Up the Plot Scale.** You can set up the scale relation between your drawing view and your plotting area by using AutoCAD's **Fit** which fills the plotting area with the largest view that fits inside the area. Or you can specify scale with by setting the Number of plotting units = Number of drawing units.

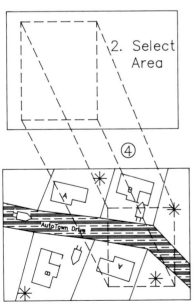

2. Select Area

3. Select View

4. Establish Scale

Four Steps to Plotting

Of course, you can use AutoCAD <default>s for all these settings except for physically readying the plotter. When you configure the plotter for use with AutoCAD, you set up <default> plotting parameters for plotting area, view, and scale, as well as physical plotting parameters like pen speed and linetype. Occasionally, you may want to change these physical settings.

As a fifth step you can change:

☐ Plot origin, plot rotation, plotter pen width, pen speed, and linetype parameters.

Unless you specifically change the settings for the plotter, AutoCAD assumes the setup parameters from your previous plot or your configuration setup. For the HI DMP 52, these are:

SAMPLE AutoCAD DEFAULT PLOT ASSUMPTIONS

☐ DMP Model 52.

☐ Change pens while plotting—YES. If color pens are selected, we WILL change pens while plotting. (If this was set NOT to change pens, all colors in the drawing file would be drawn with whatever color pen is in the plotter pen holder.)

☐ The plotter is calibrated.

☐ Plots are written to the plotter, NOT to a disc file.

☐ Plotting units are measured in Inches.

☐ Plot origin (in inches) is at 0.00,0.00.

☐ Plot size (in inches) is the MAXimum size, 34.00,21.50.

☐ 2D plots are plotted normally, NOT rotated 90 degrees.

☐ The pen width (in inches) is 0.010.

☐ Area fill boundaries are NOT adjusted for pen width.

☐ Hidden lines are NOT removed. (This only applies to 3-D views.)

☐ Scale is to Fit the MAXimum plotting area.

AutoCAD stores these plotting parameters in a file created at configuration.

You have the option of changing any of these parameters by answering **Y** to the plot change prompt:

```
Do you want to change anything? <N>:
```

AutoCAD provides this prompt for each plot. If you make changes, AutoCAD will store your new settings as <defaults> in the configuration file for your next plot.

In the first AutoTOWN DRIVE plot, you did not have to change any <default>s since the drawing was sized to **Fit** the MAXimum plotting area.

Plotting Exercises

Plotting requires some trial and error until you arrive at plot settings that fulfill your needs. In the rest of the Chapter, we will set out some plotting examples for you to tailor the plot parameters to get different types of plots.

The examples are to:

☐ Plot AutoTown Drive at 1 drawing file unit = 1/2- plotting-inch.

☐ Plot the AutoTown View (saved as ROADTURN) to **Fit** an 8 1/2″ × 11″ sheet.

☐ Plot the same ROADTURN View on an 8 1/2″ × 11″ printer plotter (dot matrix plotter).

☐ Change plotter parameters to use a plotter Line Type to represent the AutoTown colored layer BOUNDARY.

☐ Plot the Widget Drawing in color by layer.

☐ Place a standard title block on the Widget drawing and plot it at maximum size.

☐ Place two small **detail** drawings on a single plotting sheet by adjusting their plot origins.

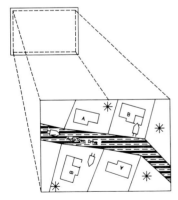

Setting the Plot Scale
(MAX Fit of AutoTOWN Plot)

SETTING THE PLOTTING SCALE

In your first plot, you used the <default> **Fit** to plot the entire drawing in the <default> MAXimum plotting area. Here's how AutoCAD determined how big to make the drawing. Using AutoTown's drawing Extents of 49 units in X, and 34.5 units in Y, AutoCAD determined the best **Fit** scale:

☐ MAX plot width: **Q.** How many times does 49 units go into 34″ ? **A.** 0.694 times.

☐ MAX plot height: **Q.** How many times does 34.5 units go into 21.50″ ? **A.** 0.623 times.

☐ MAX scale factor: **Q.** Which scale factor is smaller? **A.** Y scale of 0.623.

☐ AutoCAD sets plot size to: $0.623″ × 49 = 30.54$ Wide by $0.623″ × 34.5 = 21.50$. High.

AutoCAD shows you these calculation results during plot preparation. FIT MAXIMUM SCALE pictorially shows how AutoCAD **Fits** this 49 × 34.5 unit drawing into a 30.54 × 21.5 plot on a 34.00″ × 21.50″ size drawing area.

Setting the Scale

In many cases, getting the MAXimum plot size is not what you want. Usually you have a specific scale in mind for the final plotted drawing. Examples of some specific scales are:

EXAMPLES OF SPECIFIC PLOTTING SCALES

DRAWING TYPE	LIMITS Lower left: Upper right:	PLOTTED SCALE	PLOT DIMENSIONS
Electronic Schematic in millimeters	0.00,0.00 400.00,300.00	1:1	400 X 300 mm*
Piping Schematic "D" size drawing	0.00",0.00" 3'0.00",2'0.00"	MAX to 1:1	36 X 24* inches
Mechanical in metric	0.000,0.000 100.000,75.000	10:1	10 X 7.5 cm*
Mechanical in English	0.000",0.000" 22.000",1'10.000"	1:1	22 X 22* inches
Architectural large buildings	0' ,0' 120',80'	1/4"=1'	30 X 20* inches

*If the plot dimensions exceed the plotter's currently selected or maximum plot area the portion of the plot beyond the plot area will be **clipped** and not plotted.

To set your own scale, you must not let AutoCAD go through its MAX Fit <default> calculations. Instead, you set the **scale** function in response to AutoCAD's prompts:

```
Specify scale by entering:
Plotted units = Drawing units or Fit or ? <Fit>:
```

To specify scale, you simply type the number of output (plotter) units you want equal to one drawing file unit. Here are some examples:

Plotter Units	=	Drawing File Units
0.25		12
1/4"		1'
1 (cm)		0.254 (inches)
1 (mm)		1 (mm)

Plotting AutoTown Drive by Changing Scales

Let's plot AutoTown Drive at 1 drawing file unit = 1/2-plotting-inch.

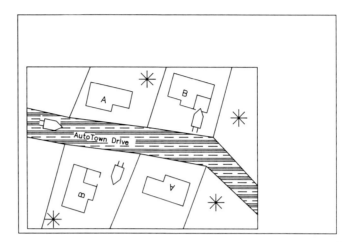

AutoTOWN Plotted = 1/2 Plotting Inch

SETTING PLOTTING SCALE

Select 3 from the Main Menu.

Enter Selection: **3 (RETURN)**

Enter NAME of drawing <AUTOTOWN>: **(RETURN)**

Specify the part of the drawing to be plotted by entering:
Display, Extents, Limits, View, or Window <E>: **E (RETURN)**

Plot will NOT be written to a selected file
Sizes are in Inches
Plot origin is at (0.00,0.00)
Plotting area is 34.00 wide by 21.50 (MAX size)
Plot is NOT rotated 90 degrees
Pen width is 0.010
Area fill will NOT be adjusted for pen width
Hidden lines will NOT be removed
Plot will be scaled to fit available area

Do you want to change anything? <N> **Y (RETURN)**

(AutoCAD displays the current settings for plot parameters.)

Entity Color	Pen No.	Line Type	Pen Speed	Layer Color	Pen No.	Line Type	Pen Speed
1 (red)	1	0	16	9	1	0	16
2 (yellow)	1	0	16	10	1	0	16
3 (green)	1	0	16	11	1	0	16
4 (cyan)	1	0	16	12	1	0	16
5 (blue)	1	0	16	13	1	0	16
6 (magenta)	1	0	16	14	1	0	16
7 (white)	1	0	16	15	1	0	16
8	1	0	16				

```
Line types: 0 = continuous line          Pen speed codes:
            1 = . . . . . . . . . . . . . . . . . .
            2 = .  .  .  .  .  .  .  .  .  .       Inches/Second:
            3 = - - - - - - - - - - - - - - - - - -    1, 2, 4, 8, 16
            4 = -  -  -  -  -  -  -  -  -  -
            5 = --  --  --  --  --  --  --  -      Cm/Second:
            6 = ---  ---  ---  ---  ---              3, 5, 10, 20, 40
            7 = --  -  --  -  --  -  --  -
            8 = __--__--__--__--__-
```

Enter line types, pen speed codes
   blank=go to next, Cn=go to Color n,
   S=Show current choices, X=Exit
Do you want to change any of the above parameters? <N>
   N (RETURN)

Write the plot to a file? <N> **(RETURN)**
Size units (Inches or Millimeters) <I>: **(RETURN)**
Plot origin in Inches <0.00,0.00>: **(RETURN)**

Standard values for plotting size

Size	Width	Height
A	10.50	8.00
B	16.00	10.00
C	21.00	16.00
D	33.00	21.00
MAX	34.00	21.50

Enter the Size or Width,Height (in Inches) <MAX>: **(RETURN)**

Rotate 2D plots 90 degrees clockwise? <N>: **(RETURN)**
Pen width <0.010>: **(RETURN)**
Adjust area fill boundaries for pen width? <N> **(RETURN)**
Remove hidden lines? <N> **(RETURN)**

Specify scale by entering:
Plotted Inches = Drawing Units or Fit or ? <F>: **.5=1 (RETURN)**

Effective plotting area: 24.50 wide by 17.25 high
Position paper in plotter.
Press RETURN to continue or S to Stop for hardware setup
   S (RETURN)
Do hardware setup now.
Press RETURN to continue:

(Check plotter readiness and hit (RETURN).)
   (RETURN)

Processing vector: nn   (AutoCAD cycles through whole drawing)

Install pen number 1, color 7 (white)
Press RETURN to continue: **(RETURN)**

(Plotting takes place.)

Plot complete.
Press RETURN to continue:

(To get back to the Main Menu hit (RETURN).)
   (RETURN)

CHANGING THE PLOTTING AREA

In the previous example, notice one of the parameters you can change is the plotting area. You can select how big you want your final drawing to be—independent of its View size.

Take the View of AutoTown, saved as ROADTURN and **Fit** it to an 8 1/2″ × 11″, "A" size plotting sheet, with a plotting area of 10.50″ × 8.00″, to leave some border room around the drawing.

SETTING THE PLOTTING AREA TO FIT A NAMED VIEW

```
Select 3 from the Main Menu.

Enter Selection: 3 (RETURN)

Enter NAME of drawing <default AUTOTOWN>:  (RETURN)

Specify the part of the drawing to be plotted by entering:
Display, Extents, Limits, View, or Window <E>:
   V (RETURN)
View name: Roadturn (RETURN)

Plot will NOT be written to a selected file
Sizes are in Inches
Plot origin is at (0.00,0.00)
Plotting area is 34.00 wide by 21.50 (MAX size)
Plot is NOT rotated 90 degrees
Pen width is 0.010
Area fill will NOT be adjusted for pen width
Hidden lines will NOT be removed
Scale is 0.5=1

Do you want to change anything?  <N> Y (RETURN)

(AutoCAD displays the current settings for plot parameters.)
```

Layer Color	Pen No.	Line Type	Pen Speed	Layer Color	Pen No.	Line Type	Pen Speed
1 (red)	1	0	16	9	1	0	16
2 (yellow)	1	0	16	10	1	0	16
3 (green)	1	0	16	11	1	0	16
4 (cyan)	1	0	16	12	1	0	16
5 (blue)	1	0	16	13	1	0	16
6 (magenta)	1	0	16	14	1	0	16
7 (white)	1	0	16	15	1	0	16
8	1	0	16				

```
Line types: 0 = continuous line        Pen speed codes:
            1 = . . . . . . . . . . . . . . . . .
            2 = .  .  .  .  .  .  .  .  .        Inches/Second:
            3 = -------------------                 1, 2, 4, 8, 16
            4 = -  -  -  -  -  -  -  -
            5 = -- -- -- -- -- -- -- -          Cm/Second:
            6 = --- --- --- --- ---                 3, 5, 10, 20, 40
            7 = -- - -- - -- - -- -
            8 = __ -- __ -- __ -- __ --__ -
```

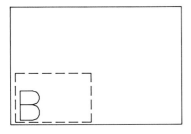
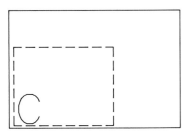
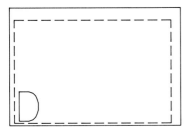

Plotting Areas A—D and MAX

```
Enter line types, pen speed codes
   blank=go to next, Cn=go to Color n,
   S=Show current choices, X=Exit
Do you want to change any of the above parameters? <N>
   N (RETURN)

Write the plot to a file? <N> N (RETURN)
Size units (Inches or Millimeters) <I>: (RETURN)
Plot origin in Inches <0.00,0.00>: (RETURN)

Standard values for plotting size

Size           Width            Height

A              10.50             8.00
B              16.00            10.00
C              21.00            16.00
D              33.00            21.00
MAX            34.00            21.50

Enter the Size or Width,Height (in Inches) <MAX>:
   A (RETURN)

Rotate 2D plots 90 degrees clockwise? <N>: (RETURN)
Pen width <0.010>: (RETURN)
Adjust area fill boundaries for pen width? <N> (RETURN)
Remove hidden lines? <N> (RETURN)

Specify scale by entering:
Plotted Inches = Drawing Units or Fit or ? <0.5=1>: Fit
(RETURN)

Effective plotting area: 10.50 wide by 7.56 high
Position paper in plotter.
Press RETURN to continue or S to Stop for hardware setup
   S (RETURN)
Do hardware setup now.
Press RETURN to continue:

(Check plotter readiness and hit (RETURN).)
   (RETURN)
```

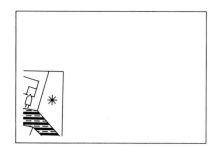

AutoTOWN "ROADTURN" Detail

```
Processing vector: nn     (AutoCAD cycles through whole drawing)

Install pen number 1, color 7 (white)
Press RETURN to continue: (RETURN)

(Plotting takes place.)

Plot complete.
Press RETURN to continue:

(To get back to the Main Menu hit (RETURN).)
   (RETURN)
```

Generating a PRPLOT of the Roadturn Detail

Let's try a printer plot of the same Roadturn Detail that we just plotted on the pen plotter. Since the printer plotter is a simpler device, the prompts for printer plotting are simplified.

Here goes:

PRPLOT OF ROADTURN DETAIL

Select **4. Printer Plot a drawing** from the Main Menu.

Enter Selection: **4 (RETURN)**

Enter NAME of drawing <default AUTOTOWN>: **(RETURN)**

Specify the part of the drawing to be plotted by entering:
Display, Extents, Limits, View, or Window <D>: **V (RETURN)**
View name: **Roadturn (RETURN)**

Plot will NOT be written to a selected file
Sizes are in Inches
Plot origin is at (0.00,0.00)
Plotting area is 8.00 wide by 11.00 (MAX size)
2D Plots are rotated 90 degrees clockwise
Hidden lines will NOT be removed
Scale is 1=1

Do you want to change anything? <N> **Y (RETURN)**
Write the plot to a file? <N> **(RETURN)**
Size units (Inches or Millimeters) <I>: **(RETURN)**
Plot origin in Inches <0.00,0.00>:

Standard values for plotting size

Size   Width   Height
MAX   8.00   11.00

Enter the Size or Width,Height (in Inches) <MAX>: **(RETURN)**
Rotate 2D plots 90 degrees clockwise? <Y> **(RETURN)**
Remove hidden lines? <N> **(RETURN)**

Specify scale by entering:
Plotted Inches=Drawing Units or Fit or ? <1=1>: **Fit (RETURN)**
Effective plotting area: 7.92 wide by 11.00 high
Position paper in printer.
Press RETURN to continued:

Processing vector: nn   (AutoCAD cycles through the drawing)

Printer Plot complete.

Press RETURN to continue: **(RETURN)**

(Main Menu appears)

CHANGING PHYSICAL PLOTTING PARAMETERS—PLOTTER LINE TYPE

So far the plots you have created have ignored layer and entity colors originally set up in the drawing file. Recall that AutoTown's outer boundary was set in blue on a layer named BOUNDARY and that the paving (cross hatching) was set on a layer named SHADING in a color of your choice.

You can do two things with layer and entity color—assign a pen number to that color to plot a different color or a different line weight; and/or assign a plotter line type to that color. In this exercise you will use the same pen, but assign a different line type to represent the blue color. In the next exercise, you will use a different color pen for each layer color.

Do not confuse plotting Line Types with AutoCAD's drawing layer or entity LINETYPE. A **Line Type** is a line pattern created by the **plotter**.

The HI DMP plotter supports several different Line Types. So far we have simply assigned all layer colors to Pen No. 1 with a DMP Line Type of **0 = . CONTINUOUS**. Now, let's assign the color blue to Pen No. 1 with a DMP Line Type of **5 = Dashes**.

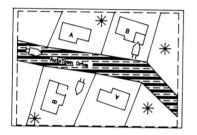

AutoTOWN with Dashed Boundaries

Changing the Plotter Line Type to Represent the AutoTown Colored Layer Boundary

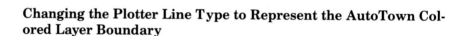

CHANGING LAYER COLOR INTO A PLOTTER LINE TYPE

Select 3 from the Main Menu.

Enter Selection: **3 (RETURN)**

Enter NAME of drawing <default AUTOTOWN>: **(RETURN)**

Specify the part of the drawing to be plotted by entering:
Display, Extents, Limits, View, or Window <V>: **E (RETURN)**

Plot will NOT be written to a selected file
Sizes are in Inches
Plot origin is at (0.00,0.00)
Plotting area is 10.50 wide by 8.00 (A size)
Plot is NOT rotated 90 degrees
Pen width is 0.010
Area fill will NOT be adjusted for pen width
Hidden lines will NOT be removed
Plot will be scaled to fit available area

Do you want to change anything? <N> **Y (RETURN)**

(AutoCAD displays the current settings for plot parameters.)

Entity Color	Pen No.	Line Type	Pen Speed	Layer Color	Pen No.	Line Type	Pen Speed
1 (red)	1	0	16	9	1	0	16
2 (yellow)	1	0	16	10	1	0	16
3 (green)	1	0	16	11	1	0	16
4 (cyan)	1	0	16	12	1	0	16
5 (blue)	1	0	16	13	1	0	16
6 (magenta)	1	0	16	14	1	0	16
7 (white)	1	0	16	15	1	0	16
8	1	0	16				

```
Line types:  0 = continuous line          Pen speed codes:
             1 = ...................
             2 = . . . . . . . . . .        Inches/Second:
             3 = -------------------           1, 2, 4, 8, 16
             4 = - - - - - - - - - -
             5 = -- -- -- -- -- -- -        Cm/Second:
             6 = --- --- --- --- ---           3, 5, 10, 20, 40
             7 = -- - -- - -- - -- -
             8 = __--__--__--__--_-
```

Enter line types, pen speed codes
   blank=go to next, Cn=go to Color n,
   S=Show current choices, X=Exit
Do you want to change any of the above parameters? <N>:
   Y (RETURN)
Enter values, blank=Next value, Cn=Color n,
   S=Show current values, X=Exit

Layer Color	Pen No.	Line Type	Pen Speed	
1 (red)	1	0	16	Pen number <1>: **C5 (RETURN)**
5 (blue)	1	0	16	Pen number <1>: **(RETURN)**
5 (blue)	1	0	16	Line type <0>: **5 (RETURN)**
5 (blue)	1	5	16	Pen speed <16>: **X (RETURN)**

Write the plot to a file? <N> **N (RETURN)**
Size units (Inches or Millimeters) <I>: **(RETURN)**
Plot origin in Inches <0.00,0.00>: **(RETURN)**

Standard values for plotting size

Size	Width	Height
A	10.50	8.00
B	16.00	10.00
C	21.00	16.00
D	33.00	21.00
MAX	34.00	21.50

Enter the Size or Width,Height (in Inches) <A>: **MAX (RETURN)**

```
Rotate 2D plots 90 degrees clockwise? <N>:  (RETURN)
Pen width <0.010>:  (RETURN)
Adjust area fill boundaries for pen width? <N>: (RETURN)
Remove hidden lines? <N>:  (RETURN)

Specify scale by entering:
Plotted Inches = Drawing Units or Fit or ? <F>:  (RETURN)

Effective plotting area: 30.54 wide by 21.50 high
Press RETURN to continue or S to Stop for hardware setup
   S  (RETURN)
Do hardware setup now.
Press RETURN to continue:

(Check plotter readiness and hit (RETURN).)
   (RETURN)

Processing vector: nn    (AutoCAD cycles through whole drawing)

Install pen number 1, color 7 (white)
Press RETURN to continue:  (RETURN)

(Plotting takes place.)

Plot complete.
Press RETURN to continue:  (RETURN)

(Main Menu appears.)
```

You assign a plotter Line Type to a drawing "color" and everything in that color will plot with that Line Type, regardless of scale. If you plot an AutoCAD layer or entity LINETYPE with a plotter Line Type, you will get an odd combination of the two.

The last exercise showed how plotter Line Types work, however, we recommend that you use AutoCAD's software Linetypes. AutoCAD's Linetypes have several advantages over plotter Line Types:

☐ Plotter Line Types must be set with every plot while AutoCAD's are set when the entity is created.

☐ Plotter Line Types do not usually close or meet at corners while AutoCAD's meet correctly.

☐ Plotter Line Types affect everything of that color, while AutoCAD ignores color and always plots text with a continuous line, regardless of linetype or color.

☐ AutoCAD's Linetypes can be scaled in the drawing and you can create new linetypes.

Sticky Plotting Default Settings

Notice that this last time through the plotter routines, AutoCAD presented you with several <default> settings that were not the same as the originals in the first plot of the Chapter. For both the PLOT and PRPLOT routines, AutoCAD maintains your most recent plot parameters from plot to plot and from one AutoCAD use session to the next.

This saving of defaults is advantageous, but can be problematic.

The advantage is apparent whenever you take several attempts to get your plot correct. The first time through you can set your plot parameters and try out the plot. Then if you have to make a few changes to the plot parameters, you do not have to go back to ground zero and set all the parameters over again.

A problem may arise when you do not use the plotting routines for a while (like a few days) and you forget what the parameter settings were. In this case, you do not have a standard set of <defaults> to work from. Instead, what you have is whatever you set last time. You can set AutoCAD to save and use several sets of defaults, using configuration subdirectories. See **Configurations—multiple** in the AutoCAD Reference Manual Index.

You always have the option of viewing all the defaults or current parameter settings and making whatever changes are necessary. Just keep an eye on them!

PLOTTING IN COLOR

Just as you assigned the layer BOUNDARY blue color to come out in dashed lines, you could assign it to come out in a different color or line weight. By specifying a different pen number for each color in the drawing file, AutoCAD knows to switch pens when plotting. The alternate pen(s) can be a different color or a different line weight.

Whether you have a single pen plotter (like the DMP 52), or a multiple pen plotter, AutoCAD will select the correct pen. With a multiple pen plotter, AutoCAD switches pens automatically. With a single pen plotter, AutoCAD plots one pen color first, pauses and prompts you to change the pen, and then continues plotting in the next color.

Plotting the Widget Drawing in Color

Let's use the Widget Drawing to create a color plot.

In this example, you will plot in multiple colors, and we suggest that you slow down the green pen plotting speed.

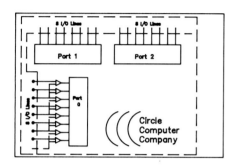

Black and White Drawing of Color Widget

As you test your pens, you will learn which ones require plotting at a slower speed. AutoCAD can control the speed of the pen as it creates a plot. From trial and error (and advice from friends and INSIDE AutoCAD), you will eventually determine the best plotting speed for different pen combinations and media.

The <default> plotting speed for the DMP is 16 inches per second. We have found that too fast for the .35 mm (0.010″) ink pens. The AutoCAD drawings in the Book were plotted at 6 inches per second.

The Widget drawing has a **Sandbox** on layer 0. To get around the Sandbox, you can plot the drawing with layer **0** turned Off.

CHANGING COLOR AND PEN SPEED FOR PLOTTING

Select 2 from the Main Menu.

Enter Selection: **2 (RETURN)**

Enter NAME of drawing <default AUTOTOWN>: **WIDGET (RETURN)**

    (Image appears in the drawing editor.)

ZOOM All

Turn all layers On.

Turn layer **0** Off.

Execute the PLOT command from the Root Menu or by typing

Command: **PLOT (RETURN)**

What to plot -- Display, Extents, Limits, View, or Window <E>:
  D (RETURN)

    (FLIP SCREEN appears.)
Plot will NOT be written to a selected file
Sizes are in Inches
Plot origin is at (0.00,0.00)
Plotting area is 34.00 wide by 21.50 (MAX size)
Plot is NOT rotated 90 degrees
Pen width is 0.010
Area fill will NOT be adjusted for pen width
Hidden lines will NOT be removed
Plot will be scaled to fit available area

Do you want to change anything? <N> **Y (RETURN)**

(AutoCAD displays the current settings for plot parameters.)

Entity Color	Pen No.	Line Type	Pen Speed	Layer Color	Pen No.	Line Type	Pen Speed
1 (red)	1	0	16	9	1	0	16
2 (yellow)	1	0	16	10	1	0	16
3 (green)	1	0	16	11	1	0	16
4 (cyan)	1	0	16	12	1	0	16
5 (blue)	1	5	16	13	1	0	16
6 (magenta)	1	0	16	14	1	0	16
7 (white)	1	0	16	15	1	0	16
8	1	0	16				

Line types: 0 = continuous line   Pen speed codes:
          1 = ...
          2 = ...   Inches/Second:
          3 = ------------------   1, 2, 4, 8, 16
          4 = - - - - - - - - - -
          5 = -- -- -- -- -- -- -   Cm/Second:
          6 = --- --- --- --- ---   3, 5, 10, 20, 40
          7 = -- - -- - -- - -- -
          8 = __--__--__--__--__-

Enter line types, pen speed codes
   blank=go to next, Cn=go to Color n,
   S=Show current choices, X=Exit
Do you want to change any of the above parameters? <N>
     Y (RETURN)
Enter values, blank=Next value, Cn=Color n, S=Show current
     values, X=Exit

Layer Color	Pen No.	Line Type	Pen Speed		
1 (red)	1	0	16	Pen number <1>:	**2 (RETURN)**
1 (red)	2	0	16	Line type <0>:	**(RETURN)**
1 (red)	2	0	16	Pen speed <16>:	**(RETURN)**
2 (yellow)	1	0	16	Pen number <1>:	**3 (RETURN)**
2 (yellow)	3	0	16	Line type <0>:	**(RETURN)**
2 (yellow)	3	0	16	Pen speed <1>:	**(RETURN)**
3 (green)	1	0	16	Pen number <1>:	**4 (RETURN)**
3 (green)	4	0	16	Line type <0>:	**(RETURN)**
3 (green)	4	0	16	Pen speed <16>:	**4 (RETURN)**
4 (cyan)	1	0	16	Pen number <1>:	**(RETURN)**
4 (cyan)	1	0	16	Line type <0>:	**(RETURN)**
4 (cyan)	1	0	16	Pen speed <16>:	**(RETURN)**
5 (blue)	1	5	16	Pen number <1>:	**5 (RETURN)**
5 (blue)	5	5	16	Line type <5>:	**0 (RETURN)**
5 (blue)	5	0	16	Pen speed <16>:	**(RETURN)**
6 (magenta)	1	0	16	Pen number <1>:	**X (RETURN)**

Write the plot to a file? <N> **N (RETURN)**
Size units (Inches or Millimeters) <I>: **(RETURN)**
Plot origin in Inches <0.00,0.00>: **(RETURN)**

```
Standard values for plotting size

Size            Width           Height

A               10.50            8.00
B               16.00           10.00
C               21.00           16.00
D               33.00           21.00
MAX             34.00           21.50

Enter the Size or Width, Height (in Inches) <A>:
   MAX  (RETURN)

Rotate 2D plots 90 degrees clockwise? <N>:  (RETURN)
Pen width <0.010>:  (RETURN)
Adjust area fill boundaries for pen width? <N>  (RETURN)
Remove hidden lines? <N>  (RETURN)

Specify scale by entering:
Plotted Inches = Drawing Units or Fit or ? <F>:  (RETURN)


Effective plotting area: 29.87 wide by 21.50 high
Press RETURN to continue or S to Stop for hardware setup
   S  (RETURN)
Do hardware setup now.
Press RETURN to continue:  (RETURN)

(Check plotter readiness and hit (RETURN).)


Processing vector: nn    (AutoCAD cycles through first color)
(Plotting takes place.)

(When AutoCAD is through with the first pen it will
prompt for a new pen number and color. Change pens and
proceed with the plot.)

Install pen number 4, color 3 (green)
Press RETURN to continue:  (RETURN)
Processing vector: nn    (AutoCAD cycles through green color)

Install pen number 3, color 2 (yellow)
Press RETURN to continue:  (RETURN)
Processing vector: nn    (AutoCAD cycles through yellow color)

Install pen number 2, color 1 (red)
Press RETURN to continue:  (RETURN)
Processing vector: nn    (AutoCAD cycles through red color)

Install pen number 5, color 5 (blue)
Press RETURN to continue:  (RETURN)
Processing vector: nn    (AutoCAD cycles through blue color)
Plot complete.
Press RETURN to continue:  (RETURN)

(To get back to the Drawing Editor hit (RETURN).)
   (RETURN)

(Drawing editor appears.)
```

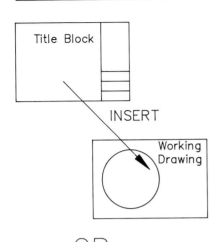

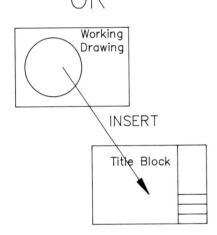

Title Block Placements

TITLES, SETUPS AND REGULAR FORMATS

One important aspect of plotting is creating **finished** drawings with title, title blocks, and other presentation embellishments. AutoCAD makes you a pro at delivering presentation quality drawings.

Over time you will develop a repertoire of title blocks, logos, and different presentation styles. We will give one example here using the title block you created and stored as TITLEBLK.

Overlaying a Title Block on a Check Print

In order to satisfy the Board of Directors of the Honeycomb Corporation, you need to merge your **WIDGET** file with the **TITLEBLK** file.

There are two ways to do this—put the title block on top of the Widget drawing, or put the Widget into title block drawing. Either way works. The following exercise lays out the first way.

Here are the steps for the plot:

HONEYCOMB BOARD OF DIRECTORS PLOT

1. Make a copy of the WIDGET file. Call it **HONEY**.
   This saves the original as a separate file for future use.
   You can use the MS-DOS **COPY**, or AutoCAD's **File Utility**.

2. Enter the drawing editor to edit the EXISTING file **HONEY**.
   Set LIMITS to lower left -5",-5", and upper right
   50",35".

3. Turn the important layers On. Set up a new layer called
   Title with <default> white color. Set layer TITLE Current.

4. Insert **TITLEBLK** as block on the **HONEY** drawing.
   Place and size the block with DRAG. If you want
   to change anything in TITLEBLK, use *INSERT.

   The negative LIMITS are handy here. INSERT the Titleblk
   at -1,-1 so that it does not bump into any Honey (Widget)
   Drawing entities. Use DRAG mode and stretch the Titleblk
   until it comfortably surrounds your Widget drawing. Use
   <0> rotation for INSERT.

5. Fill in title information (date, revision number,
   signatures, and company information) by placing text
   on the TITLE layer. Try sketching a signature.

6. SAVE (not END) the merged drawing so that it is still
   showing.

7. ZOOM Extents.

8. Plot the merged drawing to the MAX size, with scale fit,
   and appropriate pen or color assignments. Plot the TITLE
   layer in black.

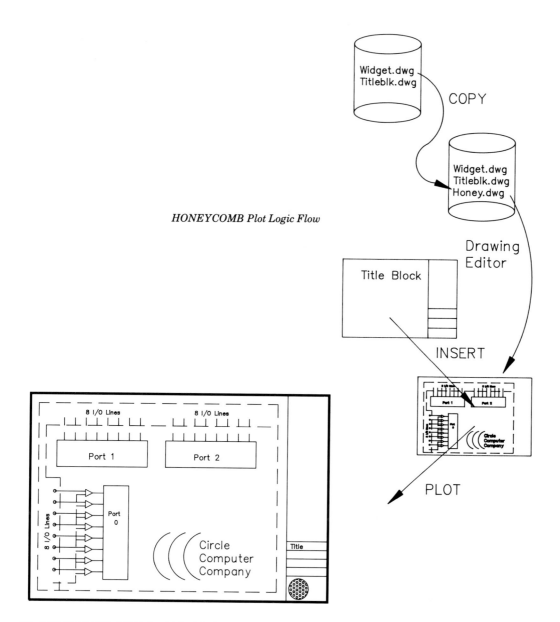

HONEYCOMB *Plot Logic Flow*

The HONEYCOMB BOARD of DIRECTORS Plot

Overlaying a Check Print into Title Block

Putting a drawing into a TITLE Block drawing allows you to do all your scaling on-screen and then plot at 1:1 scale. When you plot Extents at 1:1 scale that places the lower left corner of the TITLE Block at the plot origin and yields an appropriate border.

If your plot comes out slightly too big or too small on your plotter, you can STRETCH the top and left sides of the Title Block and move the left corner as needed. You also can adjust the plot position relative to the plot origin by saving and plotting a VIEW with its lower lefthand corner placed at the plot origin.

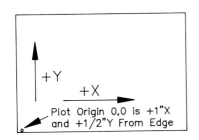

Plot Origin and Drawing File Origin

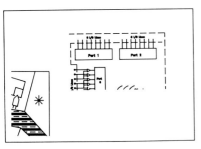

Multiple Image Sheet with ROAD-TURN and WIDGET Details.

CREATING A DETAIL OR MULTIPLE SHEET DRAWING

There is another plotting sequence that you will use frequently. This is creating multiple images on the same plotting paper. You plot multiple images by changing the plot origin parameter.

The logic behind multiple plots on a single plot sheet is simple:

☐ Get a View or drawing editor screen image ready for plotting.

☐ Decide what size the image should be on the paper (like MAX or "A" or "B" size).

☐ Decide where on the plotter paper you want this image to go. Make a note of the **origin point** or lower left hand corner for your prepared image. Record this location in inches or mm depending on your plotter setup routine.

☐ Run the plot utility as normal except for the plot origin location. In earlier examples you let AutoCAD use <0.00,0.00> as a default. Now insert your location and proceed as usual.

Try a multiple sheet by plotting the AutoTown ROADTURN View in an "A" size starting at a 0.00,0.00 origin. Plot a **portion** of the Widget drawing at "B" size at a 12.00,10.00 origin.

SUMMING UP

If you followed all the examples through this Chapter you should have eight separate plotter sheets:

☐ AutoTown in its entirety (and in all its glory).

☐ AutoTown at 1/2-scale.

☐ AutoTown Roadturn View at "A" size.

☐ AutoTown Roadturn View on the printer plotter.

☐ AutoTown with a dashed border.

☐ The Widget drawing in its entirety in full color.

☐ The Honeycomb Corporation full color presentation with a title block.

☐ A multiple detail sheet with Roadturn at "A" size and a portion of the Widget drawing at "B" size.

If you have extra trial and error sheets you may want to consider a few plotting tips:

TIPS FOR PLOTTING

☐ Think Ahead About Plotting.

   ☐ Plan ahead for scale, pen types and color. When you set up your drawing file, you should have an idea about how it eventually will be plotted out.

☐ Organize layers to set up efficient plotting for separate colors. If you have not kept all your color- specific entities on a single layer, use the CHANGE Command to regroup. Remember that colors are for pen line weights too, not just pen colors.

☐ Think ahead about leaving room for a title block. Make your LIMITS your paper size, sizing and positioning your title block to match the plotter plot area and borders. Plot Extents or View at 1:1 as a good standard.

☐ Plotter Maintenance is Essential.

☐ Pen plotters are mechanical beasts.

☐ Keep paper and pen supplies stored in proper humidity. It really helps. Your paper and pen supplier should know the proper storage requirements. A dust free environment helps keep pens from clogging.

☐ Clean the paper path to keep dust from abrading the underside of your sheets. Brush the paper or mylar before plotting. Finger prints can cause skips. Rubbing alcohol removes finger prints.

☐ Cap pens when not in use. They dry out quickly. Worse, they can get partially clogged and skip in the last minute of a twenty-minute plot. Disposables may pay for themselves by lessening trouble.

☐ You Can Optimize Your Plotting Speed.

☐ This takes a little practice, but you will soon learn the maximum speed for plotting without pen skipping. Ask your supplier what pens work best with which ink/media combinations—it is a 3-way balance.

☐ Continuous lines improve plot speed. If you can minimize the amount of running around the plotter does with the pen **up**, then you will speed up your plots.

☐ For **finished** copies it pays to slow the plotter way down to improve line definition. Once slow is better than twice fast.

☐ Learning To Control Plot Origin Will Save Time.

☐ For multiple image sheets—lay them out ahead of time using a scrap sheet of paper. Write in the plot origin of each detail, scale, linetype, etc.

☐ You can avoid merging a title block with another drawing file by plotting the two separately. You just have to plan ahead for proper overlap and plot origin.

☐ Don't confuse AutoCAD's Layer/Entity Linetype with Plotter Line Type.

☐ AutoCAD's linetypes are unaffected by plot setup. AutoCAD will send a linetype (in any color) to the plotter the same way it sends a normal line. If you send a dashed layer linetype to a dashed plotter Line Type, the results are unpredictable.

☐ Use the plotter's continuous Line Type for all AutoCAD broken linetypes.

☐ Plotting Multiple Colors with a Single Pen Plotter.

   ☐ It's important not to move, remove, or alter the paper's position in the plotter. The layers will not line up (register) if you move the paper.

   ☐ Some plotters require resetting between plotting colors. First, try multiple colors without resetting. If that doesn't work, reset between colors.

   ☐ Don't forget to change the pen! Sometimes you get caught up in getting the correct screen image, and you forget to replace the pen.

☐ A skip in a Plot. If you get a skip in a long plot, WBlock the affected portion of the drawing to a new file and plot it with the same settings on the same sheet.

☐ Take Advantage of Your Printer Plotter.

   ☐ Use the printer plotter for quick, easy, and inexpensive check plots.

   ☐ It also is useful for 8 1/2″ × 11″ details.

   ☐ Remember! Control Q (^Q) within the drawing editor gets text screen information out on the printer.

Lines on paper. That's what it's all about. Or is it? Lines on paper are two-dimensional. In the next Chapter you will take a behind-the-lines-look at AutoCAD's third dimension.

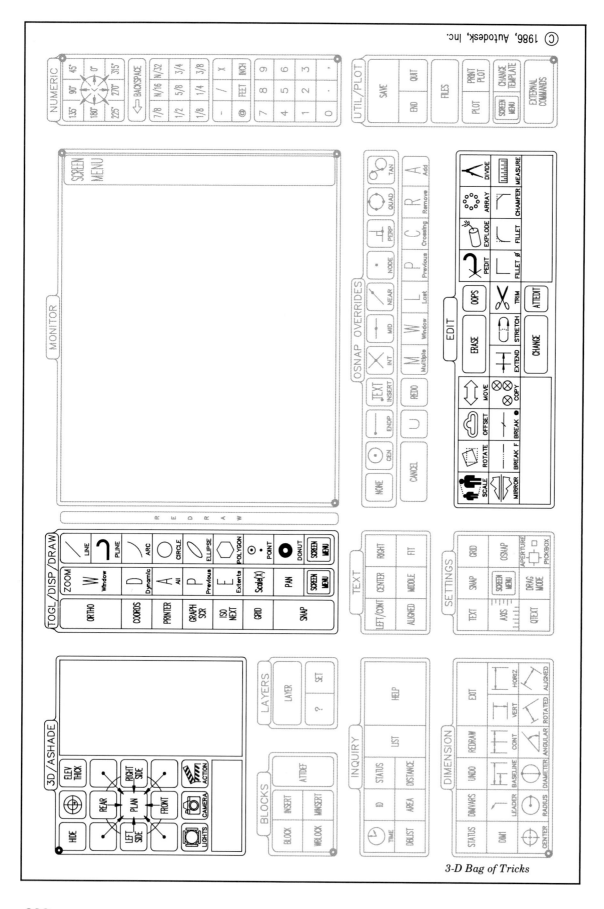

© 1986, Autodesk, Inc.

3-D Bag of Tricks

CHAPTER 9

3-D—MAKING YOUR DRAWINGS STAND OUT

▶ **Do You Really Have 3-D?** ▶ **The 3-D Bag of Tricks.** ▶ **Isometric Drawing With Iso-Grid and Iso-Snap.** ▶ **Generating 3-D Models.** ▶ **Editing 3-D Models.** ▶ **Understanding The 3-D Model Commands: VPOINT and HIDE.** ▶ **Making 3-D Images More Realistic With Hidden Line Removal.** ▶ **Creating an Ergonomic Chair With 3-D.** ▶ **Tips for Making 3-D Work For You.**

DO YOU REALLY HAVE 3-D?

Take a look at the SHADY 3-D IMAGE. Is it really a 3-D image? It certainly looks like it is standing out from the page. But the page is a flat 2-D surface. The drawing is printed flat on the page. So is the drawing 2-D or 3-D?

What you see is a 2-D representation of a 3-D image. The representation is a trick of the drafting trade—a trick to make your eye see depth in an image that is really flat.

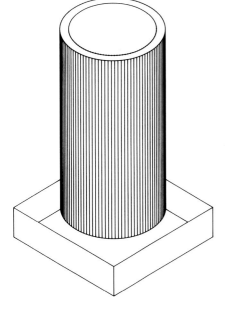

Now the idea behind the image is 3-D. Your eye can see from looking at the drawing that the picture shows a hollow cylinder sitting on top of a cubic base. From visual training and observing depth in our everyday environment, we can form a mental image of what the picture wants us to see—for example a cup with a base for holding pencils.

Most drafters can sit down and draw a SHADY 3-D IMAGE quickly, and come up with a pretty realistic looking 3-D image. The question is how fast can you redraw the image to look at it from another angle? From along side? From top down?

If a design is created in a CAD system that holds 3-D images, then all the information necessary to generate any view is readily available at any time. But, just as you can draw a realistic SHADY 3-D IMAGE on a flat piece of paper, some CAD systems can get away with creating a 2-D image that looks like 3-D—but really isn't.

Shady 3D Image

What you SEE is not necessarily what you HAVE.

—The CAD 3-D Rule

With AutoCAD you can create both 3-D drawings and 2-D drawings that look 3-D. The 2-D tools that make images look 3-D are isometric tools to help the eye see depth.

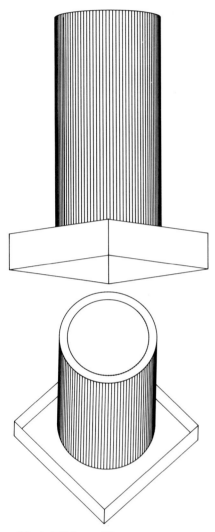

For 3-D drawing AutoCAD currently has simplified tools for defining 3-D shape models, and then viewing these models from any vantage point. The tools fall into two categories, those for creating the model, and several for setting up a viewing position to look at the model.

Wireframes

Of course, no matter how good a 3-D model you build in you drawing file, you still have to look at it on a 2-D surface—the screen or a plotted output. You also have to settle for a representational view of a 3-D surface. For example, if SHADY 3-D IMAGE was fully and truly a 3-D image, the edges of the cube base and the outside of the cylinders would appear solid. You have to settle for a few lines—or **wire frames** in CAD lingo—to represent the boundaries of the 3-D surface.

Whatever tricks you use to get the images to look 3-D, using 3-D is an important part of communicating with the drawing community. Whether you soup up your 2-D drawings with isometrics, or take the time to build 3-D models, storing as much 3-D image in the CAD system helps to generate 3-D views faster than ever done in a manual mode.

Take a look again at SHADY 3-D IMAGE once again, and then look at the SHADY 3-D IMAGE VIEWS. The view series images were generated from the same 3-D model as the first drawing **in about one minute each** — without having to add or subtract a single line from the CAD drawing. Therein lies the beauty and benefit of using 3-D CAD.

Shady 3-D Image Views

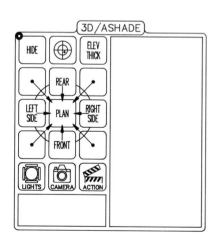

3-D Tablet Commands

THE 3-D BAG OF TRICKS

AutoCAD's 3-D Tablet Menu Commands are shown in THE 3-D TOOL-CHEST at the beginning of the Chapter.

The **ELEV**ation Command lets you set a current elevation to your drawing and an extrusion **thickness** to objects which you create. Changing the elevation changes the Z-plane (Z coordinate direction) that an object is drawn on. Assigning a plus or minus distance in the Z-plane gives an object thickness when it is **extruded** for viewing in 3-D.

VPOINT provides a series of Commands for visualizing your 3-D images. **HIDE** gets rid of wireframe "hidden" lines when you elect to use it to help visualize a VPOINT of your 3-D image.

ISOMETRIC DRAWING WITH ISO-GRID AND ISO-SNAP

One way to make 2-D drawings look 3-D is by using an isometric view. In an isometric view, angles and lines are aligned to give the impression that some lines are boundaries for each of a front, top, and side view of the object being drawn.

The CUBE AND ASSORTED ISOMETRICS drawing shows several examples of isometrics.

The key to drawing isometrics is keep your lines and angles aligned so you do not draw entities that would wreck the 3-D illusion. AutoCAD provides a series of tools to save time when drawing isometric projections.

Just like SNAP helps keep you drawing within a specified accuracy, setting SNAP to **Style** with **ISO** sets up a drawing mechanism that keeps you drawing in isometrics. The SNAP Style option toggles between isometric drawing control and a Standard SNAP/GRID. Once within isometric drawing, you control which face of the drawing (top, left, right) you are drawing on with the **ISOPLANE** Command.

When in isometric mode, AutoCAD displays a grid that is angled and offset to match the angles and lines you might want to draw. This is just like tracing over isometric or 30-60 degree tracing paper. If you want to draw isometrics, you are probably familiar with manual techniques, AutoCAD's isometric techniques are quite similar.

Let's try an isometric drawing example. Many of the drawing exercises in this Chapter are based on the image of the cylinder and a cube-like pedestal. We like to think that you have to design this pencil holder to hold all of your old, left-over pencils when you switched to CAD drawing.

Cube and Assorted Isometrics

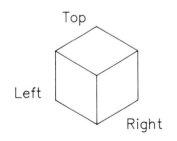

ISO Planes

USING ISOMETRIC SNAP/GRID TO DRAW A CUBE AND A CYLINDER

Use Main Menu 1. Begin a new drawing, call it ISOCUP.

Leave UNITS and LIMITS to default. Toggle COORDS On.

```
Command: GRID (RETURN)
Grid spacing (X) or ON/OFF/Aspect <0.0000>: .5 (RETURN)
Command: SNAP (RETURN)
Snap spacing or ON/OFF/Aspect/Rotate/Style <1.0000>:
Style (RETURN)
Standard/Isometric <S>: Isometric (RETURN)
Vertical spacing <1.0000>: .5 (RETURN)
Command:
```

Notice that the GRID is now aligned in a 30-60 degree arrangement and that the crosshair is skewed. You are now in ISOPLANE LEFT, with the crosshair aligned to draw on the left face of a drawing. The toggle for ISO-PLANE is Control-E (^E).

Pedestal

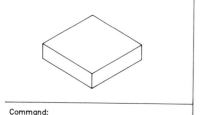

Pedestal Pick Points

THE ISOPLANE TOGGLE

Find the ISOPLANE Toggle command, and toggle it a few times.

Try to get a feel for the different "faces" of isoplane. When you are through, leave the toggle in ISOPLANE LEFT.

For beginners, the best way to draw in isometric is with SNAP and ORTHO turned on. Try drawing the pedestal base now, first the left, then the top, and finally the right faces.

DRAWING THE PEDESTAL

Command: **ORTHO (RETURN)**   (Or pick the ORTHO toggle.)
ON/OFF <Off>: **On (RETURN)**
Command: **LINE (RETURN)**
From point: <Coords on> **6.0622,2.0000 (RETURN)**   (Make sure
   the digital coordinate readout tracks where you are. You may
   not have to type the coordinates if you can pick this snap
   point. Then look at PEDESTAL PICK POINTS for reference.)

To point: (Eight grid/snap points up and to the left = digital
   readout 4.0000<150).
To point: (Two grid/snap points down.)
To point: (Back to underneath the first point)
To point: **Close (RETURN)**
Command: **(RETURN)**   (To restart LINE)
From point: **Continue (RETURN)**
To point: <Isoplane Top>   (First toggle ISOPLANE, then pick a
   point eight grid/snap points up and to the right = digital
   readout 4.0000<30.)
To point: (pick the back corner.)
To point: (join back to the corner of the left face.)
To point: **(RETURN)**   (To end continuous lines.)
Command: **(RETURN)**   (To restart the LINE command.)
From point: <Isoplane right>   (First toggle ISOPLANE, then
   pick the pedestal front bottom corner.)
To point: (Pick the right bottom back corner)
To point: (Join the right rear face to the top.)
To point: **(RETURN)**   (To end LINE.)
Command:

Using Ellipse in ISO Mode

While most drawing primitives were designed to be used in a 2-D flat environment (except the ubiquitous LINE, of course), ELLIPSE stands out as one of those commands that works well in ISO mode. In fact, ELLIPSE has an ISO option just for times like now, when you need to draw the base of the cup cylinder.

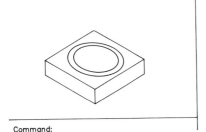

ISO Ellipse - Base of Cylinder

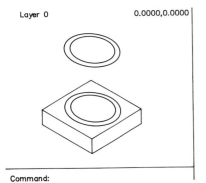

Copy Circles up 4 Units

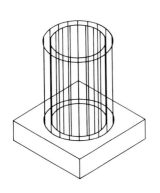

ISO Cup Pencil Holder

USING ISOMETRIC SNAP/GRID TO DRAW A CUBE AND A CYLINDER

```
Command: <Isoplane Left> <Isoplane Top> ELLIPSE (RETURN)
<Axis endpoint 1>/Center/Isocircle: Isocircle (RETURN)
Center of circle: (Pick the point in the middle of the
   pedestal top.)
<Circle radius>/ Diameter:
   (Drag to see how your isocircle is coming. Then pick a
   point three snap points away.)
Command:
```

Try the inner circle by picking another radius about 2 and 1/2 grid points away.

```
Command: <Snap off> ELLIPSE (RETURN)
<Axis endpoint 1>/Center/Isocircle: Isocircle (RETURN)
Center of circle: (Pick the point in the middle of the
   pedestal top.)
<Circle radius>/ Diameter:     (Pick a point about 2 1/2
   grid/snap points away.)
Command:
```

Using Regular 2-D Mode To Finish ISO Drawings

To finish creating this drawing, COPY the two circles (ellipses) for the top of the cylinder, DIVIDE the circles into regular intervals and drop a few wireframe lines to complete the 3-D illusion.

COMPLETING THE CYLINDER

Copy the circles up four units.

```
Command: COPY (RETURN)
Select objects: 1 selected, 1 found.   (Pick the first circle.)
Select objects: 1 selected, 1 found.   (Pick the second circle.)
Select objects: (RETURN)        (To end selection.)
<Base point or displacement>/Multiple: 0,4 (RETURN)
Second point of displacement: (RETURN)
Command:
```

Finally, create a layer for the "wireframe". Create a simple Block for wire, and DIVIDE the Circles into 18 parts with the wire Block. Then set SNAP back to Standard Style and add some text if you like.

ADDING "WIREFRAME" TO THE CYLINDER

Make a New Layer named WIREFRAME. Color it red.
Set it Current.

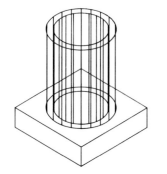

Layer WIREFRAM   0.0000,0.0000

First corner: Other corner:

"Wire" Block Creation

Create a Block that is simply a 4 unit high vertical red line,
call it Wire and give it an insertion base point at its top.

Command: **DIVIDE (RETURN)**
Select object to divide: (Pick the upper, outer circle)
Divide into how many parts / Block: **Block (RETURN)**
Block name to insert: **Wire (RETURN)**
Align block with object? <Y> **N (RETURN)**
Divide into how many parts: **18 (RETURN)**

(If you want you can DIVIDE into 36 parts. Then erase all
the "wires" that extend above the horizontal center line of
the circle. Then DIVIDE the upper inner circle with 18
segments. This will give the drawing a "cleaner" look.

Command:

Your pencil holder should now look like ISO CUP PENCIL HOLDER.

Reset from ISO to 2-D mode.

Command: **SNAP (RETURN)**
Snap spacing or ON/OFF/Aspect/Rotate/Style <0.5000>:
   Style (RETURN)
Standard/Isometric <I>: **Standard (RETURN)**
Vertical spacing <0.5000>: **(RETURN)**
Command:

Play around with ISOCUP. Add some text. Try a PRPLOT,
then END to clear the way for another exercise.

ISO Cup Pencil Holder

ISO Has Limitations: Static Images and No Hidden Line Removal

As you can see from ISO PENCIL HOLDER, working with ISO and regular
2-D commands is limited. But you can throw together a pretty good looking
drawing in a hurry if you need to get a feel for how something "looks in 3-
D" from a single view point.

If you like, you can remove those segments in the drawing that would not
be seen if the cylinder were solid by using BREAK, TRIM, and EXTEND.
It is a lot of work, and there is another way.

If you wanted to look at a bird's eye plan view, or another frontal view, you
would have to start all over again and draw a new picture. That's why you
should look into....

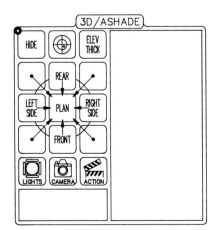

Figures with Different Elevations and Thicknesses

Tablet ELEV/Thickness Command

GENERATING 3-D MODELS

So far in AutoCAD, every entity you have created has been in X and Y in a flat plane—the Z value for all of these entities has been 0. But just as you have control over X and Y locations for entities, AutoCAD gives you limited control of the Z value for purposes of extruding X-Y planar objects out of the Z = 0 flat plane.

While you do not have control over every nuance of how an image will be built in 3-D, AutoCAD does allow you to give flat images a "bottom" and "top" by setting an **ELEVATION** and a **thickness**. See FIGURES WITH DIFFERENT ELEVATIONS AND THICKNESSES.

Take a look at the current settings for ELEVATION and thickness:

SETTING UP A 3-D MODEL-LOOKING AT ELEVATION AND THICKNESS

```
Use Main Menu 1.  Begin NEW Drawing to start a new file
  called 3DCUP.

Command: SNAP (RETURN)
Snap spacing or ON/OFF/Aspect/Rotate/Style <1.0000>:
  0.5 (RETURN)
Command: GRID (RETURN)
Grid spacing (X) or ON/OFF/Aspect <0.0000>: On (RETURN)
Command:

Now take a look at ELEVATION and thickness.

Command: ELEV (RETURN)
New current elevation <0.0000>:  (RETURN)
New current thickness <0.0000>:  (RETURN)
Command:
```

To build a 3-D model, you usually create the plan view (X-Y view) of a shape first, then look at it in 3-D. When you create the plan view shape, you set ELEVATION and thickness for each object. Then, when viewed in 3-D, each object hovers in Z-space according to the elevation and thickness that you set.

Try creating the same cup you did in the ISO exercises using 3-D models. The base pedestal starts at elevation = 0 and has a thickness of 1.0. The cylinder starts at an elevation of 1.0 and has a thickness of 6.0.

CREATING THE PENCIL CUP IN 3-D MODEL

First the pedestal.

Layer 0   0.0000,0.0000

```
Command: ELEV (RETURN)
New current elevation <0.0000>: (RETURN)
New current thickness <0.0000>: 1 (RETURN)
Command: LINE (RETURN)
From point: 3.5,1 (RETURN)
To point: 7.5,1 (RETURN)
To point: 7.5,5 (RETURN)
To point: 3.5,5 (RETURN)
To point: Close (RETURN)
Command:
```

Command:

Plan View—Base and Cylinder

Now the cylinder.

```
Command: ELEV (RETURN)
New current elevation <0.0000>: 1 (RETURN)
New current thickness <1.0000>: 6 (RETURN)
Command: CIRCLE (RETURN)
3P/2P/TTR/<Center point>: 5.5,3 (RETURN)
Diameter/<Radius>: 1.5 (RETURN)
Command: (RETURN)
3P/2P/TTR/<Center point>: @ (RETURN)
Diameter/<Radius>: 1.25 (RETURN)
Command:
```

Want to take a quick look in 3-D?

```
Command: VPOINT (RETURN)
Enter view point <0.0000,0.0000,1.0000>: 1,1,1 (RETURN)
Regenerating drawing.
Command:
```

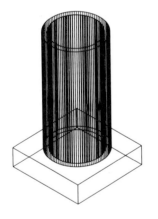

3D Image Target Drawing

Pretty quick, huh? Pretty neat, too. You can set a VPOINT just about anywhere to have your eye "walk around" the drawing. AutoCAD will obediently figure out the "view" and regenerate the drawing for you. Try a few VPOINTs to see how this works. Try a few negative VPOINTs if you are daring.

Keep an Eye on ELEVATION and Thickness

Now you see that creating 3-D models is as easy as drawing 2-D objects with proper elevation and thickness. But you have to be careful to keep in mind just what the current elevation and thickness are before you draw objects.

The settings for elevation and thickness are not a part of the Status Line, but you can find out the current settings for these parameters in two convenient ways:

☐ Execute the ELEV command and see the current default.

☐ Do a STATUS and find elevation and thickness in the listing. (Why don't you try one now?)

You can also find out the elevation and thickness of an object that you have already created in two easy ways:

☐ Do a LIST and pick the item on the screen. The LISTing will tell you both settings for that object.

☐ Do a CHANGE Properties and pick the item on the screen. CHANGE will ask you what property you want to edit. When you respond **Elevation** or **Thickness**, you will be prompted with the <current default>.

Try changing the elevation and thickness of the inner circle of the cylinder.

EDITING 3-D MODELS

Making changes to your 3-D model is simple as changing the shape of the plan view objects that you extruded in the Z-direction. You edit these objects just the same way you edit any 2-D image.

You can edit the shape of a 3-D object when it is projected into 3-D. (Notice the crosshair provides a viewing aid as in ISO.) However, many users find it easier to flatten the image first, make the necessary edits, and then reproject into 3-D.

Try changing the shape of the pedestal by erasing the square and replacing it with a pentagon.

Layer 0   0.0000,0.0000

Command:

Polygon Base—Plan View

EDITING THE PENCIL CUP HOLDER

First flatten the image.

```
Command: VPOINT (RETURN)
Enter view point <X,Y,Z -- your last setting>: 0,0,1 (RETURN)
Regenerating drawing.
Command:
```

ZOOM All and then change the square to a pentagon.

```
Command: ERASE (RETURN)
Select objects: 1 selected, 1 found.
  (Pick the four sides of the square.)

Select objects: (RETURN)     (To end selection)
Command: ELEV (RETURN)
New current elevation <1.0000>: 0 (RETURN)
New current thickness <6.0000>: 1 (RETURN)
Command: POLYGON (RETURN)
Number of sides: 5 (RETURN)
Edge/<Center of polygon>: 5.5,3 (RETURN)
Inscribed in circle/Circumscribed about circle (I/C):
  C (RETURN)
Radius of circle: 2 (RETURN)
Command:
```

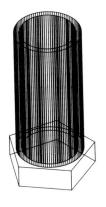

Polygon Base—in 3D

Take a look:

```
Command: VPOINT (RETURN)
Enter view point <0.0000,0.0000,1.0000>: 1,1,1 (RETURN)
Regenerating drawing.
Command:
```

UNDERSTANDING THE 3-D MODEL COMMANDS: VPOINT AND HIDE

Aside from the ELEV command which controls object elevation and thickness, AutoCAD currently has only two other commands for controlling 3-D.

☐ **VPOINT**—or View**POINT**—controls from where you look at your image. AutoCAD helps you get a handle on setting viewpoint with several visual and tablet cues.

☐ **HIDE**—eliminates hidden lines from a 3-D generated view. Solving the mathematics to get rid of hidden lines is a rather complex problem. In the current version of AutoCAD, the program gets rid of most, but not necessarily all, hidden lines.

Getting Around With VIEWPOINT

In 3-D mode, the default VPOINT is 0,0,1. AutoCAD considers your entire drawing to be located at 0,0,0. VPOINT = 0,0,1 is directly above—looking down. This is called the **Plan View**.

So long as you are directly above your drawing (sitting on the Z-axis) looking down , everything you create (regardless of elevation and thickness setting) looks flat. You are looking at the Plan View of your objects.

In order to "see 3-D" you have to get off of this Z-axis and look "from the side". In VPOINT terms, you must have a non-zero X or Y or both. For example, a 1,1,1 setting gives you a 45 degree angle looking back at 0,0,0 where your image is located. You can't get "inside" the object and view it.

You can set VPOINT to any X,Y and Z location you please. The best way to get conceptually past VPOINT is to try to develop an intuitive sense for VPOINT. Try assigning a few VPOINT values with the 3DCUP drawing. In the last part of the Chapter, you will complete a 3-D drawing of a chair—something more interesting to look at in 3-D.

While you are thinking through VPOINT locations, you might want to try using two tools that AutoCAD provides for setting up VPOINTs.

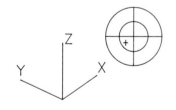

VPOINT Screen Prompt

Using the VPOINT Prompt Screen To Select a VPOINT

The first tool is the **VPOINT** Screen Prompt that you see in the VPOINT SCREEN PROMPT drawing. You can get this image up on your screen several ways:

☐ Picking the concentric circle diagram in the 3-D section of the Tablet Menu.

☐ Picking VPOINT from the Screen Menu and then picking the **axes** screen subcommand.

☐ Getting the VPOINT prompt on the Command: line and then hit a (RETURN). (A second (RETURN) executes the command.)

Here's how to use the VPOINT Prompt Screen.

Consider your drawing to be located at the center of the earth. The concentric circles on the screen represent the earth, the center point equals the north pole and the outer circle equals the south pole.

When you move the cursor around, you move around the outside of the earth's sphere. If the cursor is in the inner circle, you are looking from the northern hemisphere. If the cursor is in the outer circle, you are looking from "under" your drawing or from the southern hemisphere.

The dynamically moving X,Y and Z axis which shows on your screen reflects the position of your VPOINT. For some people, this is an intuitive way to select a VPOINT.

By positioning the cursor in the concentric circles on the VPOINT Prompt Screen and then picking, you will select a VPOINT in response to the VPOINT prompt. Your drawing is regenerated to reflect your VPOINT position.

Using the VPOINT Tablet Prompts to Select a VPOINT

The second tool that AutoCAD provides for figuring out VPOINTs is a series of tablet boxes and "VPOINT calculators" built into the commands behind those boxes. Find the 3-D section of your Tablet Menu. It looks like AutoCAD 3-D TABLET MENU.

The top three boxes are straight forward—HIDE issues the HIDE Command, the concentric circles gets you the VPOINT Prompt Screen discussed above, and the ELEV/THICK button executes the ELEV command.

Now look at the nine boxes below. The PLAN box sets VPOINT to 0,0,1, the Plan View or default VPOINT for working in 2-D. All of the other eight boxes position you away from your drawing at the sides noted, looking back at your drawing.

As soon as you pick a side to look from, you get a screen menu that asks you to select a height to look up or down from.

After you select a "side" and "height", AutoCAD calculates the VPOINT from your selections and regenerates the drawing.

Try playing with VPOINT using both the VPOINT Screen Prompt and VPOINT Tablet Prompts. If you get lost in outer space, you can always return to Plan View by picking the tablet PLAN box or by resetting VPOINT = 0,0,1.

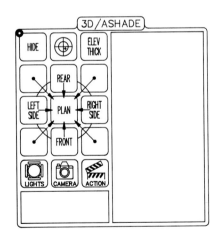

3-D Tablet Commands

MAKING 3-D IMAGES MORE REALISTIC WITH HIDDEN LINE REMOVAL

While you were playing around with VPOINT and different views of the 3DCUP drawing, AutoCAD was responding with screen images that showed a wireframe representation of the drawing file. All of those wire edges help you to visualize just how the pencil holder appears in 3-D space.

When AutoCAD generates a wireframe image, it does not stop to think whether a piece of the frame would be visible from your viewpoint or not. It puts up all the wires indiscriminately, even those that would be hidden from view if your object was a solid.

Once you get a VPOINT image on the screen that you like, you can **HIDE** those hidden lines from view. This gives you an image that is likely to deceive the eye even more into thinking that the flat screen 2-D plane is jumping out at you.

The command is very simple:

USING HIDE TO GET RID OF HIDDEN LINES

```
Get a VPOINT = 1,1,1.

Command: HIDE (RETURN)
Removing hidden lines: nn (AutoCAD gives you a count.)

(Old image disappears, new one appears after a while...)

Command:
```

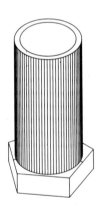

3D and Hidden View

Calculating a hidden line removal can take a long time. AutoCAD tells you that it is processing hidden lines with a number count — don't despair, eventually you will get your hidden line view.

What Gets Hidden With HIDE

Here's a way to think about hidden lines. If you were to cover your view of a 3-D wireframe model with a tight-fitting piece of cloth, you would only see the sides of the cloth facing you, and nothing behind the cloth. In effect, AutoCAD attempts to hide all lines from view that would be on the backside of the model.

Hiding all those lines doesn't always work. Calculating hidden lines can be a complex mathematical process. In the current release of AutoCAD the authors of the program state that small round-off errors may cause problems with touching or intersecting lines.

> There's no hiding from the fact that HIDE only gives a representational
> 3-D image.
>
> — The Second Rule of 3-D

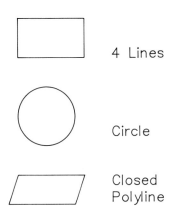

4 Lines

Circle

Closed
Polyline

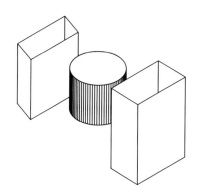

HIDE Examples—Closed and Open Surfaces

Most AutoCAD users find that the amount of line hiding that AutoCAD does is more than adequate for getting a feel for how 3-D models will look in real life. If you need to turn out a highly exact drawing, you can always use an editing command like ERASE to remove any lines that AutoCAD leaves in place.

(Yes, all normal editing commands work on 3-D generated images!)

When considering HIDE, it helps to know how AutoCAD treats surfaces when it calculates hidden line removal. AutoCAD puts a non-see-through cap on the bottom and top of most graphic primitives that surround an area.

For example, a circle, solid, trace or wide polyline will have surfaces that hide lines behind the surface. Lines have no top or bottom and therefore do not hide lines enclosed within, even when the line is extruded as if it were a "wall-like" part of the model.

A polyline only hides what is behind its extrusion or concealed by its width, but it has no top or bottom even when closed. This is why the top of the cylinder appeared solid in the POLYGON BASE DRAWING, yet you can see the back of the base therough its "top" of lines. To create a solid base, use a SOLID or wide PLINE. To get the expected cylinder effect, redraw the cylinder with DONUT.

Using Hidden Layers To See Hidden Lines

What happens to all those hidden lines? When generating a HIDE view, AutoCAD discards the vectors that would be hidden. They are not part of the image on the screen, and they cannot be edited. With one exception...

Let's say you build your plan view 3-D model entities on a layer called **Stuff**. If you also create a layer called **Hiddenstuff**, all hidden lines will get put on the Hiddenstuff layer when you use HIDE to generate a hidden line view.

Any layer in your drawing file can have a hidden line counterpart — even layer 0 (**Hidden0**). All you need to do is create a layer that has the same name as your drawing layer with the letters **h-i-d-d-e-n** as a prefix.

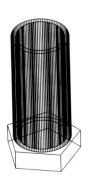

3-D Cup with Hidden Lines

You can control hidden layers just as you would with a drawing layer. You can turn them On and Off, and give them colors and linetypes. A popular use for hidden layers is to construct a 3-D view, HIDE it, and look at the screen view or plotted view of the drawing with the hidden lines in a different color and/or linetype than those used in the viewed drawing.

IN SEARCH OF THE WILD HIDDEN LAYER

Try creating a HIDDEN0 layer and regenerating the 3DCUP model. When the image is on the screen, change layer HIDDEN0 color or linetype, or turn it Off altogether.

When you are through playing around, END to get out of the drawing editor and SAVE your drawing.

Plotting in 3-D

Getting 3-D model views from the screen to the plotter is easy. Once you have the 3-D image in front of you, simply execute a PLOT or PRPLOT command and follow the usual prompts.

You can use a VIEW (if you defined one) to get a PLOT or PRPLOT of a 3-D model from the Main Menu PLOT or PRPLOT. Otherwise, AutoCAD will use the view point set at the time the file was SAVEd, WBLOCKed, or ENDed.

When you are plotting a 3-D model, the default plotting prompts tell you that **Hidden lines will NOT be removed**. You can remove hidden lines at the time of plotting. When the plotting prompts ask **Do you want to change anything?**, answer **Yes** and change the hidden line setting to **Hidden lines WILL be removed**. Remember that removing hidden lines takes time, so removing them at the time of plotting will make plotting calculations longer.

CREATING AN ERGONOMIC CHAIR WITH 3-D MODELLING

Just as you needed to design a pencil holder to hold all the pencils you won't be needing any more, you have to design a comfortable chair to sit in while you watch your CAD screen do all of your work. Every CAD system should have a five-legged ergonomic chair.

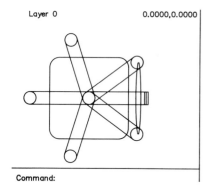

In this exercise you will create the chair from bottom up, starting with the casters, and ending with the seat back. For each part, you will have to set the ELEVATION and thickness, and place the Plan View of each part in relation to the others.

CHAIR 3-D VIEW shows how your chair will eventually look. CHAIR PLAN VIEW shows how all the parts line up in relation to one another. The following text gives you the information you need to know to construct the chair drawing.

Plan View all Components

BUILDING A 3-D CHAIR MODEL

Use Main Menu 1.
Begin a NEW Drawing to start a file called CHAIR

Use the screen menu SETUP to get a "Full" Scale drawing on a 36" x 24" D size sheet.

Leave UNITS alone. You have a 36.0000 x 24.0000 area to work in. Don't bother turning on Inches.

Turn GRID On. Set spacing to 1.0000.

Turn SNAP On. Set spacing to 0.25.

Get the status line digital read out to track your cursor. All of the absolute coordinates given below can be picked with the current SNAP setting, just line up using the digital readout.

Create the casters.

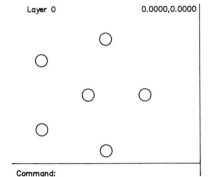

Layer 0   0.0000,0.0000

Command:

Casters and Pedestal—Plan View

```
Command: ELEV (RETURN)
New current elevation <0.0000>: (RETURN)
New current thickness <0.0000>: 2.5 (RETURN)
Command: CIRCLE (RETURN)
3P/2P/TTR/<Center point>: 28,12 (RETURN)
Diameter<Radius>: 1.25 (RETURN)
Command: ARRAY (RETURN)
Select objects: Last (RETURN)
1 found.
Select objects: (RETURN)    (To end selection.)
Rectangular or Polar array (R/P): Polar (RETURN)
Center point of array: 16,12 (RETURN)
Number of items: 5 (RETURN)
Angle to fill (+=CCW, -=CW) <360>: (RETURN)
Rotate objects as they are copied? <Y> (RETURN)
Command:
```

Next create the center pedestal.

```
Command: ELEV (RETURN)
New current elevation <0.0000>: 2 (RETURN)
New current thickness <2.5000>: 15.5 (RETURN)
Command: CIRCLE (RETURN)
3P/2P/TTR/<Center point>: 16,12 (RETURN)
Diameter<Radius>: 1.25 (RETURN)
Command:
```

Now for the legs...

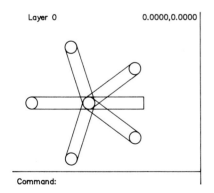

Layer 0   0.0000,0.0000

Command:

Legs and Back Support

```
Command: ELEV (RETURN)
New current elevation <2.0000>: 2.5 (RETURN)
New current thickness <15.5000>: 1.5 (RETURN)
Command: LINE (RETURN)
From point: Quad (RETURN)
of    (Pick top of center pedestal circle.)
To point: Quad (RETURN)
of    (Pick top of caster circle to the right.)
To point: (RETURN)  (To end continuous lines.)
Command: LINE (RETURN)
From point: Quad (RETURN)
of    (Pick bottom of center pedestal circle.)
To point: Quad (RETURN)
of    (Pick bottom of caster circle to the right.)
To point: (RETURN)  (To end continuous lines.)
Command: ARRAY (RETURN)
Select objects: 1 selected, 1 found.  (Pick one leg line.)
Select objects: 1 selected, 1 found.  (Pick the other leg
line.)
Select objects: (RETURN)  (To end selection.)
Rectangular or Polar array (R/P): Polar (RETURN)
Center point of array: 16,12 (RETURN)
```

```
Number of items: 5 (RETURN)
Angle to fill (+=CCW, -=CW) <360>: (RETURN)
Rotate objects as they are copied? <Y> (RETURN)
Command:
```

Next the back support base.

Because we are used to working with ORTHO and horizontal lines extending from the center pedestal, we can ROTATE what we've built so far to clear this work area to build the back support base.

```
Command: ELEV (RETURN)
New current elevation <2.5000>: 17.25 (RETURN)
New current thickness <1.5000>: 0.75 (RETURN)
Command: Rotate (RETURN)
Select objects: Crossing (RETURN)
First corner: Other corner: 16 found.   (Pick a  Crossing
  window to include all the objects on the screen.)
Select objects: (RETURN)   (To end selection.)
Base point: 16,12 (RETURN)
<Rotation angle>/Reference: 36 (RETURN)     (Half a chair
  leg rotation.)
Command: LINE (RETURN)
From point: Quad (RETURN)
of    (Pick the top of the center pedestal circle.)
To point: 12,0 (RETURN)
To point: 0,-2.5 (RETURN)    (That's a negative 2.5.)
To point: Quad (RETURN)
of    (Pick the bottom of the center pedestal circle.)
Command:
```

Now the seat itself.

```
Command: ELEV (RETURN)
New current elevation <17.2500>: 18 (RETURN)
New current thickness <0.7500>: 1 (RETURN)
Command: LINE (RETURN)
From point: 8,4 (RETURN)
To point: 24,4 (RETURN)
To point: 24,20 (RETURN)
To point: 8,20 (RETURN)
To point: Close (RETURN)
Command: FILLET (RETURN)
Polyline/Radius/<Select to objects>: Radius (RETURN)
Enter fillet radius <0.0000>: 2 (RETURN)
Command:
Fillet the four corners of the seat.
Command:
```

Now try the back support upright.

```
Command: ELEV (RETURN)
New current elevation <18.0000>: (RETURN)
New current thickness <1.0000>: 13 (RETURN)
Command: LINE (RETURN)
From point: 28,10.75 (RETURN)
To point: 28,13.25 (RETURN)
To point: 27.25,13.25 (RETURN)
To point: 27.25,10.75 (RETURN)
To point: Close (RETURN)
Command:
```

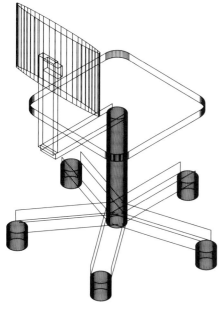

Chair 3-D View

There's a little block between the back support upright and the back.

```
Command: ELEV (RETURN)
New current elevation <18.0000>: 28.5 (RETURN)
New current thickness <13.0000>: 1.5 (RETURN)
Command: LINE (RETURN)
From point: 27.25,10.75 (RETURN)
To point: 27.25,13.25 (RETURN)
To point: 26.5,13.25 (RETURN)
To point: 26.5,10.75 (RETURN)
To point: Close (RETURN)
Command:
```

And finally the back itself.

```
Command: ELEV (RETURN)
New current elevation <28.5000>: 25.5 (RETURN)
New current thickness <1.5000>: 9 (RETURN)
Command: ELLIPSE (RETURN)
<Axis endpoint 1>/Center: 26.5,12 (RETURN)
Axis endpoint 2: 25.5,12 (RETURN)
<Other axis distance>/Rotation: 7 (RETURN)
Command: SAVE (RETURN)
File name <CHAIR>: (RETURN)
Command:
```

Sit back in your chair and have a look!

```
Command: VPOINT (RETURN)
Enter view point <0.0000,0.0000,1.0000>: 1,1,1 (RETURN)
Regenerating drawing.
Command:
```

To get the grid dots back down on earth...

```
Command: ELEV (RETURN)
New current elevation <25.5000>: 0 (RETURN)
New current thickness <9.0000>: 0 (RETURN)
Command:
```

Sit back with your chair and take a look from all over. When you get views you like, try the HIDE command to clean up hidden lines. When you're through, END.

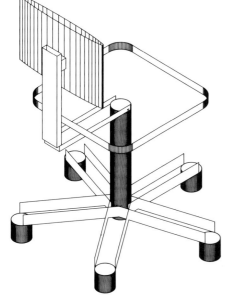

3D Chair—Hidden

255

TRICKS AND TIPS FOR MAKING 3-D WORK FOR YOU

☐ Isometric is Just One Kind of 3-D

☐ Even though AutoCAD has no special tools for building perspectives, you can create one-point, two- point, and axonometric perspectives in AutoCAD. Use the same mechanical drafting techniques you would use on your drawing file but let AutoCAD help with the angles and construction lines.

☐ Isometric mode is best for production drawing, while 3-D may be best for design and presentation. You can't annotate 3-D drawings easily.

☐ Isometrics, 3-D and Text.

☐ Isometric Text. To create Isometric Text which is not just aligned with the isometric grid, create angled text STYLEs. For example, use -30 degrees for the LEFT Side and Top aligned with the Right side.

☐ 3-D Text. Text and dimensions are normally in the X-Y plane., and correctly skewed when seen from a 3-D VPOINT. Sharp viewing angles in the X or Y axis can create unreadable text. There is no straight-forward way to put text in the Z axis, or to annotate a 3-D View with normal text.

☐ Text in 3-D. Text ignores the Thickness setting when created. If you want text with a 3-D thickness, use the CHANGE command after creating the text.

☐ Making Sense of VPOINT.

☐ What you are looking at is always located at 0,0,0.

☐ You move around the drawing, not the other way around.

☐ If you are having trouble picking a VPOINT, try to pinpoint the VPOINT angle (X and Y) first and then adjust the VPOINT Z.

☐ Dynamically Viewing Without Adjusting VPOINT.

☐ Find a good standard VPOINT that you like (like 1,1,1) and VPOINT your drawing to make sure it gives you a good view. Then BLOCK your entire drawing (or a part) into a single block. INSERT it back into the drawing.

☐ Use ROTATE, SCALE, and MOVE to manipulate the 3-D image while still in 3-D and without changing VPOINT.

☐ 3-D Has its Limitations and Is Not Perfect.

☐ Projections, VPOINT generations, and HIDEs are close, but not exact.

☐ Instead of depending on perfect 3-D output from AutoCAD, use AutoCAD 3-D images as a reference drawing for preparing presentations and renderings.

☐ In the current version of AutoCAD a single object has a single Elevation and Thickness across its entire entity. There is no tapering in the Z-direction.

☐ Tricks For Improving and Working With HIDE.

☐ Turn off layers that contain extra information before attempting a HIDE. It takes long enough to do a HIDE, there is no reason to have AutoCAD spend time removing hidden lines unnecessarily.

☐ If you have top and bottom surfaces that are created with single linetype entities and that do not hide lines behind them, try soldifying the surface boundary with circles, solids, traces or wide polylines.

☐ While regular VPOINT 3-D views are dynamically editable, views that have had hidden lines removed are not—you can edit them, but when you do, you may loose the hidden property. If you have to edit a hidden view, execute HIDE when you are through editing, to regenerate the hidden view correctly.

☐ Spruce Up Your 3-D and ISO Images By Using Surface Boundaries as a Edges for Hatching or Color Solids.

More lines on paper. AutoCAD's 3-D shows there is a lot going on behind-the-scenes in your drawings. In the next Chapter we take a behind-the-scenes-look at spatial intelligence and dimensioning.

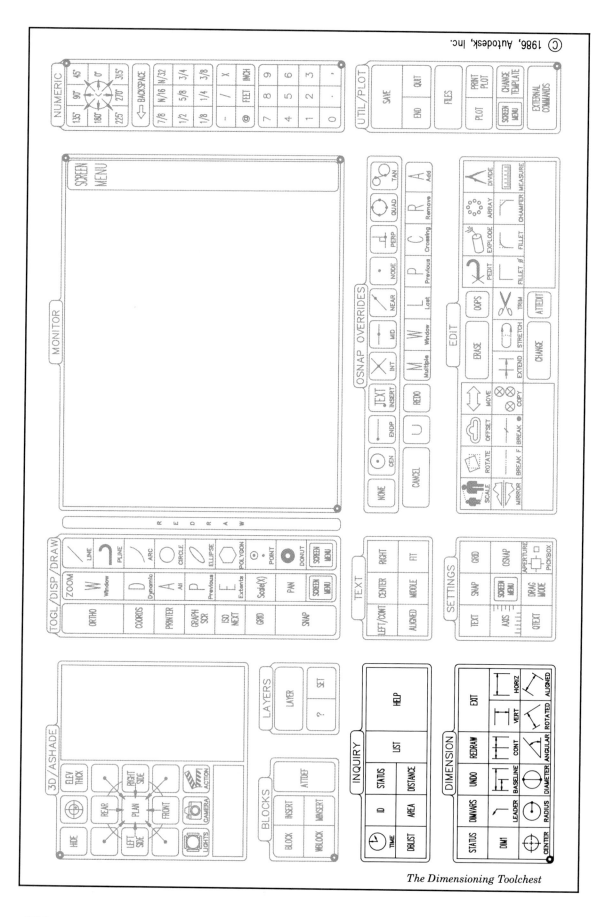

The Dimensioning Toolchest

CHAPTER 10

DRAWING INTELLIGENCE

ADDING "SMARTS" TO YOUR DRAWING

Spatial Intelligence—Dimensioning. The Dimensioning Toolchest. Dimension Examples. Dimensioning Some Circles—And More Circles. Dimensioning Polygons. Aligned Dimensions. Angle Dimensions. ▶ Alternative Text For Dimensioning. How to Scale Dimensions. ▶ One More Dimensioning Example. ▶ Other Intelligence. ▶ Summing Up With Dimensioning Tips.

SPATIAL INTELLIGENCE—DIMENSIONING

For professional designers, the drawing is a communication medium. To make a drawing actually communicate a design idea, the drawing must represent the design idea accurately, and contain enough information to get the design points across.

Isolated lines, arcs, symbols, and text often are not enough to communicate the whole idea. Graphic elements have a spatial relationship to each other which are important. While a graphics image may be worth a thousand words, there are still literally thousands of words that are required to explain and support professional designs.

You can store both spatial relations and non-spatial information inside AutoCAD drawing files. That's what we mean by adding intelligence—"smarts"—to the drawing.

A spatial relationship describes how one graphic element in the drawing file physically relates to another. The most common spatial relationships appear in a drawing as dimension lines measuring the distance between two points or the curve of an arc. This Chapter describes AutoCAD's ability to dimension drawings and measure other spatial, graphic intelligence.

Non-spatial information also makes a drawing communicate. An example of non-spatial information is text or an attribute in a drawing that describes a graphic element, but has no bearing on the spatial intelligence of that element. "Phone number 1234", "Aluminum #8 Flat Head Screw", and "80386 Processor" are examples of non-graphic intelligence that can be added to an AutoCAD drawing file. The next Chapter, ATTRIBUTES, describes AutoCAD's ability to handle non-spatial, non-graphic intelligence.

Spatial Intelligence

When lines are placed into a drawing file, they often represent distances and locations with **real world** relationships. Helping the drawing reader understand these spatial implications is part of creating a good drawing. Tools for working with spatial information are part of AutoCAD (or any CAD system worth its salt). These tools fall under the rubric—**DIMENSIONING**.

```
AutoCAD
* * * *
SETUP

BLOCKS
DIM:
DISPLAY
DRAW
EDIT
INQUIRY
LAYER:
SETTINGS
PLOT
UTILITY
3D

SAVE:
```

```
AutoCAD
* * * *
AREA:
DBLIST:
DIST:
HELP:
ID:
LIST:
STATUS:
TIME:




—LAST—
DRAW
EDIT
```

```
AutoCAD
* * * *
DIST:







—LAST—
DRAW
EDIT
```

ROOT to INQUIRY to DIST

AutoCAD knows quite a bit about the spatial relationships between points in a drawing file before you even add a graphic representation like a dimension line. To prove this point try this example:

INSIDE AutoCAD DISTANCES ARE A SNAP

Enter the Main Menu. Begin a new drawing. Call it TRYDIM.

Set SNAP to .25. Set GRID to 1. Toggle COORDS On.
Leave UNITS at default.

Draw a LINE from **3,1** to **6,7**

Now Pick INQUIRY on the ROOTMENU, and the DIST Command from the INQUIRY Screen Menu.

SNAP endpoint to pick the lower endpoint of the line, and again to pick the upper endpoint of the line.

Command: DIST First point: (pick) Second point: (pick)

Distance = 6.7082   Angle = 63
Delta X = 3.0000   Delta Y = 6.0000

Command:

When you are through with this example SAVE your drawing and clear the decks for another exercise.

Command: **SAVE (RETURN)**

Layer 0 Snap   0.0000,0.0000

Distance = 6.7082   Angle = 63.00
Delta X = 3.0000   Delta Y = 6.0000
Command:

DIST with Two Pick Points Delivers a
Distance

You see AutoCAD already knows a lot about that line, even without a formal description of all of the spatial intelligence imbedded in the drawing file. The **INQUIRY** key list of commands includes several tools for Non-destructive Testing of the AutoCAD drawing file. Using inquiry commands, you can measure, identify, and generally **find out** about what's in a drawing file.

Our goal for this Chapter is to turn spatial intelligence into drawing embellishments. Much of the time AutoCAD already knows spatial intelligence (entity relationships) from the way you placed drawing elements. In these cases, you just have to get it to show what's in the drawing file. Other times, you have to describe relationships and add this information to the file.

THE DIMENSIONING TOOLCHEST

Let's take a look at the **DIMENSION**ing tools available with AutoCAD. DIMENSION routines allow you to place extension lines, arrows, and label text around any graphic element, or group of elements. In order to DIMENSION a graphic element, you have to set a series of parameters, just as you have to set parameters for a MOVE or TEXT command.

Dimensioning has a mode and a vocabulary all its own. Here are a few definitions:

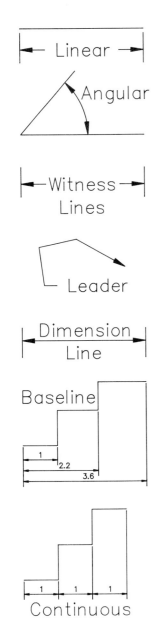

Primer Examples

DIMENSION VOCABULARY PRIMER

☐ Linear—A set of dimension lines, extension lines, arrows, and text that measures distance between two (or more) points in a straight line.

☐ Angular—A set of dimension lines, witness lines, arrows and text that measures the angle encompassed by an arc, circle, or two joining lines.

☐ Extension Lines—Also Called Witness Lines — Short line segments that show the drawing reader what is measured by dimension lines.

☐ Leader—A special single dimension line that joins dimension text with an element being dimensioned or annotated.

☐ Dimension Line—A line that shows what distance or angle is measured by the dimension process. It usually has arrows at the ends.

☐ Baseline Dimensions —A series of dimension lines, starting at the same witness line, that measure successive linear distances.

☐ Continuing Dimensions—A series of dimension lines that follow one another along successive linear distances.

Dimensioning Commands

If you can draw it, you can measure it. If you can measure it, you can dimension it. AutoCAD provides dozens of ways to measure and draw dimension lines. In addition, you have complete control over the way the dimension graphics look. In dimensioning, you can decide:

☐ How big and what the arrows look like (if you decide to use arrows).

☐ How big and what Style the text will be.

☐ If there will be tolerance ranges included with the text.

☐ Where the dimension text will go.

Because dimensioning is so flexible and has so many command options, AutoCAD sets up a new mode for dimensioning.

The DIM Prompt

Once you enter dimensioning, you'll see a new prompt, **Dim:**, instead of the usual AutoCAD **Command:** prompt on the prompt line. As you might suspect, when in **Dim:** you can't execute the regular AutoCAD commands. This means no ZOOMing, DRAWing, etc. If you have to get regularAutoCAD work done, do it before you execute the DIM command from the ROOTMENU, or Exit or CANCEL back to the Command: prompt.

If you know that you only want to perform one DIMensioning subcommand, you can use the special **DIM1** command. Instead of keeping you in DIM: prompt mode after the execution of one DIMensioning subcommand, DIM1 returns you to the Command: prompt.

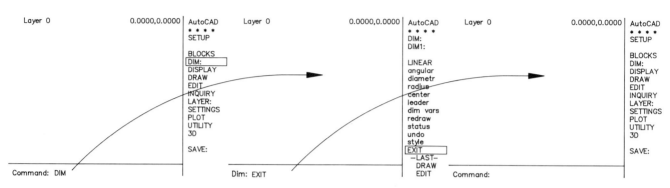

DIM: takes you from the regular Command: prompt to the Dim: prompt. Exit (^C) returns you to the Command: prompt.

Like DRAW's list of commands, DIM comes with its own list of commands. You can group these loosely into three classes:

DIMENSIONING COMMAND CLASSIFICATION

☐ Distance Between Two Points.

    ☐ LINear—A group of commands which measure between two points. The points can be endpoints, intersections, arc chord endpoints, or just about any two points you can identify.

    ☐ DIAmeter—Measures between two diametrically opposed points on the circumference of a circle.

    ☐ RADius—Measures from an arc or circle centerpoint to a circumference point.

☐ Angle Between Two Non-Parallel Lines.

    ☐ ANGular—Measures the inner or outer (Acute or Obtuse) angle between two specified lines.

☐ Other Dimensioning Commands.

    ☐ CENter—Puts a cross at the center of an arc or circle.

    ☐ LEAder—Allows you to create an extended arrow to place dimension text away from the immediate objects being dimensioned.

    ☐ Undo— As with the LINE command, Undo in DIM is forgiving. But instead of taking out the last object, DIM's Undo removes all objects (witness lines, arrows, text, etc.) from the last DIM try. You can only Undo one time, like OOPS.

    ☐ REDRAW—Is just like the regular REDRAW command.

    ☐ STATUS and DIM VARS—These two commands display and control all the settings for variable DIM features like arrow, and text size.

    ☐ EXIT—A handy command in DIM. EXIT gets you out of the DIM: mode and back to the regular AutoCAD Command: mode.

Dimensioning Example Diagrams

Dimensioning inside AutoCAD is very flexible. While AutoCAD makes it easy to create dimension lines, extension lines, and arrows by using extensive <default> settings, you have complete control over all of the dimension parameters. Some dimension parameters require values (like the size of an arrow), while others toggle only between **On** or **Off**. These parameters are called **DIM**ension **VAR**iable**S** and they are listed below along with their default settings:

DIMENSION VARIABLES WITH DEFAULT SETTINGS

DIM VARS Name	Default Value	Description
DIMSCALE	1.0000	Overall scale factor.
DIMALT	Off	Alternative text adjacent to standard.
DIMALTF	25.4	Multiplier for DIMALT measurements.
DIMALTD	2	Number of decimals in DIMALTF measurement.
DIMASZ	0.1800	Arrow size.
DIMBLK	. (period)	Block name of customized arrowhead.
DIMCEN	0.0900	Center mark size.
DIMEXO	0.0625	Extension line origin offset.
DIMDLE	0.0000	Dimension line extension through ticks.
DIMDLI	0.3800	Dimension line increment for CONTINUation or BASELINe commands.
DIMEXE	0.1800	Extension beyond dimension line.
DIMLFAC	1.0000	Overall linear units multiplier factor.
DIMRND	0.0000	Overall rounding tolerance for measurements.
DIMTP	0.0000	Plus tolerance.
DIMTM	0.0000	Minus tolerance.
DIMTXT	0.1800	Text height.
DIMTSZ	0.0000	Tick size.
DIMTOL	*Off	Add +/- to dimension text.
DIMLIM	*Off	Shows the dimension text as two values using DIMTP and DIMTM.
DIMTIH	On	Horizontal text inside extensions.
DIMTOH	On	Horizontal text outside extensions.
DIMSE1	Off	Suppress first extension line.
DIMSE2	Off	Suppress second extension line.
DIMTAD	Off	Puts text above the dimension line.
DIMZIN	Off	Suppress 0" after feet.

*Either DIMTOL or DIMLIM can be on at the same time -- not both.

Layer 0   0.0000,0.0000

Command:

Basic Dimension Diagram

DIMENSION EXAMPLES

To illustrate AutoCAD's dimension tools, you will create dimension types—one at a time—to see how they're done. First create a drawing with some parts in it. Then dimension a number of possible combinations with the aid of a diagram. Not all by any means. But a fair number. The diagram you will use is shown in BASIC DIMENSION DIAGRAM.

Create the the BASIC DIMENSION DIAGRAM by typing the coordinates in the SETUP (below) to get exact distances.

DIMENSIONING EXAMPLE SETUP

Recall your drawing called TRYDIM.
ERASE everything in your drawing.

Set GRID at 1. Set SNAP at 0.25. Leave UNITS and LIMITS at default.

Leave the rest of setup to default values.

```
Command: CIRCLE (RETURN)
3P/2P/TTR/<Center point>: 5,7 (RETURN)
Diameter/<Radius>: 1.25 (RETURN)
Command: LINE (RETURN)
From point: 2,4 (RETURN)
To point: 9,4 (RETURN)
To point: @0,-2 (RETURN)
To point: @-2,0 (RETURN)
To point: @-0.5,1 (RETURN)
To point: @-3.5,0 (RETURN)
To point: @-1,-1 (RETURN)
To point: c (RETURN)
Command:
```

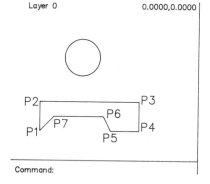

Layer 0   0.0000,0.0000

Command:

Dimensioning Example Setup

Now you are all set to practice dimensioning. Here are nine dimension examples:

DIMENSION EXAMPLES

☐ Dimensioning the circle with a radius.

☐ Dimensioning the circle with a diameter.

☐ Dimensioning the circle overall.

☐ Dimensioning the polygon overall with horizontal dimensions.

☐ Dimensioning the polygon with overall vertical dimensions.

☐ Dimensioning the polygon with horizontal continuing dimensions.

☐ Dimensioning the polygon vertically from a baseline with overall vertical dimensions.

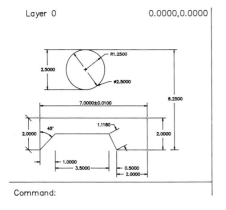

Layer 0   0.0000,0.0000

Command:

Target Dimension Drawing

☐ Aligned dimensions.

☐ Angle dimensions.

Let's step through each of the nine examples in sequence. The basic dimensioning command flow is as follows:

DIMENSIONING LOGIC FLOW

☐ Set up the basic parameters to tell AutoCAD **how** you want it to draw dimension lines.

    ☐ Arrowhead Type.

    ☐ Arrowhead Size.

    ☐ Witness Line Offset.

    ☐ Placement of dimension lines and text.

☐ Then identify **what** it is you want to measure.

    ☐ Pick endpoints, arcs, or other points of existing drawing elements, using OSNAP if needed.

☐ Tell AutoCAD **where** you want the dimension line and text located.

☐ Approve AutoCAD's measurements as dimension text, or type in your own text.

AutoCAD makes very good <default> assumptions about dimension setup parameters. For the first few examples, you won't need to change the **how** parameters. When you start to change these parameters, you will see how these affect the dimension process and you can tailor the dimensioning process to your needs.

In the examples, we will set up different ways to put in dimensions. This is for two reasons:

☐ So you can see how to clean up mistakes in DIM. When dimensioning, you place many lines, arrows, and text in the drawing file at one time. If you make a mistake you need to know how to get rid of these elements all at once.

☐ So you can see how carefully you have to choose dimensioning parameters, and what happens if you just assume that you can overcome AutoCAD's dimensioning logic flow.

You can type the commands, or pick them from the screen or tablet menus.

Let's start with simple circles.

DIMENSIONING SOME CIRCLES—AND MORE CIRCLES

Circle Radius

First let's put a CENter mark in the center of the circle.

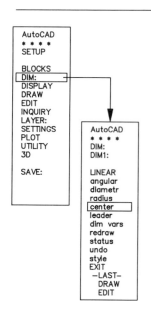

Layer 0   0.0000,0.0000

Dim: CENTER Select arc or circle:

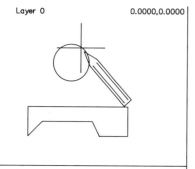

Layer 0   0.0000,0.0000

Dim:

Center Sequence

PLACING A CENTER MARK

Pick DIM from the ROOTMENU to get the DIM screen menu.

Command: **DIM (RETURN)**
Dim: (Notice the Dim: instead of the Command: prompt.)

Type **CEN** or pick CENter from the screen menu.

Dim: CENTER Select arc or circle

Pick any point on the circumference of the circle.

(A center mark appears.)

Next put in the **RADIUS** dimension line and measurement. Remember, first you tell AutoCAD what it is you want to dimension, then you tell it where to place the dimension elements.

PLACING A RADIUS DIMENSION -- FIRST TRY

Type **RAD** or pick RADius from the screen menu.

Dim: RAD Select arc or circle:

Select the circle using a point near the 0 degree point on the circumference.

Dim: RAD Select arc or circle: (pick circle near 0 degrees.)
Dimension text <1.2500>: **(RETURN)**
Text does not fit.
Enter leader length for text: **1 (RETURN)**
Dim:

AutoCAD has politely measured the radius for you, and offered you the correct dimension text it will use in drawing the dimension. Notice, however, that the **1.2500** is in brackets (<1.2500>). This means AutoCAD's suggested text is a <default> prompt.

You can always change a <default> dimension text prompt. For example, you would change a <default> text if you wanted different measurements, units or rounding, or if you wanted a note instead of numbers.

AutoCAD tried to put the dimension lines, arrow, and text inside the circle, but they wouldn't fit. So AutoCAD asked you to decide where the text should go. By entering a **1** from the keyboard you set up an offset distance to place the text away from the circle. You also could pick the leader length with your pointer, but not the angle.

Your screen drawing results should look like the FIRST TRY RADIUS drawing.

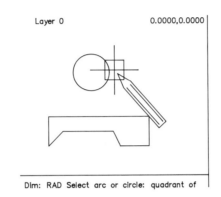

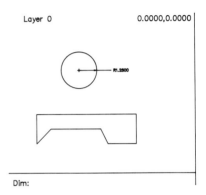

Radius Dimension—First Try

This is all well and good. But it's not quite where you wanted the radius dimension to end up. (See the TARGET DRAWING.) AutoCAD used the pick point as the circumference location for the radius dimension.

Let's undo that radius, and put in the correct one. Type **U** or pick Undo from the screen menu. All the radius dimension elements will go away—that is the dimension line, the leader, the arrow, and the text.

AN IMPORTANT NOTE ABOUT Undo IN DIMENSION

Undo executed from within the DIM: command remembers only one previous DIM: command. You cannot keep going back a step at a time as you can in the LINE command.

If you EXIT from DIM: and re-enter DIM: mode, AutoCAD forgets the last dimension item to undo. You can always use ERASE Last several times to wipe out each dimension element—text, arrow, and leader.

BE CAREFUL if you use UNDO: from the Command: level prompt immediately after EXITING from DIM:, you will wipe out all of your DIM: activites in one UNDO: back up. You can avoid this by using DIM1 to do one dimension at a time.

Execute the RADIUS command again. This time select the circle by picking the 60 degree point on the circumference. Use **0.5** as the unit leader length. You should get the drawing shown in RADIUS DIMENSION SECOND TRY.

PLACING A RADIUS DIMENSION -- SECOND TRY

(Did you Undo the first try? -- If not, do so now.)

REDRAW to make the center mark reappear (after being wiped out by the undo erasures.)

Type **RAD** or pick RADius from the screen menu.

Dim: RAD Select arc or circle: **5.750,8.000** **(RETURN)**
    (Or pick the location.)

Dimension text <1.2500>: **(RETURN)**
Text does not fit.
Enter leader length for text: **0.5** **(RETURN)**
Dim:

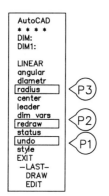
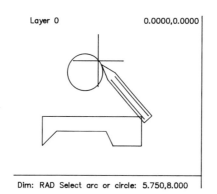
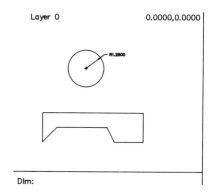

Radius Dimension—Second Try

Notice AutoCAD moves the leader line 0.5 units away from the circle, and then adds a little horizontal bar before the **R1.2500** text.

Unless you change DIM VARS, AutoCAD always writes dimension text horizontally—even angular dimensions. You'll run into problems if your current text style is vertical. You must reset the text style to horizontal before executing the Dim: commands.

Circle Diameter

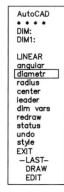

Try the DIAmeter command next. DIAmeter is similar to RADius. When identifying the circle to dimension, DIAmeter uses the point you pick as a diameter endpoint. AutoCAD automatically figures out where the second endpoint goes. (If the **Text does not fit**, a leader will also stem from this picked point, not the opposite end of the diameter).

Run the diameter dimension lines from a circumference point at approximately 120 degrees to 300 degrees:

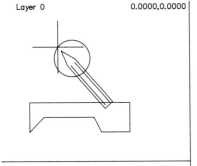

Dim: DIAM Select arc or circle: 4.250,8.000

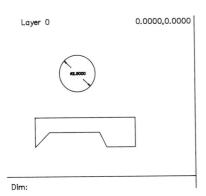

Dim:

Diameter Dimension—First Try

PLACING A DIAMETER DIMENSION -- FIRST TRY

PLACING A DIAMETER DIMENSION -- FIRST TRY

Type **DIA** or pick DIAMETR from the screen menu.

Dim: DIAM Select arc or circle: **4.250,8.000 (RETURN)**
(Or pick the equivalent screen location with SNAP on.)

Dimension text <2.5000>: **(RETURN)**
Dim:

AutoCAD determines everything fits and draws the dimension text. The drawing is shown in DIAMETER FIRST TRY.

This is different from your TARGET drawing. You want the diameter text to go outside the lower right hand part of the circle, not inside the circle.

Let's Undo and start over.

Use DIAmeter again and pick the circle at the same point. Then instead of accepting the prompt for the dimension text, disarm automatic text placement by hitting the **space bar** so that you can display it where you want it.

Use the LEAder command to place the text:

PLACING A DIAMETER DIMENSION -- SECOND TRY

(If you have not done so, Undo the first try.)

Type **DIA** or pick DIAMETR from the screen menu.

Dim: DIAM Select arc or circle: **4.250,8.000 (RETURN)**
(Or pick the equivalent screen location with SNAP on.)

Dimension text <2.5000>: **(SPACE) (RETURN)**
Dim:

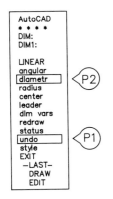

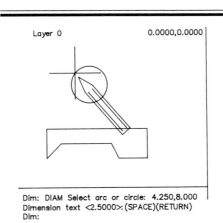

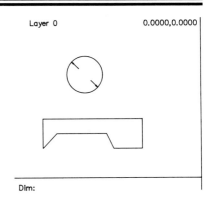

Diameter Dimension—Second Try

AutoCAD fills the circle with a textless diameter dimension line. What you've done, in effect, is replace **2.5000** with " " (space).

Now use the LEAder command to place the text. Select LEAder from the screen menu. LEADER is a special version of LINE. It lets you create a **call out** (starting with an arrowhead) to **point** the dimension text at a specific location. You can make a leader line have many continuous segments. This is sometimes necessary to snake the leader line away from dense drawing parts. AutoCAD prompts for a starting point for the leader line.

Use the OSNAP INTersec to pick the point where the diameter arrow and the circumference point come together—at the lower right side of the circle.

Then extend (drag) the leader line from this first **Leader Start:** point to a **To point:** that positions the dimension text in a readable place:

ADDING A LEADER TO THE DIAMETER DIMENSION

Type **LEA** or pick LEADER from the screen menu.

```
Dim: LEADER Leader start:  intersec (Type INT.)
of  (pick starting point.)
To point: 6.50,6.25 (RETURN)    (A good point.)
To point: (RETURN)        (To end leader extension.)
Dimension text <2.5000>: (RETURN)
Dim:
```

```
AutoCAD
* * * *
DIM:
DIM1:

LINEAR
angular
diametr
radius
center
leader
dim vars
redraw
status
undo
style
EXIT
—LAST—
DRAW
EDIT
```

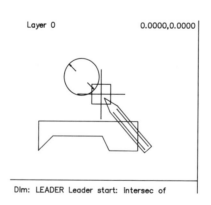

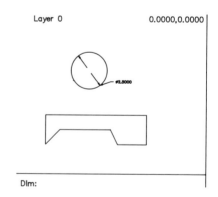

Adding a LEADER

AutoCAD remembers the last dimension text it measured (**2.5000**), and prompts you with it. You can accept it with a **(RETURN)**. AutoCAD does the rest. It puts a horizontal bar at the end of the leader line, remembers the text was diameter and puts in the diameter symbol. Your second try should look like DIAMETER SECOND TRY drawing.

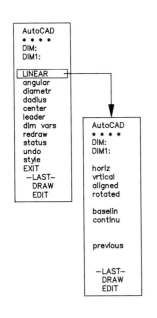

DIM to LINEAR

Circle Overall

Let's move on to measuring the circle overall. This is a LINEAR dimension, using the circle's top and bottom as starting points for witness lines. Extension lines, also called witness lines, show the drawing reader what the dimension lines measure.

If you select LINEAR from the dimension screen menu, you get the following choices:

LINEAR DIMENSION OPTIONS

☐ HORIZ—Creates horizontal dimension lines.

☐ VERTICAL—Creates vertical dimension lines.

☐ ALIGNED—Creates dimension lines that are aligned to an object or two points which you specify.

☐ ROTATED—Creates dimension lines rotated to an angle which you specify.

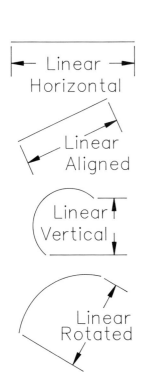

Linear Examples

Start with VERTICAL, since you want a vertical dimension to the circle's left. (See the TARGET DIMENSION DRAWING.) Type **VER** or select VRTICAL from the screen menu.

Vertical gives you two options for dimensioning:

☐ Locating the origins of two extension lines that mark the boundaries of the dimension line.

☐ Picking an object (like a line, arc, or circle) and dimensioning the full length of that object. Examples are the diameter of a circle, the length of a line, and the chord of an arc.

In either case, once you've selected what you want to dimension, AutoCAD prompts you for the location of the dimension line.

In this example, select the whole circle for a vertical dimension, and place the dimension line about one unit to the left of the circle:

DIMENSIONING THE CIRCLE OVERALL

Type **VER** or pick LINEAR and VRTICAL from the screen menus.

```
Dim: VER
First extension line origin or RETURN to select: (RETURN)
Select line, arc, or circle:   (pick any circle point.)
Dimension line location:   (pick a point 1 unit to the
  circle's left or type 2.750,7.000 (RETURN).)

Dimension text <2.5000>:  (RETURN)
Dim:
```

You should get the drawing shown in CIRCLE OVERALL.

Notice that AutoCAD does not use the diameter symbol in the text string. This text string was derived as a linear dimension, not a diameter text string.

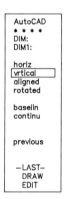

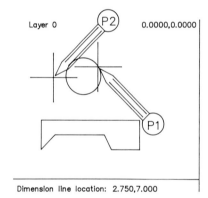

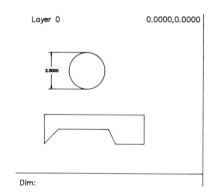

Circle Overall

DIMENSIONING POLYGONS

Polygon Horizontal With Overall Dimensions

To illustrate a few more dimension possibilities, let's go to work on the polygon in the lower portion of the screen. In this example you'll use a HORizontal LINEAR dimension. Instead of selecting an object to dimension (like the whole circle in the last example) you select endpoints for the line you want to dimension.

In the process, you will also change a few of the dimension parameter settings to fine tune the dimension process.

POLYGON HORIZONTAL OVERALL

Type **HOR** or pick LINEAR and HORIZ from the screen menus.

```
Dim: HOR
First extension line origin or RETURN to select:   (pick
the upper left corner of the polygon. Use OSNAP if you
need to. It is a SNAP point.)

Second extension line origin:   (pick the upper right corner
  of the polygon.)

Dimension line location:   (pick a point 0.75 units above
the polygon. You can count 3 SNAP ticks up.)

Dimension text <7.0000>:  (RETURN)
Dim:
```

Let's take a look at the first try. It's shown in the POLYGON HORIZONTAL FIRST TRY drawing.

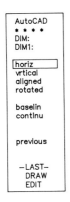
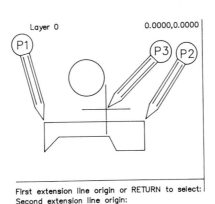
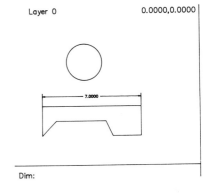

Polygon Horizontal—First Try

AutoCAD breaks the dimension line to leave room for the dimension text. Looking at your TARGET DRAWING, this is not what you want. The TARGET DRAWING also shows that you want tolerances with the dimension text.

It's time to take a look at AutoCAD's **DIM**ension **VAR**iable**S**. There are a lot! Look at the ones which allow you to control tolerance text.

Select DIM VARS from the screen menu. You'll get a list of the dimension variables. Select DIMTAD. That's short for **DIM**ension **T**ext **A**bove the **D**imension line. You want to turn DIMTAD **On**. You also want to set DIMTOL, short for **DIM**ension **TOL**erance, **On**.

Next select DIMTP for **DIM**ension **T**olerance **P**lus. Give it a value of **0.01**. Do the same for DIMTM, **DIM**ension **T**olerance **M**inus.

The prompt sequence looks like this:

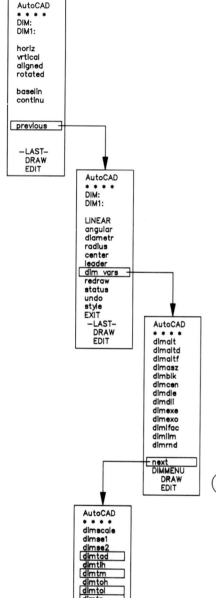

Getting to DIM VARS

SETTING A FEW DIMENSION VARIABLES

Type U or pick Undo from the DIM menu to clean up
the first try.

Get the DIM VARS list by picking DIM VARS from the DIM menu.

Dim: DIMTAD Current value <Off> New Value: On/Off: **On**

The menu returns you to the main Dim: menu. Repeat the process
for the rest of the DIM VARS.

Dim: DIMTOL Current value <Off> New Value: On/Off: **On**
Dim: DIMTP Current value <0.0000> New Value: **0.01** **(RETURN)**
Dim: DIMTM Current value <0.0000> New Value: **0.01** **(RETURN)**
Dim: (Get back to Dim:.)

POLYGON HORIZONTAL -- SECOND TRY

Type **HOR** or pick LINEAR and pick HORIZ.

Use the same two extension points and dimension line location
as in the first try.

Accept the default text.

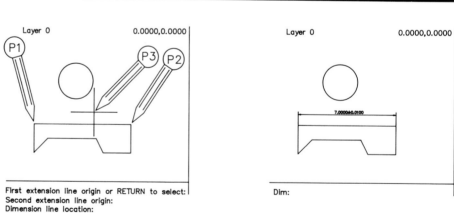

Polygon Horizontal — Second Try

Your drawing should look like the drawing shown in POLYGON HORIZON-
TAL SECOND TRY.

Notice, you get text on top of the dimension line, tolerance included. AutoCAD
combines the tolerance symbol to ± **0.01** because the values are the same.
If they were different, AutoCAD would put plus and minus text lines adjacent
to the **7.0000** value.

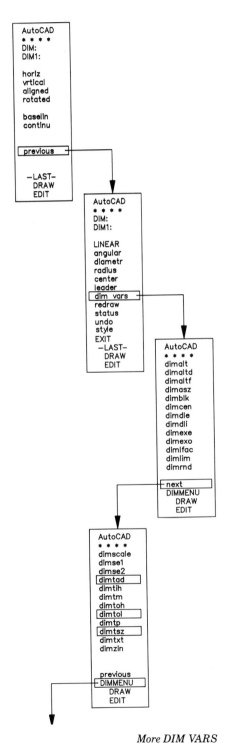

More DIM VARS

Polygon Vertical Overall

To create the left vertical polygon dimension, make use of the VERTical LINEAR commands again. Let's think ahead about what you want by studying the TARGET DRAWING.

First, you don't want tolerances in this dimension. So use DIM VARS to get to DIMTOL, and toggle it **Off**.

Second, you want the dimension text to break the dimension line, so toggle DIMTAD to **Off** as well.

Finally, you want this dimension line to end in **tick** marks, not arrows. As you might guess, there is a DIM VARS for ticks—**DIMTSZ** (**DIM**ension **T**ick **SiZ**e). It takes a value. Select DIMTSZ and give it a value of **0.18** as the tick size.

Whenever DIMTSZ has a value greater than **0**, ticks are drawn instead of arrows.

Here's the corresponding prompt sequence:

SETTING DIM VARS FOR POLYGON VERTICAL DIMENSIONS

Pick DIM VARS to get to the DIM VARS menu.

```
Dim: DIMTOL Current value <Off> New Value: On/Off: Off
Dim: DIMTAD Current value <Off> New Value: On/Off: Off
Dim: DIMTSZ Current value <0.0000> New Value: 0.18 (RETURN)
Dim:
```

Now you're ready to draw the dimension line.

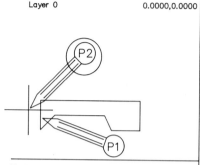

Layer 0   0.0000,0.0000

First ext. line origin or RET. to select:(RETURN)
Select line, arc, or circle:
Dimension line location:

POLYGON VERTICAL OVERALL

Type **VER** or pick LINEAR and pick VRTICAL.

Use a **(RETURN)** to select an object.

First extension line origin or RETURN to select: **(RETURN)**

Select the left line.

Pick a point 0.75 units to the left of the polygon.

Accept the default text.

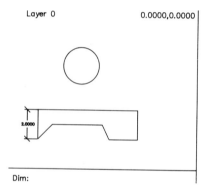

Layer 0   0.0000,0.0000

2.0000

Dim:

Polygon Vertical Overall

Your drawing should look like the POLYGON VERTICAL OVERALL drawing.

Polygon Horizontal With Continuing Dimensions

To start the continuing horizontal dimension string below the polygon, use linear dimensioning again.

POLYGON HORIZONTAL -- FIRST SEGMENT

Get back to DIM VARS.
Toggle the ticks **Off** by setting DIMTSZ to **0**

Dim: DIMTSZ Current value <0.1800> New value: **0**

Type **HOR** or pick LINEAR and pick HORIZ.

Pick the lower left corner of the polygon for the first extension line origin.

Using the crosshair as a guide (and SNAP points), follow the continuous horizontal and pick the next point directly below the first angle, but on the same horizontal as the first pick point.

Give a dimension line location 0.750 units or three SNAP points below the polygon.

Accept AutoCAD's text default.

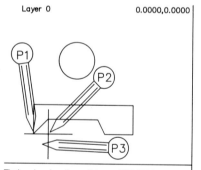

Layer 0   0.0000,0.0000

First extension line origin or RETURN to select:
Second extension line origin:
Dimension line location:

Your drawing should look like POLYGON HORIZONTAL CONTINUING— FIRST SEGMENT. Notice, AutoCAD put the **1.0000** outside the witness line because it could not fit into the dimensioned space. If you want the text on the left side, just reverse the order of the two points.

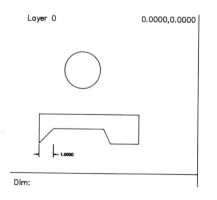

Layer 0   0.0000,0.0000

1.0000

Dim:

Polygon Horizontal Continuing

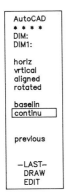

```
AutoCAD
* * * *
DIM:
DIM1:

horiz
vrtical
aligned
rotated

baselin
[contiпи]

previous

—LAST—
DRAW
EDIT
```

Layer 0   0.0000,0.0000

Second extension line origin:

Polygon Horizontal Setup for Continuing

Layer 0   0.0000,0.0000

Dim:

Polygon Continuing Complete

Continuing The Horizontal Dimension With the CONTINUE Command

AutoCAD provides a feature that allows you to continue dimensioning along successive linear points in the same horizontal line. **CONTINUE** starts a new dimension line where the last dimension line left off, using the old witness line as the first witness line for the new dimension line. You CONtinue to add new **second** witness lines.

POLYGON HORIZONTAL CONTINUING

Continue dimensioning along the same horizontal line.

Type **CON** or select CONTINU from the screen menu.

Second extension line origin: (Pick the next point over to the right, the next angle.)

Accept AutoCAD's text.

Notice AutoCAD automatically put the new dimension line below the first one. The distance between the two dimension lines is controllable. The distance is called DIMDLI for**DIM**ension **D**rawing **L**ine **I**ncrement and can be adjusted through the DIM VARS menu and prompts.

POLYGON CONTINUING COMPLETE

To finish the continuing dimension line, select CONTINU twice more, giving the appropriate extension line origins.

A **(RETURN)** repeats the previous Dim: command.

When you're done your drawing should look like POLYGON CONTINUING COMPLETE.

Polygon and Overall Vertical—Using the BASELINE Command

Now you want to come up the polygon's right side, and get the overall vertical dimension for both the polygon and the circle.

First start by putting in a normal vertical dimension:

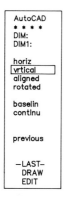

AutoCAD
* * * *
DIM:
DIM1:

horiz
vrtical
aligned
rotated

baselin
continu

previous

—LAST—
DRAW
EDIT

POLYGON VERTICAL -- FIRST SEGMENT

Type **VER** or select LINEAR and VRTICAL.

Select the First extension origin at the bottom right corner of polygon.

Pick the top right corner of the polygon to get the Second extension origin.

Pick a Dimension line location one unit to the right.

Accept the default text.

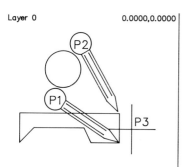

Layer 0   0.0000,0.0000

First extension line origin or RETURN to select:
Second extension line origin:
Dimension line location:

Once the first vertical dimension line is in place, use the menu feature called **BASELINE**. The BASELINE command continues extension lines just like CONTINUE, but BASELINE uses the first or **base** extension line as the origin for all successive dimension calculations and line placement.

USING BASELINE TO CONTINUE THE VERTICAL POLYGON DIMENSION

Type **BAS** or select BASELIN from the screen menu.

BASELIN prompts for a second extension line origin.

Second extension line origin   (To get the correct baseline pick the topmost point on the circle circumference. Use OSNAP QUAdrant, if you need to.)

Accept the default text.

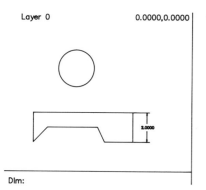

Layer 0   0.0000,0.0000

2.0000

Dim:

Polygon Baseline Sequence

Your results should look like the POLYGON BASELINE DIMENSIONS drawing.

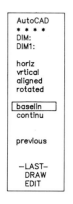

AutoCAD
* * * *
DIM:
DIM1:

horiz
vrtical
aligned
rotated

baselin
continu

previous

—LAST—
DRAW
EDIT

Polygon Baseline Dimensions

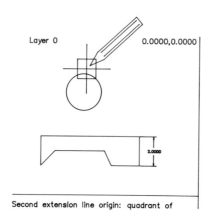

Layer 0   0.0000,0.0000

2.0000

Second extension line origin: quadrant of

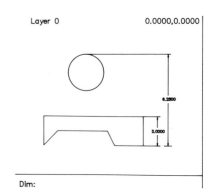

Layer 0   0.0000,0.0000

6.2500

2.0000

Dim:

ALIGNED DIMENSIONS

Now you want to measure the right downward facing slope in the lower half of the polygon. To do this, you use the **ALIGNED** dimension command. If you used the VERtical command, you would get the height from the polygon bottom to where the slope starts. What you want is the length of the slope itself. This is what you get from ALIgned.

```
AutoCAD
* * * *
DIM:
DIM1:

horiz
vrtical
aligned
rotated

baselin
continu

previous

—LAST—
   DRAW
   EDIT
```

DIM to ALIGNED

ALIGNED DIMENSION

Type **ALI** or pick from the DIM menu.

Pick the lowest point on the slope, and the uppermost point on the slope as the extension line origins.

Use **7.25,2.75** as the dimension line location.

Accept AutoCAD's text prompt.

And Voila! You've got an ALIGNED DIMENSION.

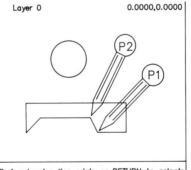

```
Layer 0                    0.0000,0.0000          Layer 0                    0.0000,0.0000
```

```
First extension line origin or RETURN to select:      Dim:
Second extension line origin:
Dimension line location:  7.25,2.75
```

Aligned Dimension

ANGLE DIMENSIONS

Last but not least, measure the angle in the polygon's lower left corner. This, of course, is an ANGULAR dimension. Not a linear dimension.

Select **ANGULAR** from the screen menu. With ANGular AutoCAD prompts for the two lines necessary to measure the angle. ANGular only works with lines or polylines as take off points for the angle measurement. Pick the left polygon side and the slope, responding to AutoCAD's prompts.

(Of course, there are two angles. The inner acute angle. And the outer obtuse angle. AutoCAD prompts for the angle decision.)

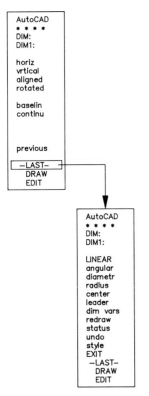

DIM to ANGULAR

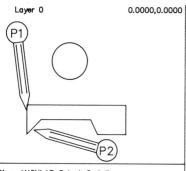

Dim: ANGULAR Select first line:
Second line:
Enter dimension line arc location: 2.5,3.0
Dimension text <45°>: (RETURN)
Enter text location: 2.50,3.25

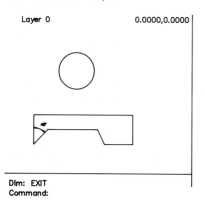

Dim: EXIT
Command:

Angle Dimension

ANGULAR DIMENSION

Type **ANG** or pick ANGULAR from the screen menu.

Pick the leftmost vertical line of the polygon.

Pick the leftmost polygon sloped line.

Enter dimension line arc location: (Pick a point inside
   the angle, 2.5,3 is a good looking location.)

Accept the default text.

Place the dimension text at 2.5,3.25

(Exit and end the dimension session.)

Dim: **EXIT (RETURN)**
Command: **END (RETURN)**

If you pick a point in the obtuse angle, you'll get the big arc dimension. If you pick a point in the acute angle, you'll get the small arc dimension. (Which is what you did.) The dimension arc will pass through the pick point. The point, **2.5,3**, typed from the keyboard will give you a good arc.

The ANGLE DIMENSION is shown in the ANGLE DIMENSION drawing.

Take a look at the TARGET DRAWING again.

These are most, but not all of the dimensioning possibilities that AutoCAD offers.

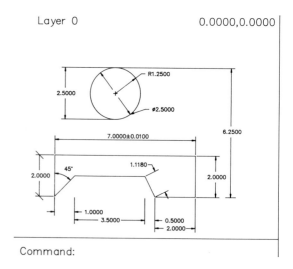

Command:

Target Drawing

ALTERNATIVE TEXT FOR DIMENSIONING

In the Dimensioning example you took advantage of AutoCAD's feature known as "semi-automatic" dimensioning. This means that you let AutoCAD make (fairly good) assumptions about where to put the dimensioning elements. In some cases you overrode these assumptions and gave AutoCAD more specific, manual locations.

But in all cases you accepted AutoCAD's measurements as the default values to be put in the text portion of the dimensioning detail. There will be times when you want numbers or text different from what AutoCAD proposes as the default. You may want to:

☐ Use a text STYLE with a "width" factor of 0.75 to condense your dimension text into less space.

☐ Embellish the default numbers with a suffix or prefix like "about" or "give or take".

☐ Place your own numbers or text like "This measurement is not important" or "three widths".

☐ Replace all numbers that AutoCAD proposes as defaults by multiplying them by a standard factor. For example, replace the default of $<7.05\,''>$ with the metric equivalent (17.907 cm) by multiplying the default by 2.54.

☐ Use the AutoCAD defaults and an alternate form at the same time. For example, have the text line read 7.05″ (17.907cm).

Of course you can always use DIM to get witness and dimension lines and use the TEXT command to place the alternative text forms.

Personalized Dimensioning Texts, Prefixes and Suffixes

Whenever AutoCAD suggests <default> dimension text, you can reject the default in two ways:

☐ Use the **space bar** followed by a RETURN to put in blank dimensioning text.

☐ Type your own text and a RETURN. AutoCAD will use your text in place of the default.

You also can customize the dimension line by adding a suffix, prefix or both, surrounding AutoCAD's <default> dimension text. To do so, simply type your custom characters before or after a $<\,>$ at the dimension measurement text prompt:

ALTERNATIVE EXAMPLES

When AutoCAD offers this	Type this	To get this
Dimension text <2.5000>:	**space** (RETURN)	
Dimension text <2.5000>:	Not important	Not important
Dimension text <2.5000>:	<> inches	2.5000 inches
Dimension text <2.5000>:	about <>	about 2.5000
Dimension text <2.5000>:	about <>"	about 2.5000"
Dimension text <2.5000>:	roughly <>"	roughly 2.5000"

Dimension Measurements Times a Standard Factor

Normally AutoCAD uses the UNITs settings and actual distances you set up when drawing entities to calculate dimensions. If these units are not the lengths you want shown in dimensioning, you can apply a standard multiplier to alter the default AutoCAD calculations.

To get AutoCAD to multiply all linear <default> dimensioning measurements by a standard factor, use the DIMLFAC in DIM VARS. When **DIMLFAC** is non-zero, AutoCAD uses the factor as a multiplier before presenting you with a <default> text to use. DIMLFAC has no effect on angular dimensioning.

Use Two Systems of Measurement At The Same Time

To get AutoCAD to display two alternative dimension text strings on a dimension line, you must set DIMALT **On**. When you do, AutoCAD prepares two <default> numbers for display in the dimension screen.

The first number is the standard dimension measurement (multiplied by DIMLFAC if it is non-zero). The second number is shown in [brackets] and is the first number, multiplied by DIMALTF (DIM ALTernative Factor), with the number of decimals as set by DIMALTD (DIM Alternative Decimals). The <default> for DIMALTF is 25.4, the number of millimeters in an inch. The <default> for DIMALTD is 2 decimal places.

HOW TO SCALE DIMENSIONS

For almost all dimensioning examples you've run through, you let AutoCAD use the <defaults> for any sizes called for in DIM VARS. You've seen that you have substantial control over any dimension variable that needs a size or offset specification.

But what about the cases where you're working with a different set of units, or a large limits setting? You've seen that AutoCAD's default settings for the examples have been okay.

With very large limits or differing units, the default settings for the dimension variables may not make the dimensions visible. In a 60-foot by 100-foot facilities planning drawing, the default arrow is 0.18 millimeters—invisible for the drawing scale at almost any scale.

You could go around and reset all the dimension variables to get the right size. But this could drive you up the wall, particularly if you change units and limits frequently.

AutoCAD's answer is **DIMSCALE**.

Every scalar dimension variable gets multiplied by DIMSCALE before it is applied to the drawing. The default scale is—**1.0000**. Unless you invoke it, DIMSCALE has no effect on the dimension variables. DIMSCALE acts as a **filter** for all dimension variables as shown in the DIMSCALE FILTER drawing.

If you want larger arrows (and the other dimension variables changed), you can change the DIMSCALE value.

Dimension variable values are balanced with respect to each other, so one DIMSCALE change should be balanced for all the dimension variable settings.

Here are a few DIMSCALE settings you may want to try:

SAMPLE DIMENSION SCALE VALUES

To Get an ARROW This Big:	Use a DIMSCALE of:
0.18 mm	1.0000
0.25 mm	1.3888
0.50 mm	2.7777
1.00 mm	5.5555
1/4"	3.5277
1/2"	7.0555
1"	14.1111

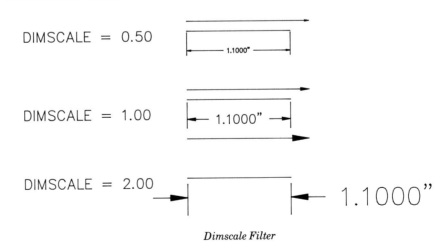

DIMSCALE = 0.50

DIMSCALE = 1.00

DIMSCALE = 2.00

Dimscale Filter

Note. If you're working in architectural units with 1/4″ as the smallest unit, don't be surprised to see DIMASZ (arrow size) displayed at 1/4″. The default DIMASZ arrow is really smaller, but the 1/4″ units cut-off overrides the arrow size and the smaller arrow size isn't displayed.

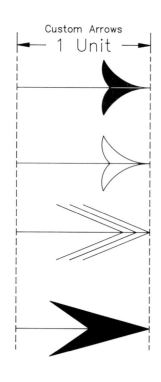

DIMBLKS Examples

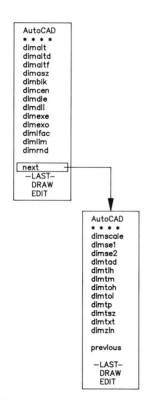

DIM VARS Screen Menu

Custom Arrow Shapes

In addition to controlling the size of AutoCAD's default arrowhead or tick length, you can create your own dimensioning arrowhead. If the DIM VAR called **DIMBLK** (DIM BLOCK) contains the name of a block, AutoCAD will use that block as your dimensioning arrowhead.

You create your custom arrow as a right arrow. AutoCAD will flip it 180 degrees for the left arrow (or rotate it for angular dimensions).

DIMBLKs can be any shape you wish. A few examples are shown in DIMBLKs EXAMPLES. There are a few guidelines you should use when designing your own DIMBLK.

☐ Make your arrowhead one drawing unit wide. AutoCAD will draw the dimension line or leader up to one unit away from the extension line. If your arrowhead is not one unit wide, there will be gap between the arrowhead and the dimension line.

☐ Make the arrow's tip your block insertion point.

☐ If you do not plan to use a filled arrow, consider including a line from the arrow tip to where your custom arrow will join the dimension line.

Other Dimensioning Options

There are subtleties that we haven't tried to include. You should try them on your own.

☐ ROTATED—A LINEAR option that allows angle specification instead of VER, HOR, or ALIgned.

And lots more DIM VARS:

OTHER DIMENSION VARIABLES

☐ DIMSE1—Suppresses drawing of the first extension line. An On/Off toggle switch.

☐ DIMSE2—Suppresses drawing of the second extension line. An On/Off toggle switch.

☐ DIMTIH—Keeps text inside a dimension line horizontal when On (Normal). When Off, the angle of the text takes the angle of the dimension line.

☐ DIMTOH—Same as DIMTIH, but keeps text from interrupting the dimension line.

☐ DIMLIM—Adds the DIMTP and DIMTM to the text instead of a ± listing.

☐ DIMASZ—Similar to DIMTSZ, but this one sets the arrow size.

☐ DIMTXT—Sets the dimension text size.

☐ DIMCEN—Sets the size of the center marker. If you give it a negative value, the center mark is replaced by lines.

☐ DIMDLE—Extends the dimension line through tick marks by DIMDLE amount when ticks are on.

☐ DIMEXO—Sets how far extension lines start away from the dimensioned object (where you pick).

☐ DIMEXE—Sets how far the extension line extends beyond the dimension line.

☐ DIMRND—Rounds all dimension measurements to this setting.

☐ DIMZIN—Turns off zero-inch (1'—0") display to show feet only (1') when using architectural units.

ONE MORE DIMENSIONING EXAMPLE

In the Chapter on CAD TECHNIQUES you created a drawing of a storage tank called MockUp. The dimensions in the MOCKUP TARGET DRAWING contained essential information not only for helping place the graphic entities in the drawing file, but for helping "read" the finished drawing.

See if you can add the necessary dimensions to the MOCKUP drawing file. Use the MOCKUP TARGET DRAWING as a guide. You may want to add other dimensions using the tools you have exercised in this Chapter.

Don't forget special dimensioning tools like BASELINE and CONTINUE as well as radius and diameter for the flange cut.

When you are through dimensioning, use TEXT to add notes to the drawing, and plot the whole file.

Mockup with Dimensions

OTHER INTELLIGENCE

AutoCAD provides a number of spatial intelligence features that are not dimensioning related.

In the beginning of this Chapter, you used the DISTance command to obtain distance information on a line. DIST is one of the INQUIRY commands which return spatial information about the AutoCAD drawing file.

If you want to test the INQUIRY commands, recall the TARGET DRAWING and test the other INQUIRY commands to see what other spatial information you can acquire from an AutoCAD drawing file.

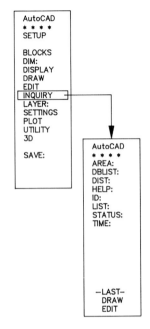

ROOT to INQUIRY

INQUIRY COMMANDS

☐ AREA—Gives the area surrounded by a straight sided polygon. The "sides" are defined by temporary points. The "sides" are not saved or displayed.

☐ DBLIST—Gives a complete data listing on every entity in the drawing file.

☐ DIST—Gives the distance between two points.

☐ ID—Returns the X,Y,Z location of a point.

☐ LIST—Gives a complete listing of all selected elements, including spatial intelligence about where the elements are located. Listing a closed polyline will give its area, including curves.

☐ STATUS—Gives information about major AutoCAD setup parameters.

☐ TIME—Gives you a listing of times and dates about your drawing and editor sessions. These include: the current system time; the date and time a drawing was created; the date and time of the last update; time in the editor; and an "elapsed timer".

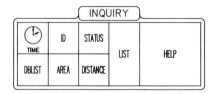

Tablet INQUIRY Commands

Time

TIME is also an INQUIRY command. It is not a spatial intelligence command—unless we are talking about a space/time continuum.

Using TIME's ON, OFf, and Reset commands, you can control the "elapsed" timer as a stopwatch to measure your drawing activity.

WHAT TIME IS IT?

Command: **TIME (RETURN)**

```
Current time:                    07 JUN 1986 at 16:44:37.987
Drawing created:                 15 MAR 1986 at 09:23:12.045
Drawing last updated:            06 JUN 1986 at 12:52:24.541
Time in drawing editor:          0 days 00:43:15.267
Elapsed time:                    0 days 00:19:23.887
Time on.
```

SUMMING UP and a FEW DIMENSIONING TIPS

Here are a few DIM tips:

DIMENSIONING TIPS

☐ Put your DIMENSIONs on a separate layer with a different color than the main body of your drawing. This way extension lines and dimensions stand out and are not mistaken for actual drawing elements.

☐ Review your dimension variable settings frequently. It's easy to make changes and forget about them.

☐ It helps to set up the dimension variables before you start dimensioning. You don't have to stop and set them in the middle of a Dim: command.

☐ Adjusting dimension text to the same height as your annotation text makes text changes and additions easier.

☐ Use CONtinue and BASeline dimensions to save time by keeping track of extension line locations.

☐ Watch for appropriate places to save time with ALIgned and ROTated dimensions.

☐ You can use more than one set of units for dimensioning by controlling DIMALT. You can display both metric and English units, for example.

☐ If you have created your drawing file in one scale and would like your dimensions to read a different scale, use DIMLFAC to multiply all AutoCAD drawing file units by a standard factor before including them in dimension text.

☐ As you become more proficient, you can make **setup** files to save dimensioning variables in a prototype drawing to preset any dimension variables before you start a new drawing.

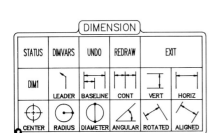

Tablet DIMENSIONING Commands

You have had a chance to look at spatial intelligence in an AutoCAD drawing. Now, let's look at non-graphic intelligence, or — as AutoCAD calls them— Attributes.

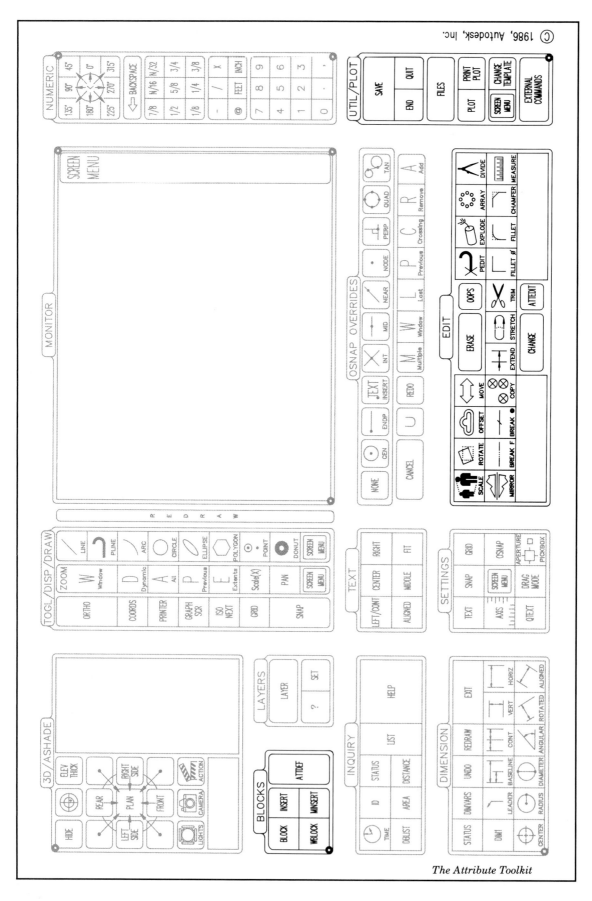

The Attribute Toolkit

CHAPTER 11

ATTRIBUTES

ASSIGNING INFORMATION TO GRAPHIC ELEMENTS

IN YOUR DRAWINGS (AND GETTING IT OUT AGAIN)

Non-Graphic Intelligence. The Attribute Toolkit. Setting Up For Attributes. Creating a Workstation With Many Attributes. Controlling Attribute Visibility. Attribute Editing. Global Attribute Editing. Data Extraction and Attribute Reporting. ▶ Summing Up—Attribute Tips.

NON-GRAPHIC INTELLIGENCE

Every tutorial example so far has been based on a graphic entity (like primitives or blocks) or on a spatial relationship between graphic entities. There's more to creating a full picture than just these graphic entities and their spatial relationships.

AutoCAD allows you to add ATTRIBUTES to graphic drawing entities to give these entities a richer vocabulary in communicating drawing information. For example, in the AutoTown subdivision map you created a few Chapters back, you could have added "House Model Name", "House Size (Sq. Ft.)" and "House Exterior Finish" to each house block to give the drawing reader more information than just graphic blocks.

Just think of the convenience of tagging your drawing file elements with attributes. Automatic Bills-of-Materials, schedules, lists of data—all can be extracted from the drawing file in tabular as well as graphic form.

ATTRIBUTE data are not necessarily displayed on the drawing. Often it is stored **Invisibly** in the drawing file along with the graphic elements it describes. Rather than clutter the drawing display with additional information, the ATTRIBUTES are usually stored away, ready to be turned into a report. A report on AutoTown might look something like this:

AutoTOWN HOUSE REPORT

House Code	House Model	Location xxxx	yyyy	Size (Sq. Ft)	Exterior Finish
A	Colony	11.5	26.5	1200	Texture 1-11
A	Colony	33.5	10.5	1200	Clapboard
B	Grand	28.5	27.5	1450	Red Aluminum
B	Grand Deluxe	12.0	4.0	1450	Brick, T1-11

Just about any graphic element can enjoy an attribute. Attributes can be their own entities in the drawing file—meaning they do not have to be associated with graphic elements. In fact, only one restriction applies to how an attribute can be placed in the drawing file:

"An ATTRIBUTE must be part of a BLOCK."

—The Only Attribute Rule

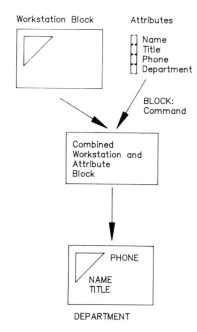

*Combined Graphic BLOCK and
ATTRIBUTE Make a New BLOCK*

Tagging Graphic Elements With Attributes

An attribute such as **Name** is stored in a block much the same way graphic elements are stored in a block. Just as you create and carefully layout graphic elements before inclusion in a block, you must set up "room" or a template for attribute text prior to creating an attribute-laden for insertion.

You enter an attribute in the same general location in the drawing file—treating the attribute as one of the elements included in the block definition. When you use the BLOCK command to herd all the different graphic elements together to form a block, you sweep the attribute element into the same block definition.

Often you want to tag a group of graphic symbols that already are complex enough to form a block. In such cases, you form a new (nested) block by including the attribute text and the original block in a new block definition. See the drawing COMBINED GRAPHIC BLOCK AND ATTRIBUTE MAKE A NEW BLOCK for a clearer picture of how this is done.

For example, if you're a Printed Circuit Board Designer, you may want to assign labels to an integrated circuit (IC) chip such as manufacturer, pin assignment, and clock speed information. If you're doing Facilities Management Planning, you may want to label a desk/workstation with an employee's name, title, department, phone, and desk description. If you're doing an open furniture plan assignment, you'll want to attribute label each desk/workstation occurrence.

Chances are the employee desk/workstation (or IC chip for the PC board) is already stored as a block. When you add attributes to the graphic block and **nest** into a new block, you create a new attribute-laden block.

It is possible to form an attribute block that has no graphic elements in it. This can be used to automate text entry and to associate invisible or non-graphic information in a drawing.

You can place attribute text in a drawing file by placing it as the only element in a block and later insert the block in the drawing file. For these non-graphic attribute blocks, instead of a graphic symbol appearing on the screen, you place the attribute data directly at the insertion point.

THE ATTRIBUTE TOOLKIT

To store and use attributes in the drawing file you use many already familiar commands like BLOCK and INSERT. Attributes have their own special commands as well. See THE ATTRIBUTE TOOLKIT at the beginning of this Chapter for the Tablet Menu listing of commands.

ATTDEF on Tablet Menu

THE ATTRIBUTE COMMANDS

☐ ATTDEF— Defines how attribute text will be stored.

☐ ATTDISP—Controls how attribute text will appear on the screen.

☐ ATTEDIT—Allows you to change attribute text once it has been inserted in your drawing (just like CHANGE for regular text).

☐ ATTEXT—Extracts attribute text and formats the text into a report.

SETTING UP FOR ATTRIBUTES

You need a drawing file to accept your attribute information. The CIRCLE COMPUTER COMPANY LAYOUT shows the room and desk layout of the computer company that designs and builds the widgets you drew in the EDITing Chapter. In the CIRCLE COMPUTER drawing you can see several desks and phones. Our goal is to **tag** those items with attribute information like phone extension, name of employee, desk type, etc.

Here's the attribute information we want to store:

Simple Company Layout

COMPANY LAYOUT REPORT

Name	Title	Phone Ext.	Desk-type
Mary Janes	Head Honcho	396	Engineering
Mark Elliot	Keyboard Div. Manager	247	Engineering
Susan Driscoll	Keyboard Div. Drafting	248	Engineering
Harriet Sands	Display Div. Manager	388	Engineering
David Jones	Display Div. Drafting	117	Engineering

In this Chapter we are not concerned as much with graphics as we are with the text associated with the graphics. The SIMPLE COMPANY LAYOUT will get you by for this exercise. Here's the prompt sequence to get started. You will add to the drawing file as you learn to define and use attributes.

SETUP FOR SIMPLE COMPANY LAYOUT

Begin a NEW drawing file called LAYOUT

Leave UNITS and LIMITS at <default>.

Set a GRID to 1 Unit.

Set SNAP to .25 Unit.

Create the desk using a rectangle BLOCK.

```
Command: INSERT  (RETURN)
Block name (or ?): rectang  (RETURN)
Insertion point: 3,4  (RETURN)
X Scale factor <1> / Corner / XYZ: 3  (RETURN)
Y scale factor <default=X>: 2  (RETURN)
Rotation angle <0>:  (RETURN)
Command:
```

Create the phone using LINE.

```
Command: LINE  (RETURN)
From point: 3.25,4.75  (RETURN)
To point: @0,1  (RETURN)
To point: @1,0  (RETURN)
To point: C  (RETURN)
Command:
```

You are now ready to give attributes to the phone and desk.

Setup for Simple Company Layout

Workstation with Template Attributes

Your screen should look like the SETUP FOR SIMPLE COMPANY LAYOUT.

Variable attributes are really just text **blanks** waiting for text. When you insert a block with a variable attribute in it, AutoCAD asks you to **fill in the blanks** before inserting the block into the drawing file.

In order to set up an attribute, you have to **format a template** for the text. This means that you have to give AutoCAD the blanks that will be filled in upon attribute block insertion. In addition, you need to set the normal text parameters to show how the attribute text will appear on the screen (and in the drawing file).

The ATTDEF Command

To create an attribute you use ATTDEF, the (**ATT**ribute **DEF**inition) command. Let's learn about ATTDEF by setting up the **Name** attribute on the workstation. Here's the prompt sequence. Type the responses as shown after you have read the descriptions for each prompt:

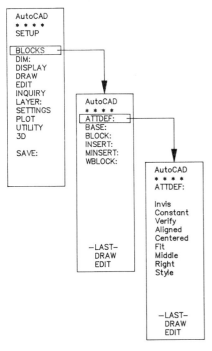

ROOT to BLOCKS to ATTDEF

SETTING UP THE EMPLOYEE NAME ATTRIBUTE

```
Command: ATTDEF (RETURN)
Attribute modes -- Invisible:N  Constant:N  Verify:N
Enter (ICV) to change, RETURN when done: (RETURN)
Attribute tag: Name (RETURN)
Attribute prompt: Type Name Here... (RETURN)
Default attribute value: Nobody (RETURN)
Start point or Align/Center/Fit/Middle/Right/Style:
   3.75,4.75 (RETURN)
Height <0.2000>: 0.15 (RETURN)
Rotation angle <0>: (RETURN)
Command:
```

AutoCAD places the Name attribute tag at 3.75,4.75
in the drawing.

Attribute Modes

AutoCAD is asking you how you want to control the appearance of the attribute text. In addition to the normal text parameters, it is possible for attributes to be **Invisible** on the screen or on a plot. Invisible is useful when you want to store a lot of data with graphic elements in the drawing, but you don't want to display all the data.

Use **Constant** attribute mode to write boilerplate parts of the attribute text **tag**. A Constant attribute can never be edited once it is inserted as a block without redefining the block.

Verify mode gives you a chance to edit variable attribute text before inserting it into the drawing file. This allows you to see what you've typed for attribute text, check for errors, and correct them before the attribute is inserted. If an attribute has the Verify mode, AutoCAD will display the attribute text on the prompt line after you type it. AutoCAD will ask you if everything is ok, and wait for a **(RETURN)** before inserting the text.

Attributes can be Constant, Invisible, or Verified at the same time—or in any combination. To change one of the ATTDEF modes, simply type **I, C,** or **V** followed by a **(RETURN)**.   AutoCAD will redisplay the mode's prompt with a **Y** (for Yes!) next to the item. In the NAME example above, you just use <default> settings.

Attribute Tag—No Blanks Allowed

An attribute tag is the name of an attribute. "Name", "Employee-No.", "Phone-Extension", and "Part-Numbers" are all valid tags. Think of a tag as the name of the text that you want to insert as an attribute (like block names).

The only restriction on tag names is that they cannot include blanks. In the examples, a hyphen is used in place of a blank (**Employee-No.**, etc.) to separate the name tag elements. AutoCAD translates all tags into upper case letters whether you type CAPS or not.

Attribute Prompt

In addition to naming the attribute tag, you can assign an **instructional prompt** to the tag. You use this prompt at insertion time. For example, you might assign the **Enter the Part Number of this widget here** to the tag name, **Part-Numbers**.

You can use anything you want for prompts. "Gimme the number now, Dummy" is as valid as "Would you please enter the number here...". If you feel that the attribute tag name says it all, you don't need to enter the added prompt. The attribute tag name is the <default> prompt. To use it instead of entering another prompt, simply enter a (**RETURN**) in response to the Attribute prompt: prompt.

Default Attribute Value

AutoCAD will ask you what the attribute will say and how it will appear in the drawing.

Useful <defaults> are **Not Yet Filled In** or **XXX.NN**. Remember, these will show up in the drawing if you (**RETURN**) accept the <default> instead of filling in the attribute at time of insertion.

Attributes Display Just Like Text

After assigning the attribute value, AutoCAD prompts you for the information about how to display attribute text and store it in the drawing file. This series of AutoCAD prompts is identical to the standard TEXT prompts.

If you define a CONSTANT attribute instead of asking for a text string, AutoCAD uses the Value or Constant text string at the time of insertion.

Workstation with Name setup

Once you've set all the attribute parameters AutoCAD will display the attribute tag on the screen just like it does with text. It will appear at the proper location with the proper text parameters (height, aligned, centered, etc.).

The first attribute you have created, **Name**, should be on your screen as a result of going through the attribute prompt sequence. Your screen should look like WORKSTATION WITH NAME SETUP.

CREATING A WORKSTATION WITH MANY ATTRIBUTES

Before you build the block called **WKSTATN**, you need to analyze the data types that you will include in the attribute tags.

Here's another look a the COMPANY LAYOUT REPORT as a guide to the attribute definitions that follow. We've abbreviated the Titles to make them fit inside the desk space on the screen:

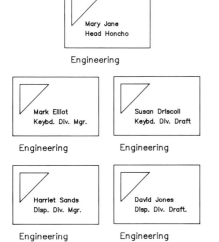

Simple Company Layout with Attributes

COMPANY LAYOUT REPORT

Name	Title	Phone Ext.	Desk-type
Mary Janes	Head Honcho	396	Engineering
Mark Elliot	Keybd. Div. Mgr.	247	Engineering
Susan Driscoll	Keybd. Div. Draft.	248	Engineering
Harriet Sands	Disp. Div. Mgr.	388	Engineering
David Jones	Disp. Div. Draft.	117	Engineering

First, let's establish a policy that says all desks in the Engineering Department look alike. (They usually do anyway.) Given the sameness, you can establish **Desk-type** as a Constant attribute for the desk workstation. The rest of the attribute tags have different values, so make them variable.

You want to create a drawing to show name, title, and Desk-type. Telephone extensions are important to store, but set them to **Invisible** to reduce the desk clutter.

Create The Rest of The Attributes

In order to get to the SIMPLE COMPANY LAYOUT and COMPANY LAYOUT REPORT, go through the rest of the ATTDEFs in the following exercise. Look for different attribute modes, tags, and <defaults>:

SETTING UP THE REST OF THE ATTRIBUTES

A. The Title Attribute

You can restart ATTDEF to get a second line of text just below the first (like TEXT). Just answer all the Attribute specific prompts first. When the text "Start point..." prompt appears, AutoCAD will highlight the last ATTDEFed line on the screen. If you simply hit a (RETURN), the current ATTDEF will go immediately under the old one.

```
Command: (RETURN)
ATTDEF
Attribute modes -- Invisible:N  Constant:N  Verify:N
Enter (ICV) to change, RETURN when done: (RETURN)
Attribute tag: Title (RETURN)
Attribute prompt: Type Title here... (RETURN)
Default attribute value: NoTitle (RETURN)
Start point or Align/Center/Fit/Middle/Right/Style: (RETURN)
Command:
```

A. Workstation with Name and Title

B. The Desk-Type Attribute

Command: **(RETURN)**
ATTDEF
Attribute modes -- Invisible:N Constant:N Verify:N
Enter (ICV) to change, RETURN when done: **C (RETURN)**
Attribute modes -- Invisible:N Constant:Y Verify:N
Enter (ICV) to change, RETURN when done: **(RETURN)**
Attribute tag: **Desk-type (RETURN)**
Attribute value: **Engineering (RETURN)**
Start point or Align/Center/Fit/Middle/Right/Style:
   3.25,3.50 (RETURN)
Height <0.1500>: **0.20 (RETURN)**
Rotation angle <0>: **(RETURN)**
Command:

B. Workstation with Name, Title, and
   Desk-Type

C. The Phone Attribute is Invisible

Command: **(RETURN)**
ATTDEF
Attribute modes -- Invisible:N Constant:Y Verify:N
Enter (ICV) to change, RETURN when done: **C (RETURN)**

(**Constant** is left over from **Desk-type**.
   you have to toggle it Off before toggling **Invisible** On.)

Attribute modes -- Invisible:N Constant:N Verify:N
Enter (ICV) to change, RETURN when done: **I (RETURN)**
Attribute modes -- Invisible:Y Constant:N Verify:N
Enter (ICV) to change, RETURN when done: **(RETURN)**
Attribute tag: **Phone (RETURN)**
Attribute prompt: **Type Phone extension here... (RETURN)**
Default attribute value: **0000 (RETURN)**
Start point or Align/Center/Fit/Middle/Right/Style:
   4.5,5.5 (RETURN)
Height <0.2000>: **(RETURN)**
Rotation angle <0>: **(RETURN)**
Command:

Note AutoCAD places the attribute tag at 4.5,5.5 even
though the attribute will be Invisible when blocked.
This is for your reference.

C. Workstation with all Attributes Setup

Your screen should now look like WORKSTATION WITH ALL ATTRI-
BUTES SETUP.

Herding Graphics and Attributes Into A Block

The next step is to herd all the graphic (desk and phone) and non-graphic
(defined attributes) elements together into a block.

Once the attributes are blocked, the definitions of the attributes cannot be
edited without a block redefinition. Right now you can edit the attribute
definitions with the CHANGE command just as you would strings of text on
the screen. You can also erase and redefine them with ATTDEF if you made
a mistake or need to make changes.

Let's block our workstation using the desk lower left corner for an Insertion base point:

HERDING GRAPHICS AND ATTRIBUTES INTO A BLOCK

```
Command: BLOCK (RETURN)
Block name: WKSTATN (RETURN)
Insertion base point: 3,4 (RETURN)
Select objects: W (RETURN)
First corner:    (pick) Other corner: (pick)  8 found.

  (Pick a lower left and upper right corner to include
  everything on the screen.)

Select objects: (RETURN)

  (All the graphic elements and attributes tags disappear,
  just as in normal block creation.)

Command:
```

Use a Window to Herd Graphics and Attributes into a Block

Congratulations! You have just formatted your first attribute-laden block! There is nothing special about attribute block creation—you can BLOCK, INSERT, WBLOCK, and redefine an attribute block the same way you would a normal block.

Now let's move on and give the five stalwart workers a place to work by inserting their workstations into the display area. (You may want to clean up the pointers left by the block work by REDRAWing before moving on.)

INSERTING WORKSTATIONS INTO THE DRAWING

A. Start by inserting Mary Janes

```
Command: INSERT (RETURN)
Block name: WKSTATN (RETURN)
Insertion point: 1.80,7.0 (RETURN)
X scale factor <1> / Corner / XYZ:  (RETURN)
Y scale factor <default=X>:  (RETURN)
Rotation angle <0>:  (RETURN)
Enter Attribute values
Enter Phone extension here...<0000>: 396 (RETURN)
Enter Title here...<NoTitle>: Head Honcho (RETURN)
Enter Name here...<Nobody>: Mary Janes (RETURN)
Command:
```

Layout Series for Five Workstations

```
The Workstation block will appear on the screen with all
the attributes displayed in their correct positions. The
phone extension will remain Invisible. It is stored in the
correct position, but not displayed.
```

Repeat the insert process for the other four employees, using the data from the following tables.

B. Mark Elliot at   0.25,4.0
C. Susan Driscoll at   3.50,4.0
D. Harriet Sands at   0.25,1.0
E. David Jones at   3.50,1.0

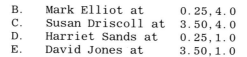

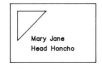

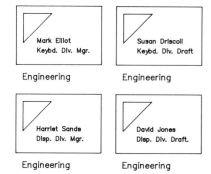

Workstation Attribute Example

COMPANY LAYOUT REPORT

Name	Title	Phone Ext.	Desk-type
Mary Janes	Head Honcho	396	Engineering
Mark Elliot	Keybd. Div. Mgr.	247	Engineering
Susan Driscoll	Keybd. Div. Draft.	248	Engineering
Harriet Sands	Disp. Div. Mgr.	388	Engineering
David Jones	Disp. Div. Draft.	117	Engineering

When you get through placing all five workstations, your screen should display all the workstations.

Notice that you were prompted for the attributes in the reverse order of their creation. Plan ahead if you want a particular order in the prompt sequence.

You screen should look like the WORKSTATION ATTRIBUTE EXAMPLE.

CONTROLLING ATTRIBUTE DISPLAY VISIBILITY WITH ATTDISP

You can control the Visibility of an attribute using the ATTDISP (**ATT**ribute **DISP**lay) command. ATTDISP can temporarily reverse a Visible setting turning Invisible attributes **ON**, or Visible attributes **OFF**; or it can return to the condition set with the ATTDEF command, **N** (Normal).

Try the ATTDISP command using the ON option now. This will cause a REGEN of the screen forcing all attributes display **ON**, whether or not they are Normally Invisible. When the screen is regenerated, you'll see whether you've stored the phone extensions in the proper place. These are shown in WORKSTATIONS WITH PHONE EXTENSIONS SHOWING.

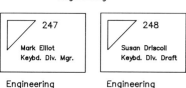

Workstations with Phone Extensions Showing

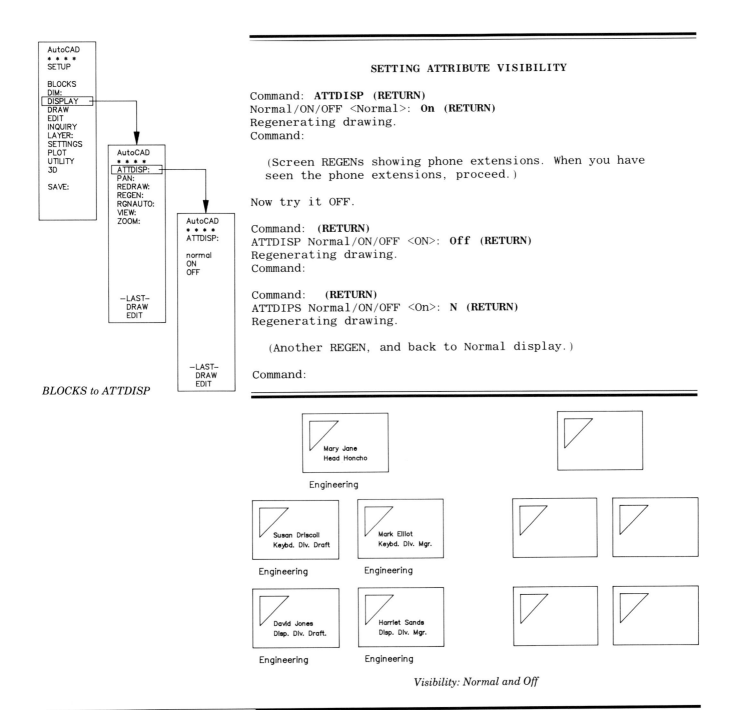

```
AutoCAD
* * * *
SETUP

BLOCKS
DIM:
DISPLAY
DRAW
EDIT
INQUIRY
LAYER:
SETTINGS
PLOT
UTILITY
3D

SAVE:
```

```
AutoCAD
* * * *
ATTDISP:
PAN:
REDRAW:
REGEN:
RGNAUTO:
VIEW:
ZOOM:




−LAST−
DRAW
EDIT
```

```
AutoCAD
* * * *
ATTDISP:

normal
ON
OFF




−LAST−
DRAW
EDIT
```

BLOCKS to ATTDISP

SETTING ATTRIBUTE VISIBILITY

Command: **ATTDISP** (RETURN)
Normal/ON/OFF <Normal>: **On** (RETURN)
Regenerating drawing.
Command:

   (Screen REGENs showing phone extensions. When you have
  seen the phone extensions, proceed.)

Now try it OFF.

Command: **(RETURN)**
ATTDISP Normal/ON/OFF <ON>: **Off** (RETURN)
Regenerating drawing.
Command:

Command: **(RETURN)**
ATTDIPS Normal/ON/OFF <On>: **N** (RETURN)
Regenerating drawing.

   (Another REGEN, and back to Normal display.)

Command:

Mary Jane
Head Honcho

Engineering

Susan Driscoll
Keybd. Div. Draft

Engineering

Mark Elliot
Keybd. Div. Mgr.

Engineering

David Jones
Disp. Div. Draft.

Engineering

Harriet Sands
Disp. Div. Mgr.

Engineering

Visibility: Normal and Off

ATTRIBUTE EDITING

Well as sure as there are raises and office romances, you can bet there will be changes in the old organizational chart. No sooner is the layout complete, than Mary Janes gets promoted from Head Honcho to Chief Honcho. What's needed is a new graphic. What do you do?

Edit the attribute, of course!

You've already seen AutoCAD's CHANGE command, a great tool for fixing mistyped TEXT or making general corrections to the drawing file contents.

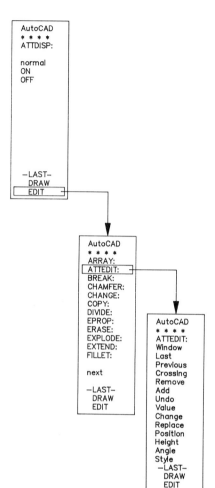

ATTDISP to EDIT to ATTEDIT

Unfortunately we cannot use CHANGE on attributes after they are blocked because—attributes are parts of blocks — and the components of a block are not individual entities.

The ATTEDIT Command

The **ATT**ribute **EDIT** command is the change command for attributes. With ATTEDIT you can select attributes for editing in the normal ways (object or Window or Last).

But ATTEDIT doesn't stop there. ATTEDIT provides additional selection tools. In the current example you don't need special selection. You can simply pick Head Honcho and change it to **Chief Honcho**:

```
            INDIVIDUAL ATTRIBUTE SELECTION

Command: ATTEDIT (RETURN)
Edit attributes one at a time? <Y>: (RETURN)
Block name specification <*>: (RETURN)
Attribute tag specification <*>: (RETURN)
Attribute value specification <*>: (RETURN)
Select Attributes or Window or Last:

   (pick a point on the text string Head Honcho and (RETURN))

1 attributes selected.
Val/Pos/Hgt/Ang/Style/Lay/Clr/Nxt <N>: V (RETURN)
Change or Replace? <R>: C (RETURN)
String to change: Head (RETURN)
New string: Chief (RETURN)
Val/Pos/Hgt/Ang/Style/Lay/Clr/Nxt <N>: (RETURN)
Command:
```

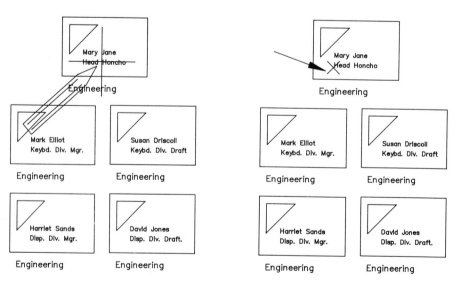

Using the Crosshair to Select an Individual Attribute for Editing

Editing MARK Example

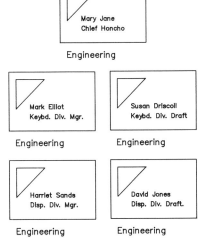

Partially Edited Attributes

Notice two nice features. First, AutoCAD temporarily highlights the attribute to be edited. Second, AutoCAD asks if you want to change part of the attribute text string or completely replace it. We changed part. An **X** mark appears on the screen adjacent to the current attribute to be edited.

The Power of ATTEDIT Selection

That was a simple change. But what about these scenarios:

☐ Change **Div.** in all titles to **Grp.**

☐ Change **Div.** to **Grp.** only in the Keyboard Division.

In your drawing with only five workstations, individually picking each attribute for editing would not be a problem. But what if you had five hundred workstations?

You could gather all the tags named **Title** and do the replacement in one window. Or could you? You could if you were able to specify to AutoCAD exactly which characters in the title attribute you wanted to edit.

In other words, you need to set up an editing buffer filled with just the precise group. Regular editing buffer techniques (object or Window or Last) are just too imprecise.

Rather than having to individually pick attributes from the screen, you can use a large Window and ATTEDIT selection to zero in on the edits you want to make. ATTEDIT allows you to select a group of attributes to edit. Here are some options:

☐ Select all attributes within blocks with a name you specify or all blocks using *.

☐ Select all attributes by tag name using a name you specify or all tag names using *.

☐ Select all attributes that have a value you specify or all values using *.

☐ Further narrow the selection process by picking an individual attribute object or Window or Last.

☐ Any and all combinations of these selections.

You can narrow the field of attributes that AutoCAD will prompt you to edit by narrowing the selection specification from the wildcard everything (*) to some specific value.

Making Attribute Edits

Once you have successfully collected attributes for editing, AutoCAD prompts you to edit them. If you have asked for individual editing (the default), AutoCAD prompts for your changes one at a time. You can tell which attribute you are editing by looking for the highlighting or **X** on the screen.

For each edit you can change Value (the text string itself) or any of the other normal text parameters.

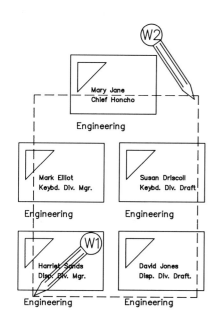

Use a Window to Select Workstation Titles to Edit

More Specification Power

To demonstrate AutoCAD's attribute-edit-specification-power, let's change Susan's title from **Keybd. Div. Draft.** to **Gen. Draft.**

Here's the process:

☐ Edit attributes one at a time.

☐ Have AutoCAD present only Titles to you to edit.

☐ Use a window to select all five workstations.

☐ Watch the screen to know which attribute AutoCAD wants you to edit.

☐ Use the <N>, (Next default), to skip to Susan's title.

☐ Change the Value of Susan's title.

☐ Use the <N> to skip past the rest.

The following prompt sequence sets up the attribute selection. You have to watch the highlighting and prompts to change Susan's title. Window picks are shown in USING A WINDOW TO SELECT WORKSTATION TITLES TO BE EDITED:

SPECIFYING ATTRIBUTE EDIT BY SELECTING A SPECIFIC TAG

```
Command: ATTEDIT (RETURN)
Edit attributes one at a time? <Y> (RETURN)
Block name specification <*>: (RETURN)
Attribute tag specification <*>: Title (RETURN)
Attribute value specification <*>: (RETURN)
Select Attributes or Window or Last: W (RETURN)
First corner:   (pick)    Other corner:   (pick)

(See drawing for window picks.)

5 attributes selected.
Val/Pos/Hgt/Ang/Style/Lay/Clr/Nxt <N>: (RETURN)
Val/Pos/Hgt/Ang/Style/Lay/Clr/Nxt <N>: (RETURN)

  (Hit (RETURN) for N until you get to Susan, then use V)

Val/Pos/Hgt/Ang/Style/Lay/Clr/Nxt <N>: V (RETURN)
Change or Replace? <R> (RETURN)
New attribute value: Gen. Draft. (RETURN)
Val/Pos/Hgt/Ang/Style/Lay/Clr/Nxt <N>: (RETURN)

  (Hit (RETURN) for N until you get through all the rest.)

Val/Pos/Hgt/Ang/Style/Lay/Clr/Nxt <N>: (RETURN)
Command:
```

If you created a COMPANY LAYOUT REPORT here, it would look like this:

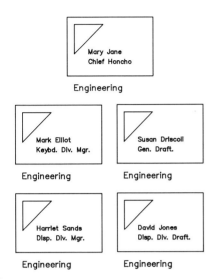

Company Layout Report

COMPANY LAYOUT REPORT

Name	Title	Phone Ext.	Desk-type
Mary Janes	Chief Honcho	396	Engineering
Mark Elliot	Keybd. Div. Mgr.	247	Engineering
Susan Driscoll	Gen. Draft.	248	Engineering
Harriet Sands	Disp. Div. Mgr.	388	Engineering
David Jones	Disp. Div. Draft.	117	Engineering

Let's try one more. A Display Division-wide reorganization has changed all Display Divisions to Display Groups. You need to change **Div.** to **Grp.**, but only for the **Disp.** Division.

Instead of going through each one individually as we did in the last example, you can use a global search and change all **Disp.** titles with **Div.** to **Grp.** Here's the prompt sequence:

A GLOBAL EDIT
ZEROING IN FURTHER
SPECIFYING ATTRIBUTE EDIT BY SELECTING A SPECIFIC TAG
AND A SPECIFIC STRING OF TEXT

```
Command: ATTEDIT (RETURN)
Edit attributes one at a time? <Y> N (RETURN)

Global edit of Attribute values.
Edit only Attributes visible on screen? <Y> (RETURN)

    (All the occurrences are on the screen, but it is nice
     to know that you have the option!)

Block name specification <*>: (RETURN)
Attribute tag specification <*>: Title (RETURN)
Attribute value specification <*>: Disp.*(RETURN)
Select Attribute or Window or Last: W (RETURN)

    (Use a window to collect all workstations.)

2 attributes selected.

    (AutoCAD highlights both.)

String to change: Div. (RETURN)
New string: Grp. (RETURN)

    (Edits take place.)

Command:
```

This is the last attribute exercise, save your work.

```
Command: SAVE (RETURN)
File name <LAYOUT>: (RETURN)
```

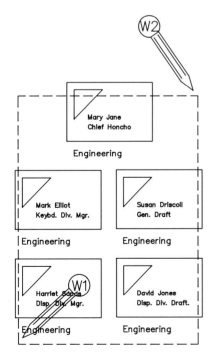

The Windows for a Global Edit should be big enough to include all the edits you want to make.

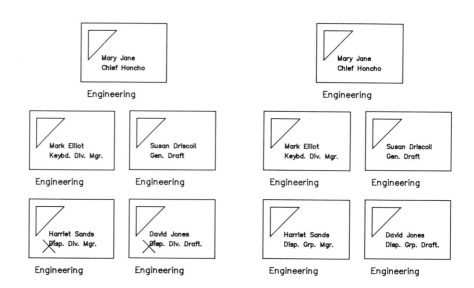

EDITED ATTRIBUTES

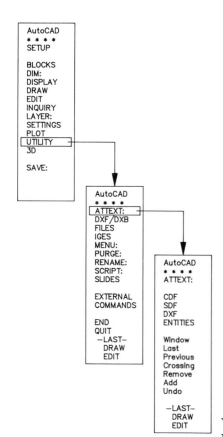

UTILITY to ATTEXT

DATA EXTRACTION AND ATTRIBUTE REPORTING—THE ATTEXT COMMAND

The ATTEXT command often misleads users into thinking it represents—at text—some kind of text operation. The command stands for **ATT**ribute **EXT**raction. ATTEXT provides a way to extract information from the drawing file and print out that information in a report.

Bill of Materials (BOM), Listings, and Specifications

In setting up the ATTRIBUTE EXAMPLE DRAWING, we listed a data table for the names, titles, division, and extension for each of our five stellar employees at Circle Computer Company. We presented the data in simple table form. (See the ATTRIBUTE DATA TABLE.)

Similar kinds of tables regularly accompany professional drawings. Known as Bill of Materials (BOM), Listings, and Specifications, or by a variety of reporting names, these tables organize the attribute value data scattered around the drawing file.

AutoCAD currently provides three ways to extract attribute text from a drawing file and format it in a disc file. You can print these lists or operate on the data in other programs like dBASE II, or III or Lotus 1-2-3. You also can put the list into a table and bring it back into your drawing.

CDF and SDF extraction formats can be read by other microcomputer programs. DXF extraction format is a database listing for programmers—we will not treat it here.

You can extract data in whatever format is suitable for your application. Many users (and vendors of third party software) now have applications built around AutoCAD using the data extraction interfaces provided by AutoCAD.

Extracting Attribute Data with CDF or SDF

CDF creates a file that has commas separating the data fields in the attribute extraction. A simple example is:

CDF FORMAT

```
'Name1','Title1','Extension1'
'Name2','Title2','Extension2'
. . .
. . .
. . .
'Name9','Title9','Extension9'
'Name10','Title10','Extension10'
```

Formatting extract files gets down to the nitty-gritty placement of alphanumeric characters, commas, spaces, and other bits and bytes.

In the CDF format, each data field is separated by a comma, and the spacing of the data field is dependent on the data width within the field—meaning **Title10** takes up more room than **Title9**.

The SDF format creates a file similar to CDF, but without commas and with a standard field length and spacing:

SDF FORMAT

```
Name1         Title1         Extension1
Name2         Title2         Extension2
. . .         . . .          . . .
. . .         . . .          . . .
Name9         Title9         Extension9
Name10        Title10        Extension10
```

Here the data field length is **standardized**, preformatted to a standard value, regardless of the data value length. If the data exceeds the value, the data is truncated.

AutoCAD needs a **Template file** in order to create an SDF or CDF file. The template file is a format instruction list telling AutoCAD where to put what in the extract data file. A template file that might be used with the attributes you have been using is shown below. You can create such a file with a line editor or word processor or, if you use dBASE, get dBASE to create a template for AutoCAD to use.

Here's how you would create an SDF or CDF file with a template:

```
Command: ATTEXT (RETURN)
CDF, SDF, or DXF Attribute extract (or Entities) <C>:
 C or S (RETURN)
Template file <default>: Template.txt (RETURN)
Extract file name <drawing name>: Newfile (RETURN)

 (AutoCAD produces Newfile on disc.)

Command:
```

Here's a **Template file** format for your EXAMPLE data. The template assumes that **Name** comes first, **Title** second, and **Extension** third.

Use a text editor/word processor to create a plain ASCII file. ATTEXT is touchy—make sure you end the last line with a **(RETURN)**. Also, make sure you do not have any extra spaces at the end of lines, or extra lines after the last line of text.

SDF TEMPLATE FILE FOR ATTRIBUTE EXAMPLE DATA

```
BL: NAME          C015000
BL: X             N006002
BL: Y             N006002
DUMMY             C002000
NAME              C015000
TITLE             C015000
EXTENSION         N005000
```

If you look closely at the right hand column you might recognize formatting information. The first **C** or **N** says this is Character or Numeric information. The next three digits (**015** in the **BL:NAME** line) tells how much room to leave for the data. The final three digits specify the number of decimal places for numeric data. The dummy line forces two blank spaces between the X,Y coordinates (BL:X,BL:Y) and the NAME, making the output easier to read.

The extracted SDF Report File is shown in the SDF REPORT EXAMPLE:

SDF REPORT EXAMPLE FOR ATTRIBUTE DATA EXTRACTION

```
WORKSTATION   1.80  7.00  Mary Janes      Chief Honcho      396
WORKSTATION   0.25  4.00  Mark Elliot     Keybd. Div. Mgr 247
WORKSTATION   3.50  4.00  Susan Driscoll Gen. Draft.       248
WORKSTATION   0.25  1.00  Harriet Sands   Disp. Grp. Mgr.  398
WORKSTATION   3.50  1.00  David Jones     Disp. Grp. Draf 117
```

Notice the extracted data gives useful spatial information about this drawing as well as the attribute data. The WORKSTATION column is set up to **dump** the name of the block acting as the attribute data source. The WORKSTA-

TION has character data (see the **C** in the template), and a 15-character print width.

The next two columns give the **X** and **Y** location of the block insertion point in numeric form (see **N** in the template). The **X** and **Y** data have 3 decimal places, including the decimal point, and a 6-character print width. The other extracted attribute fields are in the last three columns, two **character** fields and one **numeric** field. (Notice two of the titles are truncated by the print width.)

AutoCAD provides additional facilities for extracting spatial data from the drawing file. Block layers, block level (for nested blocks, block rotation and scale) are extractable. These spatial attributes are useful for handing data off to engineering programs where the block orientation or relationship among drawing entities is as critical as the text or numeric data associated with the block.

SUMMING UP WITH ATTRIBUTE AND EXTRACTION TIPS

Attributes provide the ultimate flexiblity in annotating your drawings and producing reports. Attributes make AutoCAD's drawings dynamic. An AutoCAD drawing with attributes is a living electronic model of your design when compared to a static sheet produced by manual methods.

In this sense, AutoCAD is a manager for both graphic and non-graphic information.

In order to manage information with AutoCAD you have to be organized. Here are some information management tips for organizing attributes:

ATTRIBUTE TIPS

☐ Proper layout and design of your attribute fields is a critical element in creating a useful attribute file.

☐ AutoCAD asks you for tag values in reverse order from the way you entered tag names. (Last one in—first one asked.)

☐ The names you use for tags are important so keep them brief but explanatory.

☐ The tag name is the <default prompt> when no other prompt is given.

☐ Group common attribute tag names with similar beginning characters to speed editing later with wildcards (*).

Example: "Partnum" and "Partname" can later be edited with a sweep for "Partn*" which will get "Partnum" and "Partname" but not "Partdescrip".

☐ Tag names are used as handles for your attribute text. This means that you have to type the tag name when setting up reports or edits. Keep the names as brief as practical to save on keystrokes.

☐ Break your attribute data into useful fields.

☐ Use enough fields to capture all the variable information you need.

☐ Avoid fields that are filled with extra-long strings of output.

☐ Plan ahead for attribute editing with ATTEDIT.

☐ ATTEDIT is an extremely flexible and powerful tool. Novice users (or even unsuspecting experienced ones) should treat it with care. You may need Undo to repair damage, if you create havoc in a single pass.

☐ Group common edits by the tools available to save time and typing. You can have AutoCAD prompt you for all the changes if you take advantage of grouping edits by layer, tag name, value, etc.

☐ Set up report formats at the same time you do attribute definition.

☐ Do not give your extract file the same name as your template. It will overwrite the template file.

☐ Scratch out a rough table and make your .TXT extract template first. This will help you plan ahead for field name, size, and prompting.

☐ Test your report extraction procedure before you fill up your drawing with information in a format you can't use.

Are you ready to create your own drawing files, attributes and reports? You now have the tools, you just need some practice.

In the next Chapter, you can get a little more practice while you learn to personalize AutoCAD and, at the same time, show off your AutoCAD skills by making a slide show for your friends.

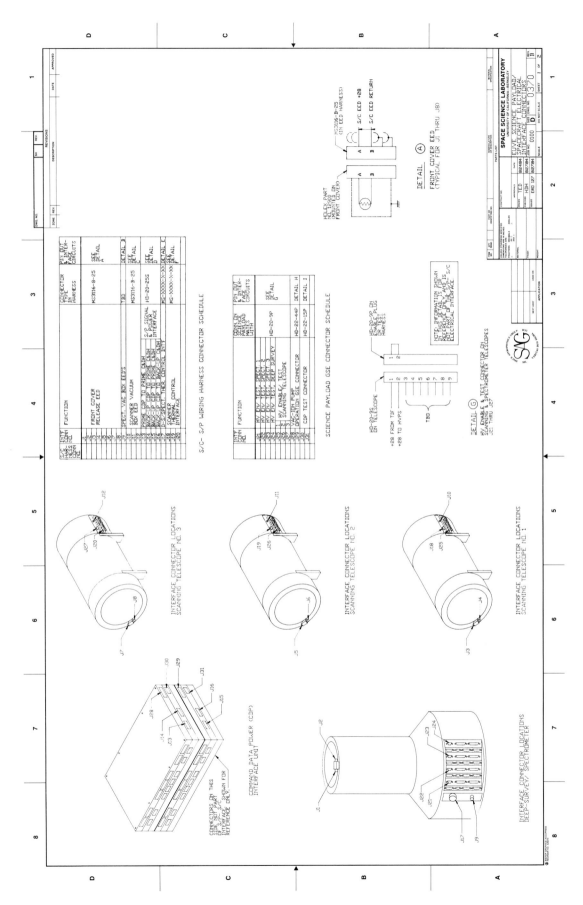

Electrical Housing Drawn with AutoCAD (Courtesy of Autodesk, Inc.)

309

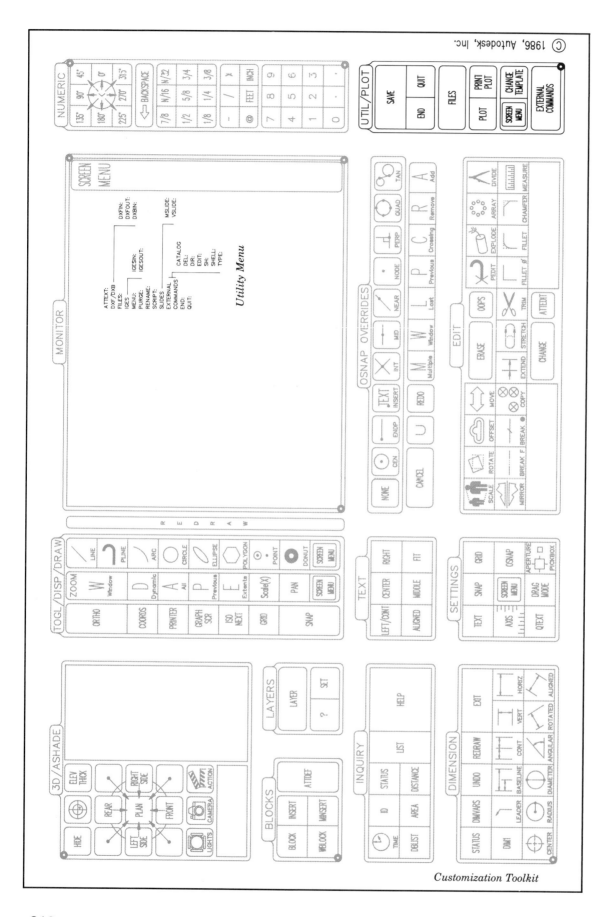

Customization Toolkit

CHAPTER 12

CUSTOMIZATION

AutoCAD AND ME

The User Environment—Standard and Custom. Creating Your Own Diploma. SLIDES—Show and Tell Time. ▶Mastering The Prototype Drawing. How Menus Are Set Up. Creating Your Own Menus. Creating Your Own Symbol Libraries. ▶ System Variables—The SETVAR Command. ▶ Beyond The Standard Environment. Player Piano CAD —SCRIPTS. Macros, Intelligent Symbols, and Parametric Programming. ▶ AutoCAD Variables and LISP. ▶Summing Up.

THE USER ENVIRONMENT—STANDARD AND CUSTOM

For most of the Book you have been on a guided tour through AutoCAD land. You started with a cab ride up town with a cabbie who barely spoke your language. By now you have covered a lot of territory, picked up many commands, and explored many screen menus. Besides, the taxi meter has run up—check the digital readout.

The guided tour is over. Now is the time to customize AutoCAD and to get around on your own.

Customizing AutoCAD

Customization draws from a bag of tricks—several AutoCAD commands, a line editor or word processor, and common sense in keeping everything in order. The AutoCAD commands used for customization are shown in THE CUSTOMIZATION TOOLCHEST at the beginning of the Chapter.

The funny part about customizing AutoCAD is that you already know how to do it. The most important tools you will use in customization are the ones you already know. When you set up custom menus, you will create command and key lists of commands that you have been using all through INSIDE AutoCAD. At this stage the trick is getting them to work 100%.

When you create symbol libraries, you will call on old friends like WBLOCK and INSERT. When you create macros, you will simply duplicate commands you have been picking or typing, by writing them down in sequence.

AutoCAD still has a couple of new tricks up its sleeve. **SLIDES** are **freeze frames** of what's on your screen that you store on disc and **play back**. **SCRIPTS** are like scrolls from player pianos that can give you an animated look at how drawing files go together.

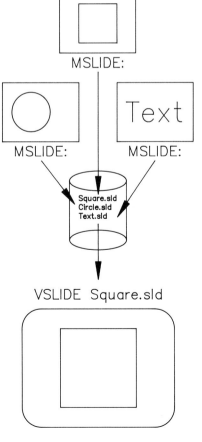

SLIDE Images are Copied to Disc and Later Replayed

Two Levels of Customization

There are two ways to look at customizing the AutoCAD program. The first is to shape the working environment that you work in. The second is to have AutoCAD do more of the work for you altogether.

Customizing at the first level is like burrowing in—getting to know the AutoCAD environment so well that you surround yourself with comfort. When AutoCAD was written, the authors of the software knew they had created a good general purpose drafting program. But they also realized that drafting lacks universal standards. They assumed that you would want to burrow in and adapt AutoCAD to fit your standards.

Customizing at this level involves:

☐ Getting to know all the default settings in the Prototype drawing and how to change them.

☐ Understanding how screen, tablet, and pointing device menus work, and how you can tailor them to your liking.

☐ Setting up your own symbol libraries and including them in screen menus.

☐ Learning how to observe and set the system variables that work beyond the scenes in the AutoCAD program.

The second level of customization is getting AutoCAD to do more work for you—in effect to get AutoCAD to become a user alongside you. Here too, the authors of AutoCAD assumed that some users would want to take control of the program's features, going beyond a standard AutoCAD working environment.

Customization at this advanced level requires a degree of programming knowledge and precision. At this level customization involves:

☐ Creating SCRIPTS or program sequences captured in text files that you "play-back" or execute like player piano CAD.

☐ Creating screen and tablet menu macros that ask for information and then execute commands based on the input.

☐ Creating whole application environments using AutoLISP that take over control of the program, run series of calculations and logical programs to execute commands, draw pictures, and create reports and databases.

The Benefits of Customization

We will show you how some users are turning out entire drawings by typing four numbers and the name of a **macro**. You will see how to rearrange screen menus into groups of commands that you use frequently and, how symbol libraries can be set up to increase efficiency. Your ultimate benefits are finding ways to type less and do more.

You will want to know how to satisfy the growing number of over-the-shoulder lookers by giving them their own show-and-tell SLIDES show of the drawings you have made.

CREATING YOUR OWN DIPLOMA

Hopefully you now think that working with AutoCAD is fun. No one said it was going to be simple. If you've gotten this far, be proud. You deserve commendation. Customization takes a degree of organization and precision. Here's your degree:

CREATE YOUR OWN DIPLOMA

```
Begin a NEW drawing file named DIPLOMA

Leave UNITS and LIMITS as they are.

Set GRID to 1, and SNAP to .5

Create a border.

Command: PLINE (RETURN)
From point: 1,1 (RETURN)
Current line-width is 0.0000
Arc/Close/Halfwidth/Length/Undo/Width/<Endpoint of line:
   W (RETURN)
Starting width <0.0000>: .2 (RETURN)
Ending width <0.0000>: (RETURN)
Arc/Close/Halfwidth/Length/Undo/Width/<Endpoint of line>:
   @10,0 (RETURN)
Arc/Close/Halfwidth/Length/Undo/Width/<Endpoint of line>:
   @0,7 (RETURN)
Arc/Close/Halfwidth/Length/Undo/Width/<Endpoint of line>:
   @-10,0 (RETURN)
Arc/Close/Halfwidth/Length/Undo/Width/<Endpoint of line>:
   C (RETURN)
Command:

And another border.

Command: LINE (RETURN)
From point: 1.5,1.5 (RETURN)
To point: @9,0 (RETURN)
To point: @0,6 (RETURN)
To point: @-9,0 (RETURN)
To point: c (RETURN)
Command: LINE (RETURN)
From point: 2,2 (RETURN)
To point: @8,0 (RETURN)
To point: @0,5 (RETURN)
To point: @-8,0 (RETURN)
To point: C (RETURN)
Command:

And fill in the border.

Command: HATCH (RETURN)
Pattern (? or name/U, style): zigzag (RETURN)
Scale for pattern <1.0000>: (RETURN)
Angle for pattern <0>: (RETURN)
Select objects: W (RETURN)
First corner 0,0 (RETURN)
Other corner: 11,8 (RETURN)
8 found.
Select objects: (RETURN)
```

313

(Zigzag pattern fills inner boundaries.)
Command:

Create an appropriate text Style.

Command: **STYLE** **(RETURN)**
Text style name (or ?): **Standard** **(RETURN)**
Font file <TXT>: **Italic** **(RETURN)**
Height <0.0000>: **(RETURN)**
Width factor <1.00>: **(RETURN)**
Obliquing angle <0>: **(RETURN)**
Backwards? <N>: **(RETURN)**
Upside-down? <N>: **(RETURN)**
Regenerating Drawing.
STANDARD is now the current text style.
Command:

Shower on the appropriate accolades.

Command: **TEXT** **(RETURN)**
Start point or Align/Center/Fit/Middle/Right/Style:
    2.5,6.25 **(RETURN)**
Height <0.2000>: **.25** **(RETURN)**
Rotation angle <0>: **(RETURN)**
Text: **New Riders Publishing Company** **(RETURN)**
Command: **TEXT** **(RETURN)**
Start point or Align/Center/Fit/Middle/Right/Style:
    4.5,5.5 **(RETURN)**
Height <0.2500>: **(RETURN)**
Rotation angle <0>: **(RETURN)**
Text: **Congratulates** **(RETURN)**
Command:

Your name in lights!

Command: **TEXT** **(RETURN)**
Start point or Align/Center/Fit/Middle/Right/Style:
    A **(RETURN)**
First text line point: **3,4.5** **(RETURN)**
Second text line point: **9,4.5** **(RETURN)**
Text: **(Your Full Name here)** **(RETURN)**
Command:

The serious text.

Command: **TEXT** **(RETURN)**
Start point or Align/Center/Fit/Middle/Right/Style:
    2.5,3.75 **(RETURN)**
Height <0.2500>: **0.15** **(RETURN)**
Rotation angle <0>: **(RETURN)**
Text: **On Completing the INSIDE AutoCAD Tutorial** **(RETURN)**
Command:

Your humble teachers.

Command: **TEXT** **(RETURN)**
Start point or Align/Center/Fit/Middle/Right/Style:
    2.5,3.25 **(RETURN)**
Height <0.1500>: **(RETURN)**
Rotation angle <0>: **(RETURN)**
Text: **%%oDan Raker   %%o** **(RETURN)**
Command: **TEXT** **(RETURN)**

```
Start point or Align/Center/Fit/Middle/Right/Style:
  2.5,2.75  (RETURN)
Height <0.1500>:  (RETURN)
Rotation angle <0>:  (RETURN)
Text: %%oHarbert Rice        %%o  (RETURN)
Command: TEXT  (RETURN)
Start point or Align/Center/Fit/Middle/Right/Style:
  2.5,2.25  (RETURN)
Height <0.1500>:  (RETURN)
Rotation angle <0>:  (RETURN)
Text: %%oMayor of AutoTown%%o  (RETURN)
Command:
```

Finally the official seal.

```
Command: ARC  (RETURN)
Center/<Start point>: 8.5,2.5  (RETURN)
Center/End/<Second point>: C  (RETURN)
Center: 8.25,3  (RETURN)
Angle/Length of chord/<End point>: 8,2.5  (RETURN)
Command: LINE  (RETURN)
From point: 8,2.5  (RETURN)
To point: 7.75,1.25  (RETURN)
To point: 8.25,1.75  (RETURN)
To point: 8.75,1.25  (RETURN)
To point: 8.5,2.5  (RETURN)
To point:  (RETURN)
Command:
```

And now a little pizzazz.

```
Command: MSLIDE  (RETURN)
Slide file <DIPLOMA>: Diploma1  (RETURN)
Command: HATCH  (RETURN)
Pattern (? or name/U,style): Stars  (RETURN)
Scale for pattern <1.0000>:  (RETURN)
Angle for pattern <0>:  (RETURN)
Select objects: W  (RETURN)
First corner: 7.5,1  (RETURN)
Other corner: 9.5,3.75  (RETURN)
5 found.
Select objects:  (RETURN)
```

   (Stars pattern fills seal boundaries.)

Now, set up a WBLOCK and a SLIDE for a later trick.

```
Command: WBLOCK  (RETURN)
File name: STARS  (RETURN)
Block name:  (RETURN)
Insertion base point; 0,0  (RETURN)
Select Objects: L  (RETURN)
1 found.
Select objects:  (RETURN)
Command: OOPS  (RETURN)

Command: MSLIDE  (RETURN)
Slide file <DIPLOMA>: Diploma2  (RETURN)
Command: END  (RETURN)
Command:
```

Congratulations!

SLIDES—SHOW-AND-TELL TIME

It's time to impress your friends and influence your boss. Give them a slide show of wonderful AutoCAD images that they can watch over and over again.

SLIDES gives a stored screen view that AutoCAD can paint on the screen. When you make a SLIDE, you **freeze** a screen image in such a way that AutoCAD can recreate the screen image quickly. Using the **MSLIDE** (**M**ake **SLIDE**) command, you create a disc file called Yourname.SLD. AutoCAD does not store all drawing file information in a .SLD file—only enough to paint the screen quickly.

You already made two slide disc files in the diploma exercise, **DIPLOMA1.SLD** and **DIPLOMA2.SLD**.

To recall a disc-stored .SLD file you use the **VSLIDE** (**V**iew **SLIDE**) command. This recalls the screen image file from the disc and paints the screen with it. Since even VSLIDE takes a little time to load Yourname.SLD from disc, you can **preload** an image by placing an asterisk in front of the disc file name:

LOOKING AT SLIDES OF YOUR ACCOMPLISHMENTS

```
Command: VSLIDE (RETURN)
Slide file <DIPLOMA>: Diploma1 (RETURN)

     (Puts the first slide on the screen as soon as possible.)

Command: VSLIDE (RETURN)
Slide file <DIPLOMA>: *Diploma2 (RETURN)

     (Loads slide2 but does not put it on the screen until:)

Command: VSLIDE (RETURN)

     (Puts slide2 on the screen.)

That's all for now.

Command: END (RETURN)
```

You can also enhance your slide show by having a SCRIPT file repeat itself continuously until you stop it. Later in the Chapter, you will learn how to turn your diploma into a movie script.

The menu diagram on the left side of the page:

```
AutoCAD
* * * *
SETUP

BLOCKS
DIM:
DISPLAY
DRAW
EDIT
INQUIRY
LAYER:
SETTINGS
PLOT
UTILITY
3D

SAVE:
```

```
AutoCAD
* * * *
ATTEXT:
DXF/DXB
FILES
IGES
MENU:
PURGE:
RENAME:
SCRIPT:
SLIDES

EXTERNAL
COMMANDS

END
QUIT
—LAST—
DRAW
EDIT
```

```
AutoCAD
* * * *
MSLIDE:

Yes
No

VSLIDE:




—LAST—
DRAW
EDIT
```

ROOT to UTILITY to SLIDES

MASTERING THE BASICS OF A PROTOTYPE DRAWING

The first time you turn on AutoCAD and get into the drawing editor, the program establishes a default working environment with now-familiar settings for basic variables such as GRID, SNAP, and UNITS. These defaults are stored in a file called ACAD.DWG that comes with the AutoCAD program. ACAD.DWG is listed in Appendix A.

The AutoCAD Reference Manual lists default settings for all system variables, and tells which are stored in ACAD.DWG, and which are stored in the AutoCAD configuration files.

Here's how to create your own prototype drawing and use it to initialize your drawings:

☐ Create your prototype drawing file as you would any other drawing.

☐ Save it on disc. Call it **MASTER**.

☐ Invoke it when you start a new drawing. You can invoke it either optionally or automatically.

To optionally invoke it, you enter selection **1** from the Main Menu.

```
Enter selection: 1 (RETURN)     (Begin a NEW drawing)
Enter NAME of drawing: Newfile=MASTER
```

AutoCAD puts you into the drawing editor and copies all your MASTER prototype settings into **Newfile**.

You can set up AutoCAD to automatically use MASTER for your new drawing in two ways. One is to use MASTER as a prototype for all of your new drawings by making a copy of it named **ACAD.DWG** on the same disc as your AutoCAD program files. The other is to use AutoCAD's Configuration options (Main Menu **5**) which allow you to set the default drawing prototype as an operating parameter.

If you want to restore the standard ACAD.DWG prototype drawing, just begin a new drawing named **ACAD=**, and then END it.

Obviously there is a lot more you can do with AutoCAD. You can go to graduate school with the rest of the Chapter. Your next course is on the **MENU**.

HOW MENUS ARE SET UP

From the beginning of this tutorial we have been using screen and tablet menus that came with AutoCAD from the factory. There is nothing magical about these menus or how they are put together. On the screen we are used to seeing a nice, neat listing of command and key names. Behind the scenes, a menu file looks like this:

```
UTILITY  SCREEN  MENU  --  .MNU  VERSION

**UT 3
[ATTEXT: ] $S=X  $S=ATTEXT   ^C^CATTEXT
[DXF/DFB] $S=X  $S=DXF
[FILES: ] ^C^CFILES
[IGES ] $S=X  $S=IGES
[MENU: ] $S=X  $S=CHTEMP  ^C^CMENU
[PURGE: ] $S=X  $S=PURGE  ^C^CPURGE
[RENAME: ] $S=X  $S=RENAME  ^C ^CRENAME
[SCRIPT: ] $S=X  $S=SCRIPT  ^C^CSCRIPT
[SLIDES ] $S=X  $S=SLIDES

[External] $S=X  $S=EXCOMDS
[Commands] $S=X  $S=EXCOMDS

[END: ] $S=X  $S=END
[QUIT: ] $S=X  $S=QUIT
```

```
AutoCAD
* * * *
ATTEXT:
DXF/DXB
FILES
IGES
MENU:
PURGE:
RENAME:
SCRIPT:
SLIDES

EXTERNAL
COMMANDS

END
QUIT
—LAST—
 DRAW
  EDIT
```

UTILITY Menu

The UTILITY SCREEN MENU—.MNU VERSION is a piece of a file named **ACAD.MNU** on your AutoCAD disc. You can look at this file by exiting from the Main Menu and issuing the following commands from the MS-DOS operating system:

```
C> Type (RETURN)
File to list  ACAD.MNU  (RETURN)

    (The file will begin to appear on your screen.)

    Use ^S to toggle (start and stop) the flow of
    characters scrolling on your screen.
```

Take a look at UTILITY SCREEN MENU—.MNU VERSION. There are several unfamiliar notations in the file. The most obvious are **[brackets]** around words, ^C, **, and **$S =**. These are explained in ACAD MENU CODES.

ACAD MENU CODES

☐ **[brackets]**. An AutoCAD screen menu item can only have eight characters and still fit on the screen. If your item name is longer than eight characters or, you want to call a command something other than its actual name, put the name to appear on the screen in [brackets].

☐ An examples is: [SLIDES]$S = X $S = SLIDES

□ **^C^C.** Here's where AutoCAD shows how forgiving it can be. If you are active in the middle of a command (say the LINE command) but you want to do something else (say DRAW a CIRCLE), first you have to CANCEL the active command before starting the second. Usually you do this by picking the CANCEL command or typing (RETURN), (SPACE) or ^C. If you put a ^C^C at the beginning of your screen menu command, the screen menu item will first CANCEL whatever is going on, then execute its commands. (It takes two ^Cs to cancel modes such as DIM:.)

□ ****.** This is the name of a subsection of a screen menu. In the UTILITY example, this entire listing is actually a submenu to the ROOT MENU. When you pick the **UTILITY** key from the screen ROOT MENU you call for the **UT submenu.

□ *****.** This is the name of a major section of a .MNU file. .MNU files can be divided into as many as seven major sections. Each section describes commands or keys that can be **picked** from a different input device as follows:
***SCREEN—Screen menu area.
***BUTTONS—Pointer device (puck or mouse) buttons.
***TABLET1—First tablet menu area.
***TABLET2—Second tablet menu area.
***TABLET3—Third tablet menu area.
***TABLET4—Fourth tablet menu area.
***AUX1—An extra. It can be a **function box** or other input device.

□ **(Backslash).** When used on a command line, it causes AutoCAD to stop and accept data entry from the crosshair location or keyboard.

□ **; (Semicolon).** Performs the same function as typing **(RETURN)** or hitting the space bar from the keyboard. This is useful for executing a command without waiting for input or for accepting defaults.

□ **$S =.** This is the way you get AutoCAD to jump to a new screen submenu. Within the screen menu you can jump from submenu to submenu.

□ An example is: [UTILITY]^C^C$S = UT

From the ROOTMENU, this first CANCEL:s, then jumps to the submenu named **UT**.

□ **+.** (Plus sign). The + is used to split long menu items into two or more lines in the .MNU file. The + is inserted at the end of a line to tell AutoCAD to continue to the next line. It will not cause a space or **(RETURN)**.

□ **Other Control Characters. ^B, ^G, ^O, etc.** To get a control character into a .MNU command, type the up caret ^ followed immediately by the letter (just like you see it here). This will be translated by AutoCAD's menu processor into a single control character—for example, Control-X.

Other examples are: [ORTHO]^O toggles the ORTHO command. [GridFlip]^G toggles the GRID command.

If you are familiar with word text editing and/or word processing, you can edit .MNU files or create new ones.

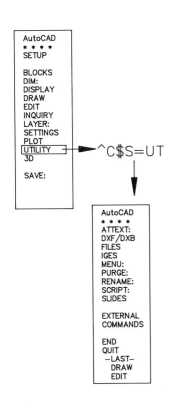

ROOT to UTILITY Jump is caused by "C$S = UT" which is stored behind "UTILITY" on the ROOT MENU

CREATING YOUR OWN MENUS

Armed with how an AutoCAD .MNU file is put together, you can analyze the ACAD.MNU file to see how your key and command structure has been supporting you all along. If you feel comfortable creating your own menus, or adding to ACAD.MNU here are a few tips:

TIPS FOR CREATING YOUR OWN MENUS

☐ **Direct from the AutoCAD Authors:**

"NOTE: If you intend to supply command parameters (options, etc.) as part of a menu item, you must be very familiar with the sequence in which that command expects its parameters. Every character in a menu item is significant, even the blank spaces. From time to time as AutoCAD is revised and enhanced, the sequence of prompts for various commands (and sometimes even the command names) may change; your custom menus may require minor changes when you upgrade to a new version of AutoCAD. Such changes can usually be made with a word processor global replace."

☐ If you choose to modify ACAD.MNU, start with a copy of ACAD.MNU. Using this copy as a base, you can add your own screen submenus at the bottom of the ROOTMENU. Then fool around with your own submenus (and successive submenus from there) instead of changing the core of the AutoCAD provided ACAD.MNU. In any case—make copies of all factory-supplied files for backup.

☐ Give your menu items useful names. You want to be able to find and use these items again and again. [EDIT1] and [EDIT2] don't say much. [2ptLINE] or [CUTerase] are more informative.

☐ Organize menus logically. You will notice that the primary keys and commands in ACAD.MNU are alphabetical. Doesn't this make sense? Try to impose some logical order on your menus as well.

TIPS FOR USING A WORDPROCESSOR OR LINE EDITOR TO CREATE OR EDIT MENU FILES

☐ Make sure you are creating simple ASCII or **program** files. These are called DOS text files, programmers mode, or non-document files. In Wordstar, for example, you want to edit **N**, a non-document file (instead of **D**, a document file). Be sure it doesn't insert extra formatting characters.

☐ Use existing menu items as templates. It is often easier to overtype or copy complex text like commas, control characters and [brackets] than to type anew.

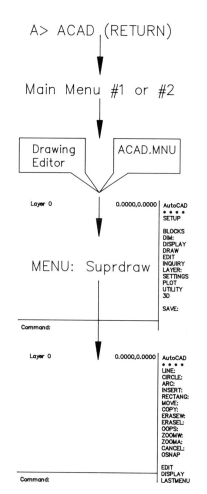

The Menu File is normally loaded from an .MNU File Specified during the Original Configuration of AutoCAD

☐ When you create menu items, you need to write them, load them, try them, correct, reload, and try them again. To get around ending your drawing and exiting AutoCAD to get to your text editor, you can use a "Desktop" text editor like Sidekick from Borland. This allows you to flip back and forth between AutoCAD and the text editor. You may need to FLIP SCREEN to the text screen before invoking Sidekick.

☐ Set up **dummy** .MNU files or portions of files with Main Menus, submenus, and sub-submenus. Then insert your specific commands into the appropriate sections.

☐ Be careful not to leave any extra spaces at the end of the line, AutoCAD will read them as SPACEs, generally the same as (RETURNS).

How To Invoke a Menu

AutoCAD provides two methods for loading your .MNU files and making them active within the AutoCAD drawing editor:

☐ When configuring AutoCAD, you can give the name of the .MNU file you want to use instead of ACAD.MNU which is the default.

☐ When within the drawing editor, you can use the MENU command from the UTILITY screen submenu. This command simply asks you for the name of the .MNU file and loads it.

If you create new menus, you can access your menu items from the Drawing Editor by placing them in a completely separate .MNU file. Say you name it MYACAD.MNU. You invoke the new menu to replace the current screen, tablet, and pointing device menu settings, using the **MENU** command.

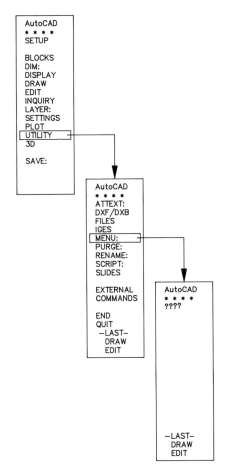

Additional .MNU Functions can be Loaded with the MENU Command

```
Command: Menu (RETURN)
Menu file name or . for none <current>: MYACAD (RETURN)
Command:
```

AutoCAD displays the name of the current .MNU file as a default option. You only need to type **MYACAD** since AutoCAD assumes a .MNU file type.

You also can access your menu items by integrating them into another menu, even into ACAD.MNU. If you use ACAD.MNU, we suggest you make a copy of ACAD.MNU before you play around with it. Again call your copy something like MYACAD.MNU so you don't get the two confused. Then load your modified menu with the MENU command.

SUPRDRAW—An Examples of A Useful Menu

Here's an example of a menu that you might put together.

```
Layer 0          0.0000,0.0000   AutoCAD
                                 * * * *
                                 LINE:
                                 CIRCLE:
                                 ARC:
                                 INSERT:
                                 RECTANG:
                                 MOVE:
                                 COPY:
                                 ERASEW:
                                 ERASEL:
                                 OOPS:
                                 ZOOMW:
                                 ZOOMA:
                                 CANCEL:
                                 OSNAP

                                 EDIT
                                 DISPLAY
Command:                         LASTMENU
```

SUPRDRAW Menu

SUPRDRAW

This is a sample of frequently used drawing, editing and display commands put together on a single screen menu. It can be called from the ROOTMENU using a SUPRDRAW key at the bottom of the normal AutoCAD ROOTMENU.

Screen Appearance	.MNU Version
	**SUPRDRAW 3
LINE:	[LINE:]^C^CLINE
CIRCLE:	[CIRCLE:]^C^CCIRCLE
ARC:	[ARC:]^C^CARC
INSERT:	[INSERT:]^C^CINSERT
RECTANG:	[RECTANG:]^C^CINSERT RECTANG;
MOVE:	[MOVE:]^C^CMOVE
COPY:	[COPY:]^C^CCOPY
ERASEW:	[ERASEW:]^C^CERASE W;
ERASEL:	[ERASEL:]^C^CERASE L;
OOPS:	[OOPS:]^C^COOPS
ZOOMW:	[ZOOMW:]^C^CZOOM W;
ZOOMA:	[ZOOMA:]^C^CZOOM A;
CANCEL:	[CANCEL:]^C^C
OSNAP	[OSNAP]$S=X $S=O
EDIT	[EDIT]$S=ED
DISPLAY	[DISPLAY]$S=DS
LASTMENU	[LASTMENU]$S=

Screen Appearance	Description and Function
LINE:	Invokes LINE command
CIRCLE:	Invokes CIRCLE command and turns on DRAG
ARC:	Invokes ARC command and turns on DRAG
INSERT:	Invokes INSERT command
RECTANG:	Invokes INSERT, Inserts a RECTANGle in DRAG
MOVE:	Invokes MOVE command
COPY:	Invokes COPY command
ERASEW:	Invokes ERASE command in Window mode
ERASEL:	Invokes ERASE command in Last mode
OOPS:	Invokes OOPS command
ZOOMW:	Invokes ZOOM command in Window mode
ZOOMA:	Invokes ZOOM command in All mode
CANCEL:	Invokes CANCEL (^C) command
OSNAP	Brings up standard OSNAP screen menu
EDIT	Brings up standard EDIT menu
DISPLAY	Brings up standard DISPLAY menu
LASTMENU	Goes back to the last screen menu

CREATING YOUR OWN SYMBOL LIBRARIES

One of the most frequently used AutoCAD customization procedures is to make your everyday symbols (BLOCKS) more accessible than having to type their names every time you INSERT. Setting up a symbol library is easy now that you know how to create your own menus.

Here's a part of a tablet menu that helps you insert furniture blocks. It could just have easily been a screen menu, too.

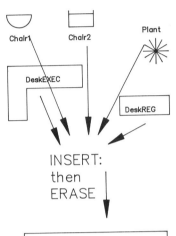

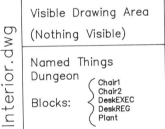

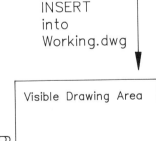

INTERIOR FURNITURE MENU

```
[Chair1] ^C^CINSERT CHAIR1;
[Chair2] ^C^CINSERT CHAIR2;
[DeskEXEC] ^C^CINSERT DESKEXEC;
[DeskREG] ^C^CINSERT DESKREG;
[Plant] ^C^CINSERT PLANT;
[LINE: ] ^C^CLINE
```

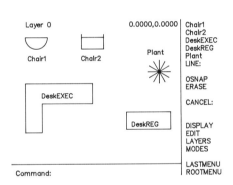

Interior Furniture and Screen Menu

TIPS FOR CREATING SCREEN SYMBOL LIBRARY MENUS

☐ Create a logical order for your library screen menus.

☐ Give your symbols unique yet explanatory names. "DESK1" and "DESK2" don't say much. "DeskEXEC" and "DeskREG" are more descriptive.

☐ Store your symbol blocks with a WBLOCK command to get them out of the current disc file and available for use in other drawing files.

☐ You can group all symbols from a common library together in a single drawing file called something like "Furnitur" or "Circuits". If you erase them all—their definitions will remain "invisibly" in the library file. Then INSERT the common library file into your working files. The block definitions will remain in the block storage area until you need them or purge them.

Group Separate WBLOCK Created Symbols into a Common Library File of Symbols

323

AutoCAD SYSTEM VARIABLES AND THE SETVAR COMMAND

Behind the scenes in the AutoCAD program are hundreds of internal settings that make the program work. You have already seen many of these in the prototype drawing and the defaults that appear on the prompt lines while you are using the program. But there are many more.

The **SETVAR** (SET VARiable) command allows you to peek at the inner workings of AutoCAD to see how it controls various commands. It lets you see and often change the setting of an internal AutoCAD parameter. Let's take a look at one of these variables:

SETTING THE MIRRTEXT VARIABLE WITH SETVAR

```
Command: SETVAR (RETURN)
Variable name or ?: MIRRTEXT (RETURN)
New value for MIRRTEXT <1>: 0 (RETURN)

Command:
```

Here we asked AutoCAD to SETVAR MIRRTEXT, to find out the current setting of the MIRRor TEXT variable. If you remember when you passed text through a MIRROR it inverts the text along with all the other objects passed through the mirror.

When MIRRTEXT is set to **1**, mirrored text is inverted. When MIRRTEXT is set to **0**, text is passed through the mirror to the proper location, but not inverted.

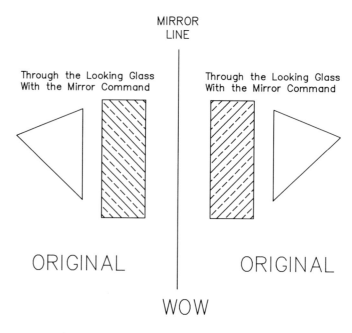

MIRROR Text — Non-inverted

What other AutoCAD variables can we see and alter? Just about every command that you used in this Book has at least one variable behind it. But not all of the variables can be altered — some are "read only" so that AutoCAD can keep at least some parts of your drawing environment constant.

If you are curious about the names and settings of the AutoCAD variables in your drawing file, do a **SETVAR ?** to get a listing of variables and current settings.

The AutoCAD Reference Manual "Special Features" Section can help you understand more about how each of the variables plays a role in the running of the program.

Here are a few AutoCAD variables that you may occasionally want to change or look at with SETVAR:

COMMON AUTOCAD VARIABLES TO CHECK WITH SETVAR

Variable Name	Explanation
APERTURE	Object snap target size in pixels
DWGNAME	Name of current drawing (read only)
GRIDMODE	0=Off, 1=On
LTSCALE	Current setting of linetype scale
QTEXTMODE	0=Off, 1=On
TEXTSIZE	Current height of TEXT
PICKBOX	Object selection pick box size (pixels)
SKPOLY	SKETCH draws polylines if set to 1
PDMODE	Controls style of POINT entity
PDSIZE	Controls size of POINT entity

GOING BEYOND THE STANDARD WORKING ENVIRONMENT

Here comes the fun part—getting AutoCAD to do more work while we sit back and watch commands fly by on the prompt line and drawings appear on the screen. You should learn a little about SCRIPTS if for no better reason than to have a few standard routines ready to run that make you look busy when the boss walks by.

PLAYER PIANO CAD—SCRIPTS

AutoCAD provides a utility for hands-free operation called the **SCRIPT**. A SCRIPT is a listing of commands, input, and responses that is stored in a text file and **played** as if it was typed directly at the keyboard.

Creating scripts has the same restrictions as creating menu files: be careful about specifying exactly how AutoCAD should **read** the command. Watch for AutoCAD revisions that might require an adjustment to your script; and keep scripts as logical and as simple as possible.

All script files have to have the extension **.SCR** (just like all menus have **.MNU**). Two script name examples are MAKEBOX.SCR or SAMPLE.SCR.

It's simple to start a script file running:

```
Command: SCRIPT (RETURN)
Script file <default>: MAKEBOX (RETURN)
                        (Extension .SCR is assumed)

  (Script commands appear and are executed.)
```

You can stop a script that is running by hitting the **BACKSPACE** key on the keyboard. This causes the script to finish the command it is working on and return the **Command:** prompt to you on the prompt line. You can then do some work and pick up where you stopped the script with the RESUME command.

If a script has an error, it will not run to completion. Instead AutoCAD will stop when it encounters the error and return control to you at the prompt line. You then need to correct the script.

SCRIPTS were designed to control VSLIDE shows. Here is a script for a generic recirculating slide show with preloading. You can insert your own slide names.

SCRIPT FOR A GENERIC RECIRCULATING SLIDE SHOW WITH PRELOADING AND DELAY

Adjust the slide names and delay as necessary. If you have a text editor, create this script and store it as SLIDSHO.SCR.

```
vslide slide1
vslide *slide2
delay 2000
vslide
vslide *slide3
delay 2000
vslide
vslide *slide4
delay 2000
vslide
vslide *slide5
delay 2000
vslide
vslide *slide6
delay 2000
vslide
delay 2000
rscript
```

Recirculating SLIDE Show (BACK-SPACE Gets You Out)

Slide flow diagram: SLIDE1 → SLIDE2 → SLIDE3 → SLIDE4 → SLIDE5 → SLIDE6 → RSCRIPT (recirculating back to top). Backspace to stop.

Lets see how VSLIDES and SCRIPT work by scripting a diploma show.

A Fancier Diploma

If you want to have the seal on your diploma flash on and off, use your word processor to set up two slide-script-files.

DIPLOMA. SCR

```
VSLIDE DIPLOMA1
INSERT   STARS 0,0
                   (blank line for X-scale)
                   (blank line for Y-scale)
                   (blank line for rotation)
ERASE L
                   (blank line to end selections)
SCRIPT FLASH
                   (be sure to (RETURN) after FLASH)
```

Here is the second script file.

FLASH. SCR

```
OOPS
ERASE L
                   (blank line to end selections)
RSCRIPT
                   (be sure to (RETURN) after RSCRIPT)
```

Do not leave trailing spaces or extra blank lines at the end.

The DIPLOMA.SCR file loads the VSLIDE and sets INSERT and ERASE before invoking the FLASH.SCR script file. Run the script file in AutoCAD like this:

```
Command: SCRIPT (RETURN)
Script file <default>: DIPLOMA (RETURN)

DIPLOMA.SCR Runs and starts up FLASH.SCR

FLASH flashes and clycles over and over.

A BACKSPACE or ^C will get you out of the loop!

A RESUME command will restart it.
```

If you want your diploma in living color, try putting the stars on another layer with a color of your choice. Save that layer as a slide or WBLOCK and cycle SCRIPTS through all three slides! Remember, you will have to modify your SCRIPT file, and go back to the original drawing file to do this.

Notes on SLIDES and RSCRIPTS.

☐ Slides cannot be edited. If you want to adjust a slide, you must first edit the drawing file that was used to create the slide and, then create a new one.

☐ A slide temporarily takes over the screen, but whatever drawing file you are working on remains intact and active.

☐ Any command that forces a REDRAW or REGEN will cause AutoCAD to leave the slide mode and return to the normal underlying screen, but the SCRIPT will continue running.

☐ Pressing BACKSPACE or ^C interrupts a running script.

☐ A RESUME will start a script stopped by a key from the keyboard.

MACROS, INTELLIGENT SYMBOLS AND PARAMETRIC PROGRAMMING

Using custom menus, prototype drawings, and scripts (sometimes), you can create very sophisticated AutoCAD activities, store them away, and then **use** them anytime.

We know of many users who turn out standard **Custom Drawings** through customization and macros. When an order for a new widget comes in, they simply execute their macros, let AutoCAD do its thing, and plot the "Custom Drawing" for the customer.

The macros can stop to ask the customer's name and any relevant "custom" information. This information is included in the resulting drawing file.

Here is a routine that creates a custom size circle for a customer. The screen menu item, **CUSTOM-O** sets limits and a plot VIEW, creates a user defined circle, places it in a previously stored title block, and inserts text.

The **C-PLOT** item invokes a script to do a plot. This is a good use of a script, since it can pass to and control the plotting menu—something menu macros cannot do.

Here are the custom screen menu commands:

CUSTOM CIRCLE AND PLOT MENU ITEMS

```
[CUSTOM-O] ^C^CLIMITS 0,0 36,24; +
VIEW W PLOT 1,1.25 @34,21.5; +
INSERT TITLEBLK 0,0 ;;;ZOOM A CIRCLE 16,12 \DTEXT M 16,12.75 ;
[C-PLOT  ]SCRIPT C-PLOT
```

Here is the script.

C-PLOT SCRIPT

```
PLOT V PLOT Y N N I 0,0 D N .01 N N 1=1
                    (and a blank line to start the plotter)
                    (and a blank line to return to the drawing)
```

Macros and Parametric Programming

Macros are collections of commands that are executed together regularly—regularly enough that you don't want to be bothered typing all the characters over and over again.

Intelligent Symbols

When a macro involves placement of a block into the drawing file, you often save time by using a standard symbol and your own intelligent input.

For example, the only difference between a 30-inch door and a 36- inch door is the width. If you store a door block with a single unit value (a one-inch door) and insert it using a **30**- or **36**-scale factor at the time of insert, then you do not need to store two separate blocks like Door30 and Door36. Furthermore, you never have to worry about remembering the name of the block if all doors stem from the same **intelligent symbol**.

In our example, a door block and an accompanying insertion screen menu command (let's call it **UNIDOR**) would be an **intelligent symbol**, one that is adaptable to your needs.

If a script or menu command requires input (like the width of the door), it is said to be parametric (requiring a parameter). Parametric programming is the pinnacle of CAD usage—a real time saver.

Here is an example of such a script and screen menu combination:

UNIDOOR

```
Here's the block definition of the unidoor. The jamb width is
not included. The prompt sequence sets up a 1" unit straight
line and a corresponding 90 degree arc.

Command: LINE (RETURN)
From point: 0,0 (RETURN)
To point: 0,1 (RETURN)
To point: (RETURN)
Command: ARC (RETURN)
Center/<Start point>: C (RETURN)
Center: 0,0 (RETURN)
Start point: 0,1 (RETURN)
Angle/Length of chord/<End point>: A (RETURN)
Included angle: -90 (RETURN)
Command: BLOCK (RETURN)
Block name (or ?): Unidoor (RETURN)
Insertion base point: 0,0 (RETURN)
```

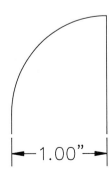

UNIDOOR, a Unit Value Door

—|← 1.00" →|—

```
Select objects: W (RETURN)
    (pick a window to include the door symbol)
First corner:    Other corner:    2 found.

Select objects: (RETURN)
```

You have now stored your door in unit format.

Here's the screen menu command:

```
[UNIDOOR: ]^C^CINSERT unidoor \\;
```

First this screen menu command sets up the insert of **unidoor**.

Then the command does several things:

☐ The first \ accepts a crosshair Insertion base point.

☐ The second \ accepts a keyboard X Scale (like 30 for 30″).

☐ The ; accepts the <default=X> Y Scale, then waits for rotation.

☐ If you use your pointer for scale, the ; will invoke the default rotation and end the command.

Notes on **Unidoor**.

☐ You can put standard **sizes** on the screen menu below the [UNIDOOR:] name like 24″, 28″, 30″, 32″, 36″, etc. Then instead of having to type these numbers, you can pick them.

☐ You can also set up individual **unidoor** commands like [UNIDR28:] and [UNIDR36:] if you use certain sizes frequently.

☐ If you are mainly inserting a symbol, such as **Unidoor** horizontally or vertically, use ^O (ORTHO) to keep the rotation drag aligned.

☐ You should figure out which permanent OSNAP will help you with this placement. You might even want to turn on a temporary OSNAP in the command line:

☐ An example is:

☐ [UNIDOOR:]^C^CInsert unidoor end\\;

☐ The **end** will turn on the aperture to help you attach **Unidoor** to the endpoint of a wall or door jamb.

Try creating your own **intelligent symbol** functions and include them in a custom screen menu.

AutoCAD VARIABLES AND LISP

Back in the beginning of this Book we promised that there would be no programming. We came close with a few SCRIPTS and MACROS, but these are really menu and command tools to help you get work done faster—not programming.

AutoCAD can be used as a programming language. Embedded in AutoCAD is a subset of the LISP programming language. Using AutoLISP and existing AutoCAD programs modules and system variables, you can put together super macros and user programs for all sorts of applications.

Using AutoLISP and variables, you could totally automate UNDIDOOR, for example, to break a hole in an existing double line wall, insert and scale, then clean up the intersections using only pointer picks as input.

But all that is beyond the scope of this Book. If you are in to programming see the Appendices and "Special Features" section of the AutoCAD Reference Manual for a full discussion on AutoCAD menus, system variables and LISP programming functions.

Expressing Yourself with Variables and Expressions

AutoCAD comes with programming capability to extend the power of scripts and parametric programming. This functionality is provided by AutoLISP which can be used to set system variables, set user defined variables, perform math and logic functions, capture pointing device and keyboard data, and execute AutoCAD commands.

Obviously AutoLISP extends the power of AutoCAD. To give you a sample of AutoLISP, we include a simple LISP routine and explanation. For more information on AutoLISP programming and handling LISP variables and expressions consult the AutoCAD Reference Manual. If you are an advanced user, you will want to consult the AutoLISP Programmer's Reference.

Putting Your Customization Together with a LISP Program

Our example routine creates a cube with the proper elevation and thickness using data you input in response to prompts built into the routine. Create the routine with a standard word processor or line editor. Invoke the routine with the LISP (load " ") function.

The file that contains the cube LISP instructions is called CUBE.LSP and is stored on disc in the same directory as the ACAD drawing files.

WHAT APPEARS ON THE SCREEN WITH THE CUBE ROUTINE

```
Command: (LOAD "CUBE") (RETURN)
Command: CUBE (RETURN)

What is the current elevation?: 0 (RETURN)
Enter lower left corner plan view: 1,1 (RETURN)
What is the length (X)?: 1 (RETURN)
What is the width (Y)?: 1 (RETURN)
What is the thickness (Z)?: 2 (RETURN)
ELEV New current elevation <0.0000>: 0 New current thickness
   <0.0000>: 2.000000000050
Command: LINE From point:
To point:
To point:
To point:
To point:
To point:
Command:
```

If you want to see the cube in 3-D use the standard VPOINT command:

```
Command: VPOINT (RETURN)
Enter view point <0.0000,0.0000,1.0000>: 1,1,1 (RETURN)
Command:
```

The LISP routine stored in the file CUBE.LSP looks like this:

CUBE.LSP

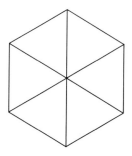

3D View

```
;This program draws a cube from elevation, length, width,
;thickness and starting point.
(defun C:CUBE ()
  (setq E (getreal "What is current elevation?: "))
  (setq pt1 (getpoint "Enter lower left corner plan view: "))
  (setq L (getreal "What is the length (X)?: "))
  (setq W (getreal "What is the width (Y)?: "))
  (setq T (getreal "What is the thickness (Z)?: "))
  (setq pt2 (list (+ (car pt1) L) (cadr pt1)))
  (setq pt3 (list (+ (car pt1) L) (+ (cadr pt1) W)))
  (setq pt4 (list ((car pt1) (+cadr pt1) W)))
  (setq H (+ E T))
(command "ELEV" E H)
(command "LINE" pt1 pt2 pt3 pt4 pt1 "")
```

In this listing E, pt1, L, W, pt2, pt3, pt4, and H are defined variables. Here is the interpretation of the other major features in the listing:

☐ ( ) Parentheses—LISP functions must all be inside parentheses. To separate functions within one line of LISP code, additional sets of ( ) are used.

☐ **setq**—setq sets the value of a user defined variable or system variable to the evaluation of a LISP expression. For example, (**setq H (+ E T)**) sets **H** to the total of **E + T**.

☐ **getpoint and getreal**—tell AutoCAD to get either a pointing device location or keyboard values as input. AutoLISP allows you to insert a string of text that will appear on the prompt line to prompt the input.

☐ **list**—puts together two or more numbers into a collection. This is useful for grouping X and Y coordinates to designate point locations.

☐ **+ − * /** —plus, minus, multiply and divide. The math symbol precedes the values operated on.

☐ **command**—invokes a standard AutoCAD command. The command instruction is given followed by the AutoCAD command in quotes, "ELEV" for example. The LISP expression gives all the parameters necessary to execute the command.

AutoLISP is powerful! It can be used for parametric and mathematical functions, including angular geometric functions (SINE, COSINE, etc.), powers, roots, conditionals, and string functions.

Some users have created database listings, bills-of-Materials, prototypical drawings, and more using AutoLISP routines.

Including LISP in Defined Menus

Many users start getting productivity mileage out of AutoCAD's LISP by including LISP expressions in their custom menus. You can see several simple examples in the standard AutoCAD menu listing.

Look at examples in the SETUP portion of the ACAD.MNU file. Copy the ACAD.MNU file into a text editor and look at the LISP function that sets the number of ENGLISH units in a horizontal layout. Look at and print the portion of the menu starting with ****SETUP 2** followed by **SHEETEN-GHORZ**. See if you understand how the variables and expressions are used to set variables for UNITS and LIMITS, and how the rectangular border is drawn.

All the SETUP functions are AutoLISP expressions!

SUMMING UP

It's been fun having you along—again.

"Never stop after just one book."

—Authors of the Sequel

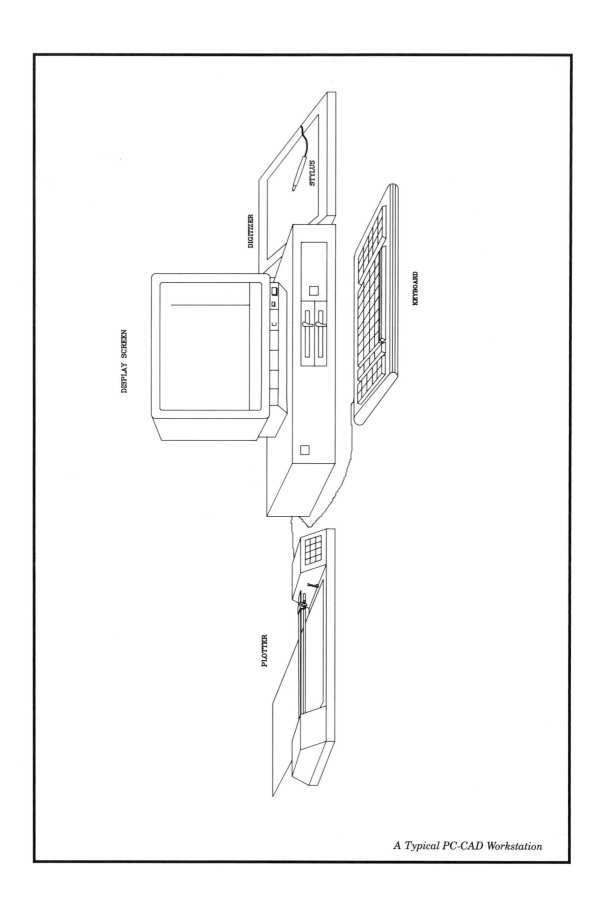

A Typical PC-CAD Workstation

APPENDIX A

MS-DOS AND CONFIGURING AutoCAD
THE INSIDE AutoCAD TEACHING CONFIGURATION

TURNING AUTOCAD ON

Getting AutoCAD going is similar to starting any other microcomputer program. You must physically turn on the computer, load the operating system from disc, then initiate the AutoCAD program from an operating system prompt. The tutorial assumes you have the hardware and software configuration described in this Appendix (A). If your workstation setup is different, take a moment now to get familiar with the differences between the Book's setup and yours.

```
          INSIDE AutoCAD TEACHING CONFIGURATION


                                 Fill in Your Configuration


PC/MS-DOS Microcomputer          ...........................
    640K Memory                  ...........................
    Math co-processor            ...........................
    Hard Disc (10MB or more)     ...........................
    Floppy disc(s)  (number)     ...........................
    360K, 720K or 1.2MB (size)   ...........................

PC/MS-DOS (Version 3.1 or later)
    Program files                ...........................
    Loaded on the hard disc (C:) ...........................
AutoCAD (Version 2.5) Hardware lock...........................
    Connected on RS-232 port (COM1).......................
AutoCAD (Version 2.5) Program files.........................
    Loaded on the hard disc (C:) ...........................
    Includes all ACAD program files as well as support files

Drawing files on hard disc (C:)  ...........................

        (Note. If you do not use a hard disc, then specify B: as
          the drawing file disc for the Book.)

Single Screen Monitor Brand Name  ...........................
        With 640 x 350 and 8 Color Display

        (Dual Screen will work as well.)

Digitizer Brand Name             ...........................
        With digitizer pointer (or mouse).

"D"  Size Pen Plotter Brand Name  ...........................

        (or other Plotter or Printer Plotter).

        (Note. The drawing sessions assume a "D" size plot.)
```

Two important notes:

☐ Make copies of the boot discs that contain MS-DOS and AutoCAD. Do not use the originals.

☐ Make sure your hardware lock is secured on the serial (RS-232) port (COM1).

MS-DOS

AutoCAD provides you with a set of drawing tools. MS-DOS is the operating system that works behind the scenes with AutoCAD as a task manager to manage and maintain your files.

Files are collections of commands and/or data on a disc. MS-DOS (and AutoCAD) files are recognized by their name extensions. The DOS name extension is the last three characters after the period in the DOS file name.

MS-DOS files have the file extension .COM (or .EXE). The DOS system is composed of the file COMMAND.COM and two hidden files. These three files boot the computer and contain common file management commands like the DIR (Directory) command. To execute a command, you type the command name at the DOS prompt followed by a (RETURN). **DIR (RETURN)** executes the DIRectory command which gives a list of the DOS files in the current directory.

Other Common DOS Commands

Commands which are resident within COMMAND.COM, like the DIR command, are called "internal" DOS commands. Besides the DIR command, other important internal DOS commands which you will use are the MD (Make Directory) command, the CD (Change Directory) command, the COPY (file) command, the REN (Rename file) command, and the DEL (Delete file) command. Make sure you are familiar with these file management commands before you attempt any extensive work with AutoCAD.

Besides these DOS resident file management commands, DOS also has other "external" file management commands which you will use in setting up and maintaining your files on disc. These also have the name extension .COM. For example, FORMAT.COM is the DOS command for formatting a data disc to accept DOS files.

To execute the command to format a data disc on drive B:, you type **FOR-MAT:B (RETURN)** at the DOS system prompt. (Remember, a disc drive is targeted in DOS by a letter and colon.) Do not FORMAT your hard disc if it has already been formatted. The FORMAT command wipes out all existing data as it formats the disc.

DISKCOPY formats a floppy disc and copies files from another disc to the target disc. The CHKDSK command lets you check the status of a data disc to determine if it has any bad files or areas. DISKCOPY.COM and CHKDSK.COM are the files names for these commands.

In all, MS-DOS (Version 3.1) contains some 33 files. Use the DIR command to examine the DOS files on the DOS system disc, or the root (or\DOS) directory of your hard disc if the DOS system is already loaded on your hard disc. Use Control S (^S) to toggle the text screen scroll on or off. Make sure you are familiar with and know how to use the basic DOS "external" file management commands.

AutoCAD Files

AutoCAD (Version 2.5) comes on seven floppy discs. It has three main types of files: program files (.EXE and .OVL files, for example), support files like help (.HLP), text (.SHX), pattern files (.PAT), and, of course, drawing files (.DWG). AutoCAD's default drawing file is called ACAD.DWG.

AutoCAD's file naming conventions are easy to follow. It is not hard to deduce file functions by looking at the name extension. ACAD.MNU is the standard menu file. (The compiled version is .MNX). Driver files (the files that control the video display, digitizer, or plotter) have the extension .DRV. AutoCAD's configuration is stored in the ACAD.CFG file.

Pre-Loaded AutoCAD Files

To run AutoCAD from a hard disc, you format the hard disc to receive DOS files, transfer the MS-DOS program files to the hard disc, and transfer the AutoCAD program and support files to the hard disc.

If your workstation has been prepared for you by a dealer, and these steps already have been done, you can start the program by turning the machine on. After a hardware self-check, the machine will search for the DOS files on the hard disc and load the MS-DOS operating system. It also is common practice for dealers to include an automatic date and time setting in the start up procedure. If this also has been done, you should see the following DOS operating system prompt on your display screen:

C>

This is your operating system telling you that everything is ready to go from the default disc drive **C:**. If you are prompted for date and time, enter the current date and current time according to your DOS manual, and you will receive the **C>** prompt.

If the AutoCAD files were placed in the root directory, you can start AutoCAD by simply typing **ACAD (RETURN)** next to the **C>** prompt. But we recommend placing AutoCAD in its own sub-directory.

Loading AutoCAD Files

If your hard disc was formatted and loaded with DOS, but AutoCAD files were not loaded, you need to load the AutoCAD files. We recommend that you follow the procedures in the AutoCAD Installation and Performance Guide for preparing your hard disc and transferring the AutoCAD files.

The best way to manage AutoCAD on a hard disc is to create a sub-directory to run AutoCAD. Use the DOS command MD (Make Directory) to create a sub-directory on your disc. Type **MD** \ followed by a **(RETURN)**.

```
C>
C>MD \ACAD (RETURN)     (Creates ACAD sub-directory.)

(A DIR command will display all the programs and directories.
 The ACAD directory will be listed at the bottom of the list.)
```

Using The DOS Change Directory Command

To load the AutoCAD program files, you want to change to the new ACAD directory. Use the DOS CD (Change Directory) command. Type **CD** \ and a **(RETURN)**. Then use the DOS COPY command to sequentially copy all the AutoCAD files from the floppy discs to the ACAD directory. We will assume that you are copying the files from the A: floppy disc drive.

```
C>
C>CD \ACAD (RETURN) (Changes to the ACAD directory.)

Place the AutoCAD EXE disc in A:

C>COPY A:*.* (RETURN)   (This copies all the files on
    the disc to the ACAD directory. When all the files are
    copied, the DOS prompt will return.)

Replace the disc in the A: drive with the next disc. Repeat the
COPY A:*.* command. Continue until all the discs are copied.
```

After the files are loaded, typing **ACAD** followed by a **(RETURN)** will load AutoCAD. The screen will display the AutoCAD's header and a message that AutoCAD is not yet configured.

```
C>  ACAD (RETURN)
```

CONFIGURING AutoCAD

If AutoCAD was not configured on your workstation, the Configuration Menu will sequentially prompt you to identify the types and selected parameters for your video display, digitizer, plotter, and printer/plotter which make up your workstation configuration.

Looking At Your Configuration

If AutoCAD was loaded and your workstation is already configured, you can look at your configuration by selecting **5** from the Main Men. AutoCAD will display your current configuration and prompt you with the Configuration Menu.

```
                    A U T O C A D

Copyright (C) 1982, 83, 84, 85, 86 Autodesk, Inc.
Version 2.5X (06/15/86) IBM PC
Advanced Drafting Extensions 3
Serial Number: 12-3456789

Main Menu

         0.  Exit AutoCAD
         1.  Begin a NEW Drawing
         2.  Edit an EXISTING Drawing
         3.  Plot a drawing
         4.  Printer plot a drawing

         5.  Configure AutoCAD
         6.  File Utilities
         7.  Compile shape/font description file
         8.  Convert old drawing file

Enter selection <0>: 5 (RETURN)
```

```
Main Menu

0.  Exit AutoCAD
1.  Begin a NEW drawing
2.  Edit an EXISTING drawing
3.  Plot a drawing
4.  Printer plot a drawing

5.  Configure AutoCAD
6.  File Utilities
7.  Compile shape/font description file
8.  Convert old drawing file

Enter Selection ____
```

AutoCAD'S Main Menu

AutoCAD is ready to configure. Pressing (RETURN) will get you AutoCAD's Configuration Menu to continue with the configuration process.

```
From the Main Menu:

Enter your selection: 5  (RETURN)

Configure AutoCAD

Current AutoCAD configuration

    Video display: ...............(lists display type)

    Digitizer: ...................(lists digitizer type.)

    Plotter: .....................(lists plotter type.)

    Printer Plotter:..............(lists printer plotter type.)


Press RETURN to continue:  (RETURN)
```

Pressing (**RETURN**) gets you AutoCAD's Configuration Menu:

```
Configuration menu

0. Exit to Main Menu
1. Show current configuration
2. Allow I/O port configuration

3. Configure video display
4. Configure digitizer
5. Configure plotter
6. Configure printer plotter
7. Configure system console
8. Configure operating parameters

Enter selection:
```

Configuring Or Reconfiguring Your System

Using the **Configure AutoCAD** utility is simple and straightforward. AutoCAD asks you several questions about your hardware setup and you respond with answers or a number selection from a list of choices that AutoCAD provides. Configuration is dependent on your hardware setup.

AutoCAD supports a number of computers and peripherals. We will not try to duplicate the large number of possible configuration combinations. AutoCAD supplies a separate User's Installation And Performance Guide for configuring your computer workstation. The Guide lists the displays and peripherals supported for each computer.

To configure or reconfigure your system, you select a menu item number. The number puts you in a submenu for each device-type and/or operating parameters. AutoCAD supplies a numbered list of devices supported. You select the individual device by number and AutoCAD prompts you for information to configure its support of the device.

Hardware Options

Option 3 configures the video display. The Book assumes AutoCAD's default values for a single video display. A dual screen works as well.

Option 4 configures the digitizer. The Book assumes you have selected and configured a brand name digitizer from the option list under Option 4.

Option 5 configures the plotter. The Book assumes you have selected and configured a brand name plotter from the option numbers listed under Option 5. Apppendix C gives additional details on setting up a Houston Instrument DMP plotter for plotting.

Option 6 configures a printer plotter. The Book does not assume you have selected a printer plotter, but does provide a printer plotter exercise in the Chapter on plotting.

Option 7 configures the system console.

Option 8 configures selected operating parameters. The submenu allows you to exit to the configuration menu, set an alarm for error messages, set up default prototype drawings, and set up AutoLISP features. Its submenu is:

```
0. Exit to the configuration menu
1. Alarm on error
2. Initial drawing setup
3. AutoLISP features
```

After exiting the AutoCAD's configuration menu, you return to AutoCAD's Main Menu. Your configuration is kept in a file called ACAD.CFG plus OVL files.

When you are through checking your system configuration, you can exit AutoCAD by selecting Option **0 Exit AutoCAD** from the Main Menu. Option **0** gets you back to the MS-DOS operating system. You will use this option every time you finish an AutoCAD session.

Function Keys

When your computer is configured, AutoCAD also sets other workstation functions. Each MS-DOS work-alike computer has a set of function keys. These keys vary from microcomputer type to type. The Book does not make extensive use of function keys, but does refer to them.

The following list gives an example setup of function keys for an IBM PC/XT. If AutoCAD has been configured for an IBM PC/XT using the configure utility, AutoCAD will automatically set up the following function keys and colors:

```
              SAMPLE  AUTOMATIC  FUNCTION  KEYS  FOR  AN  IBM  PC  SETUP

   AutoCAD Function:    IBM PC Key        Fill in your own key.

   CTRL                 CTRL              .............................
   FLIP  SCREEN         F1                .............................
   TOGGLE  COORD        F6 or ^D          .............................
   TOGGLE  GRID         F7 or ^G          .............................
   TOGGLE  ORTHO        F8 or ^O          .............................
   TOGGLE  SNAP         F9 or ^B          .............................
   TOGGLE  TABLET       F10 or ^T         .............................
   SLOW  CURSOR         Shift + Down Key...........................
                        (Num Lock Off)
   FAST  CURSOR         Shift + Up Key    .............................
                        (Num Lock Off)
   ABORT  CURSOR        End               .............................
   SCREEN  CURSOR       Home              .............................
   MENU  CURSOR         Insert (INS)      .............................
   UP  CURSOR           Up arrow          .............................
   DOWN  CURSOR         Down arrow        .............................
   LEFT  CURSOR         Left arrow        .............................
   RIGHT  CURSOR        Right arrow       .............................

   Pressing the F keys sets COORDs On,  GRID On,  ORTHO On,  and SNAP
   On.  The GRID display is set to a default value of 1.0.  The
   Insert (INS) key will execute a menu item,  if it is already
   highlighted (hit twice).

   Color Assignments:

   1 - red                       5 - blue
   2 - yellow                    6 - magenta
   3 - green                     7 - white
   4 - cyan                      colors 8 and up vary with display.
```

THE PROTOTYPE DRAWING

When you configure AutoCAD, it assumes a standard prototype drawing as its initial drawing environment. AutoCAD's default drawing is called ACAD.DWG. This is your drawing environment until you change the initial values in ACAD.DWG, or until you change your prototype drawing.

The default modes of ACAD.DWG are shown below.

DEFAULT MODES OF ACAD.DWG

Mode	Default
ATTDISP	Normal (controlled indivdidually)
AXIS	Off, spacing (0.0, 0.0)
BASE	Insertion base point (0.0,0.0)
BLIPMODE	On*
CHAMFER	Distance 0.0
COLOR	BYLAYER
Coordinate	Updated on point entry display
DIM variables	See DIMENSION Modes List
DRAGMODE	Auto
ELEV	Elevation 0.0, thickness 0.0
FILL	On
FILLET radius	0.0
GRID	Off, spacing (0.0,0.0)
Highlighting	Enabled
ISOPLANE	Left
LAYER	Current/only layer 0, On, color 7 (white) and linetype CONTINUOUS
LIMITS	Off, drawing limits (0.0,0.0) to (12.0,9.0)
LINETYPE	BYLAYER
LTSCALE	1.0
MENU	ACAD
MIRROR	Text mirrored like other entities.
ORTHO	Off
OSNAP	None
PLINE	Line-width 0.0
POINT	Display mode 0, size 0.00
QTEXT	Off
REGENAUTO	On
SKETCH	Record increment 0.10, creates polylines
SNAP	Off, spacing (1.0,1.0)
SNAP/GRID	Standard style, base point (0.0,0.0), rotation 0 degrees
STYLE	STANDARD with font file TXT, and no special modes
TABLET	Off
TEXT	Style STANDARD, height 0.20, and rotation 0
TIME	User elapsed timer on
TRACE	Width 0.05
UNITS (linear)	Decimal, 4 decimal places
UNITS (angular)	Decimal degrees, 0 decimal places, angle 0 direction to right, angles increase CCW
VIEWRES	Fast zoom on, circle zoom percent 100
ZOOM	To drawing limits

Following are the dimensioning default modes set in ACAD.DWG:

DIMENSION DEFAULT MODES IN ACAD.DWG

DIM variables		
	DIMALT	Off
	DIMALTD	2
	DIMALTF	25.40
	DIMASZ	0.18
	DIMBLK	(None)
	DIMCEN	0.09
	DIMDLE	0.00
	DIMDLI	0.38
	DIMEXE	0.18
	DIMEXO	0.0625
	DIMLFAC	1.00
	DIMLIM	Off
	DIMRND	0.00
	DIMSCALE	1.00
	DIMSE1	Off
	DIMSE2	Off
	DIMTAD	Off
	DIMTIH	On
	DIMTM	0.00
	DIMTOH	On
	DIMTOL	Off
	DIMTP	0.00
	DIMTSZ	0.00
	DIMTXT	0.18
	DIMZIN	Off

Changing The Prototype Drawing

You can modify ACAD.DWG by changing the settings and saving your updated drawing with AutoCAD's END command.

When you configure AutoCAD, you can choose a different default drawing. If you create a new prototype, you can specify a new drawing by setting your drawing = new prototype when AutoCAD prompts you for the drawing name from selection **1** at the Main Menu.

You also can create a drawing without a prototype drawing by entering your drawing name with an = sign after the drawing name prompt at selection **1** of the Main Menu. In this case, AutoCAD will use the default modes.

```
Main Menu

0.  Exit AutoCAD
1.  Begin a NEW drawing
2.  Edit an EXISTING drawing
3.  Plot a drawing
4.  Printer plot a drawing

5.  Configure AutoCAD
6.  File Utilities
7.  Compile shape/font description file
8.  Convert old drawing file

Enter Selection ____
```

AutoCAD'S Main Menu (Again)

Back to the Main Menu

Main Menu Options 1, 2, 3, and 4 are where the AutoCAD action is — we spend most of the Book on what goes inside these options.

If your computer is configured with AutoCAD, you are ready to start Chapter 1 of INSIDE AutoCAD using the standard prototype drawing.

AutoCAD SCREEN MENUS AND COMMAND STRUCTURE

INTRODUCTION TO THE AUTOCAD COMMAND STRUCTURE

There are commands and there are commands. AutoCAD has what is known in computing as a **flat** command structure. This means that just about any AutoCAD command can be executed at any time. Other programs may use a **heap** or "hierarchical" command structure.

In a heap structure you have to know exactly where you want to go in the command structure and the path to get there. Then you have to execute all the necessary steps to get to the command you want. This method is okay for a beginner who needs a lot of direction, but is cumbersome for someone who justs wants to draw a **LINE** without having to key through a command sequence just to get there.

In AutoCAD you can just type a command from the keyboard without having to step through a series of intermediate commands. Of course, this means that you have to know the name of the command you want to execute (like LINE:).

Menus, Keys, and Commands

Because we often want to group commands together for convenience (as in a heap structure), or to prompt us to use certain commands together, AutoCAD provides the capability to create menus or groups of commands.

☐ A MENU is a listing of commands or keys. This list is for convenience only and has no effect on the AutoCAD command structure.

☐ A KEY is the name of an AutoCAD menu. A key does not actually execute an AutoCAD command—instead it activates another menu.

☐ A COMMAND is what makes AutoCAD go. A command actually performs an AutoCAD function. A command has a colon, :, after it.

AutoCAD comes from the factory with a preset structure of screen menus (and a standard tablet menu). These menus list keys or commands that you can use during an AutoCAD drawing editor session. **AutoCAD** is the key of the ROOTMENU. The ROOTMENU list contains commands (words followed by a colon, like DIM: or LAYER:) and several keys (BLOCKS, EDIT, SETTINGS) to get to other screen menus.

This Appendix (B) provides a list of the primary keys and commands of the standard AutoCAD screen menus. These are shown in THE AutoCAD STANDARD SCREEN MENUS (Version 2.5). The keys and commands are grouped by menus linked back to the AutoCAD ROOTMENU.

Remember, menus are simply for convenience in grouping commands. As additional features are added to AutoCAD, the screen menus change. If you have additional features, or if customized commands have been added to your screen menus, write the screen menu words at the appropriate place in the menu list to get a complete list.

The AutoCAD Standard Tablet Menu is shown in Appendix D.

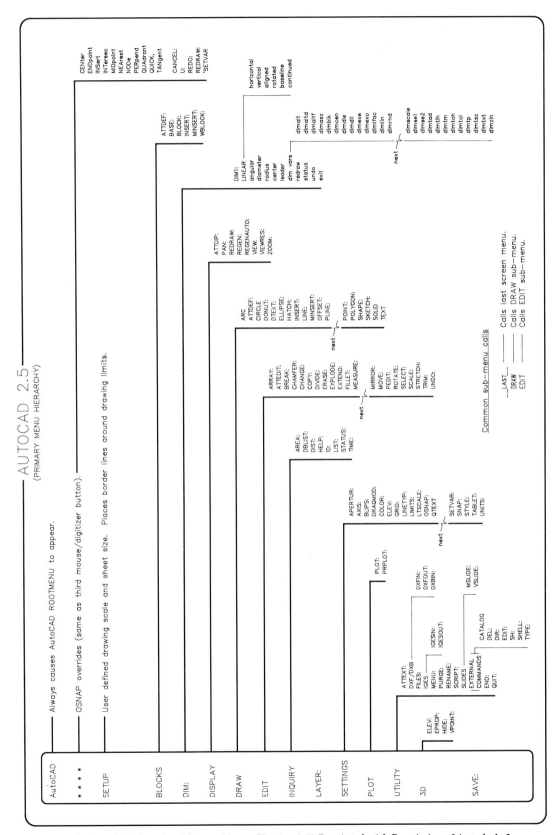

The AutoCAD Standard Screen Menus (Version 2.5) Reprinted with Permission of Autodesk, Inc.

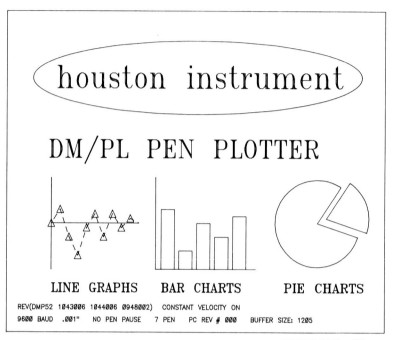

DMP Self-Test Plot

PEN DOWN VELOCITY (IPS):
2   3   4   5   6   7   <u>8</u>   9   10   11   12   13   14   15   16
PEN UP VELOCITY (IPS):
2   3   4   5   6   7   <u>8</u>   9   10   11   12   13   14   15   16
PEN DOWN ACCELERATION (G):
.5   <u>1</u>   2   3   4
PEN UP ACCELERATION (G):
.5   1   <u>2</u>   3   4
PEN DOWN DELAY (MS):
0   5   10   15   20   25   <u>30</u>   35   40   45   50   55   60   65   70
PEN UP DELAY (MS):
0   5   10   15   20   <u>25</u>   30   35   40   45   50   55   60   65   70
PAPER SIZE:
SMALL   <u>LARGE</u>
SMALL CHART FORMAT:
<u>18"x24"</u>   A2(METRIC)
LARGE CHART FORMAT:
<u>24"x36"</u>   A1(METRIC)
PEN CHANGE ACTION:
IGNORE   <u>PAUSE</u>
CONSTANT VELOCITY:
<u>ON</u>   OFF
ADDRESSING:
<u>.001IN</u>   .005IN   .1MM   .025MM
CHARACTER SET:
<u>G0</u>   G1   G2   G3   G4   G5   G6   G7
TEXT FONT:
<u>F0</u>   F1
ZERO CHARACTER:
<u>SLASH</u>   NO SLASH
BAUD RATE:
<u>9600</u>   4800   2400   1200   600   300
UART PARITY:
<u>BIT8=1</u>   BIT8=0   EVEN   ODD
HANDSHAKE RTS/DTR:
<u>TOGGLE</u>   ALWAYS HIGH
PASS-THRU PORT:
<u>TOGGLE</u>   ALWAYS ON
AUTOMATIC PEN CAPPING (SEC):
15   30   60   120   240   <u>480</u>   DISABLE
WARNING BEFORE AUTO-CAPPING:
<u>ON</u>   OFF
MACHINE TYPE:
1 PEN   <u>7 PEN</u>   14 PEN

Sample DMP 52MP Settings for Plotting with AutoCAD

APPENDIX C

GETTING A PEN PLOTTER READY TO PLOT

For discussion, INSIDE AutoCAD assumes that you have a Houston Instrument (HI) Model DMP 52 pen plotter. This is a single pen plotter which plots on "D" size paper (36″ × 24″) with an approximate maximum image size of 34″ × 21.5″.

Getting The Plotter Ready

Here's a checklist for getting the plotter ready:

PLOTTER READY CHECKLIST

☐ First Time Check.

    ☐ Is the plotter plugged in and turned on?

    ☐ Is the plotter data cable plugged into the computer port? If you use the same port for your digitizer, make sure you've switched data cables from digitizer to plotter.

    ☐ Is the paper movement path clear? No obstacles?

    ☐ Run the plotter self-test. Does the example drawing look okay? Any pen skips? Paper misalignments? (To run the plotter self-test for the HI DMP 52 see RUNNING THE HI DMP SELF-TEST.)

    ☐ Are the internal plotter settings correct? (To check these settings for the HI DMP 52 see CHECKING THE DMP 52 INTERNAL PLOTTER SETTINGS.)

☐ Every Plot Check.

☐ Is the pen in the pen holder? Is it the right pen width? Color? Have you tested the pen in the last few minutes to make sure it is not clogged?

☐ Is the paper loaded properly? Are the gripper wheels set properly? Is the paper aligned?

☐ Is the plotter set for the correct paper size?

☐ If you use a single communication port computer, is the data cable coming from the computer switched from digitizer (or other input device) to plotter?

The Self-Test

The DMP plotter has a self-contained practice plot stored internally. This practice plot tests the plotter by drawing to the full extents of the plotting area, drawing straight and curved lines, plotting text and more. Also during this test, the plotter checks its internal circuitry and lets you know if there is anything wrong.

You should run the self-test frequently. Here's how to run the self-test:

RUNNING THE HI DMP SELF-TEST

☐ Turn the plotter on.

☐ Insert any pen into the pen holder.

☐ Line up a "D" size sheet of paper. Open the paper grippers. As you face the plotter from the front, slip the paper in from the rear until it reaches the front edge of the flat bed at the front of the plotter. Align the left edge of the paper with the inside of the leftmost wide white line on the left edge of the flat bed of the plotter. Holding the paper in place, lower the left and right gripper wheels.

☐ Press the **LARGE** button on the control panel and GET OUT OF THE WAY—hands, hair, necklaces, ties, cuffs long earrings!

☐ The plotter will check paper alignment by running the paper back and forth through the plotter. If the paper falls out of the plotter or gets crooked with respect to the white lines at the edge, the alignment has failed. Repeat the paper lineup step and press **LARGE** again.

☐ Initiate the self-test by pressing the **LOCAL** button (the LOCAL button light will come on) and then press the **UP** and **DOWN** arrows at the same time.

☐ If all is well, the DMP will create the image shown in the DMP SELF-TEST PLOT. If not, check the DMP Operations Manual to find out what is wrong.

If your plotter dealer did not set the DMP with suitable settings for AutoCAD, or you use your plotter with several different computers or programs, you may need to reset the DMP internal settings.

A full discussion on the DMP internal settings can be found in Houston Instrument's publication "HIPLOT DMP-51/52 Operation Manual". The Book's discussion here is only a summary discussion.

The Plotter Internal Setup

The DMP setup program is executed using the buttons on the front panel of the plotter. The setup program first lets you know the current settings by plotting them out. Then it asks you if you want to change any settings by moving the pen to the current setting. With the arrow keys on the front panel you can change the setting by moving the pen to the desired setting and pressing **ENTER**. The setup program will prompt you for each setting.

SAMPLE DMP 52 SETTINGS FOR AutoCAD shows sample internal plotter settings as plotted by a DMP.

CHECKING THE DMP 52 INTERNAL PLOTTER SETTINGS

☐ To initiate the setup program:

  ☐ Turn the plotter on.

  ☐ Run the DMP self-test.

  ☐ To start the internal setup program press **ENTER**. The light on the ENTER button should come on. Press **SCALE UR**. The plotter should start plotting the first internal setup parameter.

  ☐ When the plotter has plotted all the options, the pen will move to the current setting and hover over that setting. You can adjust the internal setting by using the left and right arrow buttons on the front panel to move the pen to your desired setting. When you get the pen to the right place, press ENTER. The plotter records your setting by underlining it, and moves on to the next internal setup parameter.

  ☐ Check the internal setup parameters against those shown in the SAMPLE DMP 52 SETTINGS FOR AutoCAD. Move through each setting as necessary. If the setting is okay as is, simply press ENTER to move on to the next parameter.

  ☐ The internal setup program will repeat itself. If you miss a setting, you can go through the process again.

  ☐ To exit from the internal setup program press **SCALE UR** again.

☐ Save the plot of internal parameter settings for comparison with those in the SAMPLE, and for future reference.

☐ To remove the paper, gently lift the gripper wheels and pull the paper out.

☐ If you do not plan to plot again in the next few minutes, remove the pen and cap it to keep the tip from drying.

SETTING UP THE PLOTTER WITH AutoCAD

When you first configure AutoCAD for use with the plotter or a printer/plotter, you set most of the plotting parameters that you will use in plotting.

AutoCAD will prompt you through a sequence to set your initial parameters for plotting or printer/plotting. The Book uses the following default assumptions.

SAMPLE AutoCAD DEFAULT PLOT ASSUMPTIONS

☐ DMP Model 52.

☐ Change pens while plotting—YES.

☐ The plotter is calibrated.

☐ Plots are written to the plotter, NOT to a disc file.

☐ Plotting units are measured in Inches.

☐ Plot origin (in inches) is at 0.00,0.00

☐ Plot size (in inches) is the MAXimum size, 34.00,21.50.

☐ The image is plotted normally, NOT rotated 90 degrees.

☐ The pen width (in inches) is 0.010.

☐ Area fill boundaries are NOT adjusted for pen width.

☐ Hidden lines are NOT removed. (This applies only to 3-D views.)

☐ Scale is Fit to the maximum plotting area.

☐ Pen speed is 16 inches per second.

AutoCAD stores these plotting parameters in a file created at configuration.

You have the option of changing any of these parameters by answering **Y** to the plot change prompt:

```
Do you want to change anything?  <N>:
```

AutoCAD provides this prompt for each plot. If you make changes, AutoCAD will store your new settings as <defaults> in the file for your next plot.

SAMPLE PAPER DRAWING AREAS

AutoCAD supports a number of printer/plotters and plotters, handling from "A" size to "E" size sheets. The SAMPLE TABLE OF PAPER SCALES lists the paper sheet size and approximate drawing areas for different sheet sizes.

SAMPLE TABLE OF PAPER SCALES

Scale	Sheet (X x Y)		Image Drawing Area (X x Y)*
Civil Engineers	A:	12" x 9"	10" x 8"*
and	B:	18" x 12"	16" x 11"
Architects	C:	24" x 18"	22" x 16"
	D:	36" x 24"	34" x 22"
	E:	48" x 36"	46" x 34"
Mechanical	A:	11" x 8 1/2"	9" x 7"
Engineers	B:	17" x 11"	15" x 10"
	C:	22" x 17"	20" x 15"
	D:	34" x 22"	32" x 20"
	E:	44" x 34"	42" x 32"
Metric Scale	A:	280 x 216 mm	230 x 178 mm*
	B:	432 x 280 mm	380 x 254 mm
	C:	55.9 x 43.2 cm	50.8 x 38.1 cm
	D:	86.4 x 81.3 cm	81.3 x 50.8 cm
	E:	111.8 x 86.4 cm	106.7 x 81.3 cm

*Approximate drawing area. Allow 0.5" to 1" less than the sheet size as an effective image area for most plotters.

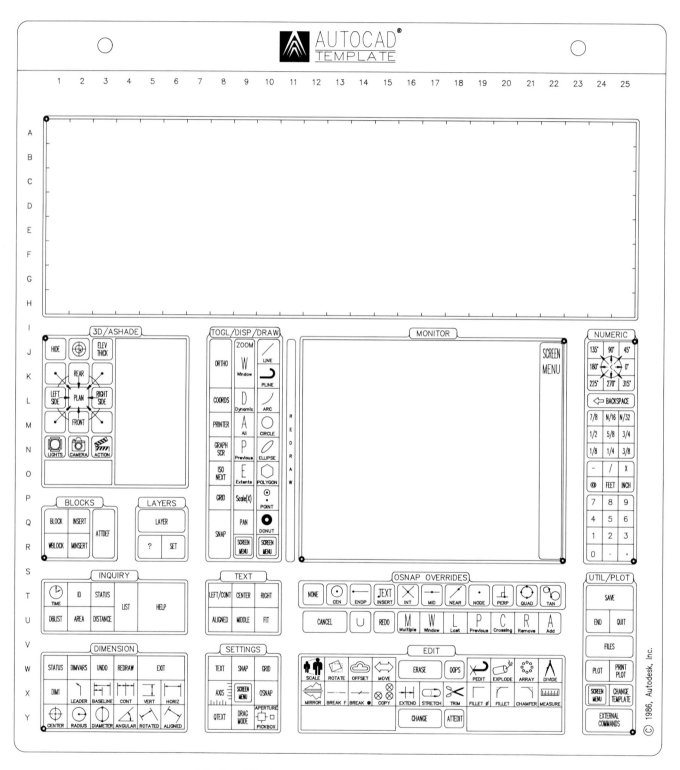

The AutoCAD Standard Tablet Menu (Version 2.5) Reprinted with Permission of Autodesk, Inc.

APPENDIX D

SETTING UP YOUR TABLET WITH THE STANDARD
AutoCAD TABLET MENU

AutoCAD Version 2.5 comes with a standard tablet menu, including a plastic template for an 11″ × 11″ digitizer tablet. To use the standard AutoCAD tablet menu, you affix the template to your digitizer, and use the AutoCAD TABLET Command to let the program know where the tablet "boxes" are located.

The TABLET.DWG Drawing

AutoCAD also comes from the factory with a drawing file named TABLET.DWG. This is a drawing file like any other AutoCAD drawing file. You can view it on the screen, edit it, and plot it. You also can use this drawing to create a template drawing for your digitizer.

Once you know how to edit drawings and customize the tablet menu, you can make your own tablet drawing and support it with your own tablet menu programs. If you do wish to customize your tablet menu, we suggest you first make a copy of TABLET.DWG, call it MYTABLET.DWG, and make your changes to the copy, not the original.

In this Appendix (D) we will step through plotting a copy of TABLET.DWG to use as the tablet overlay. Then, step through the procedures for loading the tablet menu. If you are using the standard template, proceed directly to loading the menu.

We assume that you are using an 11″ × 11″ digitizer that has been set up according to the AutoCAD Installation And Performance Guide. We also assume that you have already loaded AutoCAD, configured your system (Appendix A), read Appendix C on Plotter Setup and have a plotter ready for plotting. You will need a paper sheet (D size or 36″ × 24″ for the DMP-52) and a .35mm black plotting pen.

Plotting the TABLET Drawing

Here is the step-by-step sequence for plotting the tablet drawing. Turn on the plotter, load paper and pen, and begin the following sequence:

PLOTTING THE STANDARD TABLET MENU

Load the AutoCAD program

C:> **ACAD (RETURN)**

    Main Menu

    0. Exit AutoCAD
    1. Begin a NEW drawing
    2. Edit an EXISTING drawing
    3. Plot a drawing
    4. Printer plot a drawing

    5. Configure AutoCAD
    6. File Utilities
    7. Compile shape/font description file
    8. Convert old drawing file

Enter selection: **3 (RETURN)**

Enter NAME of drawing <default>: **TABLET (RETURN)**

Specify the part of the drawing to be plotted by entering:
Display, Extents, Limits, View, or Window <D>: **E (RETURN)**

Plot will NOT be written to a selected file
Sizes are in Inches
Plot origin is at (0.00,0.00)
Plotting area is 34.00 wide by 21.50 (MAX size)
Plot is NOT rotated 90 degrees
Pen width is 0.010
Area fill will NOT be adjusted for pen width
Hidden lines will NOT be removed
Plot will be scaled to fit available area

Do you want to change anything? <N> **Y (RETURN)**

(AutoCAD displays the current settings for plot parameters.)

Layer Color	Pen No.	Line Type	Pen Speed	Layer Color	Pen No.	Line Type	Pen Speed
1 (red)	1	0	16	9	1	0	16
2 (yellow)	1	0	16	10	1	0	16
3 (green)	1	0	16	11	1	0	16
4 (cyan)	1	0	16	12	1	0	16
5 (blue)	1	0	16	13	1	0	16
6 (magenta)	1	0	16	14	1	0	16
7 (white)	1	0	16	15	1	0	16
8	1	0	16				

```
Line types: 0 = continuous line          Pen speed codes:
            1 = . . . . . . . . . . . . . . . . . .
            2 = .  .  .  .  .  .  .  .  .  .       Inches/Second:
            3 = -------------------                 1, 2, 4, 8, 16
            4 = - - - - - - - - - -
            5 = -- -- -- -- -- -- -                Cm/Second:
            6 = --- --- --- --- ---                 3, 5, 10, 20, 40
            7 = -- - -- - -- - -- -
            8 = __--__--__--__--__-
```

Enter line types, pen speed codes
  blank=go to next, Cn=go to Color n,
  S=Show current choices, X=Exit
Do you want to change any of the above parameters? <N>
  N (RETURN)

Write the plot to a file? <N> **(RETURN)**
Size units (Inches or Millimeters) <I>: **(RETURN)**
Plot origin in Inches <0.00,0.00>: **(RETURN)**

Standard values for plotting size

Size   Width   Height

A   10.50   8.00
B   16.00   10.00
C   21.00   16.00
D   33.00   21.00
MAX   34.00   21.50

Enter the Size or Width,Height (in Inches) <MAX>: **(RETURN)**

Rotate 2D plots 90 degrees clockwise? <N>: **(RETURN)**
Pen width <0.010>: **(RETURN)**
Adjust area fill boundaries for pen width? <N> **(RETURN)**
Remove hidden lines? <N> **(RETURN)**

Specify scale by entering:
Plotted Inches = Drawing Units or Fit or ? <F>: **1=1 (RETURN)**

Effective plotting area: 24.50 wide by 11.00 high
Position paper in plotter.
Press RETURN to continue or S to Stop for hardware setup
  S (RETURN)
Do hardware setup now.
Press RETURN to continue:

(Check plotter readiness and hit (RETURN).)
  (RETURN)

Processing vector: nn   (AutoCAD cycles through whole drawing)

(Plotting takes place.)

Plot complete.
Press RETURN to continue: **(RETURN)**

    Main Menu

    0. Exit AutoCAD
    1. Begin a NEW drawing
    2. Edit an EXISTING drawing
    3. Plot a drawing
    4. Printer plot a drawing

    5. Configure AutoCAD
    6. File Utilities
    7. Compile shape/font description file
    8. Convert old drawing file

Enter selection:

The standard tablet drawing is shown in AutoCAD's TABLET DRAWING

CONFIGURING THE TABLET

Once you have plotted the TABLET drawing, trim the drawing leaving about a 1/2" border and tape it to your digitizer. Since every tablet is different and since every user trims and tapes differently, you have to let AutoCAD know exactly where the tablet commands are located on the surface of the tablet.

You use the **TABLET** Command from inside the Drawing Editor to configure the tablet. AutoCAD provides a series of **Tablet Pick Points** on the drawing (or template) as guides to loading each of the four menu areas prompted by the TABLET Command. These are donut points on the menu.

The standard menu is divided in columns and rows and four menu areas. Look at the TABLET MENU. The columns are numbered 1 to 25 across the top. The rows are lettered A to Y on the left. Menu area 1 is the top rectangular area which is left for customization. The first "donut" pick point is near A and 1 in the top left corner. Menu area 1 has 25 columns and 9 rows of menu "boxes".

To load the menu, you pick three points for a menu area, and give the number of columns and rows in the menu area:

CONFIGURING THE STANDARD TABLET

```
Go To the Main Menu

Enter selection: 1 (RETURN)

Enter NAME of drawing <TABLET>: TEST (RETURN)

(The AutoCAD drawing screen appears with the screen menu.)

Command: TABLET (RETURN)
Option (ON/OFF/CAL/CFG): CFG (RETURN)
Enter the number of tablet menus desired (0-4) <4>: (RETURN)

Digitize the upper left corner of menu area 1: (Pick point)
Digitize the lower left corner of menu area 1: (Pick point)
Digitize the lower right corner of menu area 1: (Pick point)
Enter the number of columns for menu area 1: 25 (RETURN)
Enter the number of rows for menu area 1: 9 (RETURN)

Digitize the upper left corner of menu area 2: (Pick point)
Digitize the lower left corner of menu area 2: (Pick point)
Digitize the lower right corner of menu area 2: (Pick point)
Enter the number of columns for menu area 2: 11 (RETURN)
Enter the number of rows for menu area 2: 9 (RETURN)

Digitize the upper left corner of menu area 3: (Pick point)
Digitize the lower left corner of menu area 3: (Pick point)
Digitize the lower right corner of menu area 3: (Pick point)
Enter the number of columns for menu area 3: 9 (RETURN)
Enter the number of rows for menu area 3: 13 (RETURN)
```

```
Digitize the upper left corner of menu area 4:  (Pick point)
Digitize the lower left corner of menu area 4:  (Pick point)
Digitize the lower right corner of menu area 4:  (Pick point)
Enter the number of columns for menu area 4:  25  (RETURN)
Enter the number of rows for menu area 4:  7  (RETURN)

Do you want to respecify the screen pointing area (Y)  (RETURN)

Digitize lower left corner of screen pointing area:  (Pick)
Digitize upper right corner of screen pointing area:  (Pick)
Command:  QUIT  (RETURN)
Do you really want to discard all changes ?  Y  (RETURN)

Main Menu appears.  Select 0 to exit AutoCAD.
```

The standard AutoCAD tablet menu is now configured for your digitizer and the configuration parameters are stored on your disc in a file.

To help you become familiar with the tablet menu, we have reproduced the tablet menu command areas in each Chapter of INSIDE AutoCAD—highlighting the tablet commands that are exercised in the Chapter.

INDEX

The ▶ preceding items in the INDEX indicates new material.

ORDER AND COMMENT FORM

Please send me the following NEW RIDERS Books.

CURRENT RELEASES:

    ....Copies of INSIDE AutoCAD   @ $34.95 US
        (Supports AutoCAD 2.5)   ISBN 0-934035-08-3

    ....Copies of INSIDE AutoCAD   @ $27.95 US
        (Supports AutoCAD 2.1)   ISBN 0-934035-03-2

    ....Copies of STEPPING INTO CAD   @ $24.95 US
        (AutoCAD Workbook)   ISBN 0-934035-05-9

    ....Copies of STEPPING INTO CAD   @ $24.95 US
        INSTRUCTOR'S GUIDE   ISBN 0-934035-06-7

FUTURE RELEASES:

    ....Copies of WORKING OUT WITH AutoCAD   @ $29.95 US
        (Advanced Workbook)   ISBN 0-934025-10-5
    ....Copies of THE MICROCOMPUTER CAD MANUAL @ $27.95 US
        (Manager's Guide To CAD)   ISBN 0-934035-04-0

I understand that I may return any book for a full refund if
if not satisfied.

Name:...

Address:..

....ZIP:...............

Telephone:................................EXT:...................

Californians: Please add 7% sales tax per book.

Shipping and Handling: $3.50 for the first book and $1.00 for
for each additional book.

    ......I can't wait 3-4 weeks for Book Rate Mail. Here is $5.00
        per book for Special Handling via Air Mail/UPS.

    ......Please add my name to New Riders Publishing list for
        more information on microcomputers and affordable CAD.

Please send to the Attention of Product Review.

COMMENTS (Suggestions for Improvements in INSIDE AutoCAD):.....
....
....
....
....

WISH LIST (Topics You Would Like Covered):......................
....
....
....
....

NEW RIDERS PUBLISHING
Post Office Box 4846-B
Thousand Oaks, CA 91630
Telephone (818) 991-5392

NEW RIDERS PUBLISHING
Post Office Box 4846-B
Thousand Oaks, CA 91630
Telephone (818) 991-5392